Core Concepts in Physiology

David R. Bell, Ph.D.

Associate Professor of Physiology and Biophysics
Indiana University School of Medicine, Fort Wayne, Indiana

Illustrations by
Roberta J. Sandy-Shadle
and
James E. Whitcraft

Learning Resource Center
Indiana University, Purdue University
Fort Wayne, Indiana

Lippincott - Raven
P U B L I S H E R S

New York

Acquisitions Editor: Richard Winters
Developmental Editor: Carol Field
Manufacturing Manager: Dennis Teston
Associate Managing Editor: Kathleen Bubbeo
Production Services: Textbook Writers Associates
Cover Designer: Patricia Gast
Indexer: Joan Croce
Compositor: Compset
Printer: Victor Graphics

Printed in the United States of America

9 8 7 6 5 4 3 4 2 1

Library of Congress Cataloging-in-Publication Data

Bell, David R., 1952–
    Core concepts in physiology / David R. Bell; with illustrations
by Roberta J. Sandy-Shadle and James E. Whitcraft.
      p.   cm.
    Includes index.
    ISBN 0-316-08868-4
    1. Human physiology. 2. Physiology, Pathological. I. Title.
    [DNLM: 1. Physiology. QT 104 B432c 1997]
    QP34.5.B435 1997
    612—dc21
    DNLM/DLC
    for Library of Congress   97-31210
                                   CIP

To Pam,
my wife and best friend,
for all the love and encouragement
you have given me throughout my career.

Contents

Preface

There is a sign on my office door that reads, "The main thing is to keep the *main thing* the *MAIN THING*." These twelve simple words serve as a constant reminder of where I should set my priorities before I deliver any lectures to my medical students. These words also serve as the guiding principle of this book. I have been charged with developing a text of less than 250 printed pages that can address two questions concerning teaching physiology to medical students: What do future physicians really need to know about physiology? Of all the topics that could be included in a physiology course (and potentially forgotten by a student shortly after the course is over), what key concepts would I hope future physicians *not* forget?

The goal of this book is to provide access to quick, clear, and concise information about key physiological principles and functions. However, this text was formulated with the thought that current and former students often need more than just a descriptive review of physiology. Whenever possible, this book emphasizes the "hows" and "whys" of physiology, not just the "whats." This book is intended to provide individuals with *explanations* in the area of physiology. It is hoped that this book will become the first source to which students or other individuals refer when they ask themselves the question in physiology, "Now, how did that work again?"

It is my intent that students find multiple uses for this text. Medical students should find it useful as a study aid for their Medical Board exams, as a quick read prior to attending lectures or seminars in physiology, and as a source when any need arises for a quick understanding of physiological processes. In addition, many undergraduates in nursing or allied health fields should find this book helpful. Finally, this text can be a useful resource for individuals whose primary training has been in the areas of molecular biology, genetics, and biochemistry and who now find themselves working on physiological problems as so-called "non-traditional" members of physiology departments.

Certain principles and constraints have guided the content of this book. This text is not restricted to the physiology of the well individual; whenever possible and appropriate, the physiology of disease is also discussed. This is done not only to add medical relevance to the text, but also because I have always believed that a deeper understanding of physiology can be obtained by examining the consequences of a malfunction of a physiological process as well as our body's attempt to compensate for that malfunction. Extensive use of figures has been made in this text. These figures are multipart and explanatory in nature, rather than reprints of actual physiological recordings. They are intended to aid the student's understanding of the written material, which has purposely been kept concise. Whenever possible, complete explanations of a physiological process can be found by reading one page of text associated with one figure on the facing page.

In keeping with the structure of most current U.S. medical school curriculums, which place neurosciences in a separate course, discussion of high-level central nervous system functions and special senses have been placed in a separate Core Concept text in this series; only a brief description is provided in this volume. In the area of neurosciences, this text concentrates on "how nerves work" with some additional discussion of synaptic function and the neuromuscular junction. In addition, the myriad roles of the autonomic nervous system in physiological functions have not been placed in a separate chapter, but have been dealt with on an individual basis wherever such roles impact upon specific physiological processes.

D.R.B.

CHAPTER 1

Physiology and the Concept of Homeostasis

Typical dictionaries define *physiology* as the study of processes involved with the functions of living organisms and their component parts. Unfortunately this statement does not provide insight into how these many functions allow us to cope with the complex challenges presented to our survival. It also does not convey the nature of the elegant, interrelated functions that serve to keep us alive.

Even the simplest, single-cell organism is a complex chemical and physical system. Furthermore, only certain chemical and physical conditions are compatible with the proper operation of such a living system. Maintaining these conditions in the face of an ever-changing and unpredictable external environment is not easy; it is not easy to stay alive.

As an example, take the problems faced by a single-cell organism living in a pond. ■ **Fig. 1-1a** ■ Initially this pond might provide the organism with an environment compatible with the chemical and physical composition of the cell. It also might be large enough to provide the cell with an effectively unlimited food supply, while also providing enough space to prevent buildup of harmful wastes from the cell. The cell in this environment is likely to thrive and even produce offspring, thus ensuring survival of its species.

If the temperature of the pond changed, however, or significant evaporation from the pond occurred, or any other factor altered its chemical or physical properties, the single cell might find itself surrounded by intolerable conditions. Most important, this cell would be incapable of doing anything to alter this intolerable environment. As a consequence, the cell is likely to malfunction or even die.

Human beings are not exempt from the laws of nature. As it is for the single cell, it is difficult for us to live in an unpredictable, changing environment. Unlike the single cell, however, we have an important survival advantage. We have enclosed the environment surrounding the cells of our body and have evolved mechanisms to control the chemical and physical nature of this environment. ■ **Fig. 1-1b** ■

Our cells are surrounded by an aqueous environment, called the *interstitial fluid*. This fluid communicates with the external environment through the aqueous component of blood, or *plasma,* in our cardiovascular system. Various physiological mechanisms in our bodies control oxygen and CO_2 levels, electrolyte and metabolic substrate concentrations, volume, osmolality, temperature, and pH in these two extracellular fluids. By extension, this makes easier the management of the internal environment of our cells, or intracellular fluid. This overall control of the composition of the environment within our bodies is called *homeostasis*.

The value of homeostasis to our survival grows from the fact that much of our structure and function is linked to properties of proteins. Proteins are amino acid polymers. They provide the structure for the organ systems in our bodies and thus allow these systems to carry out their functions. They control many processes at the cellular level by serving as enzymes that modulate chemical reactions, and by serving as transporters of substances into and out of cells.

It is important to note that the function of any protein is dependent on its shape, or *conformation*. Protein conformation can be altered by changes in the pH, electrical potential, ionic strength, and temperature in its surrounding environment. ■ **Fig. 1-1c** ■ Any organism that can control its internal environment therefore can prevent conformational changes in its proteins, and thus prevent malfunction of various processes within the organism.

Providing overall homeostasis in our body is a daunting task, to be sure. We are primarily warm, water-based organisms living in a cool, dry world. We must maintain the chemical environment of our bodies within narrow limits, yet our intake and output of water and electrolytes can vary enormously.

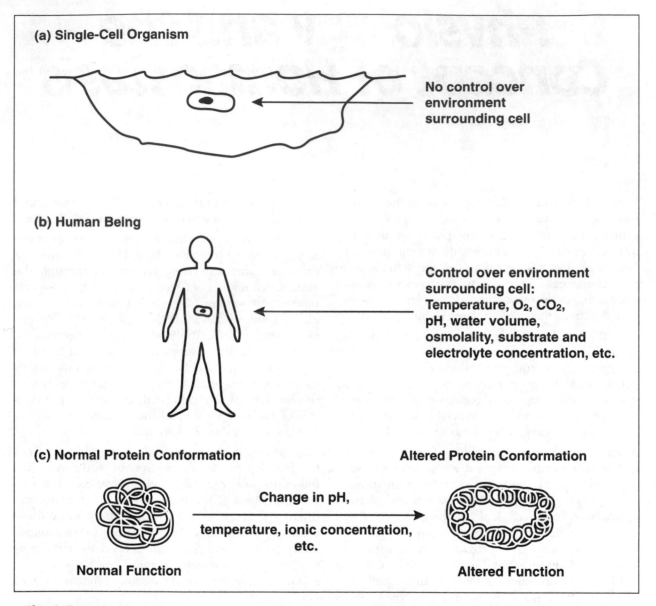

(a) Single-Cell Organism

No control over environment surrounding cell

(b) Human Being

Control over environment surrounding cell: Temperature, O_2, CO_2, pH, water volume, osmolality, substrate and electrolyte concentration, etc.

(c) Normal Protein Conformation   **Altered Protein Conformation**

Change in pH, temperature, ionic concentration, etc.

Normal Function   **Altered Function**

■ **Fig. 1-1** ■

(a) A single-cell organism in an aqueous environment. (b) A single cell within the human body. (c) The effect of physical and chemical factors on protein conformation. Conformational changes lead to functional changes.

We derive energy needed for our survival from the oxidation of chemicals within foodstuffs, yet our supply and intake of such foodstuffs is unpredictably variable. Furthermore, the oxygen needed for our metabolism cannot get to every cell by random diffusion at rates fast enough to meet our needs. We produce CO_2 when we oxidize foodstuffs, which then is converted to enormous amounts of acid that assault all our tissues.

Even the chemical environments of our extra- and intracellular fluid compartments are dissimilar. For example, sodium and chloride are the dominant electrolytes in the extracellular fluid, with small contributions from potassium, bicarbonate, and organic anions. Potassium and organic anions exist in high concentration in the intracellular fluid, with minor amounts of sodium and chloride. Thus these two compartments, in contact with one another, have a built-in deviation from equilibrium. In short, we are constantly faced with the threat of dehydration, hypothermia, acidification, and starvation, as well as water and electrolyte imbalances that are incompatible with life.

Despite these problems, homeostasis is maintained in a healthy individual. There is a respiratory system to bring oxygen into the body no matter how great the need, and a cardiovascular system that can transport that oxygen rapidly to every cell. We have elaborate systems for storing food energy in times of excess supply so that it can be released to ward off starvation in times of famine. Our kidneys and other organ systems control the water, electrolyte, and acid/base composition of the extracellular fluid with high precision. Many systems within the body maintain its internal temperature within fractions of a degree Fahrenheit despite wide variations in the temperature of the external environment. These and many other functions and systems in our bodies form the core of human physiology.

Physiology is more than the study of the function of our organ systems, however. These systems are the essential reason for our ability to stay alive and therefore are the essence of life itself. Beyond the study of the function of our individual parts, a study of human physiology is, in the end, a study of human survival.

CHAPTER 2

Transport of Materials Across the Cell Membrane

Survival of any organism is linked to its ability to transport materials into and out of its cells, across the cell membrane. Many schemes are used by cells for such transmembrane transport; some follow simple non-energy–requiring chemical and physical principles, whereas others involve complex, energy-requiring, multistep processes.

Passive Transport

At temperatures above absolute zero (−273.2°C), all molecules are in continual, random motion. Consequently, they do not congregate in one location in a system, but rather spread and distribute randomly into all available space. This "spreading out" of molecules is called *passive diffusion* and is illustrated in ■ **Fig. 2-1a** ■. In this illustration a compartment is separated into left and right chambers by an imaginary barrier, with the left chamber containing a higher concentration of molecules (dots in the figure) than the right. All the molecules are in constant random motion and can move in any direction across the barrier.

Because more molecules are in the left chamber, however, the probability of any molecule going left to right is greater than any going right to left. Consequently, the tendency initially is for the *net* movement of molecules to proceed from left to right. This tendency will exist until the probability of any molecule going in either direction is equal, which will occur when the concentration of molecules in both chambers is identical.

Thus, net movement of molecules by passive diffusion always occurs from areas of high concentration to low concentration until the concentrations are equilibrated. This process works for a single type of molecule, or for mixtures of two or more types of molecules, as shown at the middle of ■ **Fig. 2-1** ■.

It is important to note that molecular movement does not cease at equilibrium. At equilibrium in our example, molecules still move left to right and right to left between the chambers, but there no longer is a tendency to move more in one direction than another. For this reason, the equilibrium condition for molecules undergoing passive diffusion is often called *dynamic equilibrium*.

The amount of a substance diffusing across a membrane per unit of time is called its *rate of diffusion* or *flux* (designated by the letter J). See ■ **Fig. 2-1b** ■ Small (less massive) molecules diffuse more rapidly than larger, heavier molecules, and the rate of diffusion for any molecule is enhanced by an increase in temperature. Molecules moving by diffusion can cover short distances in little time (e.g., 0.1 mm in about 5 seconds) but may take hours to traverse even a few centimeters. (This is why the cells of our bodies, which exchange many substances with their surrounding environment by passive diffusion, are microscopic and generally within micrometers of a source of oxygen and metabolic substrates).

Flux of a molecule into the cell across the cell membrane is directly proportional to the difference in concentration of the molecules outside versus inside the cell, called the *concentration gradient* or *difference,* as well as to the surface area over which the molecules diffuse. Large concentration differences and large surface areas yield a higher amount of transport per unit of time. Because molecules moving into or out of the cell must traverse the cell membrane, however, the chemical nature of this membrane is also a determinant of the rate of diffusion. The cell membrane is composed mostly of a lipid bilayer interspersed with proteins. See ■ **Fig. 2-1b** ■ Lipid-soluble molecules (such as O_2, CO_2, CO, fatty acids, monoglycerides, steroids, anesthetics, and many drugs) can traverse the membrane easily by simple diffusion. Water and small water-soluble molecules (e.g., urea) also traverse the cell membrane easily by simple diffusion, though this occurs through water-filled protein pores in the membrane.

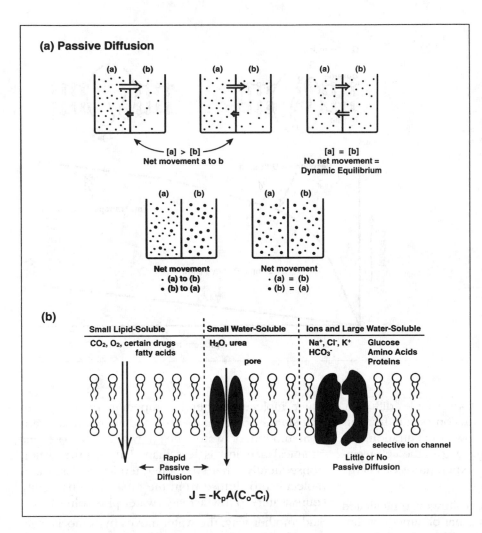

(a) Passive Diffusion

[a] > [b]
Net movement a to b

[a] = [b]
No net movement =
Dynamic Equilibrium

Net movement
· (a) to (b)
● (b) to (a)

Net movement
· (a) = (b)
● (b) = (a)

(b)

Small Lipid-Soluble	Small Water-Soluble	Ions and Large Water-Soluble
CO₂, O₂, certain drugs fatty acids	H₂O, urea	Na⁺, Cl⁻, K⁺ HCO₃⁻ / Glucose Amino Acids Proteins

pore

selective ion channel

Rapid
← Passive →
Diffusion

Little or No
Passive Diffusion

$$J = -K_pA(C_o - C_i)$$

■ Fig. 2-1 ■
(a) Passive diffusion of molecules. Molecules move by random motion from areas of high concentration into areas of low concentration until concentrations are equilibrated. (b) The cell membrane. Small lipid-soluble molecules diffuse easily across the lipid bilayer. Water and small water-soluble molecules also diffuse easily through water-filled pores. Passive diffusion of ions or large water-soluble molecules is limited across the cell membrane. Flux, J, or transport of a molecule across the membrane, is proportional to the permeability of the membrane to the molecule, the surface area over which the molecule diffuses, and the difference in concentration of the molecule outside vs. inside the cell.

In contrast, ions, large water-soluble molecules (such as glucose and amino acids), peptides, and proteins either diffuse through the cell membrane very poorly or not at all. All the physical factors determining how easily a given molecule can traverse the cell membrane are contained within a factor called the *permeability coefficient,* K_p. A large K_p indicates that a molecule can diffuse across the cell membrane relatively easily.

Overall, the rate of diffusion of a molecule is given by the equation

$$J = -K_p A(C_o - C_i)$$

where K_p is the permeability coefficient, A is the surface area of the membrane involved, and $C_o - C_i$ is the molecular concentration outside the membrane minus the concentration inside.

This equation also can be used to describe diffusion across a layer of tissue as well as across a cell membrane. For example, it is useful in describing diffusional transport of O_2 and CO_2 across the alveoli/ capillary barrier in the lung or diffusion of certain substrates across the intestinal villi. It is to an organism's advantage if it can obtain substances by passive diffusion because no energy expenditure is required for passive diffusion to occur. As a substance is used, cells can simply allow new substance to follow its concentration gradient and passively diffuse into the cell.

Facilitated Diffusion

In some instances, transport of molecules into the cell by passive diffusion alone is not sufficient to meet the cell's needs for that substance. Consequently, cells have membrane-bound protein transport systems that augment the transport of molecules across the cell membrane. See **■ Fig. 2-2a ■** Glucose, fructose, and many amino acids are "shuttled" across the cell membrane by such a system in a process

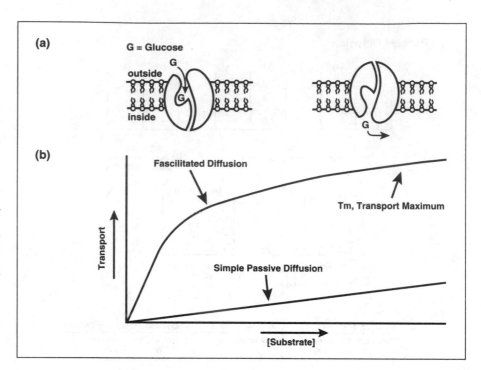

■ Fig. 2-2 ■
(a) A protein transporter that moves glucose across the cell membrane by facilitated diffusion. (b) At any concentration difference of substrate across the cell membrane, transport by facilitated diffusion exceeds that by simple passive diffusion. Facilitated diffusion transport processes exhibit transport maximums, T_m.

called *facilitated diffusion*. Like simple diffusion, net transport by facilitated diffusion occurs from areas of high concentration to low concentration, can only equilibrate concentrations across the cell membrane, and does not require expenditure of energy by the cell.

For any concentration gradient, however, facilitated transport is much greater than that obtained by simple passive diffusion. **■ Fig. 2-2b ■** Nevertheless, there are limits to this increase because the number of carrier proteins, sites on the proteins, and the shuttling rate of the protein transporter all have limits. Substances transported by facilitated diffusion thus exhibit a transport rate maximum, or T_m, as shown in **■ Fig. 2-2b ■** .

Osmosis

Many cell functions are critically dependent on the internal chemical composition of the cell. This composition can be altered indirectly by changing the amount of water in the cell. An important means of moving water into or out of a cell occurs by the process of *osmosis,* shown in **■ Fig. 2-3a ■** .

In this illustration, a cylinder of water and dissolved solute is separated from a container of pure water by a semipermeable membrane, i.e., a membrane through which water but not solute can move freely by passive diffusion. Solutes attract or "hang on to"

water molecules, thereby impeding their random diffusion in solution. As such, the energy of the random motion of water mixed with solute (i.e., its chemical activity) is less than that of pure water. Consequently, there is a net tendency for water molecules to diffuse from the area of high activity (pure water) to low activity (water plus solute).

Said another way, the water moves by osmosis from areas of low solute concentration to areas of high solute concentration. In our example, then, pure water will enter the cylinder from the container. As the water level in the cylinder rises, however, hydrostatic pressure at the bottom of this column of water, due to the effect of gravity, will increase until enough pressure builds up to push water out of the cylinder at a rate equal to the diffusional movement of water into the cylinder. The pressure reached at equilibrium in this situation is called the *osmotic pressure.*

It is important to note that the osmotic pressure driving water across the membrane depends on the number, not the chemical nature, of solute molecules present in the solution. For example, when 100 millimoles (mM) NaCl totally dissociates in water, the resulting solution contains 100 mM each of Na^+ *and* Cl^- ions. This produces a solution with a concentration of 200 mM in total solute particles. Such a solution is said to have an *osmotic concentration* of 200 milliosmoles (200 mOsm). A solution of glu-

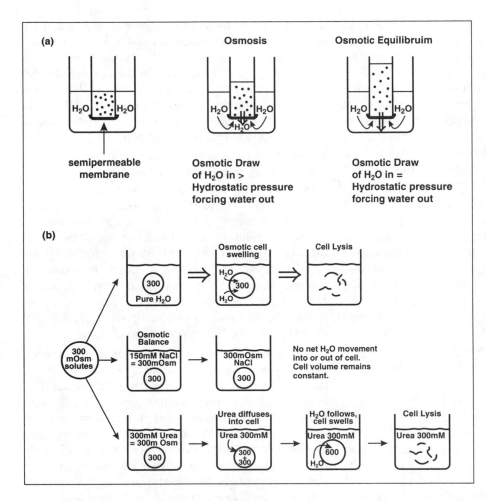

■ Fig. 2-3 ■
(a) A demonstration of osmosis. Water molecules move from areas of low or no solute concentration into areas of high solute concentration by osmosis. (b) An example of osmotic effects on cells. Cells contain osmotically active solutes trapped within their interiors. In pure water, water enters the cells by osmosis, causing the cells to swell and lyse. Molecules that are impermeable to the cell membrane (NaCl) can counteract the osmotic influx of water into the cell; cell-permeable molecules such as urea cannot.

cose, which does not dissociate in water, would have to have a concentration of 200 mM to have the same osmolar concentration as a 100 mM solution of NaCl.

In our bodies, the composition of intracellular and the extracellular fluid are quite different (see Chap. 1). Despite markedly different chemical compositions, fluid inside and outside the cell has essentially the same number of dissolved particles per milliliter of water. Thus, both water compartments are osmotically similar ($\approx$ 290 mOsm) and there is no net tendency for water to flow into or out of the cell.

In determining osmolar concentration of a solution, the molar concentration of the solute often is multiplied by an osmotic coefficient, ϕ, which represents how completely a solute dissociates in water. Salts such as NaCl, which dissociate almost completely, have high coefficients ($\approx$0.93). In contrast, $MgSO_4$, which incompletely dissociates in water, has a $\phi = 0.58$.

In physiology, one is not as interested in the osmotic concentration and pressure of a solution as much as how cells respond osmotically when placed in solu-

tions containing various solute concentrations. Physiologists are interested in whether exposure of a cell to a given solution will cause the cell to lose water, resulting in cell shrinkage and concentration of intracellular contents, or to gain water, resulting in dilution of intracellular contents, cell swelling, and eventual cell death through *lysis* (rupture). The effect of a solution on cell water volume depends on two factors:

1. The permeability of the membrane to a given solute, and
2. The difference in the effective osmotic concentrations across the cell membrane.

In **■ Fig. 2-3b ■** a cell is depicted with a internal osmotic concentration of 300 mOsm, due to all trapped intracellular solutes. If this cell is placed in a beaker of pure water (0 mOsm solutes), water will move by osmosis into the cell, from the area of high water activity to low water activity, causing the cell to swell and burst.

The cell membrane is essentially impermeable to NaCl. If a cell is placed in a solution of NaCl of equal osmolarity as the cell interior (i.e., 150 mM or ≈ 300 mOsm), there will be no net tendency for NaCl or water to move either into or out of the cell. Thus the cell volume will remain constant. A similar effect would occur if the cell were placed in any 300 mOsm solution containing solute that cannot cross the cell membrane (e.g., dextran, albumin, sucrose). Such impermeable solutes are said to exert a "full" osmotic balancing effect across the cell membrane.

Predictions of osmotic flux of water across the cell membrane are not as straightforward if cells are placed in solutions containing solutes to which the cell membrane is slightly or totally permeable. For example, our cell membranes are freely permeable to urea. A cell placed in a solution of 300 mM (300 mOsm) urea will swell and burst just as if it were placed in pure water, even though its osmotic concentration is the same as that inside the cell. See ■ **Fig. 2-3b** ■ The cell behaves as if nothing had been dissolved in the water surrounding the cell.

This example demonstrates the axiom that solutes to which the cell membrane is permeable are ineffective in balancing, or counteracting, the osmotic effect of trapped solutes inside the cell. In our example, because the cell membrane is permeable to urea, urea will passively diffuse into the cell until its intercellular concentration alone is 300 mM. At that point, the total osmolar concentration inside the cell will be 600 mOsm, whereas that outside still will be 300 mOsm. Consequently water will flow into the cell.

As can be seen, the flow of water into or out of the cell is as much a function of how permeable the cell membrane is to any solute as it is a function of the osmotic concentration across the cell membrane. To get a true measure of osmotic forces across the cell membrane, one must adjust the osmotic concentration of a solution for the permeability of its solute relative to the cell membrane. Such an adjustment is expressed in a term called the *reflection coefficient,* or σ.

The reflection coefficient is multiplied by the osmotic pressure difference across the cell membrane to give the true osmotic effect of the solute on the cell membrane. The value of σ is 1 when the membrane is totally impermeable to a given solute such as Na^+, Cl^-, peptides, or proteins; it is 0 for small permeant molecules such as lipids, water, and urea. Other chemicals will fall between these two limits and affect water flow across the membrane accordingly.

To understand effects of solutions on cell volume, it is clear that some distinction must be made between the osmolar concentration of a solution and its effect on water movement across the cell membrane. Solutions that have the same, lower, or higher osmolar concentration compared to intracellular fluid are said, respectively, to be *isosmotic, hypoosmotic,* or *hyperosmotic* relative to the cell.

By extension, because the osmolarity of the intracellular fluid and plasma are essentially the same, these terms could be used relative to plasma osmolarity as well. Instead of osmolar nomenclature, however, the term *tonicity* is used to describe the effect of a solution on cell volume. *Hypotonic* solutions cause cells to swell, *hypertonic* solutions cause cells to shrink, and *isotonic* solutions maintain cell volume. By definition, then, a solution of 150 mM NaCl, 300 mM sucrose, or 300 mM albumin is isosmotic and isotonic to our cells, whereas 300 mM urea is isosmotic but hypotonic to our cells.

In physiological systems, osmotic forces also are important determinants of water flows across tissue membranes such as at the capillary/extracellular fluid interface. Here solutes such as glucose, NaCl, other ions, and dissolved substances of the plasma can pass easily across pores in the capillary membrane. They are "permeable" to this *tissue* layer, and therefore do not exert any net osmotic force across the capillary. In this system, only molecules too large to pass through capillary clefts (e.g., albumin, globulins, and other plasma proteins) exert an effective osmotic force that retains water in the bloodstream. The importance of this osmotic effect in determining H_2O movement across the capillary is discussed in Chap. 13.

Ionic Equilibrium and Cellular Membrane Potentials

Physiologically important ions such as Na^+, Cl^-, and K^+ are highly lipophobic. Therefore their ability to diffuse across the lipid bilayer of the cell membrane is extremely limited and much less than that seen for small lipid-soluble molecules. Nevertheless, they may move through protein pores in the membrane and, because ions carry electrical charge, this movement across the cell membrane is important to the function of the body. Such electrical properties are exploited for use in basic mechanisms responsible for the function of nerves, muscles, and various other cell types.

The movement of ions across the cell membrane by passive diffusion depends on two properties:

1. The chemical concentration gradient driving the diffusion, and
2. Any electrical charge or potential, acting on, or being created by, the ion.

For example, suppose a cell with an intracellular K^+ concentration of 140 mM is placed in a solution containing 4 mM K^+, as shown in ■ **Fig. 2-4a** ■. Assume for this example that osmotic equilibrium is maintained in this cell and that K^+ can move by passive diffusion across the cell membrane. Also assume, however, that large negatively charged molecules such as proteins and organic anions (A^-) cannot cross the cell membrane.

Initially, K^+ will move out of the cell by passive diffusion. As it moves, however, it will leave the negatively charged impermeable anions behind, making the inside of the cell membrane slightly more negative and the outside slightly more positive. This negative charge will create an electrical force that will attract positively charged potassium, thus retarding its efflux from the cell. This negative charge will continue to build as K^+ continues to diffuse out of the cell, until enough *electrical* force attracting K^+ inside the cell balances the *chemical* force driving K^+ out by simple diffusion. At this point the cell will be in a dynamic electrochemical equilibrium for potassium. (To avoid confusion, note that this pro-

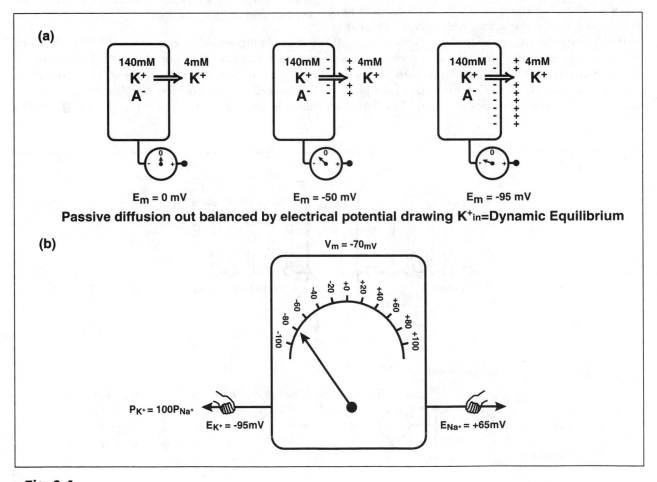

Passive diffusion out balanced by electrical potential drawing K^+in=Dynamic Equilibrium

■ **Fig. 2-4** ■
(a) The consequences of potassium diffusion out of the cell. Passive diffusion of potassium out of the cell results in a buildup of negative charge on the inside of the cell membrane, until a sufficiently large negative electrical force is created to balance the concentration diffusional force across the cell membrane. (b) In systems containing both potassium and sodium ions, the actual cell membrane potential, V_m, will reflect most closely the equilibrium potential, E_m, for the ion to which the membrane is most permeable.

cess reaches equilibrium with negligible effects on the intra- or extracellular potassium concentrations).

The electrical potential needed to counterbalance diffusional movement of any ion across the cell membrane at 37°C can be determined by the Nernst equation, which states

$$E_m = (-61.5/z)\log(C_i/C_o)$$

where E_m is the Nernst potential in mV, C_i and C_o are the concentration of the ion inside and outside the cell respectively, and z is the ion valence (e.g., $K^+ = +1$, $Cl^- = -1$, $Ca^{++} = +2$).

In our example, with a K^+ gradient of 140/4 (which is similar to the K^+ gradient across human cell membranes), the Nernst equation predicts equilibrium will be reached if the actual membrane potential is −95 mV inside versus outside the cell membrane. If the actual membrane potential for any reason were less negative than this value, there would be net diffusion of K^+ out of the cell; a more negative potential would actually cause potassium to flow into the cell, against its chemical gradient. Similarly, with $[Na^+]_i \approx 12$ mM and $[Na^+]_o \approx 140$ mM, the equilibrium potential for sodium ≈ +65 mV. If the cell membrane is less positive than this, sodium will diffuse into the cell; sodium will move out of the cell at $E_m > +65$ mV.

Of course, the extra- and intracellular fluids in our bodies contain many different cationic and anionic molecules. The actual resting membrane potential in a cell, resulting from the net diffusion of all ionic species, reflects the total effect of the concentration differences across the membrane for each ion and their relative membrane permeabilities. The more permeable the membrane is to a given ion, the more the actual membrane potential will reflect the Nernst potential for that ion.

For most purposes, the permeabilities of our cell membranes to K^+ and Na^+ are most important in determining the membrane potential at rest. The permeability of the cell membrane for K^+, however, is ≈ 100 times greater than it is for Na^+. See ■ **Fig. 2-4b** ■

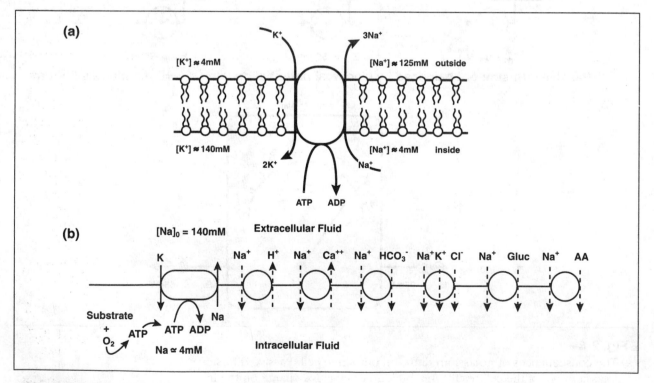

■ **Fig. 2-5** ■

(a) The sodium/potassium ATPase pump in the cell membrane. (b) Movement of sodium down its concentration gradient is used to transport several other molecules across the cell membrane via transmembrane protein transporters.

At the intra- and extracellular concentrations for these two ions given above, the actual passive membrane potential in this two-ion system will be "pulled" to more closely approximate the -95 value for K^+ than the $+65$ value for Na^+. Indeed, most membrane potentials in our cells reside between -70 and -90 mV.

It has been determined, however, that no combination of passive diffusion, electrical forces, or osmotic forces can maintain ionic concentrations for all the different chemical species involved inside and outside our cells at the values that actually exist. Clearly, a cell membrane potential of -70 mV will not keep a higher concentration of Na^+ outside than inside the cell, as is the case in our bodies. In fact, this level of negativity is not even enough to maintain the observed K^+ concentration difference across the cell membrane. At normal resting membrane potentials, Na^+ eventually will diffuse into and K^+ will diffuse out of the cell. This will depolarize the cell membrane (in this case to a more positive membrane potential), cause accumulation of intracellular Na^+ and water, and eventually cause cell malfunction and death. Other mechanisms therefore must come into play to maintain the concentration gradients for these two ions across our cell membranes.

Active Transport

All cells in the body contain proteins that transport Na^+ out of and K^+ into the cell *against* each ion's electrochemical gradient. These proteins are called *Na^+/K^+ pumps* or *Na^+/K^+ ATPases* because of their ability to enzymatically hydrolyze adenosine triphosphate (ATP) to ADP plus inorganic phosphate. Like rolling a ball uphill, moving ions against an electrochemical gradient requires the expenditure of energy. This energy is found in the high-energy phosphate bond of ATP. The hydrolysis of ATP by the sodium/potassium ATPase releases the energy from one phosphate bond on ATP. This energy produces a conformational change in the pump, which results in movement of 3 Na^+ out of the cell and 2 K^+ into the cell. ■ **Fig. 2-5a** ■ This process is called *active transport,* because it requires energy.

ATP is produced in cells primarily by the oxidation of chemical substrates such as glucose and fatty acids by oxygen (oxidative phosphorylation). Details of this process will not be elaborated upon here. It is important to note, however, that any factor that impairs the production of ATP in the cell (such as lack of O_2) will result in shutting down of

the Na^+/K^+ pump and cell death. Needless to say, this molecule has an essential survival function. Almost 50% of the O_2 consumed by our bodies is utilized to run this cell pump.

Other types of cellular ATPase pumps have additional important survival functions. For example, oxidative metabolism in our cells produces CO_2. This CO_2 combines with H_2O to form carbonic acid (H_2CO_3), which dissociates into H^+ and bicarbonate. The hydrogen ions so produced represent an acid assault on all cellular functions. But H^+ is removed readily from the intracellular fluid by the action of H^+-ATPase pumps in the cell membrane, which actively transport H^+ out of the cell against a substantial electrochemical gradient. In a similar manner, intracellular Ca^{++} is maintained in the sub-μM range against a millionfold greater extracellular concentration by a cell membrane Ca^{++} ATPase. The importance of this calcium pump will be discussed in later chapters.

Secondary Active Transport

The large electrochemical gradient for Na^+ across the cell membrane created by Na^+/K^+ ATPase pumps represents an exploitable source of potential energy for cellular processes. Specific membrane protein transporters couple energy, released from Na^+ flowing passively down its concentration gradient, to the movement of other molecules across the cell membrane. ■ **Fig. 2-5b** ■

Specific membrane protein transporters move Ca^{++} and H^+ out of the cell in exchange for sodium (countertransport process). Still other protein transporters couple Na^+ entry with uptake of gluc and amino acids by cells (cotransport processes couple Na^+ entry with entry of potassium and ride. Transport by this latter type of cotransp stimulated by cell shrinkage and helps rest volume by causing osmotic influx of wa function of specific transporters in variou logical functions will be discussed where ate in later chapters.

Although these protein transporters fu by passive ionic movements, they ulti dependent on the active transport of cell to establish a sodium electroch For this reason, such transport me sified as secondary active transp is important to note that any fa with the function of the Na^+/K feres with any other co- and co anism coupled to sodium.

CHAPTER 3

Physiology of Nerves

The Nervous System: A Descriptive Overview

The survival of an organism is enhanced by its ability to be aware of changes in the chemical and physical conditions of its external and internal environment, integrate this information, and effect an appropriate response in its body. These processes comprise the overall function of the nervous system. In the human nervous system, information about the chemical and physical condition of the external and internal environment is transmitted throughout the body, in the form of electrical signals, by specialized cells called *neurons*. See the top right of ■ **Fig. 3-1** ■ . Neurons comprise the primary functional cellular unit of the nervous system.

l signals in these nerve cells are transmitted , cylindrical projections from their cell d *axons*. Axons of some nerve cells are others can be as long as 1 m. In the electrical signals are not passed nerve cell through direct elec- ween the axon terminus of body of the next. Instead, nally by transmission of inus one nerve to a re-

in a nerve travel *neurotransmit-* to the next nal again. n nerve ignal are

several chemical and physical environmental variables and sends signals along sensory afferent nerves to the *central nervous system,* or CNS. The CNS comprises the brain and spinal cord. These organs receive and integrate these sensory signals and transmit efferent signals along motor nerves to the necessary skeletal muscles to elicit an appropriate response.

The somatosensory system obtains information about our external environment through sensation of light (sight), sound waves (hearing), and various external chemical stimuli (via taste and smell). We also receive information related to physical contact with the external environment (i.e., touch intensity, vibration, external temperature) through sensory receptors in the skin. Finally, sensory receptors also monitor muscle stretch and tension, body motion, balance, and equilibrium, as well as sense our orientation relative to gravity.

Many of our unconscious, internal, day-to-day bodily functions, as well as the control of chemical and physical variables within our bodies, are influenced by the second major subdivision of the nervous system, called the *autonomic nervous system,* or ANS. ■ **Fig. 3-2** ■ Heart rate, blood pressure, ventilation, balance of body water, electrolyte and acid-base composition, body temperature, levels of O_2 and CO_2 in body fluids, and chemical and physical processes associated with digestion are some of the variables influenced by the ANS.

The autonomic nervous system is divided into *parasympathetic* and *sympathetic* divisions. Efferent neurons from these systems first form synapses with second efferent nerve cells before innervating an effector organ. These synapses often coalesce into localized groups called *ganglia*. Ganglia of the parasympathetic division usually are located near n effector organ and thus postganglionic parasympathetic nerve fibers are short; sympathetic ganglia are predominantly grouped in chains outside the spine in the thoracic cavity (thoracic chains).

Acetylcholine is the neurotransmitter between pre- and postganglionic nerves in both divisions of the ANS. Generally, but not exclusively, acetylcholine is the postganglionic neurotransmitter in parasympathetic nerves, whereas norepinephrine serves that role in postganglionic sympathetic fibers. Often, but not always, both branches of the ANS will innervate the same effector organ and elicit opposite effects on that organ when activated. For example, stimulation of parasympathetic nerves to the heart decreases heart rate, whereas stimulation of cardiac sympathetic nerves increases heart rate.

The mode of activation of the two divisions of the ANS also differs, although both divisions are continually (or tonically) active at most effector organs. The sympathetic division of the ANS often is activated "in total" in situations generically described as requiring a "fight or flight response." The sympathetic portion of the ANS innervating many different systems (cardiovascular, respiratory, metabolic) will activate simultaneously in response to physical stress, exercise, shock, emotional trauma, or perceived threats to the whole organism. In contrast, the parasympathetic system is more involved with day-to-day regulation of metabolism, digestion, and normal cardiorespiratory function.

Knowledge of the nervous system, especially the brain, has grown so large and complex that most medical schools in the United States have taken much neuroscience instruction out of physiology courses and devoted a separate course to neuroscience alone. This division is being followed here,

The primary purpose of this chapter will be to provide an explanation of " how nerves work," with some additional explanation of synaptic transmission between nerves, and between nerves and skeletal muscle. In addition, rather than follow the common convention of including a chapter devoted to an overview of all ANS functions, the role of the ANS in any specific physiological function will be

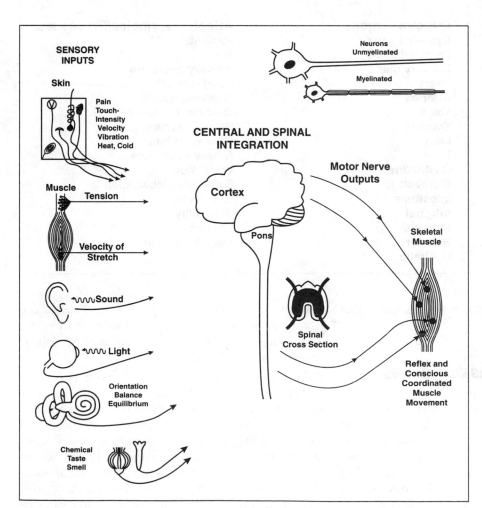

■ **Fig. 3-1** ■

A general overview of the somatosensory or motor nervous system. Several physical and chemical sensory inputs are processed by the brain and spinal cord to effect changes in movement in the body through efferent motor neurons. (See text for details.)

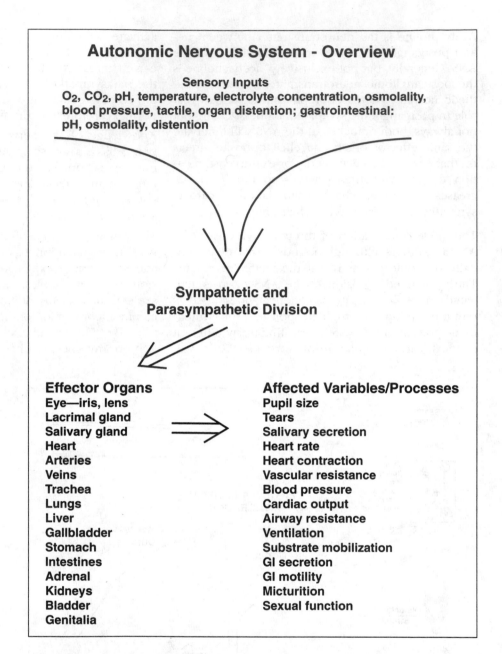

■ Fig. 3-2 ■
An overview of the sensory inputs, effector organs, and affected variables in processes affected by the autonomic nervous system.

included in the section of this text explaining that specific function.

Electrical Properties of Nerves

Nerves contain protein channels for Na^+, K^+ and Cl^-. In explaining electrophysiological phenomena in nerves the term *conductance* (signified by the letter g) often is used to describe how easily an ion crosses the nerve cell membrane; high conductance implies easy passage. Understandably, the resting conductance of the cell membrane for any ion is a function of the permeability of the membrane to that ion. As in other types of cells, gK^+ across the resting nerve cell membrane is higher than gNa^+. The resting membrane potential for most neurons is approximately -70 mV.

Electrical current can be injected into a nerve cell and cause membrane depolarization to less negative resting potentials, or cause membrane hyperpolarization to more negative resting potentials, as shown in **■ Fig. 3-3 ■**. Here, square waves of depolarizing or hyperpolarizing current are applied to the nerve and recorded by an extracellular electrode at various distances from the current source. The magnitude of depolarization or hyperpolarization at the recording site is proportional to the stimulus intensity, and therefore is called *graded response*.

The graded response spreads through the axon by a process called *electrotonic conduction*. However, its amplitude decreases exponentially as it spreads further from the initial current source; therefore it is said to be *conducted with decrement*. The distance over which the potential change decreases to 1/*e*, or 37% of its maximum value, is called the *length constant*, a value often used to compare electrical properties of different nerves.

If one progressively depolarizes a nerve cell, a threshold will be reached where the cell, without further external stimulation, will spontaneously depolarize to a positive value. Shortly thereafter there will follow successively a repolarization, hyperpolarization, and return to resting membrane potential. This response is called an *action potential* and is characteristic of all nerves. ■ **Fig. 3-4a** ■ The key features of action potentials are a reversal of the resting membrane potential to a positive value, and generation in an "all-or-none" fashion. That is, below threshold, no action potentials are created, whereas depolarization above threshold produces the same action potential no matter how strong the depolarizing stimulus.

For an action potential to be a useful means of transmitting a signal from a nerve cell body down a long axon to the nerve terminal, it is necessary that the action potential not dissipate as it proceeds down the axon. This occurs as follows: Local depolarization of the cell membrane caused by an action potential causes depolarizing current to flow within the axon. This depolarizing flow is sufficiently strong to bring the adjacent membrane to threshold, creating a second action potential of equal amplitude, downstream from the first. This then will depolarize an adjacent membrane further down, firing another action potential, and so on. As a result, unlike graded potentials in the nerve, the action potential is transmitted down the length of the axon without decrement.

Action potentials in nerves result from selective opening and closing, called *gating*, of cell membrane protein channels for Na^+ and K^+. ■ **Fig. 3-4b** ■ The Na^+ channel has two control points, analogous to the front and back door of a house. At rest, the gate facing the extracellular fluid (m gate), is closed and that facing the intracellular fluid (h gate), is open. Resting gNa^+ through the membrane is very low. As the cell membrane becomes depolarized (in this case more positive), the m gates begin to open and the h gates begin to close.

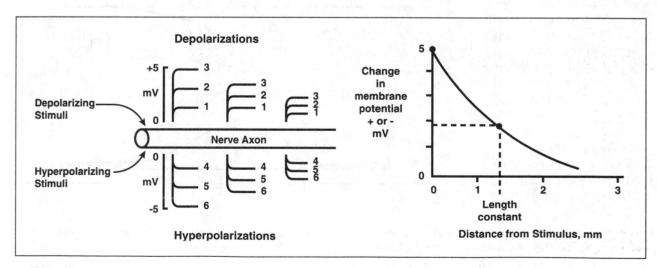

■ **Fig. 3-3** ■

The effect of injecting depolarizing or hyperpolarizing electrical currents into the nerve axon. The resulting change in the resting membrane potential is greater near the source of the current and diminishes further away from the source. The length constant is the distance from the source of the depolarization or hyperpolarization to a point where the membrane potential change has diminished to 37% of its maximum value.

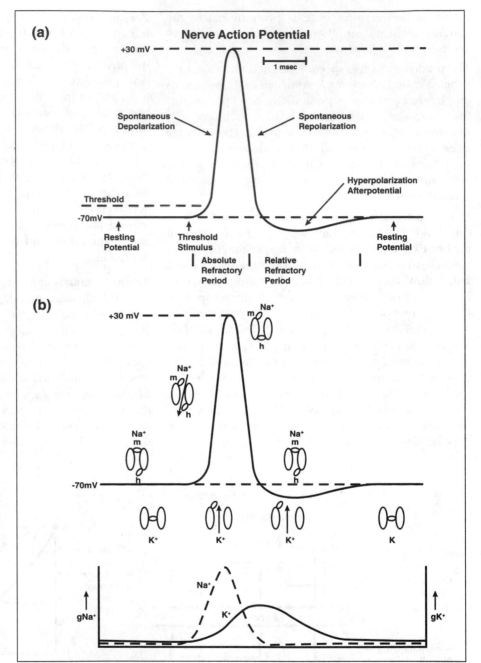

■ Fig. 3-4 ■
(a) A representation of the nerve action potential showing the resting membrane potential, the potential at which threshold is reached, membrane depolarization, and membrane hyperpolarization. (b) Representation of the opening and closing of fast sodium and potassium channels in the nerve cell during an action potential, and changes in sodium and potassium conductance during the action potential. (See text for explanation.)

Closure of the h gate, however, occurs more slowly than opening of the m gates, providing a finite window for Na$^+$ to enter the cell down its electrochemical gradient. This results in a rapid influx of Na$^+$, further depolarizing the cell, opening of more m gates, more Na$^+$ entry, and so on. The high gNa$^+$ provided by the open gates moves the membrane potential toward the positive Nernst potential for Na$^+$. With continued depolarization, however, the h

gates close, inactivating the channel and restricting further Na$^+$ influx.

At this point the cell membrane potential is positive and thus favors the extrusion of K$^+$ out of the cell, which then tends to repolarize the cell. Repolarization is facilitated by the opening of a K$^+$ channel in the membrane. This opening also is stimulated by membrane depolarization shortly after activation of the Na$^+$ channel. This increases gK$^+$ and speeds the flux of K$^+$ out of the cell, driving the membrane potential toward the negative Nernst potential for K$^+$.

In nerves, the membrane potential often becomes more negative than the resting membrane potential (hyperpolarization) before the cell returns to its resting value. When the cell membrane potential becomes less and less positive during repolarization, the m and h gates of the sodium channel reset and are then ready to initiate another action potential.

Neural Information and Refractory Periods

Because the amplitude of the action potential does not change as it is transmitted down the nerve fiber, changes in amplitude of electrical signals are lost to us as a means of conveying information through nerves. Consequently, differences in information are carried by our nerves as differences in the frequency of action potential generation (i.e., the number of action potentials generated per second). This process is limited by how fast the neuronal Na$^+$ and K$^+$ gates can be reset.

There is a period during the generation of an action potential in which absolutely no electrical stimuli, no matter how strong, can generate another action potential. This is called the *absolute refractory period* and is related to the period of time before any of the sodium gates are reset; see ■ **Fig. 3-4a and 4b** ■. As repolarization proceeds, however, some Na$^+$ gates on some channels become reset and another action potential can be generated if a stronger than normal stimulus is provided. This period is called the *relative refractory period*. The duration of a typical nerve action potential is ≈ 1 millisecond. Thus the frequency of nerve firing is limited to about 1000 impulses per second.

Determinants of Conduction Velocity in Nerves

Processing of information in the nervous system is constrained by how fast electrical potentials can travel along the axon. In order for action potentials to travel down the length of the neuron, current first must flow across the cell membrane and through the interior of the axon. Anything that increases the amount of charge that must flow across the cell membrane to produce a given amount of depolarization, or impairs movement of charge either across the membrane or within the axon interior,

will slow the conduction of electrical potentials in the nerve.

In nerves, the membrane capacitance, C_m, is representative of the amount of charge that must flow to create a given level of depolarization across the cell membrane; r_m and r_{in} represent the resistance to charge flow across the membrane and within the axon, respectively. ■ **Fig. 3-5a** ■ These factors comprise a variable called the *time constant,* which equals $(r_m r_{in})^{1/2} \times C_m$. Small time constants imply fast electrotonic conduction in nerves.

The amount of decrement of electronic conduction in nerves is another factor that determines how fast electrical potentials are conducted in the nerve. The lipid bilayer of the nerve cell is a partial insulator, that is, a little bit of current tends to leak out of the cell as it proceeds down the length of the axon, thus weakening the strength of any initial depolarization. The more insulated the cell membrane is, the farther an electrical signal can be transmitted without significant decrement.

The *length constant,* given by $(r_m/r_{in})^{1/2}$, is an indicator of the degree of electrical decrement occurring along the length of the nerve. Large length constants indicate an ability to transmit electrical potentials farther down an axon without significant decrement. This occurs with a well-insulated nerve, or in one in which resistance to current flow within the axoplasm is low. Many nerve axons are much longer than their length constants. It is the ability of nerves to form action potentials, which are transmitted down the axon without decrement, that gives nerves the necessary ability to transmit electrical information across distances much larger than their length constants.

Nerve membrane resistances and capacitances are a function of nerve axon radius. Increasing nerve radius by a factor of 2 increases capacitance and reduces membrane resistance by a similar magnitude, but reduces internal axon resistance by a factor of 4. The overall effect is that conduction velocity down an axon increases by a factor of 2 for every doubling of the cell radius.

The giant squid axon has a diameter of 500 μm and an action potential conduction velocity of 25 m/s. Many human nerves have diameters of ≈ 10 μm, which would result in conduction velocities on the order of 0.5 m/s. At this velocity a neural reflex would take 4 seconds to remove a finger from a hot flame. This is obviously too long to prevent damage to the finger.

In reality, nerves involved in such a reflex transmit action potentials at a velocity of 50 m/s. The reason for this phenomena is that many of our nerve fibers are surrounded at intervals with *Schwann cells* containing an insulating material called *myelin*. ■ **Fig. 3-5b** ■ Myelin greatly reduces membrane capacitance while reducing loss of current through the cell membrane. Myelin decreases the time constant and increases the length constant of the nerve allowing rapid electrotonic conduction along the axon with little decrement.

In addition, the insulating nature of Schwann cells only allows action potentials to be generated at gaps along myelinated nerves, called *nodes of Ranvier*. Because action potentials are restricted to the gaps in the myelin sheath, the electrical signal in the nerve "skips" from point to point along the axon, rather than having to proceed along every increment of the cell membrane. This is called *saltatory conduction*. This process increases conduction velocity, relative to that in an unmyelinated nerve, in a manner analogous to the difference in distance covered in a given time when we walk with a normal stride versus walking heel-to-toe. For any given axon diameter, myelinated axons have higher conduction velocities than unmyelinated axon. ■ **Fig. 3-5c** ■

■ **Fig. 3-5** ■
(a) Flow of positive charge across the axon membrane and through the axon interior during opening of the sodium channels in the nerve axon. (b) Local depolarization spreads to adjacent areas of the axon, bringing these areas to threshold and forming an action potential of identical magnitude and shape as that initially produced in the axon. Propagation of action potentials skips from point to point along myelinated axons, increasing conduction velocity. (c) The conduction velocity is greater in myelinated axons than unmyelinated axons for any given fiber diameter.

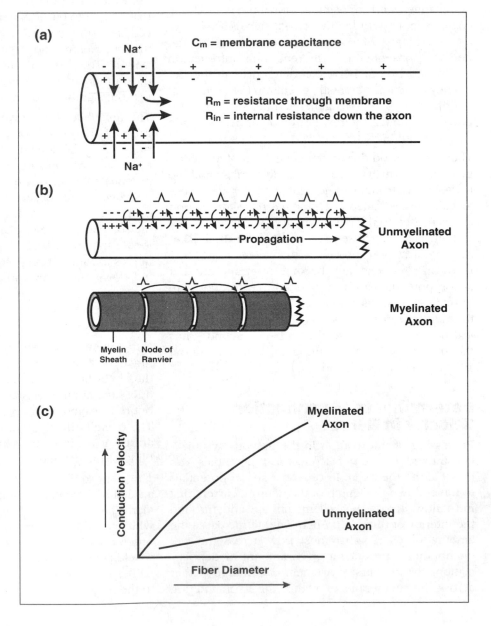

(a)

Na$^+$

C_m = membrane capacitance

R_m = resistance through membrane
R_{in} = internal resistance down the axon

Na$^+$

(b)

Propagation

Unmyelinated Axon

Myelinated Axon

Myelin Sheath   Node of Ranvier

(c)

Conduction Velocity

Myelinated Axon

Unmyelinated Axon

Fiber Diameter

Synaptic Transmission

In order to integrate sophisticated multiple sensory inputs and effector processes in mammalian systems, multiple nerve cells must be linked to one another. The connection between the axon terminal of one nerve and portions of another nerve is called a *synapse*. ■ **Fig. 3-6a** ■

Synaptic connections between nerves generally are not points where electrical activity is transmitted directly from one neuron to the next. Instead, action potentials reaching the end of the axon initiate changes in the axon terminus that release a chemical substance into the synaptic cleft. This chemical is called a *neuro-*

transmitter. A neurotransmitter binds to a postsynaptic receptor on the next neuron to elicit changes in the postsynaptic nerve membrane. This can result in either electrotonic depolarization (excitation) or hyperpolarization (inhibition) of the postsynaptic nerve.

Excitatory transmitters often induce nerve depolarization by increasing sodium conductance in postsynaptic nerves, whereas increased chloride conductance is the hyperpolarizing mechanism initiated by many inhibitory neurotransmitters. Norepinephrine, acetylcholine, glutamate, serotonin, peptides, and nucleotides are some of the types of agents employed as neurotransmitters in the nervous system.

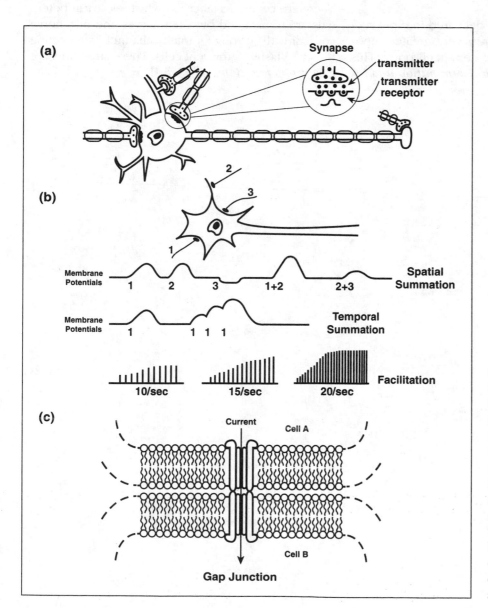

■ **Fig. 3-6** ■

(a) Synaptic connections between nerves. Synapses may be made with the nerve cell body, the axon terminus, or nerve dendrites. (b) Hypothetical effects of individual and simultaneous stimulation of several nerve projections to another nerve cell body. The lower tracing demonstrates the process of facilitation. (c) A representation of gap junctions.

The role of specific transmitters in any physiological process will be discussed where appropriate in later sections of this text.

The cell body of a single neuron can receive signals from several other neurons located elsewhere in the body. ■ **Fig. 3-6a** ■ An example of three such connections to a single neuron is shown in ■ **Fig. 3-6b** ■ . Different combinations of inputs from these presynaptic nerves can combine to create a variety of grades of electrical depolarizations or hyperpolarizations in the postsynaptic nerve body. These combinations may result in initiation or inhibition of action potential formation. This type of effect, resulting from simultaneous combined input from other neurons, is an example of *spatial summation*.

In addition, action potentials delivered in rapid succession can produce a progressively greater depolarization of the postsynaptic nerve cell body. This phenomenon is called *temporal summation and facilitation*. At some synapses in the central nervous system, this facilitation can last for hours or even days. This prolonged facilitation has been suggested as a model of memory.

Postsynaptic neurons do not exhibit sustained electrical changes to indefinite presynaptic activity. After long-term, high-frequency stimulation, response in the postsynaptic nerve may become attenuated. This phenomenon is called *synaptic fatigue* and results from depletion of neurotransmitter in the presynaptic nerve. Normal responses are not restored until neurotransmitter either is taken back up into the presynaptic nerve terminus by membrane transport mechanisms, or is resynthesized in the presynaptic nerve.

There are certain instances in which electrical potentials are transmitted between nerves and non-nerve cells directly through protein channels connecting the cytoplasm of adjacent cells. These structures are called *gap junctions*. ■ **Fig. 3-6c** ■

CHAPTER 4

Physiology of Skeletal Muscle

Synaptic Transmission Between Nerves and Skeletal Muscle

Skeletal muscle, as the name implies, refers to muscle tissues that are associated primarily with bones. Other forms of muscle (cardiac and smooth) play significant roles in the physiology of the cardiovascular, respiratory, gastrointestinal, renal, and reproductive systems. Skeletal muscle, however, is responsible for movement in response to stimuli from our external environment. These movements may be reflexive or voluntary. They can involve large muscle groups, such as those used in running or standing erect against gravity, or be responsible for fine movements of the eye and hand required to perform delicate surgery.

Body movement results from active shortening of many individual cells within a muscle. This shortening results from the generation of action potentials in the muscle cell that activate unique contractile proteins within the muscle cytoplasm, also called *sarcoplasm*. Skeletal muscle cannot generate its own action potential and contraction. It is dependent upon neurotransmitters released from efferent somatic motor nerve endings in response to nerve action potentials. Severing motor neurons to skeletal muscles renders them incapable of contraction and results in flaccid paralysis.

Action potentials are transmitted from nerve to muscle via special chemical synapses called *neuromuscular junctions*. ■ **Fig. 4-1** ■ When an action potential in the presynaptic motor axon reaches the axon terminal, it increases the permeability of the terminal to calcium. Calcium then flows down its electrochemical gradient into the terminal area, where it initiates fusion of acetylcholine containing lipid vesicles to the terminal membrane. As these lipid vesicles "blend" into the membrane lipids, acetylcholine is released into the synaptic cleft and eventually binds to receptors on specialized multiunit proteins in the muscle cell membrane, called *nicotinic receptors,* named after early observations

that this receptor can be activated or blocked by nicotine. See the bottom of ■ **Fig. 4-1** ■ .

The nicotinic receptor is an ion channel that allows passage of Na^+ and K^+ across the cell membrane when acetylcholine binds to special sites on the β-subunits of the protein. As a result, the underlying postjunctional muscle membrane, called the *motor end plate,* becomes depolarized, generating an end plate potential. End plate potentials are graded phenomena; the higher the frequency of action potential generation in the motor neuron, the more acetylcholine is released onto nicotinic receptors and the more depolarized the motor end plate becomes. The motor end plate region cannot generate action potentials, however.

The end plate potential spreads electrotonically to adjacent muscle membrane that does contain voltage-sensitive Na^+ and K^+ channels, analogous to those found in nerves. If the end plate potential is of sufficient magnitude, the adjacent muscle membrane will be brought to threshold and generate, as well as conduct, an action potential by the same mechanism seen in nerves, as discussed previously. The duration of a skeletal muscle action potential is about twice as long as that in typical nerves, but otherwise it has the same basic form as a nerve action potential.

Any factor that interferes with motor nerve transmission to muscle cells will result in inability of the muscle to contract. *Myasthenia gravis* is a disease in which a person's immune system malfunctions and attacks nicotinic receptors. As a result, those suffering from the disease have difficulty activating their muscle fibers, thus experiencing a partial flaccid muscle paralysis and weakness.

Cellular Basis of Muscle Contraction

Actual shortening of large muscles is the result of a unique interaction between two proteins, called

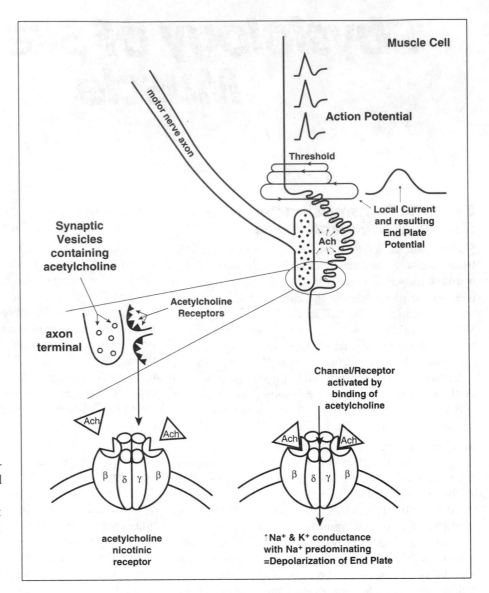

■ Fig. 4-1 ■

Depiction of the nicotinic acetylcholine receptor at the neuromuscular junction. Binding of acetylcholine to the receptor increases sodium conductance, with resulting depolarization of the motor end plate, which spreads electrotonically to the adjacent cell membrane, bringing it to threshold and initiating an action potential in the muscle cell.

---

actin and *myosin,* within muscle cells. **■ Fig. 4-2 ■** Muscle cells (or fibers) are extremely large (approximately 100 μm in diameter and up to several cm long). Muscle fibers contain myofibrils that have a unique striated appearance; hence skeletal muscle often is called *striated muscle.* These striations result from the highly organized interdigitation of actin and myosin molecules as shown in **■ Fig. 4-2 ■** .

The *sarcomere* is the term given to the contractile unit of muscle fibers and includes overlapping portions of actin and myosin, between actin attachment points (*z lines*). F-actin, sometimes called the *thin filament,* is a double-stranded polymer of G-actin protein monomers. Myosin is a thicker, heavier molecule composed of three distinct polypeptides. One

of these forms a twisted α-helical double strand of protein that associates with other such strands to form a long, thick tail region. These strands also project from the tail at intervals, each terminating in a globular head.

Two different types of myosin *light chain proteins* are associated with each globular head and are involved in control of the contractile process. The projecting head region of the myosin molecule is called a *crossbridge* because it can bind to actin and form a connection or bridge between the two molecules. Myosin also contains binding sites for ATP, ADP, and inorganic phosphate. It functions as an ATPase because it can enzymatically hydrolyze ATP to ADP and phosphate.

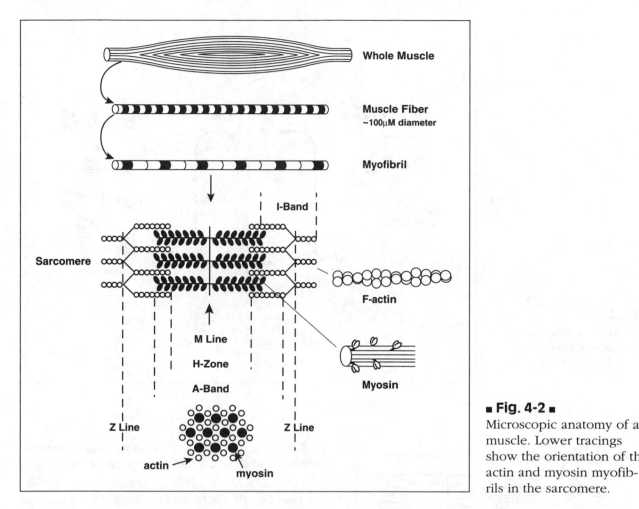

■ **Fig. 4-2** ■
Microscopic anatomy of a muscle. Lower tracings show the orientation of the actin and myosin myofibrils in the sarcomere.

Contraction of muscle results from the individual shortening of thousands of sarcomeres arranged in series within the muscle fiber. This shortening process at the molecular level is called the *crossbridge cycle* and is depicted in ■ **Fig. 4-3** ■ . When ADP and phosphate are bound to myosin, it has a high affinity for actin. As such, it binds the thin filament with its head at a 90° angle relative to the long axis of actin.

This binding, however, results in the dissociation of ADP and phosphate from myosin. This dissociation changes the conformation of the myosin head to a 45° angle, which results in stretching of the projecting myosin filaments in a manner similar to pulling on a spring. When this "spring" pulls back, a shortening of the sarcomere of about 10 nm results. In this state, the acto-myosin complex can bind ATP. When ATP binds to the crossbridge, detachment of the myosin head and ATP hydrolysis results. Energy released by the hydrolysis of ATP is believed to reset the myosin head at a 90° angle, thus completing the crossbridge cycle.

Regulation of Crossbridge Cycling

Clearly, the crossbridge cycle would proceed once and forever, until maximum sarcomere shortening occurred, were there not some means of regulating the interaction of the actin and myosin in the muscle fibers. Such regulation exists in the form of a chemical link between generation of the action potentials in muscle cells and eventual activation of the crossbridge cycle within muscle fibers. ■ **Fig. 4-4** ■

Muscle cells contain elaborate networks of *sarcoplasmic reticulum* (SR). The membrane of this organelle contains Ca^{++} ATPase pumps that actively concentrate calcium from the intercellular fluid into the SR. The muscle cell membrane projects deeply into the cell (forming a *T tubule*) and makes physical contact with the sarcoplasmic reticulum. ■ **Fig. 4-4** ■ When an action potential is generated in a muscle cell, it travels along the cell membrane and down

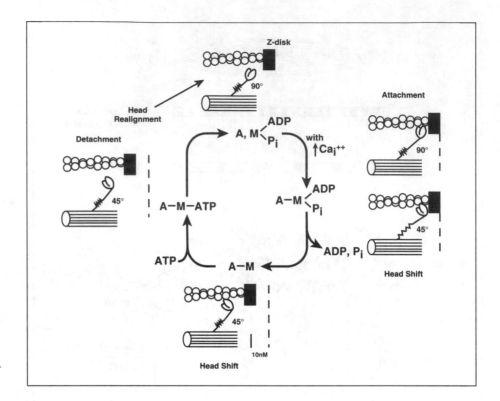

■ Fig. 4-3 ■

The crossbridge cycle in contracting skeletal muscle. (See text for explanation.)

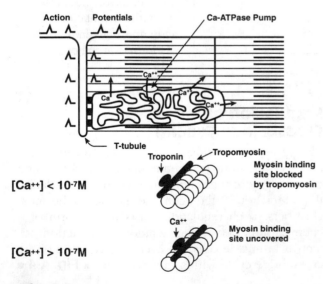

■ Fig. 4-4 ■

Demonstration of the effect of calcium released from the sarcoplasmic reticulum by action potentials in muscle cells. At calcium concentrations less than 10^{-7} M, tropomyosin blocks myosin binding sites for actin. At higher intracellular calcium concentrations, the interaction of calcium with troponin removes the inhibitory effect of tropomyosin, allowing crossbridge cycling to occur.

the T tubules to a point where it stimulates the release of Ca^{++} from the sarcoplasmic reticulum.

This release greatly elevates intracellular calcium concentration that serves as the trigger for initiating the crossbridge cycle as follows. Actin molecules are associated with a linear protein called *tropomyosin*. This molecule spans about seven G-actin monomer units and blocks the binding site on actin for myosin; see the bottom of **■ Fig. 4-4 ■**. Tropomyosin is associated with troponin, a regulatory protein. Troponin can bind calcium when levels of this ion exceed 10^{-7} M. When Ca^{++} levels increase inside muscle cells beyond this level, calcium binds to troponin, resulting in a change in the conformation of tropomyosin such that the binding sites for actin are uncovered. This then allows the crossbridge cycle to proceed.

Muscle will shorten and/or build force so long as the Ca^{++} levels are elevated and sufficient ATP is available to reset the crossbridge cycle. In the absence of such stimuli, the sarcoplasm reticulum pumps reduce intracellular calcium levels so that troponin is no longer bound with calcium and tropomyosin is allowed to block actin-myosin interaction. Also, an active crossbridge cycle eventually will stop, with crossbridges bound to actin, if ATP is not generated in the muscle cell. This occurs at death (no oxidative metabolism) and results in the condition called *rigor mortis*.

Skeletal Muscle Mechanics

A single action potential from a motor neuron results in a single action potential in each muscle fiber innervated by the neuron. This in turn leads to a single brief "twitch" contraction of muscle. ■ **Fig. 4-5a** ■ The duration of an action potential in skeletal muscle is much shorter than the duration of the twitch contraction (about 5 milliseconds versus tens or hundreds of milliseconds). Thus the absolute electrical refractory period of the muscle fiber is completed before the force generated by a single contraction dissipates. In skeletal muscle, therefore, it is possible to repeat the stimulus to the muscle

fast enough so that contractions add, one upon another. ■ **Fig. 4-5b** ■ *Tetanus, tetanic contraction,* or *fused contraction* are names given to the condition that occurs in muscle when summed contractions occur so closely together that they fuse into a smooth sustained contraction.

Motor nerve axons terminate in several branches, each of which innervate a single muscle fiber. All the muscle fibers supplied by a single axon will contract together as the action potential courses down the axon into its branches. A motor axon and all the cells with which it innervates is called a *motor unit.* ■ **Fig. 4-5c** ■ A motor unit is the smallest functional unit of a whole muscle; it is impossible to activate only some of the fibers in a motor unit. Some motor units might involve only a few muscle cells, whereas others might involve several thousand. Furthermore, large anatomical muscles such

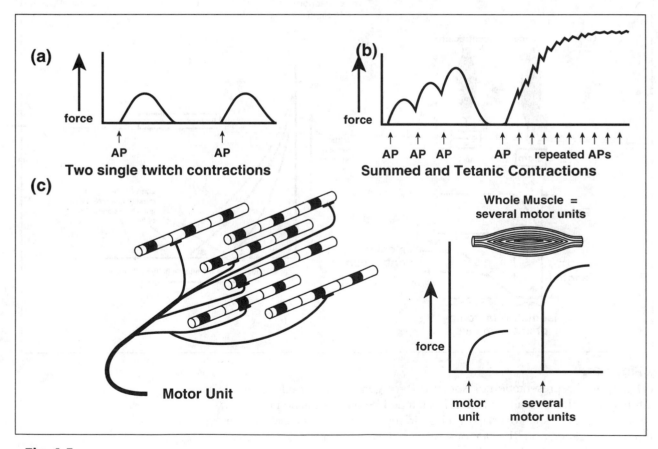

■ **Fig. 4-5** ■
(a) Force generation from two individual single contractions in a muscle cell as the result of two action potentials. (b) Resulting force generation after repetitive action potential stimulation of the muscle cell. (c) A skeletal muscle motor unit. Recruiting more motor units activates more muscle fibers and enhances the contraction of the whole muscle.

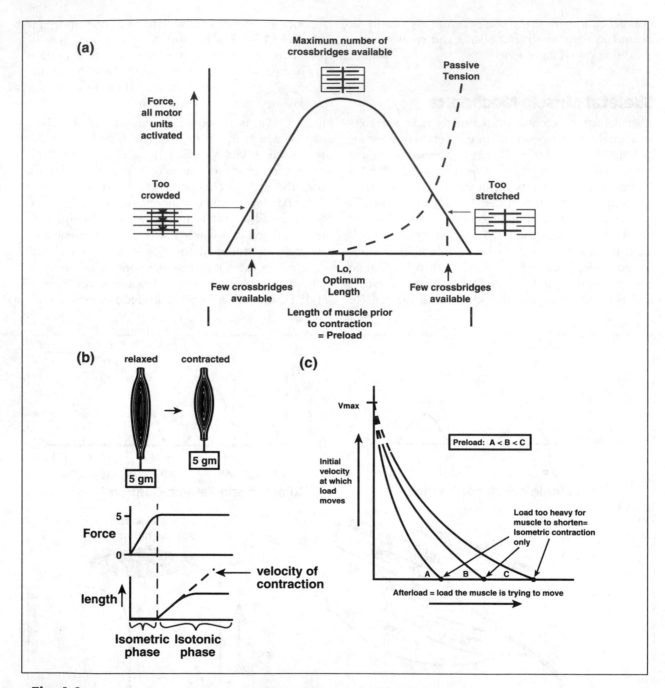

■ Fig. 4-6 ■

(a) Graphical representation of isometric force generation in skeletal muscle as a function of the length to which it is stretched before contraction (preload). Note L_o relates to ideal overlap of the actin myosin crossbridge sites and maximum force generation. (b) Demonstration of isotonic contractions of muscle with initial isometric phase followed by shortening of muscle and movement of the load. (c) The velocity at which a load is moved by a muscle contraction is inversely related to the weight of the load moved. Increasing preload on the muscle enhances the velocity at which any given load can be moved, or enhances the amount of load that can be moved at any given velocity. V_{max} = theoretical maximum velocity of contraction occurring while moving zero load.

as the biceps or gastrocnemius are composed of many motor units of varying sizes. The amount of force generated by these muscles as a whole, whether as a single twitch or a tetanic contraction, can be modified by the number and size of motor units being activated at a given time.

The nerves supplying a whole muscle contain many individual nerve fibers, each with different thresholds for activation and each innervating different motor units. Successively stronger stimuli from the central nervous system (or supplied artificially by an electrical stimulator in an experimental setting) will activate motor units in a sequential fashion, with units having the lowest threshold activated first. As more and more motor units are recruited by successively more nerve activation, the amount of force generated in the whole muscle increases. This is an example of *motor unit summation* or *motor unit recruitment*. See the right portion of ■ **Fig. 4-5c** ■.

In our bodies, muscles have two primary mechanical tasks: They generate force and can shorten to create movement. Pulling or pushing against an immovable object will develop force in the muscle without any actual muscle shortening. Similarly, holding a weight in the air against gravity requires muscle activation to prevent the weight from falling, but the muscle does not move the weight. These types of contractions are called *isometric,* or "same-length" contractions, because the muscle develops force but does not shorten.

The magnitude of force generated by an isometric contraction can be examined in single muscle cells or in isolated whole muscles. Such force is proportional to the number of crossbridges that can be activated during the contractile process. This, in turn, is a function of the length to which the muscle is passively stretched prior to generation of the isometric contraction, called the *preload.* ■ **Fig. 4-6a** ■ This passive stretch alters the amount of overlap between actin and myosin in the muscle fiber and thus the number of crossbridges available to generate force. This relationship is shown experimentally for isometric force generation in an isolated segment of muscle in ■ **Fig. 4-6a** ■.

As can be seen, there is an optimum resting length, L_o, from which the muscle produces maximum isometric force when activated. Stretching the muscle beyond this length pulls apart the sarcomere and reduces the number of crossbridges available for generating force. Compressing the muscle has a similar effect on crossbridge availability. Although most

skeletal muscles have complex geometric arrangements, muscles in simple arrangements such as those attached to long bones, usually are fixed at lengths near that for optimum force generation.

Relaxed skeletal muscle shows very little resistance to stretching until it is stretched beyond the optimum passive resting length. ■ **Fig. 4-6a** ■ Beyond this length, passive tension builds rapidly in the muscle due to elastic components in the muscle structure as a whole, in much the same way a rubber band becomes stiffer the further it is stretched.

Another function of muscle is to move a weight (or load) over a distance with a certain velocity. Consider the simple action of throwing a 1 kg weight over your shoulder. Muscles in your arms must first generate enough force to equal the weight. Once this is met, any additional activation of the muscle will result in muscle shortening and movement of the weight. This principle is shown in ■ **Fig. 4-6b** ■. The weight moved after the muscle starts to contract is often designated as the *afterload* of the contraction and the contraction that moved the load is called an *isotonic* ("same-force") contraction.

The initial velocity at which a muscle can move a load during an isotonic contraction is inversely proportional to the magnitude of load moved. ■ **Fig. 4-6c** ■ That is, the heavier the afterload, the slower the initial velocity of shortening. Velocity increases as lighter and lighter loads are moved. Theoretically, contracting a muscle against no afterload will result in the maximum possible velocity of shortening or V_{max}. V_{max} is never really attained physiologically, but it does estimate the theoretical intrinsic maximum rate of crossbridge cycling in the muscle. This value is a function of the myosin ATPase activity of a given muscle and will vary among muscle types.

Some muscle fibers, such as those required to blink the eyes, have high ATPase activities and shorten quickly, whereas those required for more sustained or slow movements, such as those of gluteal muscles used to help us stand erect against gravity, have low myosin ATPase activities. V_{max} for a given skeletal muscle type cannot be varied under physiological conditions; therefore, it is not a means by which skeletal muscle contraction can be altered.

At initial resting muscle lengths less than L_o, shortening velocity for movement of any given afterload will increase with an increase in the initial resting length of the muscle fiber; see the right portion of ■ **Fig. 4-6c** ■. Also, an increase in preload in this range will allow the muscle to move a heavier after-

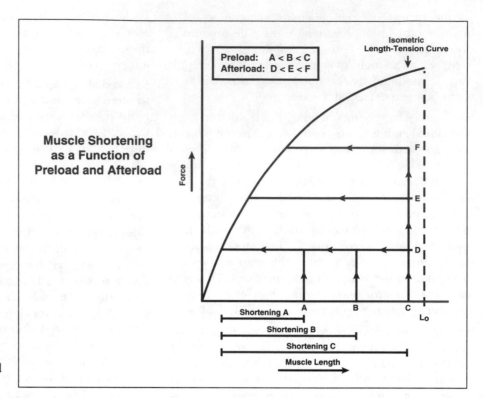

Preload: A < B < C
Afterload: D < E < F

Isometric
Length-Tension Curve

Force

F
E
D

**Muscle Shortening
as a Function of
Preload and Afterload**

Shortening A
A   B   C
Lo
Shortening B
Shortening C
Muscle Length

■ **Fig. 4-7** ■

Demonstration of isotonic muscle contractions at various levels of preload and afterload. The extent of shortening is increased by an increase in preload up to the optimum length for the muscle and is decreased by increases in afterload.

load at any particular velocity of shortening. This is simply a reflection of the principle that muscle performance is enhanced when more crossbridges are available for contraction.

The relationships between isometric force and passive length and that for shortening velocity and afterload are interrelated and determine the shortening and load-carrying capacity limits during muscle contraction. ■ **Fig. 4-7** ■ In an isotonic contraction, muscle will first develop force, then shorten; muscle length obviously decreases continuously during the isotonic contraction, however. At each successively smaller length, the maximum isometric contraction that theoretically could be developed by the muscle diminishes.

Eventually, during muscle shortening, a length is reached at which isometric force generation capa-

bility equals the load being moved. It is impossible for the muscle to shorten beyond this point, because at shorter muscle lengths the force generated by the available crossbridges would be less than the load being moved. The extent of shortening is proportional to the starting length of the muscle prior to contraction, at all values less than L_o, i.e., for a given afterload an increase in preload increases the extent of muscle shortening; this also is shown in ■ **Fig. 4-7** ■.

Again, this effect (and all skeletal mechanical properties) can be summed up as a function of the number of crossbridges activated during the contraction. A muscle with more crossbridges available for contraction can hold a heavier load and move it faster and farther than a muscle with fewer crossbridges available for contraction.

CHAPTER 5

Overview of the Cardiovascular System and Hemodynamics

The cardiovascular system typically is defined as a system that transports substances to the tissues of the body and removes byproducts of metabolism. The simplicity of this definition makes it easy to overlook the enormous importance of these functions for our survival and how the circulatory system is responsible for allowing us to exist in relatively large bodies. O_2, metabolic substrates, and the CO_2 produced by oxidative metabolism all enter or exit the cells of the body through some form of passive diffusion—the simplest, least energy-requiring cell transport mechanism available.

However, transport of molecules by diffusion is sufficiently rapid only over small distances. It takes approximately 5 seconds for an O_2 molecule to diffuse 100 microns, a distance consistent with distance between our cells. It is important to note that the time required for a molecule to diffuse given distances increases geometrically with the distance traveled; diffusion of a molecule over several centimeters can take many hours or even days. This time frame is not compatible with the metabolic needs of a body of human size.

It is the cardiovascular system that enables us to deliver O_2 and substrates into locations within our bodies where limitations to diffusion are minimized and the diffusion process can be exploited. Simply put: If, as a developing, evolving organism, we wanted to take advantage of having an enclosed, controllable internal environment, we would be restricted to a body size on the order of a microorganism were it not for our cardiovascular system. Any organism of our stature could not exist without a transport system to bring O_2 and substrates to the tissues and to remove the potential acid assault brought upon by production of CO_2. In this sense, the function of the cardiovascular system is life itself!

The cardiovascular system is a fluid transport system. The fluid component of this system, blood, is composed of about 45% oxygen-carrying red blood cells, or *erythrocytes*, small numbers of immune cells called "white" blood cells or *leukocytes,* several types of proteins suspended in solution, and water containing salts and other chemicals. The liquid component of blood is called *plasma* and consists of water, salts, proteins, metabolic substrates, and metabolic byproducts.

The cardiovascular system ■ **Fig. 5-1** ■ is composed of a muscular pump (the heart), and a blood delivery system composed of:

1. Arteries, which are tube-like conduits that bring blood to the peripheral organs
2. Capillaries, which are thin, microscopic vessels that allow for exchange of water and substances between the plasma and the interstitial fluid
3. Veins, which are vessels that return blood to the heart

The heart is a four-chambered muscular organ that contracts to pump blood and relaxes while being filled with blood, in a regular repeating cycle. Valves in the heart ensure forward flow through the chambers. The heart is really two pumps connected in series. The left heart is composed of the left atrium and ventricle separated by the mitral valve. Contraction of the left ventricle is responsible for pumping blood to all systemic organs except the lungs. Blood exits the ventricle through the aortic valve into a single-tube conduit called the *aorta*.

The aorta branches into successively smaller arteries that terminate into billions of capillaries. Blood from the capillaries of all the systemic organs is collected in veins and eventually returned to the right atrium. The right heart consists of the right atrium and ventricle separated by the tricuspid valve. The right ventricle pumps blood through the pulmonic valve into the pulmonary artery and thence into the lungs. Blood exiting the lungs is returned to the left

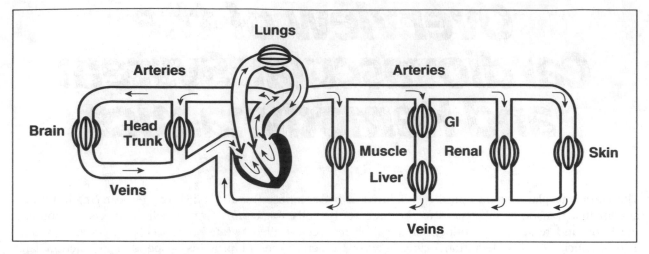

■ **Fig. 5-1** ■

A diagrammatic representation of the circulatory system. The pulmonary and systemic circulations are arranged in series, whereas most individual organ circulations are arranged in parallel.

atrium, where it passes through the mitral valve and into the left ventricle, completing the circulatory loop.

A student can gain insight into several functional aspects of the cardiovascular system simply by examining the structure of the system and its components. For example, imagine a bucket of water interposed between two pumps; one pump removes water from the bucket and returns it to the other pump, which moves the water back into the bucket. This is analogous to the situation surrounding the pulmonary circulation. It is obvious that if the outputs of the two pumps are not matched identically, the bucket could be drained dry or overflow. By analogy, should the output of the left heart exceed that of the right by as little as 2%, the pulmonary circulation would be drained of blood in less than 10 minutes.

Conversely, if right heart output exceeded the left by a similar amount, the pulmonary circulation would overflow and an individual would drown in his or her own body fluids. Clearly, neither of these situations arise in a healthy individual. Thus, the implication is that some mechanism must function to match closely the outputs of the right and left heart. Such a mechanism will be discussed in subsequent chapters.

The series arrangement of the right and left heart also implies that malfunctions in the left heart will affect the pulmonary circulation and the right heart, causing disturbances in pulmonary function. Indeed, one of the first clinical signs of left heart fail-

ure is respiratory distress. Conversely, problems in the right heart can affect the output of the left heart, imperiling the supply of blood to the systemic organs. This problem often occurs when blockages (usually blood clots) form in large veins or in the pulmonary arteries.

For the most part, the arterial system is a blood distribution system that delivers blood to organ systems arranged in a parallel, or side-by-side, network. In most cases, therefore, blood flow into one organ system is not dependent on blood flow through another organ upstream. The metabolic demands of our muscles, digestive system, brain, etc. may be different relative to one another and relative to their own resting values, depending on the activity in the organ at a given time. A parallel distribution system allows adjustment of blood flow to an individual organ to meet its needs without creating major disturbances in the blood supply to other organs.

All blood vessels except capillaries, have a similar basic structure. ■ **Fig. 5-2a** ■ The key component of the walls of arteries and veins is a circular layer of smooth muscle cells. This implies that the internal caliber of the blood vessel can be altered through contraction or relaxation of this layer. The adventitial layer of blood vessels contains elastic fibers and sympathetic nerve endings, suggesting an ANS influence over vascular function.

Finally, the inner layer of arteries and veins is lined with a single-cell layer of specialized tissue, the *en-*

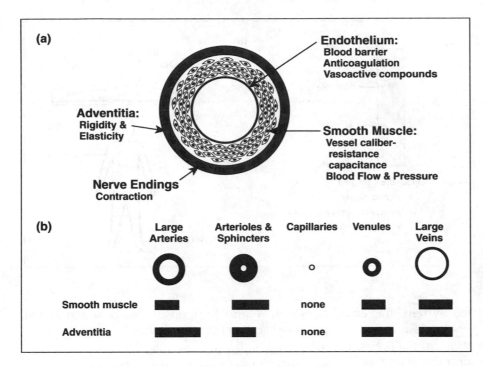

Fig. 5-2
(a) Diagrammatic representation of the blood vessel wall in an artery or vein. (b) Relative size and content (smooth muscle and adventitial) of arteries, capillaries, and veins.

dothelium. One could infer from the existence of such a lining that there is some necessity either for a barrier or a communication link between the components of blood and the vessel wall. The endothelium serves such functions, which will be discussed in subsequent chapters.

Within arteries and veins there are significant structural differences that relate to their various functions. **Fig. 5-2b** The aorta and large arteries are elastic vessels that primarily dampen pressure oscillations caused by the cyclic contraction and relaxation of the heart. They also help provide a forward flow through the capillaries during relaxation of the heart.

Small *arterioles* are the site of control of blood pressure and blood flow. They also are one factor that determines pressure and water transport across the capillaries. Precapillary sphincters determine the distribution of blood flow within the capillaries of an organ. They also influence intercapillary pressure and diffusion distances between capillaries. Oxygen, carbon dioxide, metabolic substrates and byproducts, water, and ions exchange between the circulatory system and the interstitial fluid through the capillaries.

Venules have some transport functions and serve to control intercapillary pressure. The veins and vena cava have a *capacitance,* or blood storage function.

They are one of the determinants of the filling of the heart and, hence, influence its output.

Hemodynamics

Hemodynamics is the study of the physical variables related to the containment and movement of blood in the cardiovascular system. Although the structure and function of the cardiovascular system as a fluid transport system is complex, it behaves much as if the heart were producing an average steady flow through a series of pipes, similar to flow of water through a city's water distribution system. Thus basic principles of fluid dynamics applied to the understanding of cardiovascular phenomena.

Fluid cannot move through a system unless it is applied to it. In fluid dynamics, such the form of fluid pressure (force per Many of us already are familiar with pounds per square inch of air press bile tires). Under the influence of column of fluid will exert a press tional to the depth any given la free surface of the fluid. **Fig** pressure is the product of flu beneath the free surface, an

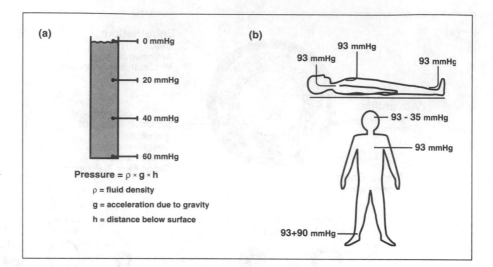

■ **Fig. 5-3** ■
(a) An example of hydrostatic pressure. (b) The effect of gravitational forces on pressure at various points in the body in the supine and upright individual.

to gravity. In the cardiovascular system, the unit used for the measurement of pressure is *millimeters of mercury,* or *mmHg.* Our average arterial pressure is about 93 mmHg. This represents the energy sufficient to raise a column of mercury, in a tube in a vacuum, a distance of 93 mm against the force of gravity.

The effect of gravity on pressure within our blood vessels is significant when we are standing. ■ **Fig. 5-3b** ■ The influence of gravity subtracts approximately 30 mmHg of pressure from the arteries and veins in the head and adds about 90 mmHg of pressure to those in the feet. This latter condition is responsible for the swelling and aching of the feet we experience after we have been standing for long periods of time. It also can result in significant pooling of blood in the lower extremities, to the extent that fainting will occur.

Pressure/Volume Relationships

In a rigid tube, volume is constant regardless of the pressure of the fluid within the tube. This is not the case with arteries and veins. Because they are flexible structures, the volume within them is related to the difference between the pressure inside the vessel and outside the vessel, the *transmural* or *cross-the-wall* pressure. See ■ **Fig. 5-4a** ■ There are a couple of ways of depicting pressure/volume interrelationships in blood vessels. The *capacitance* of a blood vessel equals the volume of blood contained in the vessel for a given transmural pressure. Sometimes, however, physiologists are interested in how volume changes in a distensible blood vessel for a given change in pressure. The

change in volume for a given change in transmural pressure is called the *compliance.*

Both capacitance and compliance can be used as measures of the flexibility of a blood vessel. For example, for vessels of equal initial internal diameters and transmural pressures, stiff vessels have a lower capacitance and compliance than flexible vessels. In general, veins are more compliant and have a greater capacitance than arteries.

Use of these variables to measure vessel flexibility fails, however, when vessels of markedly different size are compared. For example, a very large stiff-walled vessel may have a higher capacitance value than a tiny flexible vessel. For this reason, a vascular distensibility index, which is the *percent* increase in volume for a given increase in pressure, is calculated. Such an index indicates differences in vessel flexibility, even if vessels of different sizes are compared.

Even within a given vessel, capacitance, distensibility, and compliance are not constant. As transmural pressure increases, capacitance, distensibility, and compliance decrease. ■ **Fig. 5-4b** ■ Contraction of the smooth muscle within a vessel also decreases these variables and, at any given level of transmural pressure, vessels lose compliance and capacitance as we age.

Any transmural pressure within an artery or a vein exerts a force on the vessel wall that would tend to rip the wall apart were it not for opposing forces supplied by the muscle and connective tissue of the vessel wall. ■ **Fig. 5-5** ■ This force is called *tension* and is equal to the product of the transmural pressure and the vessel radius. This relationship, how-

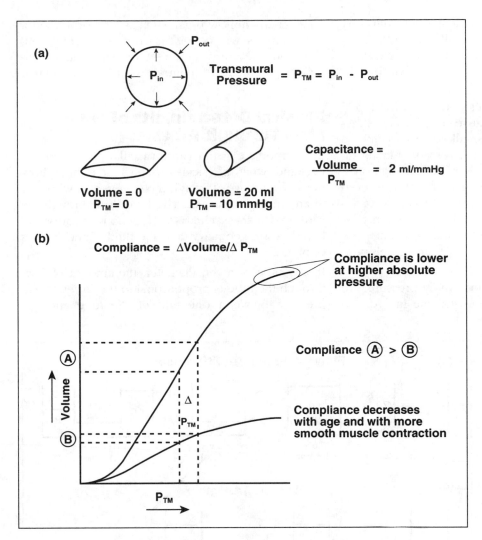

■ **Fig. 5-4** ■
(a) Representation of transmural pressure across the artery wall and its relationship to arterial capacitance. (b) Relationship between changes in volume vs. changes in transmural pressure. Compliance decreases with age and smooth muscle contraction and is lower at higher average pressures within the artery.

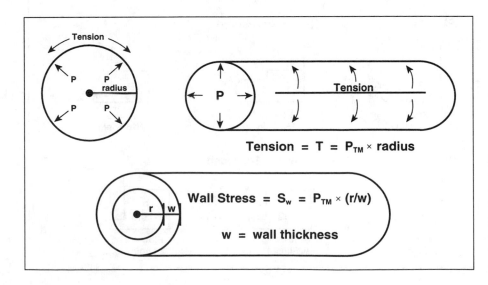

■ **Fig. 5-5** ■
Representation of wall tension in a cylinder, which is a function of transmural pressure and cylinder radius. Wall *stress* is a function of these variables divided by wall thickness.

ever, applies directly only to cylinders with very thin walls. Our blood vessel walls are sufficiently thick so that, in reality, this force is equal to a stress (the product of pressure and the radius divided by the wall thickness).

There are many consequences of this relationship in distensible tubes. First, because tension and stress are related to vessel radius, small vessels are able to withstand higher pressures than vessels of larger diameters. This allows us to have relatively high pressures within our capillaries (diameter ≈ 10 μm) even though they are a single-cell layer tissue with no muscle or adventitial components. In addition, vessels with thick walls relative to their radius also are able to withstand higher pressure than vessels with small r/w ratios.

Finally, tension and stress, not simply pressure, are the true forces that must be overcome in order to contract any hollow organ such as a blood vessel or the heart. As will be discussed subsequently, tension and stress are important determinants of energy requirements for contraction of hollow organs.

Physical Determinants of Fluid Flow Through Tubes

It is important in the cardiovascular system to understand what physical variables determine how much flow moves through the system as a whole or in any individual organ. The fluid flow through the cardiovascular system is a function of pressure, blood vessel geometry, and the fluid characteristics of blood.

In any tube of given diameter, the amount of flow through the tube is proportional to the *difference* in pressure between one end of the tube and the

■ Fig. 5-6 ■
(a) The relationship between pressure and fluid flow through a cylinder. (b) The relationship between fluid flow in a cylinder and the length of a cylinder. (c) The relationship between flow through a cylinder and the cylinder radius. (d) The relationship between flow in a cylinder and fluid viscosity, "n."

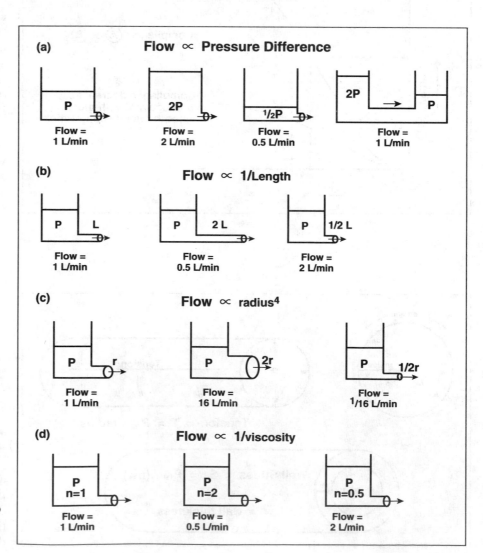

other. ■ **Fig. 5-6a** ■ Doubling the pressure difference doubles the flow; halving the difference halves the flow. Flow through a tube is *inversely* proportional to the length of the tube through which fluid flows. ■ **Fig. 5-6b** ■

Most important, flow through a tube is profoundly affected by the tube radius. ■ **Fig. 5-6c** ■ Flow trough a cylindrical tube is directly proportional to the radius raised to the fourth power, r⁴. Consequently, doubling the tube radius results in a sixteenfold increase in flow.

Finally, flow through a tube is affected by the viscosity, or the "thickness and stickiness," of the fluid. ■ **Fig. 5-6d** ■ Thick, sticky fluids will not flow as easily as thinner, water-like fluids.

Viscosity first was examined systematically by Sir Isaac Newton, who ascribed it to a "lack of slipperiness" between liquid particles that was analogous to friction between two solids. A physical description of viscosity is not necessary in this text. The units of viscosity are given in *poise,* named after Louis Poiseuille, who investigated the physical characteristics of fluid flow in tubes. Water has a viscosity of approximately 0.01 poise, or 1 centipoise. By contrast, blood plasma has a viscosity of 1.7 centipoise, and whole blood a viscosity of approximately 4 centipoise.

In the 1840s, Poiseuille conducted experiments that resulted in a mathematical relationship to describe flow in a cylindrical tube. This has become known as *Poiseuille's Law.* ■ **Fig. 5-7a** ■ Poiseuille's Law states:

$$Q = (P_1 - P_2)\pi r^4/8nl$$

where Q is flow, $(P_1 - P_2)$ is the pressure difference between the beginning and the end of the tube, r is the tube radius, l is the tube length, n is viscosity, and π and 8 are constants of proportionality.

The term $8nl/\pi r^4$ is equal to flow resistance, R, and is a measure of how easily the fluid can pass through a tube for any given pressure difference. In physiology, it is easier to calculate resistance as $(P_1 - P_2)/Q$, or mm Hg/ml/min. This term is called a *peripheral resistance unit* (pru).

Poiseuille's Law gives two of the most fundamentally important relationships used to describe flow and pressure in the cardiovascular system:

$$Q = (P_1 - P_2)/R \text{ and } (P_1 - P_2) = Q \times R$$

These equations tell us that flow is proportional to the pressure difference across a tube and inversely proportional to the resistance (i.e., as resistance in-

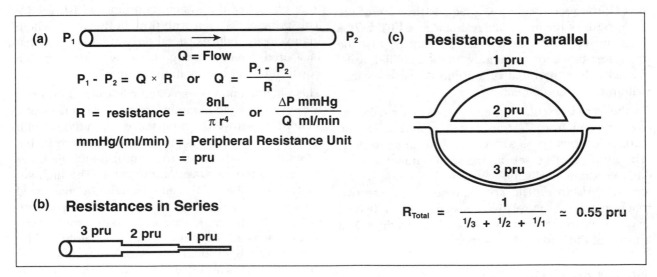

■ **Fig. 5-7** ■
(a) Poiseuille's Law. The magnitude of the pressure drop across the artery is equal to flow × resistance. Flow through an artery depends on the pressure difference between the ends of the artery divided by the vascular resistance.
(b) Calculation of resistances arranged in series. (c) Calculation of resistances arranged in parallel.

creases flow decreases). It also tells us that at any given flow, the pressure drop along the tube is proportional to resistance.

In the cardiovascular system, the final "end of the tube" is considered to be the right atrium. Pressure in the right atrium is about 2 mmHg. This is sufficiently close to zero and thus can be ignored. Therefore, P (usually mean arterial pressure) can be substituted for $(P_1 - P_2)$, yielding Q = P/R and P = Q × R. Applied to the whole cardiovascular system, the latter equation tells us that arterial pressure is the product of the flow output of the heart (the cardiac output) and the resistance to flow provided by all the blood vessels in the circulation (the *total peripheral vascular resistance* or TPR).

The cardiovascular system is composed of several vessels of different sizes and numbers. There are two simple rules used to determine how vessels of different size combine to give a single resistance to flow. ■ **Figs. 5-7b and 5-7c** ■ In a system composed of different-sized tubes arranged end to end, i.e., in series, the total resistance of that system is simply the sum of the individual resistances.

The aorta, however, branches into thousands of parallel arteries and capillaries. The total resistance in a system of parallel tubes is given by

$$1/R_{total} = \Sigma 1/R_{individual}$$

that is, the reciprocal of R_{total} equals the sum of the reciprocals of the individual resistances. ■ **Fig. 5-7c** ■ This means, under certain circumstances, that the total resistance of system of many parallel resistances is less than that of any individual resistance within that arrangement.

In the cardiovascular system vessels get smaller as we proceed from arteries down to arterioles and capillaries; this tends to increase resistance to flow. The number of vessels arranged in parallel also increases dramatically however, which tends to decrease resistance. The consequences of these two phenomena on the relative resistances of individual sections of the vasculature in our body is discussed further at the end of this chapter.

Blood Flow Velocity

In addition to the amount of blood flowing through a given vessel or organ system per minute, physiologists often are interested in how fast the blood stream is flowing (its velocity in centimeters per second). Fluid flow velocity (in centimeters per second) is given simply by flow volume per second (cm^3/s) divided by the cross-sectional area of the system through which the fluid is flowing. ■ **Fig. 5-8a** ■

If a flow of 200 mL/s in a tube is forced through another, narrower tube, the flow must go through that smaller opening faster in order to maintain a volume flow at 200 mL/s. Conversely, if this fluid is allowed to expand into a much larger cross-sectional area, it can move more slowly and still deliver 200 mL/s. At a constant flow, a decrease in the cross-sectional area through which the flow is moving increases flow velocity; an increase in area decreases flow velocity. This relationship holds whether applied to a single tube or a composite cross-sectional area of many tubes arranged in parallel, such as a cross-section of the vascular system.

The energy required to move blood at a certain velocity and the blood pressure exerted against the walls of an artery are interrelated by the *Bernoulli principle*. ■ **Fig. 5-8a** ■ The total energy of blood flow in a blood vessel is the sum of its potential energy (pressure against the vascular wall) and its kinetic energy due to its velocity (kinetic energy = 1/2 mass × velocity²). The total energy at any given point in a system is constant. This energy, however, can be transferred between pressure and kinetic components. For example, as flow velocity increases, lateral pressure must decrease in order to keep the total energy of the system constant. ■ **Fig. 5-8a** ■ This principle is seen with flow in the aorta, where high velocity reduces lateral pressure relative to that measured directly facing the flow stream, which equals the total energy in the system.

This phenomenon is exploited clinically to evaluate the severity of the hemodynamic consequences of a *stenotic* (narrowed) aortic valve. A catheter with two pressure sensors is placed in the heart in such a way that one lies within the ventricle and the other just across the narrowed aortic valve. The high-velocity jet of blood forced through the narrowed valve causes a significant drop in lateral pressure detected by the aortic sensor compared to the ventricular sensor; the hemodynamic severity of the stenosis is proportional to this pressure difference. In another medical consequence of the Bernoulli effect, blood flow forced through a narrowed portion of an artery due to an atherosclerotic plaque can result in significant reductions in lateral pressure, which, in the presence of contractile tone on the vessel, can cause vessel collapse and interruption in blood supply to the organ.

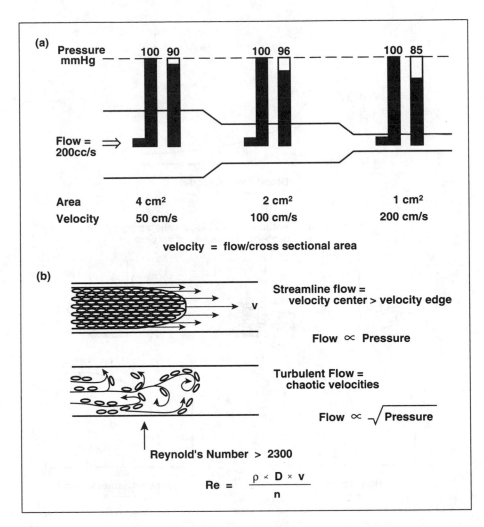

(a) Pressure mmHg

100 90   100 96   100 85

Flow = 200cc/s

Area   4 cm²   2 cm²   1 cm²
Velocity   50 cm/s   100 cm/s   200 cm/s

velocity = flow/cross sectional area

(b)

Streamline flow = velocity center > velocity edge

Flow ∝ Pressure

Turbulent Flow = chaotic velocities

Flow ∝ $\sqrt{\text{Pressure}}$

Reynold's Number > 2300

$$Re = \frac{\rho \times D \times v}{n}$$

■ **Fig. 5-8** ■
(a) The Bernoulli principle in a blood vessel. Lateral pressure decreases as flow velocity of the blood increases. (b) Streamline and turbulent flow. More pressure is lost during turbulent than during streamline flow. Turbulence occurs when the Re exceeds ≈ 2300.

Flow velocity also affects the organization of fluid layers of blood in our arteries. Normally, the cells in layers of fluid in our arteries flow with a streamlined or bullet-shaped profile. ■ **Fig. 5-8b** ■ If flow velocity becomes too high, however, these fluid layers tend to break apart and become random and chaotic. This condition, called *turbulence,* is a wasteful process that dissipates pressure energy in the cardiovascular system that otherwise could be used to produce flow.

Fluid engineers have devised a constant called the *Reynolds number,* R_e, which is a measure of the ratio of kinetic energy in the system (which will pull fluid layers apart) and the viscous component of the system (which holds the fluid layers together). R_e is the product of fluid density, vessel diameter, and average fluid velocity, all divided by fluid viscosity. Generally a value of $R_e > 2300$ indicates that turbulence will occur in the fluid stream. Clearly, large-diameter vessels, high flow velocity, or low blood viscosity favor turbulence in the cardiovascular system.

Turbulent flow creates sound in our arteries, whereas streamline, or *laminar* flow, is silent. Certain diseases, such as atherosclerosis or rheumatic fever, can scar the aortic or pulmonic valves, creating narrow openings and very high flow velocities. A clinician can detect this problem by listening to the noise created by the resultant turbulence. This noise is known as a *heart murmur.*

Rheology

Application of Poiseuille's Law to the cardiovascular system assumes that a fluid is homogeneous, i.e., its viscosity is independent of flow. Blood, being a suspension of proteins and cells, certainly is not a homogeneous fluid and its viscosity is affected by fluid flow velocity. ■ **Fig. 5-9a** ■ The presence of proteins and blood cells in blood have some important hemodynamic consequences: The hematocrit has a profound effect on blood viscosity and hence on

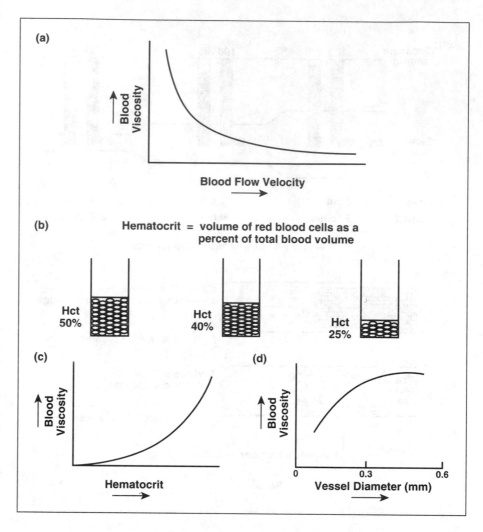

■ Fig. 5-9 ■
(a) Relationship between blood viscosity and blood flow velocity. (b) The hematocrit, or the proportion of blood volume due to the volume of red blood cells. (c) Relationship between blood viscosity and hematocrit. (d) Relationship between blood viscosity and vessel diameter.

vascular resistance. **■ Figs. 5-9b and 5-9c ■** Patients with polycythemia vera have very high hematocrits and hence very viscous blood. This creates a tremendous flow resistance against which the heart must pump.

Blood cells also tend to congregate in the center of the flow stream, leaving a thin layer of cell-free plasma against the vascular wall. This plasma has a viscosity of only 1.7 centipoise, as opposed to the 4 centipoise for whole blood. In large vessels such as the aorta, this low-viscosity layer is only a small percentage of the viscosity of the flow stream and has little effect on viscosity of blood flowing through that vessel. In small arterioles and capillaries, however, this thin layer becomes an ever-greater percentage of the total volume contained within the vessel, and viscosity of the fluid as a whole decreases. **■ Fig. 5-9d ■** Consequently, blood flowing through tiny vessels has a lower viscosity than that flowing through larger vessels. This effect makes it

easier for blood to flow through extremely small capillary networks in the cardiovascular system.

Distribution of Pressure, Flow, Velocity, and Blood Volume in the Cardiovascular System

With an understanding of hemodynamic principles, a student can gain meaningful insights into characteristics of the cardiovascular system from an examination of the distribution of flow, velocity, pressure, and volume within the system. For example, because veins are more compliant than arteries, one would expect that as the vascular system is filled with blood, the majority of this blood will end up in the veins as opposed to the arteries. This is precisely the case, as shown in **■ Fig. 5-10a ■**. Also, because cross-sectional area increases greatly from arteries to arterioles and then to the capillaries, lowest blood flow velocity occurs in the capillary network. Slow velocity through this exchange segment of the vascular system has the beneficial effect of allowing more time for exchange of material between the cardiovascular system and the extracellular fluid.

The heart is an intermittent pump, as can be seen in ■ **Figs. 5-10b and 5-10c** ■ . It generates high pressure within the ventricles when it contracts, called *systole,* which then drops to near zero when the heart relaxes, the *diastole.* Because arteries are compliant, however, some of the ejection of blood into the arteries distends these vessels, like the expansion of a water-filled balloon. During diastole, recoil of the arteries pushes blood forward against the downstream vascular resistance, generating a significant diastolic pressure.

Examination of the pressure profile across the cardiovascular system shows that the largest drop of pressure occurs across the arterioles, indicating that this is the site of greatest vascular resistance in the system. ■ **Figs. 5-10b and 5-10c** ■ Although there are many more arterioles than arteries in the cardiovascular system (resistances in parallel), this large pressure drop indicates that their reduction in individual size dominates over the addition of parallel vessels. Similarly, although individual capillaries are very small, so many of these lie in parallel that resistance across the capillaries is actually lower than that across the arterioles; hence, the pressure drop across the capillary segment of the circulation is less than that across the arterioles. Finally, since the outputs of the right and left heart are the same, the low pressure in the pulmonary circulation must indicate (by Poiseuille's Law) that vascular resistance is much lower in the pulmonary circulation than in the systemic circulation.

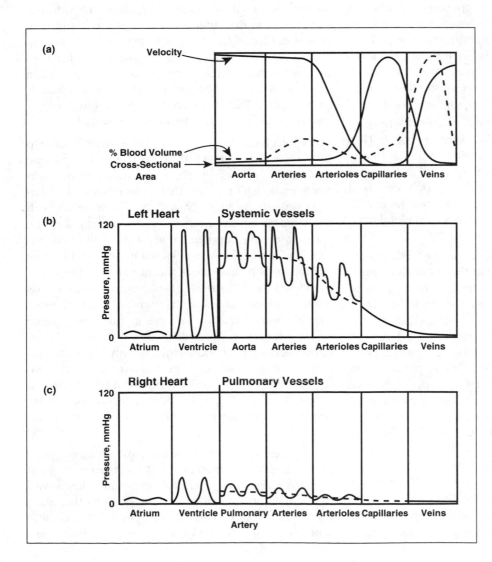

■ **Fig. 5-10** ■
(a) Profile of blood volume, blood velocity, and total vessel cross-sectional area at various locations in the cardiovascular system. (b) Pressure profile in the systemic, or left side, of the cardiovascular system. (c) Pressure profile in the pulmonary, or right side, of the circulation.

CHAPTER 6

Cardiac Electrophysiology

The heart is composed of muscle whose contractions are coupled to the generation of action potentials within its cells. Unlike skeletal muscle, however, cardiac muscle is not dependent upon innervation for generation of its electrical activity. All cardiac cells have the property of *automaticity,* the ability to generate their own action potentials, and the property of *rhythmicity,* the ability to generate these potentials in a regular, repetitive manner. Although the heart is innervated by the parasympathetic and sympathetic nervous systems, the ANS modulates and regulates cardiac performance rather than initiates contraction. (This lack of dependence on nerve connection for contraction makes heart transplant operations possible).

All myocardial cells are coupled electrically through gap junctions at points called *nexi*. ■ **Fig. 6-1a** ■ This allows generation of an action potential in one myocardial cell to spread rapidly to all cells in the heart. Thus, electrically, the heart behaves as a functional syncytium, or as if it were one large cell. There are no functional equivalents of skeletal muscle motor units in the myocardium.

The generation of action potentials in cardiac muscle cells is more complex than that of skeletal muscle or nerve and results in unique action potential forms. ■ **Fig. 6-1b** ■ There are two broad types of cardiac action potentials: Those characteristic of cardiac muscle and Purkinje fibers are called *fast response action potentials,* and those characteristic of the SA and AV nodes are called *slow response action potentials.* The fast response is divided into five phases. ■ **Fig. 6-1c** ■ The initial rapid depolarization of the cell membrane is termed Phase 0. Phase 1 represents the subsequent partial repolarization of the membrane, which is followed by Phase 2, a unique plateau region of the action potential. Phase 3 is the rapid repolarization phase of the action potential and Phase 4 is the resting membrane potential.

The resting membrane potential is primarily a K^+ diffusion potential and thus is sensitive to changes in external K^+ concentration. ■ **Fig. 6-1d** ■ Abnormal extracellular K^+ concentrations can alter cardiac function. Consequently plasma K^+ levels are monitored very carefully in a clinical setting. There is a small component of Na^+ influx to the cardiac resting membrane potential, making the resting membrane potential slightly more positive than the K^+ Nernst potential. Cardiac cells have an intrinsic buffer system that attenuates changes in membrane potential caused by changes in external K^+ concentration. Over the physiological extremes of 2 to 7 mM, K^+ conductance increases or decreases when external K^+ concentration increases or decreases, respectively. This helps counteract the effect of external K^+ alone on the membrane potential.

Many ion channels are involved in the overall makeup of the fast response. ■ **Fig. 6-2** ■ The rapid upstroke in Phase 0 occurs by the same mechanism as in nerve or skeletal muscle. That is, membrane depolarization opens voltage-sensitive Na^+ channels, which further depolarizes the membrane, causing a rapid, self-reinforcing depolarization of the cell. The cardiac Na^+ channel is also self-limiting in that the same depolarization that opens the m gates of the channel closes the h, or back gates, several milliseconds later. In nerve and skeletal muscle a K^+ channel opens soon after this Na^+ event, producing rapid cell repolarization. In cardiac cells, however, this enhancement of K^+ conductance is only transient, expressed as gK_{to}, where *to* means *transient outward.* It produces only a partial repolarization of the cell (Phase 1). For a large duration of the action potential, K^+ conductance actually is suppressed in cardiac cells.

Shortly after Phase 1 occurs, a unique channel opens in the cardiac cell membrane. This channel, termed the *L-type slow Ca^{++} channel,* opens and closes with depolarization in a manner analogous to that seen for the Na^+ channel, except its opening and closing kinetics are much slower. The electrochemical gra-

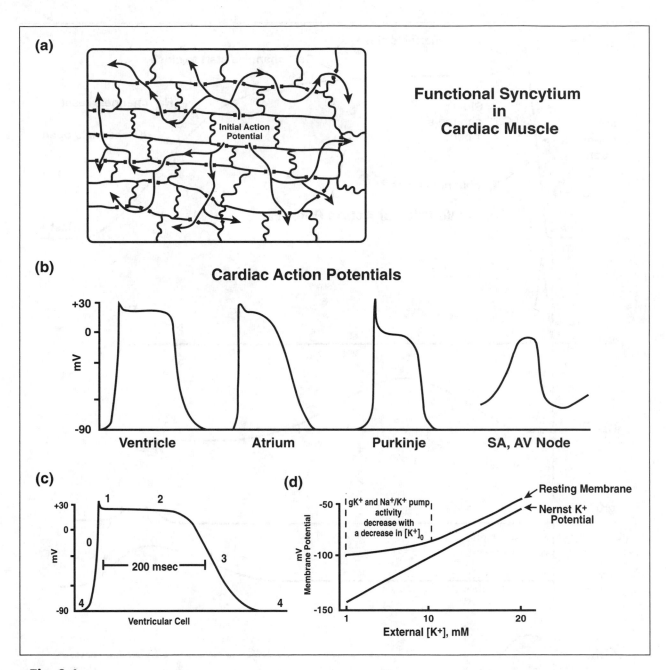

■ Fig. 6-1 ■

(a) The spread of an action potential through adjacent myocardial cells. The heart behaves as a functional syncytium. (b) Action potentials in various myocardial cell types. (c) A ventricular action potential. Point 0 = rapid up-stroke, point 1 = partial repolarization, point 2 = plateau, point 3 = rapid re-polarization, and point 4 = resting potential. (d) Relationship between cardiac resting membrane potential in external K+ concentration.

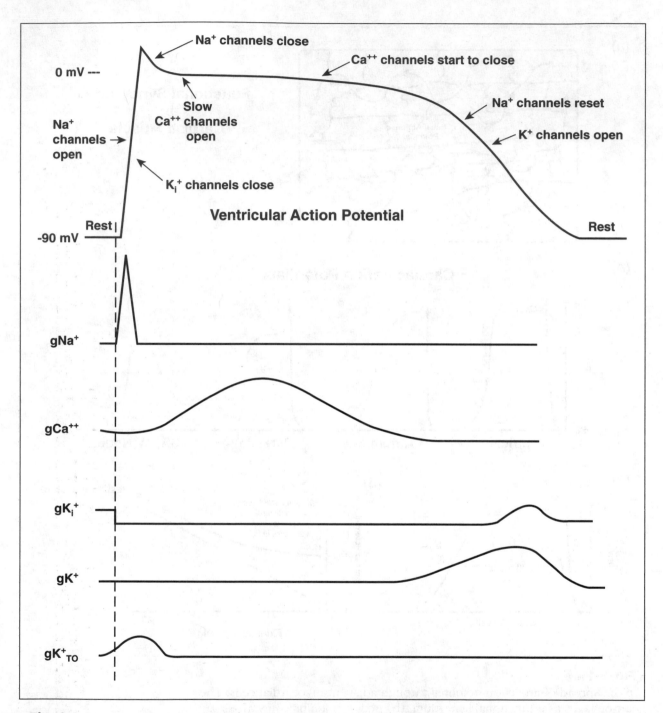

■ **Fig. 6-2** ■

Membrane conductances for sodium, calcium, and potassium during different phases of a ventricular action potential. All conductances are altered by opening and closing of specific ion gates in the cardiac cell membrane in response to different levels of membrane potential.

dient for Ca^{++} is enormous in cardiac cells; once the calcium channel opens, positive charge from Ca^{++} rushes into the cell. This positive influx approximately matches the positive efflux carried by K^+ exiting through a few open K^+ channels in the membrane. This balance causes the membrane potential to remain relatively constant at a positive value and creates the plateau, or Phase 2, of the action potential.

Eventually the Ca^{++} channels close and other K^+ channels open late in the action potential, thus bringing about a rapid repolarization of the cell membrane. Because of the plateau phase of the cardiac action potential, cardiac cells have a very long refractory period and a single contraction of cardiac muscle is completed before a second action potential can be generated. Thus, *cardiac cells cannot be tetanized,* a condition that obviously would not be compatible with the function of the heart as a blood pump.

Any condition or therapy that alters the intercellular or extracellular concentrations of Na^+, Ca^{++}, or K^+, or alters membrane permeability to these ions, can alter the electrical activation of the heart and subsequent myocardial performance. For example, catecholamines (epinephrine and norepinephrine) enhance Ca^{++} movement and increase the size of the cardiac action potential. A class of drugs called *calcium channel blockers,* often used to treat abnormal cardiac rhythms and high blood pressure, depresses Ca^{++} movement and results in small action potentials. Norepinephrine increases Phase 3 K^+ conductance, thereby shortening the cardiac refractory period. Hypokalemia and certain drugs used to treat abnormal cardiac rhythms have the opposite effect. Distension of the heart chambers, as in heart failure, or reducing the O_2 available to the heart (myocardial ischemia) partially depolarize the resting membrane potential, bringing cardiac cells closer to threshold and making it easy for even weak nonphysiological stimuli to activate the myocardium.

Initiation and Propagation of Cardiac Action Potentials

Specialized Conduction Tissue

For the heart to function as an efficient pump, action potentials and subsequent myocardial contraction must be generated and spread through the myocardium in a regular, repetitive, and organized manner. This will not occur if cardiac cells express their automaticity in a random, unpredictable fash-

ion. Normally, prior to each contraction of the heart, cardiac electrical activity is initiated by a modified set of muscle cells on the posterior aspect of the right atrium at the junction of the superior and inferior vena cava. This tissue is called the *sinoatrial* or *SA node.* ■ **Fig. 6-3a** ■

Once an action potential is initiated by the SA node, it travels through both atria at a rate of 0.1 to 1.0 m/s and coalesces at a second area of specialized conduction tissue, called the *atrioventricular,* or *AV node.* This node lies at the junction between the atria and ventricles in the ventricular septum. Conduction through the AV node is very slow (about 0.05 m/s) and delays movement of the cardiac action potential into the ventricles. This delay has the important effect of allowing more time for the ventricles to fill with blood prior to contraction. Conduction of action potentials through the AV node shows directional preference, that is, action potentials travel more easily from the atria through the AV node toward the ventricles than in the opposite direction.

Once the action potential emerges from the AV node, it enters the *bundle of His,* which splits into left and right bundle branches, which in turn give rise to *Purkinje fibers.* These fibers line the endocardial surface of both ventricles. Purkinje fibers possess the fastest conduction velocity in the heart (about 4 cm/s). Conduction through the Purkinje fibers assures that the action potential spreads to all the ventricular muscle as rapidly as possible so that it may be activated in unison. The ventricle itself is activated in the sequence of septum/papillary muscle and endocardium to the epicardium and from the apex to the base of the heart.

Action Potentials in Nodal Tissue

Action potentials generated in the SA and AV nodes have a smaller resting membrane potential than that of cardiac muscle. ■ **Fig. 6-3b** ■ Nodal tissue does not contain fast voltage-gated Na^+ channels; therefore the action potential is carried entirely by the slow voltage-dependent Ca^{++} channels and the rate of rise in Phase 0 is slower compared to ventricular cells. In addition, nodal action potentials show no plateau and a slow Phase 3.

The most unique characteristic of action potentials in the SA and AV nodes, however, is the spontaneous, progressive, and recycling depolarization that occurs in Phase 4. This forms the basis for their automaticity and rhythmicity. The ionic basis for the progressive depolarization in Phase 4 is depicted in ■ **Fig. 6-3b** ■ .

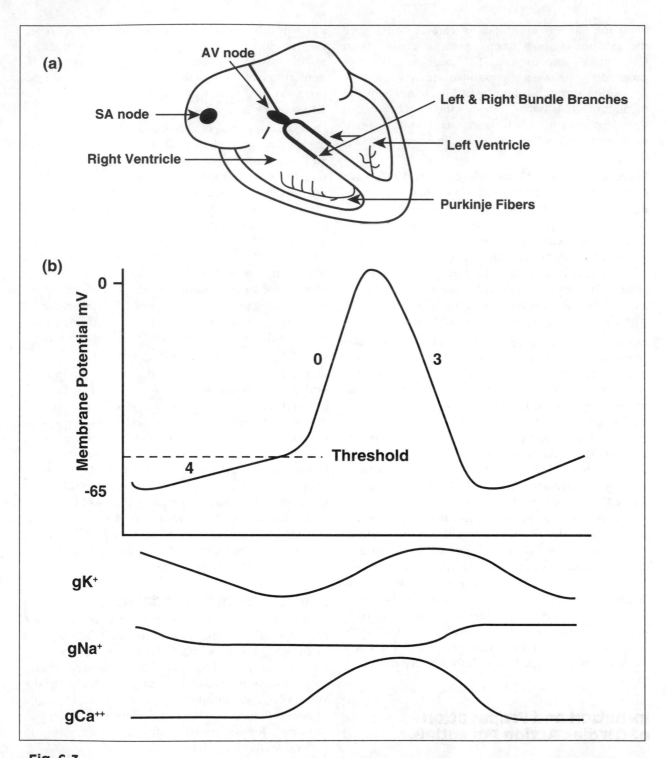

■ **Fig. 6-3** ■

(a) Specialized cardiac conduction tissues: the SA node, AV node, left and right bundle branches, and Purkinje fibers. (b) A representation of conductance changes for sodium, calcium, and potassium during an action potential in the SA node. The drifting resting membrane potential forms the basis of rhythmic activation of the myocardium.

Shortly after Phase 3 these cells experience a slight increase in Na+ conductance, which tends to halt and reverse further hyperpolarization of the cell membrane. Most important, however, there is a progressive reduction in gK+ and hence K+ efflux throughout Phase 4, which results in progressive depolarization of the cell. As depolarization begins to activate slow Ca++ channels, the membrane becomes depolarized in a reinforcing manner, resulting in the action potential. Depolarization later inactivates the Ca++ channels and the cell repolarizes due to K+ efflux. The decay of gK+ in Phase 4 then reoccurs, thus repeating the action potential cycle.

The SA node possesses the highest intrinsic rate of spontaneous action potential generation of the specialized conduction tissues. With a normal intact autonomic nervous system its rate is about 80 impulses/s. This is faster than the intrinsic rates of the AV node (approximately 50/s) or the Purkinje fibers (<20/s). Consequently, the SA node continually activates the heart before any other cardiac tissue can generate its own action potential. For this reason, the SA node is often called the *pacemaker of the heart,* as its rate of firing determines the heart rate or number of heartbeats per minute.

Phase 4 of the action potentials in the nodal tissue is affected by both branches of the autonomic nervous system. Acetylcholine from the vagus nerve that innervates the SA node slows the heart rate. Acetylcholine hyperpolarizes the resting membrane potential and decreases the slope in Phase 4; thus it takes longer for the cells to spontaneously reach threshold and fewer action potentials are generated in a given period of time. Norepinephrine or activation of the sympathetic nervous system increases the slope in Phase 4 of the SA node and hence increases the heart rate.

Acetylcholine decreases, whereas norepinephrine enhances, conduction velocity through the AV node. Conduction through the AV node also is sensitive to repetitive stimulation. Continuous stimulation at high rates results in an increased refractoriness of the nodal tissue. This helps prevent the ventricles from being driven at abnormally high rates that might impinge upon the time needed for them to fill during diastole.

Conduction of action potentials through myocardial cells is affected by characteristics of the action potentials themselves. Conduction velocity is increased when the amplitude of the action potential is increased. This may occur due to factors that enhance Na+ and Ca++ influx into the cell. Conduction of action potentials through the myocardium also is increased whenever the rate of depolarization in Phase 0 is increased (increased dV/dt). In addition, it can also occur by hyperpolarization of the resting membrane potential, which results in a larger amplitude action potential once the cell is activated. Depolarization of the cell membrane (such as that which occurs from inhibition of Na+/K+ pump activity in ischemia) will reduce the size of the action potential and reduce conduction velocity.

Conduction Abnormalities

Certain pathological conditions, such as scar tissue formation after myocardial infarction or myocardial ischemia, can result in the generation of action potentials in areas of the myocardium other than the SA node. These areas are called *ectopic foci.* Problems occur when such action potentials are generated in the myocardium in a random fashion or when the myocardium becomes paced by the ectopic foci at rates too high to allow proper filling of the ventricular chambers with blood. A type of condition that can lead to this problem is a phenomenon called *re-entry,* depicted in ▪ **Fig. 6-4** ▪. Consider action potentials proceeding down two sets of muscle pathways in the ventricle bridged by a muscle path in between. In normal myocardium, action potentials entering from the left and right paths eventually will come upon tissue refractory to additional stimulation due to the other action potential. Thus the action potentials from either branch will not cross over and proceed further.

Damaged myocardium might not conduct action potentials at all; see the center portion of ▪ **Fig. 6-4** ▪. This myocardial tissue will not contract, but action potential conduction through the remaining myocardium remains normal. In some cases, however, damaged myocardium will allow action potentials to proceed in one direction but not in the opposite direction; see the lower part of ▪ **Fig. 6-4** ▪. If an action potential is able to conduct slowly through this damaged area, it may emerge in the healthy myocardium *after* that myocardium is over its refractory period from the initial activation.

This "re-entry" action potential will reactivate the healthy myocardium, sending another action potential generation through the bridge. This process will repeat again and again in an endless circle, resulting in a repetitive contraction of the muscle. This condition is called a *circus rhythm.* Such circuits may in-

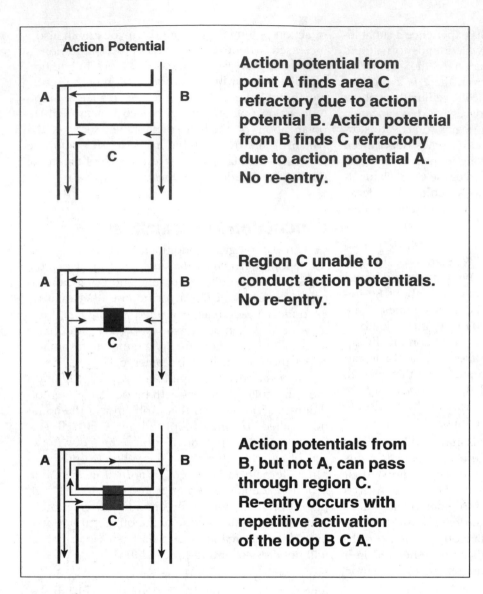

Action Potential

Action potential from point A finds area C refractory due to action potential B. Action potential from B finds C refractory due to action potential A. No re-entry.

Region C unable to conduct action potentials. No re-entry.

Action potentials from B, but not A, can pass through region C. Re-entry occurs with repetitive activation of the loop B C A.

■ **Fig. 6-4** ■
Representation of the re-entry phenomenon. Re-entry occurs when action potentials are allowed to flow preferentially in one direction through a segment of myocardium but not the other. (See text for details.)

volve a few myocardial cells, or large portions of the myocardium that then pace the whole heart at an abnormally high rate (greater than 250 beats/min). Also, because the AV node is predisposed to unidirectional conduction of action potentials, it is a common site of re-entry problems.

Ischemic conditions inhibit Na^+/K^+ pump activity in the heart. This results in accumulation of Na^+ and Ca^{++} inside the myocardial cells and progressive depolarization, which makes it more likely that they

will reach threshold and fire their own action potentials. Ischemia increases the probability of generating ectopic action potentials in myocardial cells and predisposes the heart to re-entry arrhythmias due to creation of small, slowly conducting action potentials. Formation of ectopic action potentials also are prompted by drugs such as caffeine, nicotine, and norepinephrine. Fatigue and emotional or physical stress, which activate the sympathetic nervous system, can predispose one to the formation of abnormal action potentials in the myocardium.

CHAPTER 7

The Electrocardiogram

Definition and Components of the ECG

When activated, the heart is a concentrated locus of electrical activity in the body. Of our total body mass, 60% to 70% is electrolyte solution, which is a good conductor of electricity. When a portion of the myocardium becomes depolarized its polarity is reversed, becoming positive on the inside and negative on the outside relative to neighboring inactivated tissue. This difference in polarity is transmitted through the body to the surface of the skin. ■ **Fig. 7-1a** ■ An *electrocardiogram,* or ECG, is an amplified, timed recording of the electrical activity of the heart as it is detected on the surface of the body. It results from the composite of all the different types of action potentials generated in the myocardium. ■ **Fig. 7-1b** ■ The exact mechanism by which these potentials combine to produce the pattern of a typical ECG is beyond the scope of this text. However, all normal ECGs have the same basic components. ■ **Fig. 7-1c** ■

The first sign of electrical activity in the heart revealed by the ECG is a small, rounded, upward (positive) deflection called a *P wave*. The P wave is caused by depolarization of the atria (not just the SA node). After a short interval of time, a complex, short-duration, high-amplitude, spike-like potential is observed. This potential, called the *QRS complex,* is caused by depolarization of the ventricles. By definition, within this complex the first downward deflection after the P wave is called a *Q wave,* the next upward deflection is called an *R wave* and the next subsequent downward deflection is called an *S wave*. (Depending on the location of the ECG recording on the body, the Q and S deflections might not be seen and ventricular depolarization may appear only as an R wave on the ECG. Nevertheless, such a wave is often called the QRS complex).

Following the QRS complex, the entire ventricular mass is depolarized, there is no potential difference between areas of the myocardium, and no deflections are seen on the ECG. The ECG is said to then be *isoelectric* or at *zero potential*. Once the ventricles begin to repolarize, a broad wave of modest amplitude called a *T wave* is observed. Repolarization of the atria is not seen in a typical ECG because it occurs during the same interval of time as the QRS complex and is lost in that signal.

Intervals between waves in the ECG are of physiological and clinical importance. The PR interval is the time from the beginning of the P wave to the start of the QRS complex and represents the amount of time the action potential takes to travel from the SA node through the AV node. The PR interval typically lasts 0.12–0.20 second. Since the majority of this time represents the delay of action potential conduction through the AV node, inhibition of conduction through the AV node often is reflected as a lengthening of the PR interval.

The QRS interval represents the interval of time the action potential takes to travel from the end of the AV node through the ventricles (normally 0.06 to 0.1 second). The normal conduction pathway through the bundle branches, Purkinje fibers, and ventricular muscle is the most efficient and rapid mode of action potential travel. Therefore, any pathway other than this takes longer than normal and results in an abnormally long QRS interval. The time between the initiation of the QRS complex and the end of the T wave is called the *QT interval* and is influenced by factors that alter ventricular repolarization. It is inversely proportional to heart rate and often is altered by drugs or conditions that affect the rate of myocardial repolarization (i.e., alter K^+ conductance).

Analysis of the ECG

Although it is correct to say that the electrical activity in the heart can produce an ECG, the physician looks at this process in reverse; the physician examines the ECG in order to evaluate electrical activity in the heart. The electrocardiogram is one of the most useful diagnostic tools available to the physician. Before attempting to understand how ECGs are analyzed, it is important to understand what information can and cannot be gained from the analysis of an ECG.

The ECG can be used to detect abnormalities in heart rhythm and conduction, myocardial ischemia and infarction, plasma electrolyte imbalances, and effects of numerous drugs. One also can gain information from the ECG about the anatomical orientation of the heart, the size of the atria and ventricles, and the path taken by action potentials through the heart during activation of any given part of the myocardium (e.g., the average direction of activation of the ventricles). The ECG, however, does not give *direct* information about the contractile function of the heart. Other tools must be used for such an evaluation and will be discussed in subsequent chapters.

There are two broad classes of evaluations performed using the ECG. One of these involves pattern recognition, or evaluation of abnormalities in the basic ECG form. Arrhythmias, conduction abnormalities, electrolyte disturbances, drug effects, and myocardial metabolic disorders such as ischemia can be detected as abnormal patterns from a single ECG electrode placed at almost any location on the surface of the body. Nevertheless, the amplitude, and in some cases the polarity, of various

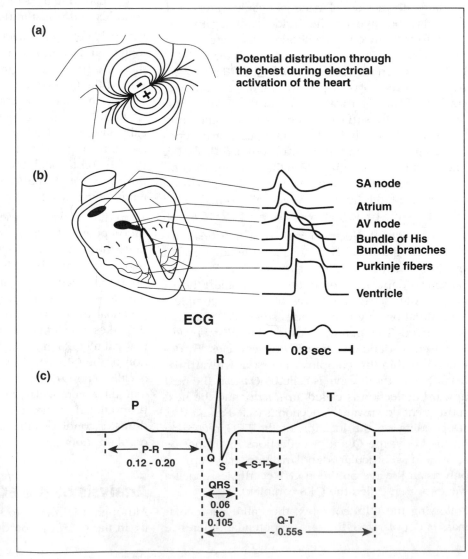

■ **Fig. 7-1** ■

(a) The spread of electrical potential through the thoracic cavity due to depolarization of a portion of the heart. (b) Action potentials at various locations in the myocardium, with the resulting composite body surface electrocardiogram. (c) A typical surface electrocardiogram: P = P wave, QRS = QRS complex, T = T wave. Numerical values list normal time intervals in seconds between wave complexes.

waveforms within the ECG will vary depending upon the location and the polarity of the recording electrode relative to the heart. For this reason, a standard system consisting of 12 specifically located *leads*, or electrode connections, has been developed.

This system offers two benefits. It provides a standard framework for identifying patterns in the ECG, thus making recognition of abnormalities easier and more consistent. More importantly, it enables an investigator to see the electrical activity in the heart from many different "views and angles" at any given point in time. Analysis of these different views is used to gain information about the orientation of the heart, the size of its chambers, and the general direction of activation in the myocardium during any interval of time.

The first ECG lead system developed was based on the precept that the heart sits at the center of a triangle in the frontal plane of the body, with vertices at the right shoulder, left shoulder, and pubic region. ■ **Fig. 7-2a** ■ In this system the arms and the legs are considered extensions of the vertices. Electrodes thus are placed on the right arm, left arm, and left leg, with the right leg serving as an electrical ground. In this system each lead is bipolar, meaning it has a positive and a negative pole. In lead I, the right arm is negative and the left arm positive. In lead II, the right arm is negative and the left leg is positive. Finally, in lead III, the left arm is negative and the left leg positive. If we imagine the frontal plane of an individual as being represented by a 360° circle, lead I has its positive pole placed at "3 o'clock" on the circle and is designated at 0°. The

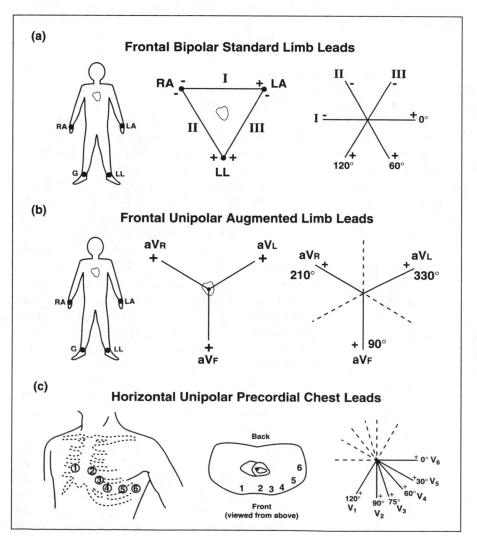

■ **Fig. 7-2** ■

(a) Orientation of the standard frontal bipolar limb leads relative to the limbs and relative to a 360° circle in the frontal plain of the chest. (b) Orientation of frontal unipolar augmented limb leads. (c) Left: Placement of horizontal unipolar precordial chest leads. Center: Placement in the horizontal plane. Right: Placement relative to a 360° circle oriented in the horizontal plane through the center of the chest.

positive pole of lead II is at 60° and that for lead III is at 120°.

Another lead system is arranged in the frontal plane of the body and consists of three unipolar leads containing a single positive pole relative to the center of the chest, which is considered zero potential. ■ **Fig. 7-2b** ■ These leads often are called *augmented leads* because the ECG recording device amplifies the signal from these leads relative to those obtained in the bipolar leads. The pole of one lead sits at the right shoulder at 210° and is called the *augmented right* or aV_R lead; another sits at the left shoulder at 330° and is called *augmented left* or aV_L. The final augmented lead is oriented at 90° in the frontal plane and is called the *augmented foot* or aV_F lead. Finally, a series of six unipolar leads are arranged in a horizontal plane around the chest as shown in ■ **Fig. 7-2c** ■ . These are sometimes called *precordial* or *chest leads* and are designated $V_1–V_6$.

During depolarization of a given portion of the myocardium, ECG leads are designed such that when the axis from the negative to positive portions of the myocardium is pointed at the positive pole of a lead, an upward deflection is recorded from that ECG lead. Another way to explain this process is to say that when a wave of depolarization in the heart is proceeding away from a negative pole and toward a positive pole of a lead, a positive deflection is seen in that ECG lead. Waves directed at a negative pole or away from a positive pole produce negative deflections in the ECG lead.

The magnitude of a deflection in the ECG caused by a given event in the myocardium (e.g., the QRS complex caused by depolarization of the ventricles) is determined both by the magnitude of the tissue involved in the electrical event and by how directly the depolarization is aimed at a given electrode. This latter factor is demonstrated in ■ **Figs. 7-3a and 7-3b** ■ .

For the sake of example only, let us imagine a wave of depolarization traveling through the ventricles as a sagittal plane, perpendicular to the ground, proceeding from the right shoulder, through the heart, toward the left shoulder, directly along lead I of the ECG. This wave of depolarization is aimed directly at the positive pole of lead I and a positive deflection of the QRS complex will be measured from this lead. For this example, let us say that this deflection is a simple R wave of 10 mm in amplitude. Should this same wave of depolarization proceed from the left to right shoulder, the wave would be aimed directly at the negative pole of lead I, resulting in a 10 mm *negative* deflection of the R wave. The amplitude of the R wave in our example will vary between −10 and +10 mm depending on the angle of the wave of ventricular depolarization relative to lead I.

Exactly what angle is being used here may be confusing to the student who realizes that the actual wave of depolarization in the normal heart is a complex, three-dimensional construct with an orientation, relative to any lead, that is going to vary every millisecond throughout the electrocardiographic cycle. Two points will help clarify this. First, it is rare that every millisecond of electrical activity in the heart is analyzed in the ECG. Instead, an event, such as depolarization of the ventricles and the resulting QRS complex, is envisioned as a single electrical vector of a given magnitude and direction in three-dimensional space. How this event results in a given QRS complex in a given ECG lead depends on how that lead "sees" this 3D vector. For example, the standard bipolar and augmented leads look at the vector as if it were projected *flat* onto a screen in the frontal plane of the body.

In explanation, imagine ventricular depolarization as a vector proceeding from the base to the apex of the normal heart. As viewed from the frontal surface of the body, this vector may appear at a 45° angle from lead I with a magnitude given as in ■ **Fig. 7-3b** ■ . If we were to shine a light up from the floor against this vector, a shadow would be cast along the length of lead I. The magnitude of the average deflection of the QRS complex in lead I of the ECG reflects the length of this shadow. In this case the vector is pointed toward the positive pole of lead I and the magnitude of the shadow cast onto lead I, and thus average QRS amplitude in that lead is 5.5 mm.

Note this *average* vector could produce a pure R wave 5.5 mm in amplitude in lead I or a QRS complex with the sum of positive and negative deflections giving a net +5.5 mm deflection; see the right portion of ■ **Fig. 7-3b** ■ . Note also that, even if the length of the vector projected on the frontal plane stays the same, the length of the shadow projected on lead I (and the magnitude of the resulting QRS complex) will vary depending on the vector's orientation relative to lead I.

Returning to the example in ■ **Fig. 7-3a** ■ , if the wave of depolarization proceeded from the right shoulder at a 30° angle relative to lead I, the resulting R wave would be positive, but with an amplitude of only +7 mm instead of the 10 mm seen when the wave was aimed at 0°; a 60° angle would

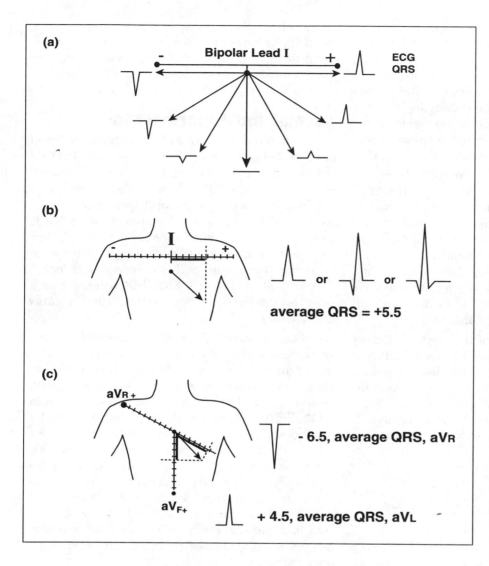

■ **Fig. 7-3** ■
(a) The effect of orientation of the wave depolarization relative to a bipolar lead on the magnitude and polarity of the QRS complex. (b) QRS complexes as measured in lead I in the frontal plane, resulting from a wave of depolarization oriented along the arrow. (c) Similar resulting QRS complexes due to a wave of depolarization proceeding down the arrow in the diagram relative to aV_R and aV_F.

result in a +3 mm deflection, and so on until the center line is met. At this point the wave of depolarization would be pointed at neither the positive nor the negative pole of lead I and no deflection would be recorded from that lead. This would result even if the wave came straight out of the chest or directly up from the ground; such waves still would be perpendicular to lead I and result in no deflection in that lead.

Clearly, because different leads are oriented at different angles relative to the QRS vector used in the example above, the same ventricular depolarization will yield different magnitude QRS complexes when recorded by different leads looking at that vector. For example, the frontal vector pictured in ■ **Figs. 7-3b and 7-3c** ■ will produce a +4.5 average QRS amplitude in lead aV_F at the same time it produces a −6.5 average QRS amplitude in lead aV_R.

Because the heart normally is activated from atria to ventricles and is tilted with the apex pointed toward the left, the normal average wave of depolarization through the ventricles proceeds at about a 60° angle from the center point of the chest, as perceived from the front of the body. ■ **Fig. 7-4** ■ As a result, the normal average QRS vector is aimed most directly at the positive pole of lead II and to a lesser extent at the positive poles in leads I and III. A useful convention states that the sum of the average magnitudes of the QRS complexes recorded in leads I and III equals the average magnitude in lead II.

Clinicians often compare the average deflections of the QRS complex in leads I, II, and III in order to work backwards and reconstruct what the average QRS vector must have looked like in an individual, when projected onto the frontal plane. An example of this process is illustrated in ■ **Fig. 7-4** ■. To determine the direction of the actual average QRS vector, the magnitude of the average QRS complex in each lead is first marked off onto each lead. Next, perpendicular lines are drawn from the ends of each of these points (dashed lines in the figure), creating an intersection. A line connecting the center of the figure with this intersection yields the actual average QRS vector in the individual as viewed from the front of the body.

A frontal depiction of the ECG using only bipolar leads I, II, and III may not provide a good evaluation of the progression of the electrical activity in the heart. The ECG also can be viewed in the frontal plane using the augmented lead system. Generally the ECG in augmented leads is similar to that in the bipolar leads, except that the QRS complex normally will appear negative in aV_R because the wave of ventricular depolarization normally proceeds away from the positive pole of that lead.

A more useful second view of the electrical activity of the heart is provided by the six horizontal chest leads. These leads all have positive polarity and are arranged such that the QRS vector is viewed in the horizontal plane, or as if the chest were cut horizontally and one viewed the vector from the top. In addition, because the heart is so close to the surface of the chest, these leads record electrical events in small portions of the myocardium directly underneath them. This allows the clinician to detect very fine changes or abnormalities in the myocardium.

Normal and Abnormal ECGs

Several different types of ECG recordings are listed in ■ **Fig. 7-5** ■ . Unless otherwise stated, these ECGs are assumed to be recorded in lead II. A normal ECG is shown in ■ **Fig. 7-5a** ■ . In the tracing found in ■ **Fig. 7-5b** ■ the pattern of P, QRS, and T waves are normal but the interval between successive P, QRS, or T waves is much shorter than normal. This represents a normal SA node-driven increase in heart rate (beats/min) and is called a *sinus tachycardia*. The tracing in ■ **Fig. 7-5c** ■ represents a slow, SA-driven heart rate and is called a *sinus bradycardia*.

The heart occasionally will be activated by the spontaneous generation of an action potential in one of the atria cells other than the SA node, resulting in a *premature atrial contraction,* or *PAC.* Such ectopic foci and its effect on the ECG is shown in ■ **Fig. 7-5d** ■ . Atrial ectopic foci often will send a wave of depolarization through the atria to the AV node and activate the ventricles before the SA node is able to do so. In our example, this activation occurred shortly after the preceding beat and rendered the SA node refractory to generation of its next impulse in the normal interval of time. This results in a pause in the heartbeat until the next normal SA node generated potential can activate the myocardium.

Ectopic foci also can occur in the ventricles, as shown in ■ **Fig. 7-5e** ■ . These result in premature ventricular contractions or PVCs. In this figure, a portion of the apex of the ventricle spontaneously fired an action potential that traveled retrograde up through the heart, resulting in a negative QRS complex. Occasional atrial or ventricular premature contractions are not uncommon in normal individuals; the probability of their occurrence is increased by cigarette smoking, nicotine in any form, physical or emotional stress, caffeine, and fatigue.

On some occasions, ectopic foci fire repetitively at an abnormally high rate, resulting in an abnormally high rate of ventricular activation. This is shown in ■ **Fig. 7-5f** ■ . Here an atrial ectopic foci fires regularly at a rate of about 200/min. This high rate of atrial activation is able to get through the AV node and activate the ventricles at the same rate. This is

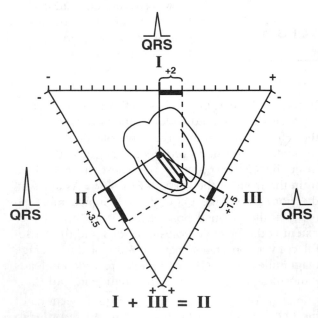

Fig. 7-4 ■

A standard mean QRS vector in a normal individual (double arrow) and resultant QRS complexes as recorded in frontal bipolar leads I, II, and III.

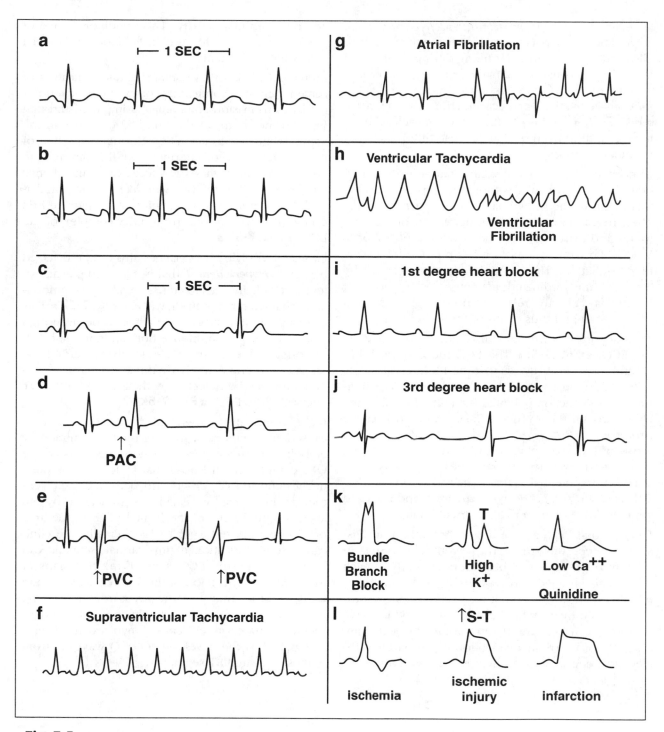

■ **Fig. 7-5** ■

Normal and abnormal ECGs. (a) Normal ECG. (b) Sinus tachycardia. (c) Sinus bradycardia. (d) Premature atrial contraction. (e) Premature ventricular contraction. (f – j) See text for details. (k) Bundle branch block and effects of changes in serum electrolytes on the ECG. (l) Progressive effect of myocardial ischemia on the ECG.

an example of *supraventricular tachycardia.* Such a condition may pace the heart at a rate too fast to allow adequate ventricular filling during diastole. Of a more serious nature, damaged atria can enter into a state of *fibrillation,* or a totally uncoordinated random activation and contraction of the atria. **■ Fig. 7-5g ■** In this situation, the ventricles are activated in a hit-or-miss fashion, resulting in a highly irregular heartbeat.

Abnormally high rates of ventricular activation generated from ventricular ectopic foci represent a serious threat to the individual. Ventricular tachycardia often results in an inefficient activation of the ventricles and extremely high heart rates. **■ Fig. 7-5h ■** Ventricular tachycardia often is a prelude to ventricular fibrillation. This condition is characterized by random, uncoordinated activation of millions of ventricular cells and results in no pumping of blood by the heart and thus death of the individual.

Conduction abnormalities also can be detected by the ECG. **■ Fig. 7-5i ■** The ECG looks normal, but careful inspection reveals that the PR interval is 0.28 second and thus outside the normal range. This indicates that the action potential is having difficulty traveling through the AV node. This condition is called *primary* or *first-degree heart block.* More serious forms of block or inhibition of transmission through the AV node can occur. Sometimes only every other atrial action potential is able to activate the ventricles. This is called *second-degree heart block* and results in a much slower than normal ventricular rate.

Finally, total blockade of action potential transmission between the atria and the ventricles results in atria and ventricles that beat independently of each other. This is called *total* or *third-degree heart block.* **■ Fig. 7-5j ■** In this condition pacing of the ventricles is taken over by the Purkinje fibers, which have an intrinsic firing rate of only about 20 beats/min. This rate of ventricular activation is just barely sufficient to keep a person alive, but is inadequate for any other normal activity. This condition is one of the major reasons for the installation of artificial electronic pacemakers.

Individual ECGs often contain telltale indicators of certain abnormal conditions. For example, action potential transmission sometimes is impaired through one, but not both, of the bundled branches in the heart. In this case, activation through one side of the ventricle proceeds normally but that through the other side must take an accessory, and hence longer, path. Thus the two ventricles are activated at slightly different times, resulting in a characteristic double R wave or split in the QRS complex of the ECG. **■ Fig. 7-5k ■**

Plasma electrolyte abnormalities also can be detected by ECGs. *Hyperkalemia,* that is, elevated plasma K^+ levels, result in a characteristic spiking or "mountain" characteristic of the T wave. **■ Fig. 7-5k ■** This is a valuable indicator to the clinician because high plasma K^+ levels can induce fibrillation in the heart. Abnormally low serum Ca^{++} levels or cardiotoxic effects of certain antiarrhythmic drugs such as quinidine can be detected by their effect on the QT interval of the ECG. **■ Fig. 7-5k ■**

Right ventricular hypertrophy, which usually is caused by pulmonary hypertension or pulmonary emboli, can create mirror-image deflections of the QRS complex in all leads. That is, lead aV_R is positively deflected, V_6 downward deflected. Left ventricular hypertrophy usually is indicated by an average QRS vector in the frontal plain in the area of 330° as opposed to 0° to 100°. Finally, the clinically useful indication of myocardial ischemia can be detected by the ECG. One of the first signs of ischemia is an inversion of the T wave, as shown in **■ Fig. 7-5l ■**. Injury to the myocardium resulting from progressive ischemia results in an elevated ST segment. Infarction, or death of myocardial tissue, is recognized by the development of Q waves in front of these elevated ST segments.**

CHAPTER 8

Cardiac Excitation-Contraction Coupling and the Cardiac Cycle

Clinical interest in cardiac electrophysiology stems from the fact that this activity is coupled to the contraction of the heart and the movement of blood through the cardiovascular system. Coupling of electrical activity in the heart to myocardial contraction uses mechanisms similar to that previously discussed for skeletal muscle.

Actin-myosin crossbridge cycling and its control through Ca^{++}/troponin/tropomyosin interactions is the basis of contraction of cardiac cells. Cardiac cells also contain an extensive network of T tubules that transmit action potentials into the cell interior and the *sarcoplasmic reticulum* (SR). Action potentials in cardiac cells stimulate the release of calcium stored within the SR and thus initiate contraction. Like skeletal muscle, Ca^+ ATPase pumps in the SR remove Ca^{++} from the intracellular fluid and accumulate it into SR interior against a concentration gradient. Ca^{++} also is removed by Ca^{++} ATPase pumps in the cell membrane.

Nevertheless, control of intracellular Ca^{++} levels and muscle contraction is more complicated in myocardial cells compared to skeletal muscle. ■ **Fig. 8-1** ■ Myocardial contraction can be modified by altering the activity of the unique voltage-dependent Ca^{++} channel in the cell membrane. These channels are opened by action potentials and result in Ca^{++} influx into the myocardial cell.

Influx through this channel is linked to contraction of the cardiac cells in an unusual fashion. Only about 10% of this Ca^{++} contributes directly to contraction of the muscle. Instead, increased intracellular Ca^{++} stimulates the release of Ca^{++} stored within the SR and stimulates the pumping of Ca^{++} into the SR by the Ca^{++} ATPase. Anything that enhances calcium influx during the action potential results in greater filling of the SR, greater release of Ca^{++} with the arrival of the next action potential, and thus a stronger subsequent contraction.

Ca^{++} influx through the voltage-dependent channels can be modified by cellular regulatory mechanisms. For example, catecholamines (like norepinephrine released from sympathetic nerve endings, or circulating epinephrine) activate β_1-adrenergic receptors on the cell membrane, which are linked to the enzyme adenylate cyclase by a stimulatory G-protein (G_s). When catecholamine binds to the receptor, the adenyl cyclase is activated and converts ATP to cAMP.

Cyclic AMP, a common chemical "second messenger" in many different cell types, functions as a communication link between extracellular events and intracellular processes. In myocardial cells, cAMP binds to a cAMP-dependent protein kinase (protein kinase A or PKA) that phosphorylates the voltage-dependent Ca^{++} channel. This phosphorylation increases the channel's probability of opening and increases the average time the channel remains open once activated. This, in turn, enhances Ca^{++} influx with every action potential, resulting in a stronger contraction in each myocardial cell, and, by extension, in the whole heart.

Most important, this enhancement of contraction occurs *independently* of any change in preload or afterload on the heart; at any given loading condition, the heart exposed to catecholamines is able to generate more isometric force and move a greater load faster and farther compared to a heart not exposed to these agents.

A modification of the contractile ability of muscle at the cellular level, independent of loading conditions, is said to be a modification of the inotropic state, or *contractility,* of the muscle. The ability to modify muscle performance by changing the inotropic state, or contractility, of individual cells is a hallmark of physiological control of myocardial contraction.

It should be noted that the term *contractility* is often applied loosely to any factor that alters contraction of the heart. This is incorrect. It is important for both physiologists and clinicians to distinguish alterations in performance of the heart due to changes in inotropic state from those changes caused by alterations in loading conditions. In this text contractility will be used to refer to the inotropic state of the heart.

Many agents and conditions can alter the inotropic state of the heart. For example, β-receptor agonists are positive inotropic agents. Conversely, agents that block Ca++ channels reduce myocardial contractility and thus exert a negative inotropic effect on the heart. Acetylcholine, released from parasympathetic nerve endings in the heart, is a negative inotropic agent. It inhibits adenyl cyclase through an inhibitory G-protein and stimulates guanylate cyclase to produce cGMP, which inhibits opening of the Ca++ channel. Ca++ channels require ATP for normal functioning. Therefore, lack of oxygen to the heart (myocardial ischemia), needed to produce ATP, results in an inhibition of the Ca++ channel

and is considered a negative inotropic condition. Also, acidosis (increased plasma H+), which often occurs in ischemic conditions, inhibits myocardial contractility.

In general, factors that alter intracellular calcium concentration can alter myocardial contractility. For example, Na+/Ca++ exchangers in the myocardial cell membrane remove Ca++ from the interior of the cell, through a secondary active transport mechanism linked to the influx of sodium moving down its electrochemical gradient. ■ **Fig. 8-1** ■ Reduction of the sodium gradient by inhibition of Na+/K+ ATPase results in Ca++ accumulation within the cell and a positive inotropic effect. This mechanism is responsible for the positive inotropic effects of cardiac glycosides such as digitalis and is the basis of their use to augment myocardial performance in heart failure. Methylxanthines such as caffeine and theophylline (an asthma medication and component of tea) inhibit the enzyme that breaks down

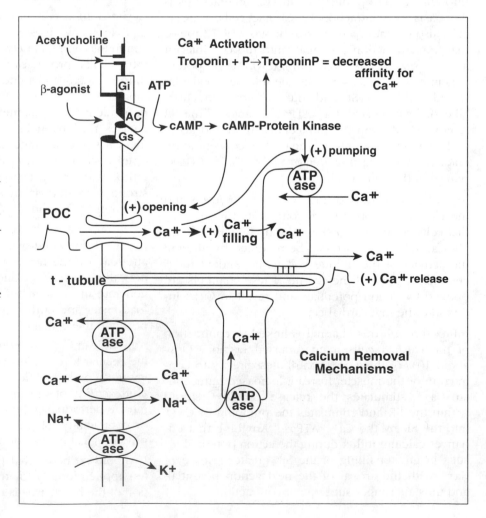

■ **Fig. 8-1** ■
Calcium handling in a myocardial cell. Action potentials increase intracellular calcium by opening potential operated calcium channels (POC) in the cell membrane. Increased calcium entry increases filling of the calcium stores in the sarcoplasmic reticulum, which are released by the action potential. Calcium influx is enhanced by β agonists through increases in cAMP. Calcium is removed by calcium ATPase pumps and by a Na+/Ca++ exchanger. AC = adenyl cyclase, Gi = inhibitory G-protein, Gs = stimulatory G-protein, (+) = stimulatory effect.

cAMP in myocardial cells, thus causing cAMP accumulation and a positive inotropic effect.

Activation of the sympathetic nervous system increases heart rate (a positive chronotropic effect) at the same time it enhances myocardial contractility. Rapid heart rates require rapid removal of calcium and inactivation of actin/myosin interactions in order to shorten diastole. Generation of cAMP and protein kinase A by norepinephrine phosphorylates Ca++ATPase pumps in the SR, which increases their pumping activity, as well as troponin, which decreases its affinity for calcium. Both these factors speed relaxation of myocardial cells.

The Cardiac Cycle

The cyclic contraction and relaxation of the myocardium sets into motion a sequence of events result-

ing in time-dependent changes in ventricular and aortic pressure, ventricular volumes, and flow into and out of the heart. Graphical representations of the variations in hemodynamic variables associated with the cardiac cycle are depicted in ■ **Fig. 8-2** ■ . Such representations usually depict hemodynamic variables in the left heart and systemic circulation along with a tracing of the ECG and heart sounds.

The peak of the R wave on the ECG is used to signify the start of systole, or the contraction phase of the cardiac cycle. This contraction increases intraventricular pressure above end diastolic levels (0–5 mmHg). When left ventricular pressure exceeds that in the left atrium, the mitral valve closes. This closure is associated with a series of broad, low-pitched sounds that are due to vibrations of blood and the chordae tendinae in the ventricles. This is called the *first heart sound.* (These sounds are *not*

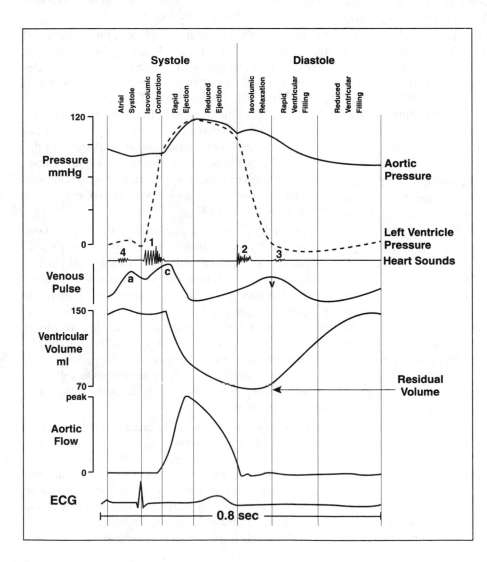

■ **Fig. 8-2** ■
A diagram of hemodynamic variables, heart sounds, and the ECG during a single cardiac cycle. (See text for details.)

made by valve leaflets "slapping against one another.") The intensity of the first heart sound is proportional to the strength of myocardial contraction; its evaluation can be employed in clinical diagnosis.

As the ventricle contracts, there is a period of time during which intraventricular pressure exceeds that in the left atrium but is less than that in the aorta. Consequently the aortic valve remains closed and the ventricle builds pressure without moving blood. This phase of systole is called *isovolumic contraction*. Once left ventricular pressure exceeds that in the aorta, the aortic valve opens and blood leaves the ventricle, initiating the ejection phase of the cardiac cycle. During systole a healthy heart ejects only 50% to 60% of the volume of blood that was in the ventricles at the end of the previous diastole.

Initially, with the opening of the aortic valve, ventricular volume decreases rapidly; about 70% of the ejected volume exits the ventricle during the first third of the ejection phase. This period is called the *rapid ejection phase*. During this phase, intraventricular and aortic pressure rise. As the outflow of blood distends the aortic wall, lateral aortic pressure may actually slightly exceed left ventricular pressure. The rapid ejection interval is followed by a *reduced ejection phase* in which aortic outflow and reduction of ventricular volume continues, but at a rate slower than that seen during the rapid ejection phase.

It is during reduced ejection phase that the T wave of the ECG begins. During reduced ejection, aortic and ventricular pressures start to decline. When ventricular pressure eventually declines below total aortic pressure (lateral and kinetic components), the aortic valve closes. The sudden cessation of ventricular outflow caused by valve closure creates a second heart sound of an intensity proportional to the intensity of the valve closure. Intensity is increased whenever aortic or pulmonary pressure is abnormally high and is taken as a clinical indicator of possible systemic or pulmonary hypertension (high blood pressure).

The closure of the aortic valve also causes a transient, small, sharp drop in aortic pressure creating a notch in the aortic pressure profile, called the *incisura*. This event sometimes is used to demarcate the transition from systole to diastole in the cardiac cycle, but systole is more correctly considered to be concluded when the T wave ends on the ECG. At the end of systole a significant volume of blood remains in the ventricles. This residual volume is decreased by increases in myocardial contractility and

heart rate, and is increased whenever the heart is weakened (e.g. heart failure) or faced with increased outflow resistance (e.g. aortic valve stenosis). Thus examination of end systolic volume has clinical usefulness as an indicator of conditions affecting the heart.

During the relaxation, or diastolic, phase of the cardiac cycle, volume and pressure changes proceed in the reverse of that seen for systole. Early in left ventricular relaxation, the aortic and mitral valves are closed and the ventricle relaxes isovolumetrically. Once ventricular pressure falls below that of the left atrium, the mitral valve opens and filling of the ventricle begins. Just prior to this occurrence, abrupt cessation of ventricular distension and the deceleration of blood creates a faint third heart sound not normally heard in healthy individuals. The third heart sound is amplified in abnormally distended ventricles, such as the condition associated with heart failure; its presence is considered an ominous sign.

During diastole the ventricles fill in a rapid, followed by a reduced, filling phase. During rapid ventricular filling, ventricular pressure actually continues to decline because ventricular relaxation occurs more rapidly than the ventricle is filled. During the reduced filling phase, sometimes called *diastasis,* ventricular pressure starts to increase. The P wave on the ECG appears and atrial contraction begins at the end of the reduced filling phase of the cardiac cycle. Atrial contraction produces a faint fourth heart sound. Diastole is considered to be concluded with the appearance of the R wave on the ECG.

Occasionally pressure waveforms in the jugular vein are depicted on cardiac cycle diagrams. These waveforms can provide clinical insights into cardiovascular disease. When the atria contract, a retrograde pressure pulse wave, called an *A wave,* is produced in the jugular vein. Factors such as tricuspid valve stenosis, which impede the flow of blood from the atria to the ventricles, increase the amplitude of the A wave. A second venous pulse wave, called the *C wave,* is seen as an increase followed by a decrease in venous pulse pressure during the early phase of systole.

The upslope of this wave is created by bulging of the tricuspid valve into the right atrium during ventricular contraction combined with transmission of the carotid systolic arterial pulse to the adjacent jugular vein. The subsequent decrease in pressure in the C wave is caused by the descent of the base of the heart and atrial stretch. Failure of the tricuspid valve to close completely during ventricular systole results in propulsion of blood back into the atrium and vena cava and results in a high-amplitude C wave. The V wave of the venous pulse is seen as a gradual pressure increase during reduced ejection and isovolumic relaxation followed by a pressure decrease during the rapid filling phase of the cycle.

This wave is created first by continual peripheral venous return of blood to the atrium against a closed tricuspid valve, followed by the sudden decrease in atrial distension caused by rapid ventricular filling. Tricuspid valve stenosis increases resistance to filling of the ventricle, which is indicated by an attenuation of the descending phase of the V wave.

CHAPTER 9

Determinants and Evaluation of Myocardial Performance

Introduction

Evaluation of the function of the heart as a blood pump is important to physiologists and physicians. The heart must be able to enhance its force generation in order to meet increased demands for blood flow during conditions such as exercise. In addition, myocardial performance is hindered in pathological conditions such as ischemia and heart failure. In skeletal muscle, force generation can be enhanced by recruitment of motor units and by generation of tetanic contractions. Motor units do not exist in the heart, however, and the cardiac muscle cannot generate tetanic contractions. (The latter, of course, would be of no value to its function as a cyclic pump).

Fortunately, the heart has two mechanisms, unavailable to skeletal muscle, by which it can alter its force of contraction. First, force generation in the heart can be altered by altering the preload on the myocardium prior to the onset of contraction. The heart is a hollow, distensible organ. Variations in the amount of filling of the heart during diastole result in variations in the initial stretch, or preload, on the cardiac muscle prior to the onset of contraction. This alters the subsequent strength of contraction in a manner similar to that represented by the length-tension relationship for isometric contraction of isolated skeletal muscle.

Second, force generation in the heart at any given set of loading conditions can be modified uniquely by altering the inotropic state of myocardial cells.

Mechanics of Isolated Cardiac Muscle

Four factors influence contractile strength of cardiac muscle:

1. Preload, or the initial length to which the muscle is stretched prior to contraction.

2. Afterload, or all the forces against which cardiac muscle must contract in order to generate pressure and shorten.
3. Contractility, or the inotropic state.
4. The inotropic effect of increased heart rate (see below).

Cardiac muscle exhibits both a length-tension and force-velocity relationship similar to that of skeletal muscle. ■ **Figs. 9-1a and 9-1b** ■ Cardiac muscle, however, is intrinsically stiffer than skeletal muscle and exhibits significant passive resistance to stretch at a length corresponding to L_o. As a result, cardiac muscle is constrained to contract from lengths $< L_o$, even though the cardiac chamber is not anchored to some fixed structure such as bone.

A key to understanding cardiac muscle contraction is to understand that any given length-tension or force-velocity relationship can be modified by the inotropic state of the heart; see the right portion of ■ **Figs. 9-1a and 9-1b** ■. At any given preload, isometric force generation of cardiac muscle is increased by positive inotropic stimuli and decreased by negative inotropic stimuli. In addition, the theoretical maximum rate of crossbridge cycling, or V_{max}, in cardiac muscle is enhanced by positive inotropic stimuli. This effectively shifts the force-velocity curve at any given preload upward and to the right. In this manner a positive inotropic agent allows cardiac muscle, at any given preload, to move heavier afterloads faster, compared to normal myocardium; see the right portion of ■ **Fig. 9-1b** ■. Negative inotropic agents obviously have the opposite effect.

How preload, afterload, and inotropic state interact to define myocardial contraction is demonstrated in ■ **Fig. 9-1c** ■. Positive inotropic stimuli shift the isometric length-tension relationship upward and to the left, enabling cardiac muscle to generate more force at any preload. As is the case with skeletal muscle, this relationship also sets the limits of mus-

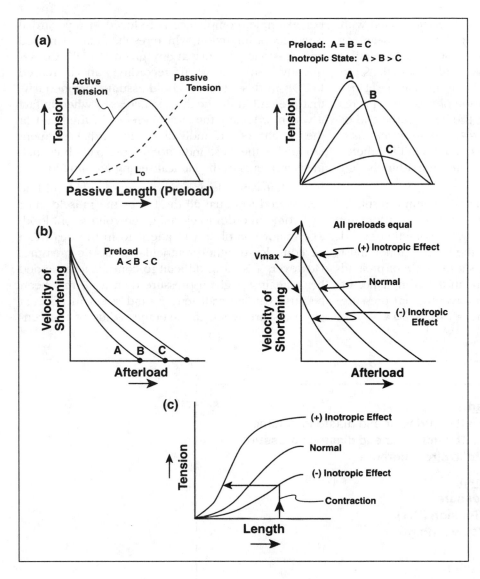

■ **Fig. 9-1** ■
(a) Left: Active and passive length tension curve in myocardial cells. Right: The effect of inotropic state on the length tension curve. (b) Left: Effect of preload and afterload on shortening velocity in the myocardium. Right: The effect of inotropic state on the force-velocity relationship. (c) Effect of inotropic state on isotonic contractions of isolated cardiac muscle.

cle shortening. Thus, compared to normal muscle, at any preload positive inotropic stimuli allow cardiac muscle to shorten more against any afterload, and it allows the muscle to shorten any set distance with a heavier load.

The strength of myocardial contraction is indirectly affected by its rate of stimulation (number of contractions/min). High-frequency activation of cardiac muscle brings Ca^{++} into the cell with each action potential at a rate faster than it can be removed. Consequently, intracellular Ca^{++} concentration increases with a resulting positive inotropic effect. This enhanced contractility helps the heart eject more blood with each contraction at high heart rates when filling time is compromised.

Mechanics of the Whole Heart

The relationships among preload, afterload, shortening, and contractility elucidated from studies of isolated cardiac muscle determine the output characteristics of the whole heart. To understand how loading conditions and contractility affect myocardial shortening and flow output, one needs to identify variables in the whole heart that are analogous to those in isolated muscle.

Stroke volume, or the amount of blood ejected with each contraction of the heart, is the whole-heart (or ventricular) analogue of muscle shortening. Similar analogues are used for preload and afterload. As the left ventricle fills with blood during diastole it becomes stretched. The magnitude of this stretch is related to the blood volume in the heart at the end of diastole, a quantity called *left ventricular end diastolic volume,* or *LVEDV.* ■ **Fig. 9-2a** ■ LVEDV therefore is used as an indicator of the preload in the left ventricle.

Because changes in end diastolic volume result in changes in end diastolic pressure, *left ventricular end diastolic pressure,* or *LVEDP,* is sometimes used as an indicator of preload on the heart. Caution must be used in applying LVEDP as a measure of preload in the whole heart. Alterations in the compliance of the left ventricle will affect intraventricular pressure at any intraventricular volume. ■ **Fig. 9-2b** ■

For example, compliance is reduced in myocardial ischemia or infarction, which results in an increased end diastolic pressure at any given LVEDV. Consequently, an individual recording an increased LVEDP in this situation could assume, erroneously, that preload in the heart was increased when in fact it was not. Ideally the circumference of the heart or the length of an individual myocardial segment would be the best indicator of preload, but such measurements in the clinical setting are limited.

In the left ventricle as a whole, afterload should be considered to equal all the forces the muscle must overcome in order to eject a given volume of blood. The major contributor to afterload in the heart can be considered either ventricular or aortic pressure. However, it is more difficult to contract a distended heart against a given pressure than a normal heart because cardiac wall tension and stress increase at any pressure when the average radius of the ven-

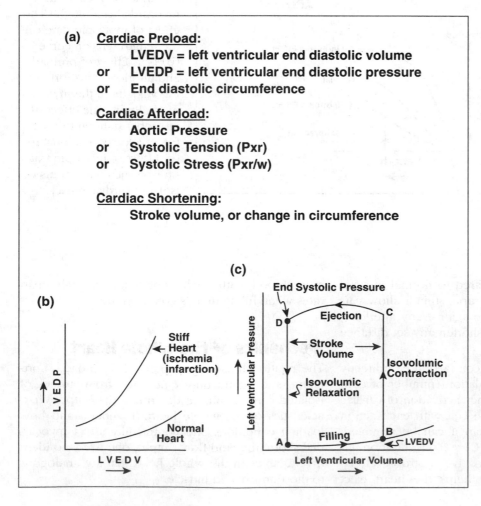

(a) **Cardiac Preload:**
  LVEDV = left ventricular end diastolic volume
or **LVEDP = left ventricular end diastolic pressure**
or **End diastolic circumference**

Cardiac Afterload:
  Aortic Pressure
or **Systolic Tension (Pxr)**
or **Systolic Stress (Pxr/w)**

Cardiac Shortening:
  Stroke volume, or change in circumference

(c)

End Systolic Pressure

Ejection

Stroke Volume

Isovolumic Contraction

Isovolumic Relaxation

Left Ventricular Pressure

Filling

LVEDV

Left Ventricular Volume

(b)

Stiff Heart (ischemia infarction)

Normal Heart

LVEDP

LVEDV

■ **Fig. 9-2** ■
(a) In situ whole-heart analogues of cardiac muscle preload, afterload, and muscle shortening. (b) Relationship between left ventricular end diastolic pressure and left ventricular end diastolic volume in the normal heart and in a heart with reduced compliance. (c) A pressure-volume loop representation of the cardiac cycle.

tricular chamber increases. Therefore, tension (T = pressure × chamber radius) or wall stress (S = pressure × chamber radius/chamber wall thickness) are considered more accurate estimators of cardiac afterload. Other forces, such as those needed to overcome blood inertia, accelerate blood, or overcome resistance of the valves, also contribute to afterload, especially in pathological conditions.

Pressure-Volume Loops and the Cardiac Cycle

The effects of preload, afterload, and contractility on stroke volume of the heart can be seen with a graph of the cardiac cycle that relates either intraventricular pressure, or wall stress, to either left ventricular volume, pressure, or circumferential length. ■ **Fig. 9-2c** ■ In this depiction of the cardiac cycle, time is not a factor. The cardiac cycle starts at point A with the beginning of diastole. Filling of the ventricle proceeds along the line connecting points A to B, where B represents LVEDV. Isovolumic contraction proceeds from this point to point C, where ventricular pressure equals that in the aorta. At this point the aortic valve opens and blood is ejected from the ventricle. The volume in the ventricle during ejection proceeds from point C to D, which then equals the stroke volume. Finally, the heart undergoes isovolumic relaxation (D to A).

The pressure and volume in the heart at the end of systole represents the point to which the heart has shortened such that the maximum force it can develop at that length equals aortic pressure. The heart cannot shorten beyond this point because, at shorter circumferences, the number of crossbridges available would not enable the heart to generate enough force to move blood against existing aortic pressure.

If one were to examine several cardiac cycles starting at various LVEDV (preloads) and proceeding against several different aortic pressures (afterloads), the points depicting pressure and volume at the end of systole would fall on a straight line like the dashed line labeled #2 in ■ **Fig. 9-3a** ■ . This line is called the *end systolic pressure-volume relationship*. At a given inotropic state it represents the most pressure the ventricle can generate with a given initial preload (estimated by LVEDV in the whole heart). This line is analogous to the length-tension curve for isolated muscle. By extension to the whole heart, it can be represented by a plot of peak isovolumic pressure in the ventricle versus LVEDV.

It is important to note that *the position of this line will be changed only by the inotropic state of the heart*. It does not matter which set of loading conditions were in place when the line was generated. As a result, the left ventricular end systolic pressure-volume relationship is considered to be an ideal indicator of the inotropic state of the heart. Relative to a normal heart, a positive inotropic influence will shift this relationship upward and to the left, whereas a negative inotropic influence will shift it downward and to the right. The consequence of such a shift for the whole heart is that, at any given afterload and preload, stroke volume is increased by a positive inotropic influence and decreased by a negative inotropic influence; see lines #3 and #1 respectively in ■ **Fig. 9-3a** ■ .

Loading conditions alone also affect the output of the heart. ■ **Fig. 9-3b** ■ In the figure, cardiac cycles 1, 2, and 3 occur with the same afterload and inotropic state but at different LVEDV and thus preloads. As LVEDV increases, the initial muscle length for myocardial contraction increases as well. Once contraction is initiated, the heart ejects blood until the pressure and volume remaining in the ventricle meets the left ventricular end diastolic pressure-volume relationship. As can be seen in the figure, greater initial LVEDV results in a greater stroke volume.

This relationship was elucidated by Starling in the early 1900s and is known as *Starling's law of the heart* or *heterometric regulation of stroke volume*. Put simply, this law states, "The more the heart fills (during diastole), the more it pumps (during systole)." This relationship between ventricular filling and the stroke output of the heart is one of the most important cardiovascular relationships for a student to remember. As will be seen in subsequent sections, this relationship is involved in both physiological and pathological conditions affecting myocardial output.

Afterload, by itself, has a negative impact on stroke volume in the heart. ■ **Fig. 9-3c** ■ The cardiac cycles in the figure all start from the same LVEDV and inotropic state, but proceed against three different afterloads. Blood cannot be ejected from the heart until LV pressure meets aortic pressure. When the ventricle contracts at higher afterloads (pressure), it will not shorten very far before encountering the left ventricular end systolic pressure volume relationship. This results in a lower stroke volume compared to contractions proceeding against lower afterloads and indicates that pumping against elevated arterial

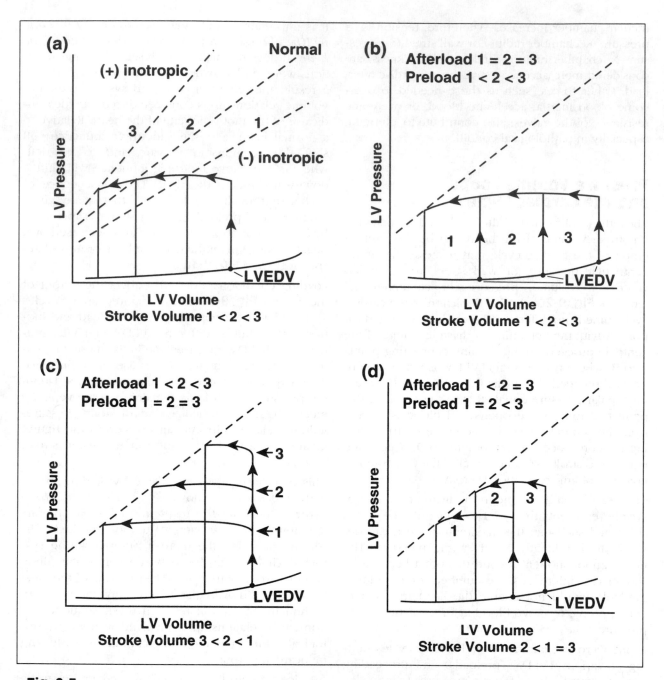

■ Fig. 9-3 ■

(a) Effect of inotropic state on stroke volume at a given left ventricular end diastolic pressure and arterial pressure. (b) Effect of changes in left ventricular end diastolic volume on stroke volume at constant arterial pressure and inotropic state (the Frank-Starling relationship). (c) Immediate effect of changes in afterload on ventricular stroke volume at constant left ventricular end diastolic volume. (d) Changes in left ventricular end diastolic volume and stroke volume subsequent to an initial increase in afterload.

pressure will have a detrimental effect on the output of the heart unless certain compensatory mechanisms are brought into play.

One such mechanism is shown in ■ **Fig. 9-3d** ■. Cardiac cycle 1 in this figure represents a contraction at normal LVEDV and against a normal arterial pressure. Loop 2 represents the first contraction against an elevated arterial pressure from the same LVEDV and results in a reduction in stroke volume. This reduced stroke volume means that the heart did not empty to its normal residual volume at the end of systole. In other words, the volume in the heart prior to it next filling is larger than normal. Thus, when the normal diastolic inflow in the next cardiac cycle is added to this increased residual volume, an increased LVEDV will be created for the next contraction (contraction 3 on the figure). By Starling's Law of the Heart, an augmented stroke volume will result. Heterometric regulation is thus a mechanism that enables the heart, within certain limits, to maintain a normal stroke volume against elevated arterial pressure.

There are other important consequences of Starling's law. For example, if output of the right heart suddenly should exceed that of the left, inflow into the left ventricle also will increase, increasing LVEDV and subsequent output of the left ventricle. In this manner, Starling's Law automatically ensures that outputs of the right and left ventricle will always match. In heart failure, the inability of individual cardiac cells to contract normally (negative inotropic effect) can be somewhat compensated for by the fact that reduced ejection allows blood to pool in the left ventricle, increasing LVEDV, and subsequently enhancing stroke volume. Also, further compensatory mechanisms in the body increase water retention and result in increased filling of the ventricle with an augmentation of stroke volume.

Clinical Evaluations of Myocardial Performance

Good evaluation of myocardial performance in patients has proven to be a challenge. There are no good measures of left ventricular volume or shortening, making difficult any evaluations based on changes in loading conditions. Furthermore, only anecdotal indices, based on experimental correlations, have been developed to estimate the inotropic state of the heart.

In the cardiac catheterization lab, clinicians can obtain a two-dimensional view of the ventricular chamber during the cardiac cycle by injecting a radio-opaque dye into the ventricle and recording the imagine on an x-ray motion picture. From this, a crude determination of ventricular chamber cross-sectional area during systole and diastole can be measured and used to estimate stroke volume in the heart. ■ **Fig. 9-4a** ■ This value is expressed as a percent of LVEDV and is called the *ejection fraction*. In normal hearts, the ejection fraction is 55% to 67%, and values less than 40% indicate impaired performance.

Clinical estimates of ventricular preload have been developed. The preload for ventricular contraction depends on how much the ventricle fills during diastole. Ventricular filling depends on the pressure difference between the left atrium and ventricle during diastole and the resistance to flow across the mitral valve. Unfortunately, the left atrial chamber is not easily accessible through a cardiac catheter (catheterizing arteries is dangerous) and venous catheters will not pass beyond the pulmonary circulation.

A catheter passed from the venous side of the circulation and "wedged" into the terminal arteriolar section of the pulmonary vasculature, however, will reflect pressure changes in the pulmonary capillaries, which in turn reflect left atrial pressure. ■ **Fig. 9-4b** ■ Pulmonary wedge pressures are used as indirect measures of left atrial pressure and ventricular filling during diastole; high pressures are assumed to result in increased filling. Stroke volume can be plotted against mean pulmonary artery wedge pressure as a means of plotting cardiac performance versus preload, according to Starling's law. Poor increases in stroke volume with increases in wedge pressure, as compared to clinically observed norms, are taken to indicate a weakened heart in an individual.

Variables that reflect changes in the inotropic state of the heart have proven difficult to develop and often are used on the basis of what works reasonably well in the clinic. For example, the peak rate of rise of pressure in the left ventricle during isovolumic contraction (peak dP/dt) has been shown to reflect alterations in myocardial contractility and to be affected little by changes in preload or afterload. A peak dP/dt < of 1200 mmHg/s indicates abnormally low myocardial contractility.

Under certain conditions, inferences about the inotropic state of the heart can be made from inspection of plots of stroke volume, cardiac output, or stroke work vs. either LVEDV, LVEDP, or pulmonary wedge pressure. For example, the only way a pa-

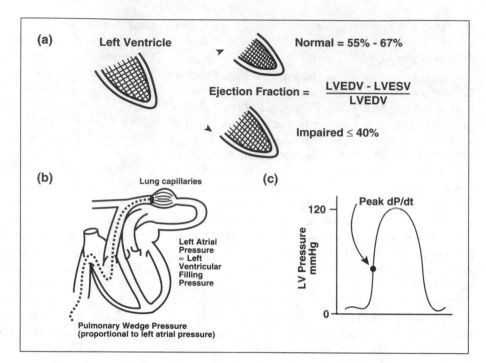

■ Fig. 9-4 ■
(a) Determination of ejection fraction by comparing cross sectional area in the ventricle during an x-ray fluorogram. (b) Method of obtaining pulmonary wedge pressure. (c) Example of peak dP/dt.

tient's stroke volume can decrease or remain unchanged in the face of an increased ventricular preload is if the patient's heart is experiencing a negative inotropic influence. Conversely, increased stroke volume in the face of an unchanged or decreased preload indicates that the heart is under a positive inotropic influence.

Because indices of cardiac performance and contractility have yet to be perfected, it is valuable to be able to identify certain physiological and pathological conditions with known changes in loading conditions and the inotropic state of the heart. For example, drugs that relax venous smooth muscle also lower central venous and ultimately right atrial pressure, thereby reducing filling of the heart and ventricular preload. Standing causes pooling of blood in the lower extremities and decreases pressure in the right atrium with a similar effect.

This effect is exacerbated by drugs that dilate veins, such as nitroglycerin used to treat angina or heart failure. Individuals taking these medication are susceptible to fainting upon standing due to excess pooling of blood in the veins that results in a precipitous drop in right atrial pressure, reduced output of the heart, and transient low blood pressure (postural hypotension). Conversely, lying down and raising the feet increases right atrial pressure and stroke output of the heart by the Starling mechanism. Also, contraction of skeletal muscle squeezes muscle veins, which results in increased venous pressure and forces blood back to the heart. This factor augments ventricular output during exercise.

Certain hormones, neurotransmitters, and drugs are known to affect contractility of the heart. Any condition that activates the sympathetic nervous system, for example, will likely enhance myocardial contractility. Conditions that activate the vagus nerve to the heart or inhibit sympathetic activity can have a negative inotropic effect. Such conditions will be discussed in subsequent chapters. Myocarditis and myocardial ischemia can be assumed to be negative inotropic influences. Certain anesthetics, such as barbiturates, antiarrhythmic drugs, and Ca++ antagonists are known negative inotropic agents.

CHAPTER 10

Cardiac Output and Cardiac Energetics

Cardiac output is defined as the volume of blood pumped by the heart per minute; it is equal to stroke volume (mL/beat) × heart rate (beat/min). Cardiac output is ≈ 4 to 5 L/min at rest in a healthy adult but can rise to more than 5 times that value during exercise. Cardiac output can be measured by a couple of methods. An older technique, called the *Fick method,* is based on the simple principle of conservation of mass. ■ **Fig. 10-1a** ■ Applying this principle to our circulation, the quantity of O_2 leav-

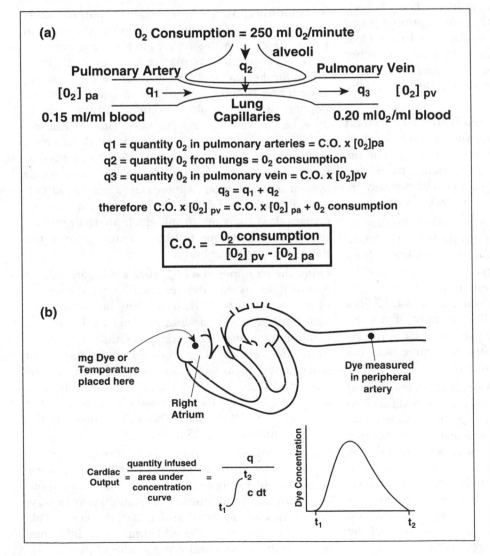

(a)

O_2 **Consumption = 250 ml O_2/minute**

alveoli

Pulmonary Artery q_2 **Pulmonary Vein**

$[O_2]_{pa}$ $q_1 \rightarrow$ $\rightarrow q_3$ $[O_2]_{pv}$

0.15 ml/ml blood   **Lung Capillaries**   **0.20 mlO_2/ml blood**

q1 = quantity O_2 in pulmonary arteries = C.O. x $[O_2]pa$
q2 = quantity O_2 from lungs = O_2 consumption
q3 = quantity O_2 in pulmonary vein = C.O. x $[O_2]pv$

$q_3 = q_1 + q_2$

therefore C.O. x $[O_2]_{pv}$ = C.O. x $[O_2]_{pa}$ + O_2 consumption

$$C.O. = \frac{O_2 \text{ consumption}}{[O_2]_{pv} - [O_2]_{pa}}$$

(b)

mg Dye or Temperature placed here

Dye measured in peripheral artery

Right Atrium

$$\text{Cardiac Output} = \frac{\text{quantity infused}}{\text{area under concentration curve}} = \frac{q}{\int_{t_1}^{t_2} c\, dt}$$

Dye Concentration

t_1 t_2

■ **Fig. 10-1** ■
(a) Calculation of cardiac output using the Fick method. (b) Measurement of cardiac output using a temperature or dye indicator dilution method. (See text for details.)

ing the pulmonary circulation must equal the sum of all sources of oxygen entering the pulmonary circulation. The quantity of O_2 entering the lung from the systemic circulation is simply the concentration of O_2 in the pulmonary artery ($[O_2]$pa in ml O_2 per ml blood) $\times$ pulmonary arterial flow (which is the same as cardiac output).

A similar equation describes the quantity of O_2 leaving the pulmonary circulation by the pulmonary vein. Oxygen also is added into the pulmonary circulation from the lungs at the pulmonary capillaries. In the steady state, this quantity is equal to whole-body O_2 consumption. With these relationship we can derive that flow (cardiac output) equals O_2 consumption / ($[O_2]$pv $-$ $[O_2]$pa). In this equation, it is assumed that an arterial blood sample reasonably reflects $[O_2]$pv. In addition, because $[O_2]$pa results from the mixing of O_2 contents of venous blood returning from all organ systems in the body (which all have different levels of O_2 consumption), only a truly mixed venous sample can be used for $[O_2]$pa. Such a sample must be obtained by a catheter either in the right atrium, ventricle, or pulmonary artery. Finally, O_2 consumption must be determined by whole-body respirometry.

Determination of cardiac output by the Fick method is accurate but cumbersome. Instead, this method often is used to calculate O_2 consumption in an organ, or organ segment, by independently measuring organ blood flow and multiplying that quantity by the difference in arterial and venous O_2 content.

Indicator-dilution techniques are more commonly used to determine cardiac output. They are based on the principle that removal of an indicator from the right atrium is proportional to cardiac output. To determine cardiac output, an indicator dye is injected into the right atrium or ventricle. ■ **Fig. 10-1b** ■ Cardiac output is equal to the quantity of dye injected into the atrium divided by the area of the arterial dye concentration versus time curve detected by a device in a peripheral artery.

Dyes recirculate in the blood stream and reappear at the detection device, however, making it difficult to determine the end point for integration. Modern cardiac output devices therefore calculate cardiac output by measuring dissipation of heat rather than a dye. A probe is inserted into the right atrium and cooled to a given temperature. The rate of change in the temperature of the probe as it warms back to body temperature is proportional to cardiac output. This method avoids the need for sampling arterial blood and the problems associated with dye recirculation.

Interplay of Cardiac Output with Venous Filling Pressure

Central venous pressure is one of the key determinants of the filling of the right heart and, by extension via Starling's Law of the Heart, a key determinant of cardiac output. However, the heart is a pump set in a *circulatory* system. Increased cardiac output into the arterial segment of the circulation must come at the expense of volume and pressure in the venous side of the circulation, yet decreased venous pressure decreases cardiac output! The poses an interesting set of questions:

1. How are values of cardiac output above or below the resting level ever achieved or maintained?
2. What determines the resting equilibrium between cardiac output and central venous pressure?

A demonstration of how cardiac output alters central venous and arterial pressure is shown in ■ **Fig. 10-2a** ■ . A theoretical circulation is depicted with a peripheral vascular resistance of 25 PRU. When the heart is stopped (cardiac output is zero), arterial and venous pressure are in equilibrium and dependent only on blood volume and the compliance of the vascular system. A.G. Guyton first reported that this value is $\approx$ 7 mmHg and described it as *mean circulatory pressure,* or *MCP.* Mean circulatory pressure is a measure of how "full" the vascular system is with blood; it increases when blood volume increases and decreases when this volume decreases. It is the value from which arterial pressure increases and venous pressure decreases once the heart starts to pump blood.

Using the example in ■ **Fig. 10-2** ■ with an MCP of 7 mmHg, let us start the heart with a cardiac output of 2 L/min. This will first translocate blood from the vein into the artery, adding pressure to the arterial component of the circulation and reducing pressure from the venous side. Let's examine the point where enough pressure difference between the arteries and veins has been created to move blood at a rate of 1 L/min across the resistance vessels in the circulation. ■ **Fig. 10-2b** ■ This will occur when the pressure difference is 25 mmHg.

The question is: How much does pressure increase in the arteries and how much does it decrease in the veins? In our example, the veins are 24 times more compliant than the arteries, or, stated another way, the arteries are 24 times stiffer than the veins. This means that for every 25 mm Hg pressure difference between the arterial and venous sides of the circula-

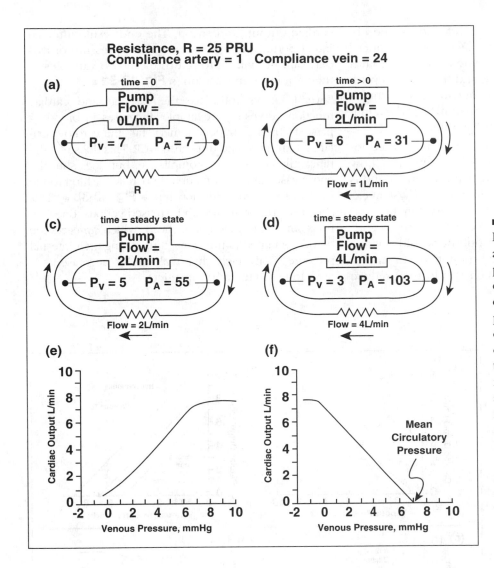

■ **Fig. 10-2** ■
Effect of cardiac output on arterial and central venous pressure. (a) At zero cardiac output all pressures equal the mean circulatory pressure. (b) Initial changes in pressures once cardiac output is increased to 2 L/min. (c) Final arterial and venous pressures after cardiac output and flow through peripheral resistance are equal at 2 L/min. (d) Final pressures in the artery and vein with the cardiac output equal to 4 L/min. (e) The cardiac function curve. (f) The vascular function curve. (See text for explanation.)

tion, 24 mmHg is added to the MCP on the arterial side (increasing its pressure to 31 mmHg) and 1 mmHg is subtracted from MCP on the venous side (reducing it to 6 mmHg).

In the steady state, when flow through the peripheral resistance and returning to the heart must equal that exiting the heart (in our example, a cardiac output of 2 L/min), arterial pressure becomes 55 mmHg and venous pressure 5 mmHg. ■ **Fig. 10-2c** ■ A cardiac output of 4 L/min would yield an arterial pressure of 103 mmHg and a central venous pressure of 2 mmHg. ■ **Fig. 10-2d** ■

In the mid 1950s A.G. Guyton described two graphical means of depicting the interrelationship between cardiac output and central venous pressure. One relationship, called the *cardiac function curve*, plots cardiac output as a function of central venous

pressure. ■ **Fig. 10-2e** ■ This is simply an extension of Starling's Law showing that factors augmenting ventricular filling result in increased cardiac output. The cardiac function curve is characteristic of the heart itself; only factors affecting the heart affect this curve. This curve can be produced even in a heart separated from the vasculature.

A second relationship, called the *vascular function curve*, shows how central venous pressure changes as a function of cardiac output ■ **Fig. 10-2f** ■ . For reasons to be seen below, and contrary to mathematical convention, the independent variable of the vascular function curve, cardiac output, is placed on the Y axis and venous pressure is placed on the X axis in this relationship. The vascular function curve is affected only by factors affecting vascular resistance, compliance, and blood volume. It is independent of characteristics of the heart and can be observed even if the heart is replaced by an artificial pump. This curve shows that when cardiac output is zero, venous pressure = MCP and that venous pressure decreases as cardiac output increases, until it results in venous collapse (≈ -2 mmHg), which limits any further increase in cardiac output.

Vascular and cardiac function curves are plotted together in ■ **Fig. 10-3** ■. This demonstrates how equilibrium between cardiac output and venous pressure is obtained. Equilibrium for this system exists at the point of intersection between the two curves. If venous pressure were to increase suddenly, an increased cardiac output would initially result. However, this elevated output would tend to reduce venous pressure, which would then reduce

cardiac output, and so on. The end result, after an initial perturbation in either venous pressure or cardiac output, will be to return these two variables to their equilibrium position. ■ **Fig. 10-3a** ■

Several factors influence the vascular and cardiac function curves. For example, increases in blood or plasma volume (hypervolemia) "fill" the cardiovascular system more and thus raise MCP. This does not significantly alter venous compliance, but does shift the entire vascular function curve in parallel fashion to the right of the normal relationship. ■ **Fig. 10-3b** ■ This shift also will be seen with increased venous tone (venous smooth muscle contraction), which *squeezes* the blood contained in the veins, thus raising their internal pressure. Conversely, hypovolemia or decreased venous tone has the opposite effect.

Fig. 10-3 ■
(a) Equilibrium resulting from normal cardiac and vascular function curves. (b) Effect of changing either blood volume or venous tone on the vascular function curve. (c) Effect of changes in arteriolar resistance on the vascular function curve. (d) Effect of changes in the inotropic state on the cardiac function curve. (e) Possible equilibrium points obtained by conjunction of altered myocardial contractility and vascular function curves. (f) Effects of alteration in vascular resistance on equilibrium points for cardiac output.

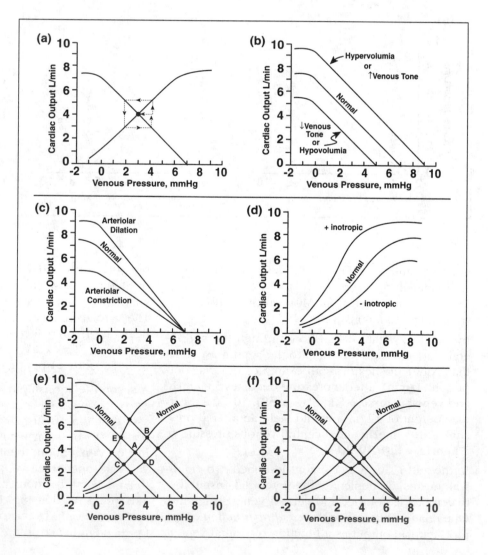

Changes in arteriolar tone have different effects on the vascular function curves. ■ **Fig. 10-3c** ■ Because little blood volume is contained in the arterioles, changes in arteriolar tone do not significantly affect MCP. However, reduced arteriolar resistance makes it easier for the heart, whereas increased resistance makes in harder for the heart to eject a given stroke volume with any venous filling pressure. Thus, at any central venous pressure, reducing arteriolar resistance augments cardiac output and increasing resistance impedes cardiac output.

Changes in the inotropic state of the heart alter the cardiac but not the vascular function curve. By definition, a positive inotropic influence will allow the heart to produce a larger output at any given venous pressure, whereas a negative inotropic influence will have the opposite effect. This axiom is reflected by the cardiac function curves in ■ **Fig. 10-3d** ■.

The net effect of changes in cardiac and venous function curves upon the equilibrium values for cardiac output and venous pressure is shown in ■ **Fig. 10-3e** ■. Point A represents the normal equilibrium. Factors that increase blood volume, like an intravenous infusion of blood or fluid, will shift the vascular function curve to the right, whereas loss of volume (i.e., hemorrhage) will shift that curve to the left. The new equilibrium points for these conditions, points B and C, respectively, correctly show the interrelationship between cardiac output and venous pressure that would be predicted by the Starling law; an increased cardiac output is associated with an elevated venous (and hence filling) pressure, and a decreased output is associated with a decreased venous pressure.

Similarly, the equilibrium points associated with changes in the inotropic state of the heart, D and E, also correspond with our understanding of the definition of contractility. A positive inotropic influence allows for an elevated cardiac output at a lower than normal venous pressure, whereas a negative inotropic influence has the opposite effect.

This illustration also shows how the body can compensate for a failing heart. ■ **Fig. 10-3e** ■ In acute heart failure a patient is likely to reside at point D on the graph, with reduced cardiac output and elevated venous pressure due to the inability of the heart to move blood from the veins to the arteries. With continued failure, however, the kidneys retain salt and water, resulting in a hypervolemic shift in the vascular function curve. This shift through the Starling mechanism helps augment cardiac output of the failing myocardium.

The effects of alterations in vascular resistance on the cardiac and vascular function curves are demonstrated in ■ **Fig. 10-3f** ■. Elevated resistance impedes cardiac output and requires a greater drop in venous pressure to occur in order to establish a gradient across the elevated resistance to produce peripheral flow matching a given cardiac output. Decreased resistance has the opposite effect. The precise location of the new equilibria depends on the relative degree to which the vascular and cardiac function curves are affected by changes in resistance.

Cardiac Energetics and Determinants of Myocardial Oxygen Consumption

Our hearts are only 0.3% of our body weights yet they use approximately 7% of the body's total O_2 consumption at rest. The energy output of a system is classically defined as the sum of heat production and work. Work in turn is defined as a force acting through a distance, or work = force × distance. In the left ventricle, work is given as the product of either arterial pressure, ventricular pressure, or wall tension during systole times the stroke volume.

From the standpoint of physics it does not matter whether cardiac work results from a large stroke volume against a low pressure or a small stroke volume against a high pressure. In the heart, energy and thus oxygen must be used to generate both pressure and pump blood. In the heart, however, *much more O_2* is required for an increase in work resulting from an increase in cardiac tension as opposed to work resulting from an increase in cardiac output. Consequently, changes in cardiac work are poor indicators of myocardial oxygen demand.

Any index that could predict cardiac O_2 demand under a variety of hemodynamic conditions would be invaluable to clinical medicine. Such an index that is both clinically practical and universally applicable to all cardiac O_2 demands has yet to be found. Much has been learned, however, about determinants of myocardial O_2 demand. Above the basal O_2 consumption needed to run membrane pumps and basic cellular activity, systolic pressure, or wall stress, the extent of muscle shortening (or stroke volume), heart rate, and the inotropic state of the heart are considered major determinants of myocardial oxygen demand.

Various investigators have used combinations of hemodynamic variables to predict O_2 demand in the heart. The double product, or systolic pressure $\times$ heart rate and the tension-time index (the area under the left ventricular systolic pressure curve) have been employed as predictors of cardiac O_2 demand. Changes in these indices reflect changes in oxygen needs of the heart caused by changes in heart rate and force generation, but they often fail in instances when certain agents, such as β-adrenergic agonists, produce positive inotropic and chronotropic effects on the heart at the same time their vascular effects cause a drop in blood pressure. Indices based on the end systolic pressure volume relationship seem promising as accurate determinants of cardiac O_2 demand. These relationships, however, are difficult to obtain in a practical way in cardiac patients.

Without a good index available as a predictor of cardiac oxygen demand, it is useful to simply recognize factors proven to alter myocardial O_2 demand. For example, hypertension, or high blood pressure, greatly increases the stress load on the heart and thus increases O_2 demand. Similarly, exercise increases heart rate, myocardial contractility and, in unconditioned individuals, blood pressure, all of which synergize to create greatly increased myocardial O_2 demand.

Due to the high O_2 requirements of the heart, this organ utilizes a wide variety of metabolic substrates. Two-thirds of myocardial energy demand is derived from metabolism of fatty acids, because on a molar basis, these compounds generate more ATP than sugars or amino acids. Metabolism of glucose supplies about 20% of the heart's energy needs, with remaining needs supplied by metabolism of lactate, pyruvate, amino acids, and certain ketones.

CHAPTER 11

Vascular Smooth Muscle and the Vascular Endothelium

Smooth muscle cells are contained in the walls of hollow organs such as arteries, veins, reproductive organs, the stomach, and intestines. Smooth muscle does not posses the complex striated appearance of skeletal or cardiac muscle, yet it is the most complex and versatile of the muscle types. This chapter will focus primarily on the function of vascular smooth muscle, although certain characteristics found in the smooth muscle of digestive or reproductive organs will be discussed where appropriate.

Contraction of smooth muscle utilizes a calcium-activated actin myosin crossbridge cycling mechanism similar to that seen in striated muscle. Little else is similar in the contractile mechanisms of the two types of muscle. ■ **Fig. 11-1a** ■ In smooth muscle, Ca++ binds to a regulatory protein called *calmodulin,* rather than troponin. The Ca++:calmodulin complex then activates an enzyme called *myosin-like chain kinase* (MLCK), which phosphorylates the myosin molecule. In smooth muscle, phosphorylation of myosin increases its affinity for actin and is a necessary step for initiating crossbridge cycling. This cycling, and resulting velocity of contraction, is much slower in smooth muscle than in striated muscle (< 1% as fast). Force-generating capacity per cm² of smooth muscle is approximately twice that of skeletal muscle, however, even though vascular smooth muscle contains only about 25% of the myosin seen in striated muscle.

Smooth muscle is unique in that the crossbridge cycle can exist in two states. Approximately 60 seconds into a sustained contraction of smooth muscle, cell O_2 consumption, ATP utilization, and intracellular Ca++ concentrations all drop to near resting levels, yet the cell is able to maintain its initial level of contraction. ■ **Fig. 11-1b** ■ This state, in which muscle contraction is maintained at lower energy utilizations, has been called the *latch state.* This state is not analogous to rigor in skeletal muscle, but instead is believed to represent a condition of either slowly cycling or noncycling crossbridges. It is important to note that arterial smooth muscle must provide a force to counteract distension of the artery due to high intravascular pressures; unlike striated muscle, it must be active *at all times.* By allowing sustained contractions with reduced energy utilization, the latch state is a valuable unique property of vascular smooth muscle.

Activator Ca++ in Smooth Muscle

Elaborate mechanisms are used in the control of intracellular calcium in vascular smooth muscle. ■ **Fig. 11-2a** ■ Four transmembrane Ca++ channels have been identified in smooth muscle and they control Ca++ entry into the cell from the extracellular fluid. There exists a potential- or voltage-activated channel that opens upon membrane depolarization. There also is a leak or passive diffusion channel that has very low conductance under normal conditions but high conductance in pathological conditions such as hypertension.

Two unique Ca++ channels exist in smooth muscle. Smooth muscle contains many different types of receptor-operated Ca++ channels. These channels open upon binding of a contractile agonist to a membrane receptor, which is linked to the channel by a G-protein. There are several different receptor-operated channel types in vascular smooth muscle (i.e., those for catecholamines, hormones, etc.) Finally, another calcium channel in the cell membrane opens whenever smooth muscle cells are stretched. Receptor- and stretch-operated channels can be activated without changes in the smooth muscle membrane potential.

Ca++ used for contraction (activator calcium) in smooth muscle also can be derived from the release of cellular calcium stores. Release of Ca++ from the sarcoplasmic reticulum (SR) occurs when a second

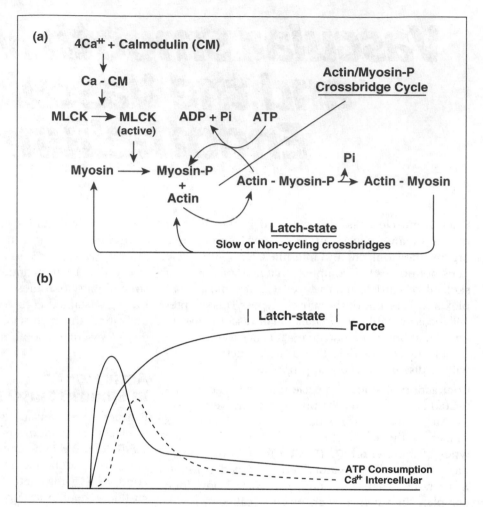

■ Fig. 11-1 ■
(a) Intracellular pathway responsible for calcium activation and crossbridge cycling in vascular smooth muscle. (b) Changes in vascular smooth muscle ATP consumption and intracellular calcium concentration during contraction, showing the latch state phenomenon.

messenger, inositol triphosphate (IP$_3$), binds to a sarcoplasmic reticular membrane receptor. IP$_3$ is formed when any of several different contractile agonists binds to a membrane receptor linked to membrane bound phospholipase C, which catalyzes the conversion of phosphotidylinositol-bis-phosphate (PIP$_2$) into diacylglycerol (DAG) and IP$_3$. Also, Ca^{++} entering through transmembrane channels can stimulate Ca^{++} release from the SR as well as from a membrane-bound store of Ca^{++}.

Electrical Properties of Smooth Muscle and Classifications of Smooth Muscle Contraction

Many smooth muscle cells are connected by gap junctions and can display syncytial electrical and mechanical properties. Smooth muscle also can fire action potentials spontaneously or in response to chemical, neural, or physical stimuli, which can then spread to adjacent cells and result in a widespread contraction. Smooth muscle action potentials are carried primarily by Ca^{++} and initiate contraction by activation of membrane potential-operated calcium channels. Action potentials can be generated individually or in bursts and correspond to single or summed tetanic-like contractions.

The syncytial and action potential characteristics of smooth muscle are more common in visceral than in vascular smooth muscle. Generally, vascular smooth muscle displays more motor–unit-like properties and is richly innervated by the sympathetic adrenergic nerves. Contractile α-adrenergic receptors predominate in the smooth muscle membranes of arteries of all organs except the brain and heart. The sympathetic nervous system is tonically active in ar-

■ **Fig. 11-2** ■

(a) Representation of calcium handling in vascular smooth muscle. Calcium may enter the smooth muscle cell through potential-operated channels (POC), leak channels, stretch-operated channels (SOC), and numerous receptor-operated channels (ROC). Activation of ROC also stimulates release of calcium from intracellular stores, production of vasoactive prostaglandins, and activation of protein kinase C (which may play a role in vascular contraction). Calcium ATPase pumps and sodium/calcium exchange mechanisms reduce vascular intracellular calcium concentration. PDE = lipid phospholipase C, IP_3 = inositol triphosphate, PIP_2 = phosphotidyl inositol bis phosphate, DAG = diacylglycerol. Ca/CaM = calcium-calmodulin complex. (b) Left: Changes in force in vascular smooth muscle due to graded changes in resting membrane potential. Right: Pharmacomechanical coupling. (+) = stimulation.

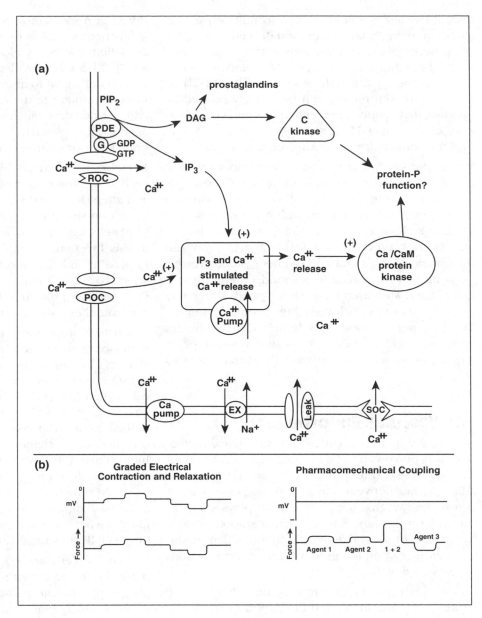

teries and veins and therefore these vessels are partially contracted by these nerves at rest. Smooth muscle has a low resting membrane potential (−65 to −50 mV), of which a large contribution (10–15 mV) comes from the electrogenic Na+/K+ pump. Inhibition of the Na+/K+ ATPase in smooth muscle leads to membrane depolarization and contraction via activation of potential-operated calcium channels in the cell membrane.

Vascular smooth muscle can contract or relax by means unique to this cell type and not seen in striated muscle. ■ **Fig. 11-2b** ■ In vascular muscle, stepwise membrane depolarization without formation of action potentials results in proportional stepwise muscle contraction (i.e., grade contraction). In addition, graded membrane hyperpolarization results in graded relaxation of smooth muscle.

Contraction of smooth muscle mediated by binding of a contractile agonist to a membrane receptor results from activation of receptor-operated membrane Ca++ channels, release of Ca++ from intracellular stores by IP_3, and activation of DAG-mediated mechanisms by means that are not yet completely understood. More important, receptor-mediated contraction often occurs without alterations in the muscle membrane potential. This is called *pharmacomechanical coupling,* at the right side of ■ **Fig. 11-2b** ■. Vascular smooth muscle can be actively relaxed by agonists that reduce intracellular calcium concentration. cAMP and cGMP both serve as vasodilator second messengers for many vasorelaxant agents.

It is important to note that vascular smooth muscle is highly heterogeneous in it properties. Crossbridge cycling and force generation development will vary with the agonist used, even within the same source of vascular smooth muscle. Norepinephrine, for example, may produce one level of activation and membrane depolarization another. Blood vessels from different organs will respond differently to a given agent and arterial muscle responds differently from that in veins. Although there are many similarities in general smooth muscle behavior in different blood vessels, the response of any vessel type to any agent should not be casually extrapolated to any other.

The Vascular Endothelium

As recently as two decades ago, vascular endothelium was perceived to be nothing more than "vascular Teflon" serving primarily as an anticoagulant and a barrier between blood and the vessel wall. It is now known that the endothelium plays a significant role in the function of vascular smooth muscle by producing several active compounds that modulate vascular contraction as well as other functions in the vessel wall.

Endothelium produces prostacyclin (PGI₂), nitric oxide (NO), histamine, and the peptide endothelin. Prostacyclin, derived from the metabolism of arachidonic acid, is produced spontaneously in endothelial cells as well as in response to certain receptor-mediated vasodilators such as acetylcholine and bradykinin. Its role in vascular contractile function is not clear, but it is a very potent inhibitor of platelet aggregation and therefore serves an important role in preventing blood clot formation in blood vessels.

The primary vasoactive component produced by the endothelium is NO, also called *endothelium-derived relaxing factor,* or *EDRF,* because of its discovery first as a mediator of vascular relaxation associated with many vasodilator agents. NO is pro-

duced in response to several receptor-mediated vasodilators, as well as by sheer stress against the endothelium caused by blood flow in the vasculature. ■ **Fig. 11-3** ■ It provides a continual, potent basal vasodilator signal to arteries and veins. It is a significant contributor to the relaxation produced by several vasodilators such as histamine, dopamine, aggregating platelets, ATP, ADP, acetylcholine, bradykinin, and thrombin.

NO also is produced by several vasoconstrictors, such as serotonin, norepinephrine, and vasopressin and attenuates the direct contractile effects of those agents on smooth muscle. NO is a potent inhibitor of platelet aggregation and will synergize with PGI₂ in this function. It inhibits the adherence of neutrophils to endothelial cells (an early step in atherosclerosis) and will react with oxygen radicals such as O_2^-, perhaps protecting the vasculature from damage from these highly reactive chemical species.

Production of nitric oxide by the vascular endothelium occurs as the result of the enzymatic conversion of L-arginine to L-citrulline and NO by a constitutively expressed enzyme within endothelial cells called *NO synthase* (ecNOS). ■ **Fig. 11-3** ■ This enzyme is activated by calcium entry into the endothelium in response to activation of receptor-operated Ca⁺⁺ channels on the endothelial cells. Intracellular Ca⁺⁺ binds to calmodulin in the endothelial cell, forming a complex that activates ecNOS. NO, being a small and highly lipophilic molecule, diffuses readily into adjacent smooth muscle where it activates guanylate cyclase to produce cGMP, which mediates vascular relaxation.

Endothelial cells are not the only source of nitric oxide synthase. Smooth muscle cells and macrophages produce an inducible form of NOS (iNOS). iNOS is usually quiescent in these tissues until they are stimulated by bacterial toxins, tumor necrosis factor, or other cytokines that are produced by the immune system in response to infectious agents. NO from these tissues appears to function as a primary or secondary bactericidal agent. NO synthase is found in the central nervous system and some peripheral nerves where it may serve as a neurotransmitter; it is the neurogenic vasodilator responsible for penile erection from nonadrenergic, noncholinergic penile nerves.

In the normal cardiovascular system, basal release of endothelium-derived NO exerts a significant anticoagulant, antiatherogenic, and antihypertensive effect. Blockade of NO synthesis causes a marked

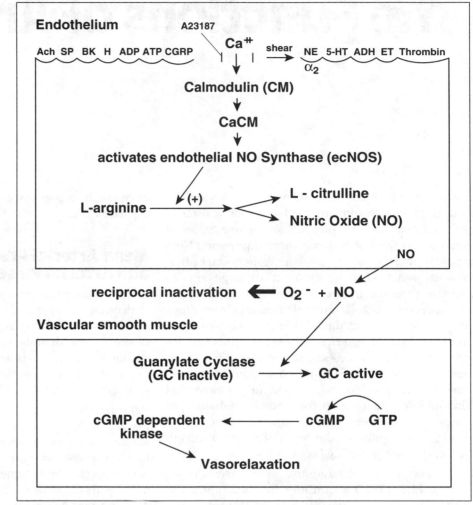

■ Fig. 11-3 ■
Mechanism of vascular relaxation by nitric oxide (EDRF). Ach = acetylcholine, SP = substance P, BK = bradykinin, H = histamine, CGRP = calcitonin gene-related peptide, A23187 = calcium ionofore, NE = norepinephrine, 5-HT = serotonin, ADH = antidiuretic hormone, ET = endothelin. (+) = stimulation.

increase in arterial pressure, or hypertension. Virtually all forms of cardiovascular disease are associated with impaired endothelial production of NO and endothelial-dependent arterial relaxation. These include acute and chronic hypertension, atherosclerosis, exposure to low-density lipoproteins, hypercholesterolemia, diabetes mellitus, heart failure, and ischemic heart disease.

The endothelium also is the source of the peptide endothelin, the most potent vasoconstrictor yet discovered, although its role in vascular function is not clearly known. Anoxia has been shown to produce an endothelium-derived constricting factor that may be O_2^- derived from prostaglandin synthesis. This factor has procoagulant and atherogenic properties that might antagonize effects of NO in the vasculature.

CHAPTER 12

The Functions of Arteries

The aorta and other large-diameter arteries do not contribute significantly to total vascular resistance and therefore do not play a role in regulation of organ blood flow or systemic arterial pressure. Nevertheless, these conduit vessels have important physiological functions. The elasticity of large arteries attenuates the rise in arterial pressure during systole and prevents diastolic arterial pressure from dropping to levels seen in the left ventricle (2–5 mmHg). Large, compliant arteries distend as pressure increases during systole, storing potential energy in their elastic walls. ■ **Fig. 12-1a** ■ During diastole, these elastic walls recoil, providing pressure that continues to push blood forward through the peripheral circulation. This ensures a steady flow through the capillaries during diastole even though the heart is not pumping blood.

The elastic nature of large arteries reduces cardiac work. ■ **Fig. 12-1b** ■ Consider the situation if the heart pumped at a constant rate of 100 mL/s into rigid arteries with a resistance of 16.6 PRU for 4 seconds. This would generate a constant pressure of 100 mmHg and cardiac work over the 4 seconds would be simply P × V or 100 mmHg × 400 ml = 40,000 units. If the heart pumps intermittently and ejects blood at 100 mL/s into rigid arteries during the first half-second of the cycle (i.e. 200 mL/s for 0.5 second), while relaxing during the last half-second, pressure will rise to 200 mmHg during each ejection and drop to 0 mmHg during relaxation. No work will be done during relaxation, but work will = 80,000 units during contraction.

If this same intermittent flow were ejected into arteries with infinite compliance (flexibility), pressure would not rise during systole or fall during diastole and would remain at an average of 100 mmHg. Work in this situation would then again be 40,000. Our arteries are neither rigid nor infinitely compliant. Clearly, however, increased arterial compliance reduces cardiac work whereas decreased compliance (such as that associated with aging) increases cardiac work.

Mean Arterial Pressure and Arterial Pulse Pressure

Arterial pulse pressure is defined as systolic pressure − diastolic pressure and is typically 40 mmHg (120 − 80 mmHg). Mean arterial pressure is not the average of systolic and diastolic pressures, because diastole is slightly longer than systole. Mean arterial pressure can be estimated as 1/3 pulse pressure + diastolic pressure and is about 93 mmHg in a normal adult.

Pulse pressure is altered by changes in arterial compliance and stroke volume. Anything that increases stroke volume or decreases arterial compliance will increase pulse pressure. ■ **Fig. 12-2** ■ During the cardiac cycle, the volume change in the arterial system equals the stroke volume minus diastolic runoff. At a constant compliance, increasing stroke volume increases mean arterial pressure by Poiseuille's law and ejects more blood into the arteries during systole, thereby increasing systolic pressure. ■ **Fig. 12-2a** ■ Runoff occurs from this higher pressure and does not reach normal diastolic levels before the next cardiac contraction.

Because compliance C = ΔV/ΔP, decreased arterial compliance results in a larger arterial pressure change for any given volume change in the cardiovascular system. ■ **Fig. 12-2b** ■ Stiff arteries have less "give" during systole and less elastic recoil during diastole. Therefore, systolic pressure increases and diastolic pressure decreases when arterial compliance is decreased; increased compliance has the opposite effect. Theoretically, pulse pressure is not affected by changes in vascular resistance. At a given cardiac output, however, an increase in resistance will increase mean arterial pressure. Because arterial compliance decreases at high arterial pressures, an increase in vascular resistance often in-

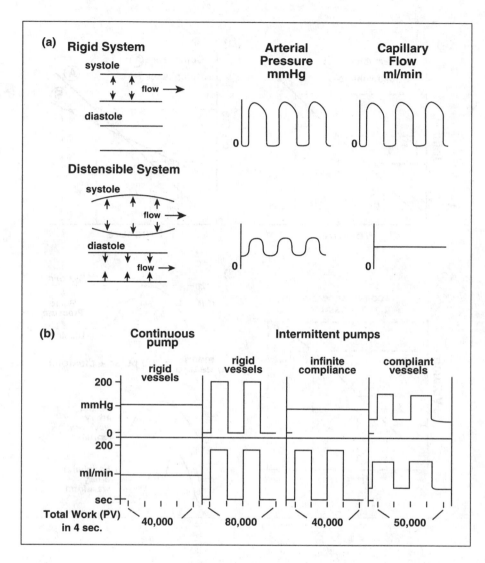

■ Fig. 12-1 ■
(a) Example of the effect of intermittent pumping of blood into rigid arteries vs. distensible arteries. Note the differences in the effect upon arterial pressure and capillary blood flow at the right. (b) Effect of intermittent pumping of blood into a rigid versus flexible vasculature on cardiac work. Increased compliance reduces myocardial workload.

creases pulse along with mean arterial pressure. **■ Fig. 12-2c ■**

Arterial Pulse Waves

The arterial pulse that one feels in the wrist or neck is not due to frank displacement of a volume of blood from one location of the cardiovascular system to the other. It is caused instead by molecule-to-molecule transmission of vibrations initiated in the aortic wall and transmitted in the walls of downstream arteries. This is similar to what one feels if one places a hand on one end of a long table while someone else pounds at the other end. The table material does not get displaced from the pounding, but the shock waves are transmitted, molecule-to-molecule, until they are felt at the other end.

The contour of the arterial pressure pulse is altered as it travels farther from the heart, due to tapering and branching of the arterial system and reflection of waves after they "hit" terminal arterioles. The result is that the pulse wave becomes steeper and foreshortened as one proceeds from the aorta to peripheral arteries in much the same way an ocean wave builds to a crest as it reaches shallower water toward the shore. This creates the somewhat confusing appearance of a higher systolic pressure in terminal arteries than in the aorta, even though mean arterial pressure is lower in the terminal vessels. **■ Fig. 12-2d ■**

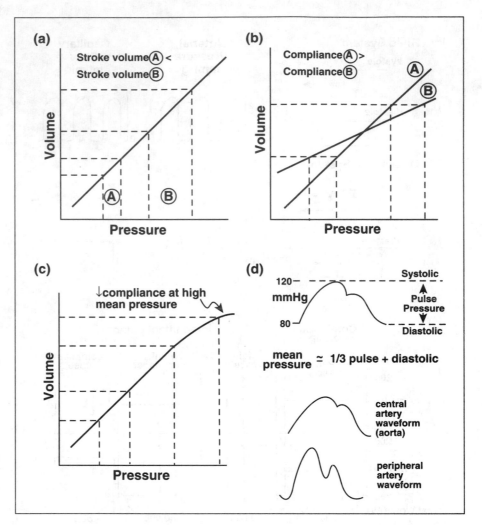

■ Fig. 12-2 ■
(a) Effect of two different stroke volumes upon arterial pulse pressure. (b) Effect of two different compliances on arterial pulse pressure at a given stroke volume. (c) Effect of a given stroke volume on arterial pulse pressure at low and high resistance. (d) Comparison of systolic, diastolic, pulse, and mean arterial pressures, and pressure pulse waveforms in the aorta and a peripheral artery.

Local Regulation of Blood Flow

The arterioles, with diameters of 10–500 μm, are the section of the vascular system with the largest flow resistance and the site of control of organ blood flow. These arteries have thick muscular walls capable of producing large changes in vessel internal radius and resistance in response to changes in the level of contraction in their smooth muscle layer. Arteriolar contraction is affected by contractile impulses from sympathetic nerves, transmural pressure, and a wide variety of local vasoconstrictor and vasodilator substances.

In passive elastic tubes, such as a vascular bed without arterial contractile activity, flow increases in proportion to perfusion pressure. **■ Fig. 12-3a ■** In fact, as pressure increases and passively distends the elastic vessels, vascular resistance starts to decrease and any further increases in pressure cause

even greater increases in flow. In most organ systems, however, blood flow is maintained relatively constant over a significant range of arterial pressure. **■ Fig. 12-3b ■**

The ability to maintain near-constant flow in the face of changes in perfusion pressure is called *autoregulation* of blood flow. Autoregulation functions in the following way. If mean arterial pressure suddenly drops from 100 to 80 mmHg, an immediate decrease in flow will result, according to Poiseuille's law. However, in many organs like the brain, heart, and kidney, this decrease in flow is followed in about 60 seconds by a return of flow to or near normal, in spite of a sustained decrease in arterial pressure.

Conversely, an increase in pressure results in an initial increase in organ flow, followed shortly thereafter by a return of flow to near its original value,

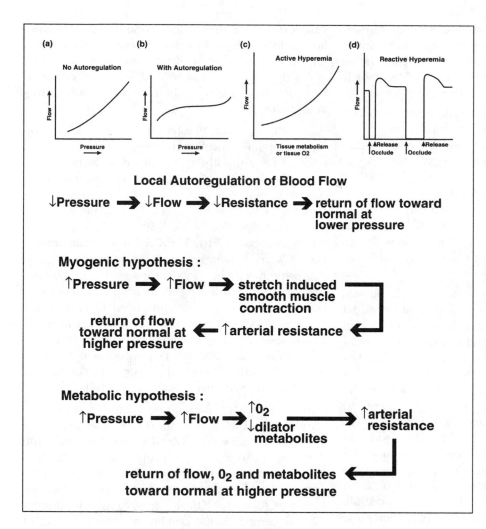

Fig. 12-3

(a) Relationship between flow and perfusion pressure in a vascular bed without autoregulation present, and (b) with autoregulation present. (c) Effect of increased tissue metabolism or decreased tissue oxygen concentration on blood flow. (d) Example of reactive hyperemia after total blood flow occlusions of two different durations. Bottom: Myogenic and metabolic hypotheses of local blood flow autoregulation. Small upward arrow = increase, small downward arrow = decrease. Heavy arrows link effects resulting from a change in the preceding variable.

even though pressure remains elevated. The mechanism ultimately responsible for autoregulation is a proportional and appropriate change in vascular resistance in response to a change in arterial pressure; that is, flow is maintained because arterial resistance increases in response to an increase in perfusion pressure and decreases in response to a decrease in pressure. This response is opposite of what would occur in a passive elastic vasculature in response to changes in arterial pressure. It implies, therefore, that arterial muscle *actively* contracts or relaxes in response to an increase or decrease in arterial pressure, respectively.

Autoregulation occurs independently of vascular sympathetic nerve activity and neural or humoral reflexes. It is abolished by anoxia or metabolic poisons such as CN^-. Autoregulation is a purely local regulatory phenomena intrinsic to the contractile ability of arterioles themselves; it is even observed in denervated vascular beds. Autoregulation is not perfect in every vascular bed; flow often returns close to, but not exactly to, normal values after a change in arterial perfusion pressure. Also, autoregulation does not function in most organs at pressures outside 60 to 130 mmHg.

Two hypotheses have been developed to explain autoregulation, as seen at the bottom of **Fig. 12-3**. One hypothesis proposes that an increase in arterial pressure stretches the arterial wall, thereby stimulating stretch-activated arterial smooth muscle Ca^{++} channels. This increases smooth muscle contraction and vascular resistance, which returns flow toward its original values.

This autoregulation mechanism was called the *myogenic hypothesis* by Baylis in the early 1900s. Baylis showed that isolated arterioles will actively contract in response to an increase in internal pressure and actively relax when internal pressure is reduced.

This theory is not wholly satisfactory in explaining autoregulation. For blood flow to remain constant at an elevated arterial pressure, the average arteriolar radius must decrease to a value *less* than that which existed prior to the increase in arterial pressure.

Once arterial contraction brings the effective radius down to its level before the pressure increase, the "stretch" on the vascular wall will be gone. It has been suggested that wall tension (pressure × radius) might be the sensed variable responsible for myogenic autoregulation of blood flow; after a pressure increase, autoregulation theoretically would reduce arterial wall tension back toward its original value. However, identification of a tension sensor mechanism in the arterial wall has not been forthcoming.

A second autoregulation hypothesis, called the *metabolic hypothesis,* proposes that a change in arterial pressure first alters organ blood flow, which in turn affects vascular resistance by changing the chemical environment surrounding the organ arterioles. For example, a drop in arterial pressure initially reduces organ blood flow, which results in a decrease in the delivery of any blood-borne vasoactive agents to the organ and increases the accumulation of any vasoactive agents surrounding the arterioles produced by the organ. Increased flow has the opposite effect. For this theory to explain autoregulation, either decreased delivery of a vasoconstrictor(s) or accumulation of vasodilator metabolite(s) is responsible for reduced vascular resistance when perfusion pressure decreases, whereas an increased delivery of vasoconstrictors and a washout of vasodilator metabolites are responsible for increased resistance in response to increased arterial pressure.

When blood flow is reduced, vasodilators such as CO_2, H^+, and K^+ (at low concentrations) accumulate around organ arterioles, while tissue O_2 (a vasoconstrictor) diminishes. None of these metabolites individually or collectively can adequately explain autoregulation of blood flow. Generally, their ability to alter vascular tone does not correspond with actual changes in their concentration during autoregulation.

It is clear, however, that tissue metabolic factors influence organ blood flow because virtually all organ systems have the ability to alter flow to match the metabolic demands of that tissue. For example, many organs show an increase in their blood flow whenever their activity is increased, for example the intestine during digestion or the heart and skeletal muscle during exercise. ■ **Fig. 12-3c** ■ This phenomenon is called *active hyperemia*. Active hyperemia suggests that some metabolic vasodilator signal must be continually produced during increased tissue metabolic activity. Berne et al. first proposed that increased tissue metabolism results in increased tissue levels of adenosine, which is a highly diffusible, potent arterial dilator. Its increase is proportional to metabolic activity in amounts appropriate to account for vasodilation seen during active hyperemia.

Occlusion of arteries for a few seconds results in increased blood flow for a short time after the occlusion is released. ■ **Fig. 12-3d** ■ The magnitude and duration of this increase is proportional, within limits, to the duration of the occlusion. This phenomenon is called *reactive hyperemia,* and it can be seen in tissues such as the heart's following restoration of normal hemodynamic conditions after a period of restricted low flow (e.g., removal of coronary artery blockages). Although myogenic mechanisms could account for the initial increase in flow upon release of the occlusion, the fact that the magnitude and duration of the increase is proportional to the period of occlusion is more indicative of accumulation of vasodilator metabolites.

CHAPTER 13

Microcirculation and Lymphatics

The microcirculation is the system of arterioles, capillaries, and venules responsible for regulation of material exchange between the plasma and interstitial fluid surrounding tissues in the body. ■ **Fig. 13-1a** ■ The major site of material exchange is the capillaries, which are small-diameter (5–10 μm) vessels composed of a single layer of endothelial cell. Capillaries in all organs except the brain contain clefts or pores between adjacent cells. ■ **Fig. 13-1b** ■ These pores are large enough in the liver and bone marrow to allow passage of proteins or cells into or out of the capillaries. Capillary pores in other organs generally exclude proteins and cells but allow passage of water, ions, amino acids, and simple sugars. Transport across capillaries also can occur through the lipid membranes of the capillary endothelium.

Not all capillaries in an organ are perfused with blood at all times. Contraction or relaxation of arterioles and precapillary sphincters control the numbers of capillaries perfused; precapillary sphincters function like "open/closed" valves opening or closing off entire sections of the capillary network. The arterioles and precapillary sphincters determine the distribution of flow within a tissue, the capillary surface area exposed to blood, the diffusion distances between capillaries and tissue, as well as help determine capillary hydrostatic pressure.

Smooth muscle tone in these vessels is affected by the sympathetic nerves (predominantly alpha-adrenergic contraction) and local factors such as O_2, CO_2, H^+, and adenosine, as well as bradykinin and histamine, which produce the vasodilation and in-

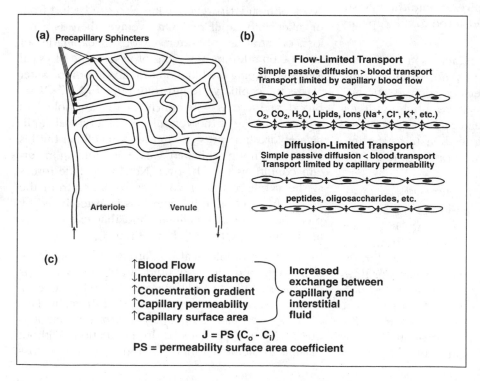

(a) Precapillary Sphincters

Arteriole   Venule

(b)

Flow-Limited Transport
Simple passive diffusion > blood transport
Transport limited by capillary blood flow

O_2, CO_2, H_2O, Lipids, ions (Na^+, Cl^-, K^+, etc.)

Diffusion-Limited Transport
Simple passive diffusion < blood transport
Transport limited by capillary permeability

peptides, oligosaccharides, etc.

(c)

↑Blood Flow
↓Intercapillary distance
↑Concentration gradient
↑Capillary permeability
↑Capillary surface area

Increased exchange between capillary and interstitial fluid

$$J = PS (C_o - C_i)$$
PS = permeability surface area coefficient

■ **Fig. 13-1** ■
(a) Diagram of the microcirculatory network. (b) Flow-limited and diffusion-limited transport across the capillaries (see text). (c) Factors that increase exchange of substances between the capillaries and the interstitial fluid. Small upward arrow = increase, small downward arrow = decrease. Flux, J, across the capillary is proportional to the concentration gradient for that substance and the combined effect of capillary permeability and surface area, as represented by the PS coefficient.

creased capillary perfusion associated with tissue injury and inflammation. Arteriolar and sphincter relaxation increases perfused capillary density, which then increases the capillary surface area available for transport while decreasing distances between the capillaries and surrounding cells. This augments transcapillary transport. Arteriolar constriction has the opposite effect.

Venules primarily control capillary hydrostatic pressure. Under certain circumstances, however, they participate in transcapillary transport of substances between blood and the interstitium.

Transcapillary Exchange

Exchange between the interstitial fluid and capillaries occurs via three processes: diffusion, filtration, and vesicular transport.

Simple passive *diffusion* is the major process by which nutrients and metabolites cross the capillary barrier. Small lipid-soluble molecules diffuse easily across the entire capillary membrane, whereas water, simple sugars, and ions diffuse easily through the capillary pores. ■ **Fig. 13-1b** ■ Transport of these substances from capillary to tissue or vice versa is not limited by their ability to diffuse across the membrane. Their transport is limited only by their rate of delivery into the capillaries from capillary blood flow (e.g., they are delivered into the interstitium as fast as they can be delivered to the capillary by blood flow).

Transport of these substances across the capillary network thus is said to occur by *flow-limited transport*. Larger lipophobic molecules such as sucrose, polysaccharides, and proteins have difficulty diffusing across the capillary membrane or pores and thus diffusion is rate-limiting in their transport into or out of capillaries. Such transport is called *diffusion-limited transport*.

Factors that affect transport of diffusible materials across capillaries are listed in ■ **Fig. 13-1c** ■ . Diffusion of a substance across the capillary is proportional to its concentration difference within and outside the vessel and inversely proportional to the distance over which diffusion must occur. For flow-limited transport substances, increased blood flow increases the effective concentration of a substance in the capillary and accelerates its outward diffusion; i.e., the faster materials are brought into the capillary, relative to their diffusion out of the capil-

lary, the higher will be the concentration of the substance inside the capillary.

In pathological conditions, substances that otherwise exhibit flow-limited transport can become diffusion-limited. This can occur when diffusion distances between capillaries and cells become too great to allow rapid exchange of materials, as seen in the lungs when transport of normally highly diffusible oxygen is impaired by infection or fluid accumulation in the pulmonary interstitium. It also can occur in any organ when the number of perfused capillaries is radically reduced (by low flow, blood clots, etc.), thereby increasing the distance between tissue cells and the nearest capillaries.

Diffusion of a substance across capillaries also is affected by the capillary surface area available for diffusion and the permeability of the capillary membrane to the substance. Surface area and permeability are combined into a proportionality constant in *Fick's law of diffusion*, which states that $J = -PS(C_o - C_i)$ where, PS is the permeability surface area coefficient and is a measure of the ease with which a substance can cross the capillary membrane.

Filtration and Reabsorption

Water diffuses back and forth across the capillary wall through pores at a rate of about 300 mL/min per 100 g of tissue. However, water also can be lost from or taken into capillaries. On average, there is a net loss, or filtration, of water out of our capillaries of about 0.06 mL/min per 100 g of tissue. The physical forces governing the filtration or reabsorption of water across the capillary are illustrated in ■ **Fig. 13-2a** ■ . Blood pressure is ≈30 mmHg at the arteriole end and ≈15 mmHg at the venous end of a typical capillary. Hydrostatic pressure in the extracellular fluid is about 0, although this may vary ± ≈ 7 mmHg in certain conditions (see below). Net hydrostatic forces at the capillary thus favor loss of water from the vessel. In addition, this water loss is exacerbated by proteins in the extracellular fluid that exert an osmotic drawing effect of about 8 mmHg.

In normal physiological conditions, the only force limiting the movement of fluid out of the capillary is the osmotic effect of plasma proteins, which exert a water retaining force equivalent to 25 mmHg. This force is often called *oncotic pressure* because it is due to just the proteins in the circulation. Without plasma proteins (primarily albumin), water loss

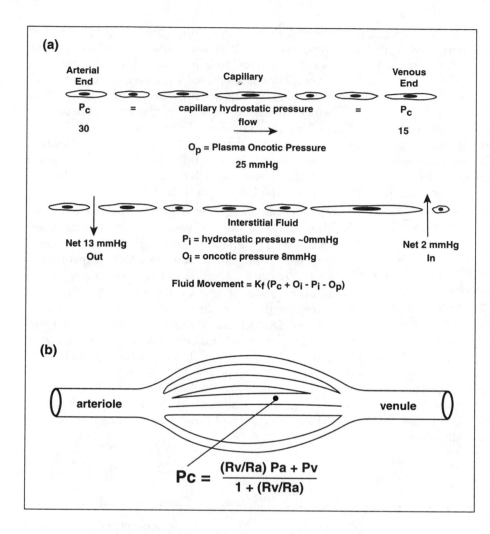

■ Fig. 13-2 ■
(a) Representation of Starling forces across a typical capillary. Capillary hydrostatic pressure is higher at the arterial end than it is at the venous end. Proteins are the only significant osmotic factor retaining fluid in the capillary. Fluid movement is proportional to the difference in hydrostatic and oncotic pressures inside vs. outside the capillaries, as determined by the conductivity of a given capillary to water. (b) Physical determinants of intracapillary blood pressure, Pc.

from our capillaries would be enormous. It is not uncommon for the net effect of all the forces influencing water movement across the capillary to favor filtration at the arterial end of the vessel and reabsorption at the venous end. In addition, some capillaries may either filter or reabsorb water across their entire length.

The forces affecting water movement across the capillary have been combined into an equation known as *Starling's law of ultrafiltration*. **■ Fig. 13-2a ■** In this equation, positive values signify filtration out of, and negative values, reabsorption of fluid into, the capillaries, and capillary hydrostatic pressure is taken to be the average value throughout the vessel. The amount of water movement across the capillaries is determined by the conductance, or ease of movement, of water across the capillaries in an organ and

is designated as K_f, or the capillary filtration coefficient. K_f is large in the intestine, liver, and kidney, and very low in skeletal muscle, skin, and brain.

Plasma and interstitial oncotic pressures and interstitial hydrostatic pressure are not physiologically controlled variables. Consequently, the only way transcapillary water movement can be altered physiologically is to alter intercapillary blood pressure (hydrostatic pressure). The average capillary hydrostatic pressure is a function of arterial and venous pressure and pre- and postcapillary resistance. **■ Fig. 13-2b ■** Pressure is increased by an increase in either arterial pressure, venous pressure, venule resistance (a damming effect), or a decrease in arteriolar resistance (increase inflow and higher pressure at the arterial end). The effect of a change in arterial pressure on capillary hydrostatic pressure is not as great as a similar change in venous pressure, however, because the former is tempered by the ratio of venule to arteriolar resistance (normally 1:4).

Lymph Vessels

Because fluid is lost via filtration at the capillaries, a mechanism must exist to return this fluid to the vascular compartment to prevent circulatory collapse. Lymphatic vessels serve this function. The lymphatic vessels are closed-end capillaries that have the primary function of returning protein, water, and electrolytes from the interstitium to the blood. ■ **Fig. 13-3** ■ Lymph vessels coalesce into larger vessels that contain one-way valves directed toward the heart. The lymphatic system terminates in the thoracic duct, which empties into the vena cava. Interspersed among lymphatics are a series of lymph nodes containing immune system cells. This function of the lymphatic system will not be covered in this text.

Total lymphatic flow is about 120 mL/h. Obviously, anything that increases filtration of water out of the capillaries will increase lymph flow. This includes any factor that increases capillary hydrostatic pressure, capillary surface area (e.g., increased organ perfusion), or capillary permeability (caused by in-

creased body temperature, toxins, histamine, and hypoxia), as well as any factor that reduces plasma oncotic or increases interstitial oncotic pressure. Lymph flow is increased by increased tissue metabolic activity. This activity causes arteriolar dilation, which increases capillary hydrostatic pressure, as well as the formation of metabolites in the interstitium, which increases tissue osmotic pressure. Lymph flow is increased by skeletal muscle contraction that compresses lymphatic channels, thereby forcing fluid back toward the heart.

Edema is a condition in which there is excessive accumulation of fluid in tissue spaces. Edema interferes with capillary transport and can cause circulatory collapse if edematous fluid forms from a loss of plasma volume. Anything that causes excess fluid filtration at the capillaries or impairs fluid transport through the lymph channels will create edema. One of the common causes of edema formation is a loss of protein, especially albumin, from the plasma. Edema will occur when albumin concentrations drop below 2.5 g/100 mL, which is common in diseases in which the liver is unable to manufacture albumin, or in kidney diseases in which albumin and other proteins are lost into the urine.

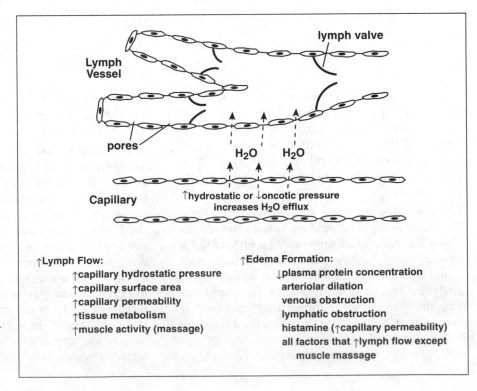

■ Fig. 13-3 ■
Water efflux from the capillary and into a lymph vessel, with a listing of factors that increase lymph flow or favor edema formation.

↑**Lymph Flow:**
↑capillary hydrostatic pressure
↑capillary surface area
↑capillary permeability
↑tissue metabolism
↑muscle activity (massage)

↑**Edema Formation:**
↓plasma protein concentration
arteriolar dilation
venous obstruction
lymphatic obstruction
histamine (↑capillary permeability)
all factors that ↑lymph flow except
   muscle massage

Burns, by destroying capillary integrity, cause edema through increased capillary permeability, loss of albumin from damaged vessels, and inflammatory vasodilation. Hives associated with allergic reactions are due to an increase in capillary permeability, venule permeability, and arterial dilation, all caused by histamine release during the allergic response. Obstruction of veins, usually from blood clot formation after surgery, is another common cause of edema.

CHAPTER 14

Neural Control of Cardiovascular Function

Role of the Autonomic Nervous System

Both parasympathetic and sympathetic nerves modulate cardiovascular function. Parasympathetic effects are primarily due to release of acetylcholine from the vagus nerve, whereas sympathetic effects result primarily from release of norepinephrine. Both ANS branches are tonically active to the heart (analogous to driving a car while depressing the brake and accelerator simultaneously). Vagal release of acetylcholine on the SA and AV nodes decreases SA firing rate, and hence heart rate, while decreasing conduction velocity through the AV node. Sympathetic stimulation has the opposite effect. Changes in heart rate are effected through a reciprocal action of both branches of the autonomic nervous system; that is, increased rate is caused by a simultaneous decrease in parasympathetic and increase in sympathetic stimulation to the heart.

Vagal effects on heart rate dominate over sympathetic effects and resting heart rate is slower than that observed if no autonomic influences were present. Maximum sympathetic stimulation of the heart cannot override maximum vagal stimulation, but maximum vagal activity can override maximum sympathetic stimulation. Continued vagal nerve stimulation actually can stop the heart from contracting for a few seconds; heart rate resumes (and at a slower rate) only if the AV node takes over as an auxiliary pacemaker. This phenomena is called *vagal escape*.

Both branches of the ANS are tonically active to cardiac muscle but sympathetic influences predominate in the control of inotropic state. Changes in inotropic state and resulting stroke volume are effected primarily through changes in sympathetic nerve activity that release norepinephrine onto β_1-adrenergic receptors in the heart. These receptors augment contraction of myocardial cells. Release of acetylcholine from parasympathetic nerves has the opposite effect, although this effect is modest and primarily directed to the atria. The negative inotropic effect of acetylcholine is due to stimulation of cGMP production, inhibition of cAMP production within ventricular muscle, and inhibition of norepinephrine release from sympathetic nerve endings.

Sympathetic nerves are tonically active to arteries and veins. There is no evidence for parasympathetic influences in the majority of the vasculature. Arterial and venous smooth muscle contains many more alpha than beta adrenergic receptors. Thus, sympathetic stimulation, which releases norepinephrine onto arteries and veins, causes vasoconstriction in most vascular beds. The brain and heart are exceptions, because the brain contains no appreciable adrenergic receptors, whereas coronary arteries contain primarily β_2-adrenergic vasodilatory receptors. The overall effect of activation of the sympathetic nervous system in the vasculature is to increase total peripheral vascular resistance and contract veins. Venoconstriction increases central venous filling pressure and therefore stroke volume and cardiac output.

Role of the Central Control Centers

The tonic activity of the ANS in the cardiovascular system is due to the combined effect of activity in three interrelated (but loosely defined) areas of the medulla and the hypothalamus. ■ **Fig. 14-1** ■ The medulla possesses a vasomotor area comprised of a pressor area that maintains tonic sympathetic outflow to the circulation, and a depressor area that inhibits the pressor area. The medulla also contains a cardioinhibitory area which, when stimulated, simultaneously increases parasympathetic and decreases sympathetic activity to the heart, thereby decreasing heart rate and myocardial contractility. Stimulation of a cardioaccelerating area in the hypothalamus has the opposite effect on nerve outflow, heart rate, and myocardial contractility.

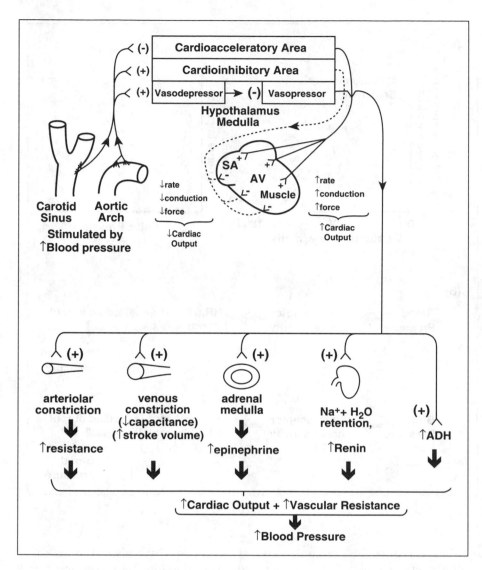

■ **Fig. 14-1** ■

Representation of the central cardiovascular control centers, their neural inputs from the carotid sinus and aortic arch, and their sympathetic and parasympathetic outputs to the heart in various other organ systems. Parasympathetic nerve outflow is indicated by a dashed line; sympathetic nerve outflow is indicated by a solid line. Stimulatory effects are indicated by a (+) sign and inhibitory effects are indicated by a (−) sign. Small upward arrow = increase, small downward arrow = decrease. Heavy arrows link effects resulting from change in the preceding variable. (See text for complete details.)

Arterial Baroreceptors and Reflex Control of Blood Pressure

The central neural control centers of cardiovascular function receive inputs from the vagus, Hering's, and glossopharyngeal nerves that are connected to peripheral pressure sensors located in the walls of the aortic arch and the carotid sinus. ■ **Fig. 14-1** ■ These sensors are spray nerve endings that are sensitive to stretch in the arterial wall and hence are sensitive to changes in arterial pressure. Thus, these sensors are referred to as *baro-* or *pressure receptors.* Increases in mean arterial pressure increase the rate of firing in the baroreceptor nerves, with the greatest increase for a given change in pressure

(i.e., sensitivity) occurring near normal mean arterial pressure. ■ **Fig. 14-2a** ■ Firing rate does not increase beyond about 160 mmHg and ceases below 70 mmHg in the aortic arch, or 50 mmHg in the carotid sinus. In addition, increases in either pulse pressure or the rate of rise of arterial pressure increases the rate of firing in baroreceptor nerves.

Impulses from baroreceptor nerves stimulate the vasodepressor and cardioinhibitory areas while depressing the cardiostimulatory area. Therefore, an initial increase in blood pressure in the carotid sinus or aortic arch acts through the baroreceptors to reflexively decrease sympathetic outflow while increasing parasympathetic outflow to the cardiovascular system. These effectively reduce vascular resistance in

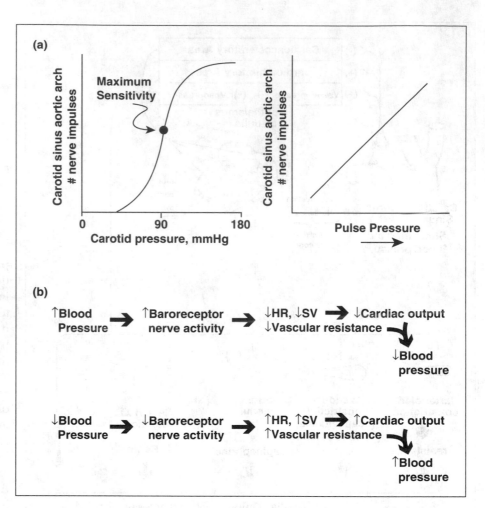

■ Fig. 14-2 ■
(a) Left: Relationship between nerve impulse frequency in the baroreceptor nerves from the carotid sinus as a function of carotid arterial pressure. Sensitivity to changes in pressure are greatest at values near mean arterial pressure. Right: Effect of pulse pressure on the number of impulses/second generated in the carotid or aortic arch nerves. (b) Examples of the function of the baroreceptor reflex. Small upward arrow = increase, small downward arrow = decrease. Heavy arrows link effects resulting from change in the preceding variable.

all organs except the heart and brain, reduce venous tone (and thus cardiac filling pressure), and reduce myocardial contractility, heart rate, stroke volume, and cardiac output. Collectively these changes aggressively act to reduce arterial pressure. Thus the baroreceptors form the sensory leg of a neural negative feedback system that controls arterial blood pressure. **■ Fig. 14-2b ■** When arterial pressure rises, the reflex alters hemodynamic variables to bring pressure back down; when pressure falls, the reflex functions to bring pressure back up.

The reflex mechanisms brought into play to correct changes in arterial pressure involve more than the cardiovascular system directly. **■ Fig. 14-1 ■** For example, sympathetic nerves also innervate the adrenal medulla and the kidney. Sympathetic stimulation of the adrenal medulla releases epinephrine into the circulation, which has positive inotropic and chronotropic effects on the heart and, at high concentrations, causes arterial and venous constriction.

Stimulation of sympathetic nerves also supports cardiac output and blood pressure by increasing Na^+ and water reabsorption by the kidney and by activating the renin-angiotensin system, which increases blood pressure through several mechanisms (see below). Decreased blood pressure also stimulates the posterior pituitary to release antidiuretic hormone (ADH, also known as vasopressin), which helps increase arterial pressure by causing direct arterial vasoconstriction and by stimulating water reabsorption in the kidney.

Other Neural/Humoral Blood Pressure Control Mechanisms

Heart rate, myocardial contraction, and peripheral resistance can be influenced through central nervous system reflexes sensitive to alterations in blood chemistry. Small organs called *carotid* and *aortic bodies* exist in the area of the carotid sinus and aortic arch. These organs are stimulated by decreased O_2, increased CO_2, or increased H^+ in the blood perfusing them. Stimulation of these *chemoreceptors* increases blood pressure by stimulating the vasomotor and cardiostimulatory centers of the brain.

Generally, blood pressure itself does not activate these receptors until the pressure drops below 80 mmHg. Therefore, this chemoreceptor reflex is not involved in the day-to-day maintenance of normal blood pressure. It becomes increasingly important, however, in maintenance of blood pressure in circulatory shock; see Chap. 16.

In addition, direct lack of O_2, increase in CO_2, or increase in H^+ ions in the brain itself elicits intense sympathetic nervous activation of the cardiovascular system. Such activation is called the *CNS ischemic response* and is a powerful reflex that can increase blood pressure as much as 270 mmHg. The reflex is activated when mean arterial pressure drops below 60 mmHg and is most active at pressures < 15 to 20 mmHg. Because this represents pressures that are below the limits of blood flow autoregulation of all organs, this reflex represents the body's last-gasp effort for survival.

Like the baroreceptor reflex, the chemoreceptor reflex and CNS ischemic response elevate vascular resistance in all organs except the brain and the heart. Indeed, all the neurogenic reflexes can be thought of as means of sacrificing other organ circulations so that adequate pressure is maintained to perfuse the heart and the brain.

The Renin-Angiotensin-Aldosterone System

The kidney contributes to the control of blood volume and is therefore a participant in the support of cardiac output and blood pressure. The kidney is the initial link in the *renin-angiotensin-aldosterone system* (RAS), which plays a significant role in the regulation of plasma sodium and water content as well as vascular resistance. ■ **Fig. 14-3** ■ The RAS is a complex hormonal feedback system with wide-ranging effects on many homeostatic processes. Only its role in blood pressure control will be dealt with in this chapter.

At the junction of the distal convoluted tubule and the afferent arteriole in the kidney there exists specialized cells, called the *juxtaglomerular (JG) apparatus,* that secrete a substance called *renin.* Renin production is stimulated by decreased wall tension in the afferent arteriole of the kidney or by an in-

crease in sympathetic nerve activity to β-receptors on the JG apparatus. Thus, renin release is stimulated by any factor that reduces mean systemic arterial pressure. Renin release also can be stimulated by a decrease in plasma Na^+ concentration.

Renin is an enzyme that converts a peptide precursor, angiotensinogen (produced by the liver), into angiotensin I. Angiotensin I travels in the blood, where it is converted to angiotensin II by a converting enzyme in the lung capillary endothelium. Angiotensin II is a highly active peptide with wide-ranging effects, all of which eventually raise arterial blood pressure. ■ **Fig. 14-3** ■ Abnormal activation of the renin angiotensin system occurs in chronic heart failure and has been implicated in several forms of hypertension, especially those associated with stenosis of the renal artery. A class of drugs called *converting enzyme inhibitors* block the formation of angiotensin II and have been employed successfully in the treatment of heart failure and hypertension.

Significance of Blood Pressure Control Mechanisms

Control of blood pressure is essential for supplying adequate perfusion pressure to support blood flow to the brain and the heart. In addition, autoregulation and other local metabolic mechanisms that control blood flow in any organ cannot work effectively if blood pressure is allowed to vary wildly from moment to moment, or if it is not maintained within the autoregulatory range.

Although neurogenic reflexes exert powerful controlling influences over arterial blood pressure, it appears that the level of mean arterial pressure is not set by the baroreceptor or other neurogenic reflexes. For example, if the baroreceptor reflex is eliminated (by denervating the carotid sinus and aortic arches), blood pressure will vary more erratically, but over any given period of time, *mean* arterial pressure will remain essentially normal. Thus the baroreceptor reflex can be considered as a blood pressure "buffer" system that prevents abnormal swings in blood pressure during the course of daily activity.

Baroreceptors also adapt whenever exposed to high arterial pressures over a period of just a few days. Therefore, their role in longterm regulation of arterial pressure is limited. It has been postulated that the kidney, through its control of water excretion and ultimately plasma volume, is most likely re-

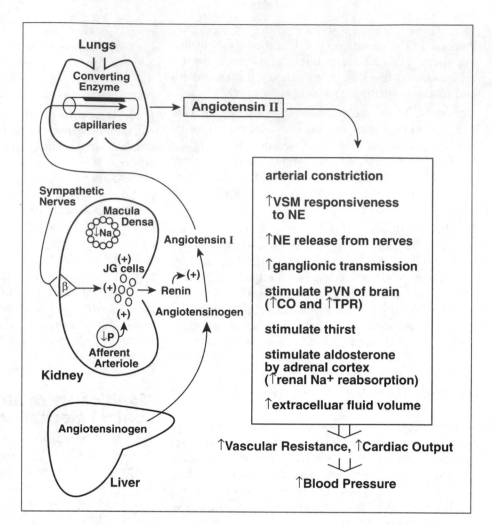

■ Fig. 14-3 ■
A summary of the renin angiotensin system and its effect on cardiovascular variables. Stimulatory effects are represented by (+) signs or small upward arrows.

sponsible for setting the level of mean arterial pressure. When arterial pressure is increased, the kidney excretes additional amounts of water in the urine until blood pressure returns to normal; decreases in blood pressure have the opposite effect. This ability of the kidney to respond to changes in blood pressure appears to be limitless; in normal individuals it will not stop excess water excretion until blood pressure is returned to normal.

Volume Receptors and CV Control

There are additional pressure receptors in the venous side of the circulation that are involved in the control of blood volume and thus indirectly, blood pressure. Excess extracellular fluid volume results in

atrial stretch, which stimulates receptors in the venoatrial junction. When stimulated, they reflexively increase heart rate by increasing sympathetic nerve activity to the SA node, the *Bainbridge reflex,* which may help remove congestion from the right side of the circulation.

Excess atrial stretch also causes the release of atrial natriuretic peptide (ANP) from the atria. ANP stimulates a brief increase in Na^+ and water excretion by the kidney (natriuresis and diuresis). The role of ANP in physiological processes is still being defined. Finally, ADH is a major factor in the kidney's ability to reabsorb water. Atrial stretch, such as that accompanied by excess plasma volume, inhibits production of ADH, thus inhibiting renal water reabsorption and allowing more water to be excreted by the kidney.

CHAPTER 15

Special Characteristics of Individual Circulations

The widely different functions of individual organ systems in the body require unique functions of their individual circulations. The unique characteristics of several individual circulations will be considered in this chapter. Pulmonary and renal circulations will be discussed in the context of those organ systems in subsequent chapters.

The Cutaneous Circulation

The skin comprises about 5% of our body weight and covers an area of about 2 m². The metabolic requirements of the skin are very low and cutaneous blood flow is little influenced by local metabolic factors. Yet the skin can exhibit one of the most variable flows in the body (50–3000 mL/min and 50% of cardiac output). The reason for this variability resides in the fact that the primary function of the cutaneous circulation is to help control body temperature by exploiting its blood flow as a means of transporting heat between the body and the external environment. The skin sits at the interface between the internal and external environment, making it an ideal location for control of heat transfer. For this purpose, the cutaneous circulation contains two specialized vascular segments in its microcirculation. ■ **Fig. 15-1** ■ An elaborate venous plexus, or network, lies parallel to the skin's surface and acts as a high-surface-area heat exchanger. Blood flow into this plexus comes directly from arteries through AV anastomoses, thus bypassing the cutaneous capillaries.

Cutaneous arterioles, veins, and AV anastomoses contain α but not β adrenergic receptors and are densely innervated by sympathetic nerve endings. Blood flow through the cutaneous circulation is dominated by the activity of these nerves. Sympathetic activity to skin vessels is quite high at rest and inhibition of cutaneous sympathetic nerve activity results in profound vasodilation. Blood flow in the cutaneous circulation is controlled by reflexes involved with body temperature regulation (discussed in the chapter on thermoregulation).

Briefly, hot and cold temperature sensors in the hypothalamus and the skin provide sensory inputs to the brain as part of a feedback loop that alters sympathetic outflow to the cutaneous circulation. When either external skin or internal body temperature decreases, sympathetic outflow to the cutaneous vessels increases, reducing the flow of heat-containing blood to the skin and thus helping maintain internal body temperature. Elevation in temperature has the opposite effect, allowing heat to escape to the environment. In addition, when temperature rises, specialized *sympathetic cholinergic fibers* (sympathetic fibers that release acetylcholine) are activated to sweat glands in the skin. In addition to producing sweat, these glands produce bradykinin, which dilates cutaneous vessels.

Sympathetic innervation is most dense in the cutaneous vessels of the extremities (hands, feet, ears, cheek, nose, etc.). This is responsible for the sensation of cold extremities whenever the body is first exposed to a cool environment. Severe cold (exposure to 0° to 15°C) results in an oscillating pattern of dilation and contraction in the cutaneous vessels, called the *hunting response*. The hunting response is thought to allow maximum heat conservation for the body while allowing a small amount of intermittent blood flow into the extremities to prevent them from freezing.

The sympathetic nerves to the skin also participate in the body's response to hypotension via neurogenic reflexes discussed in the preceding chapter. During the baroreceptor reflex, the skin contributes significantly to increased peripheral resistance and augmentation of stroke volume through venoconstriction and translocation of blood to the central circulation.

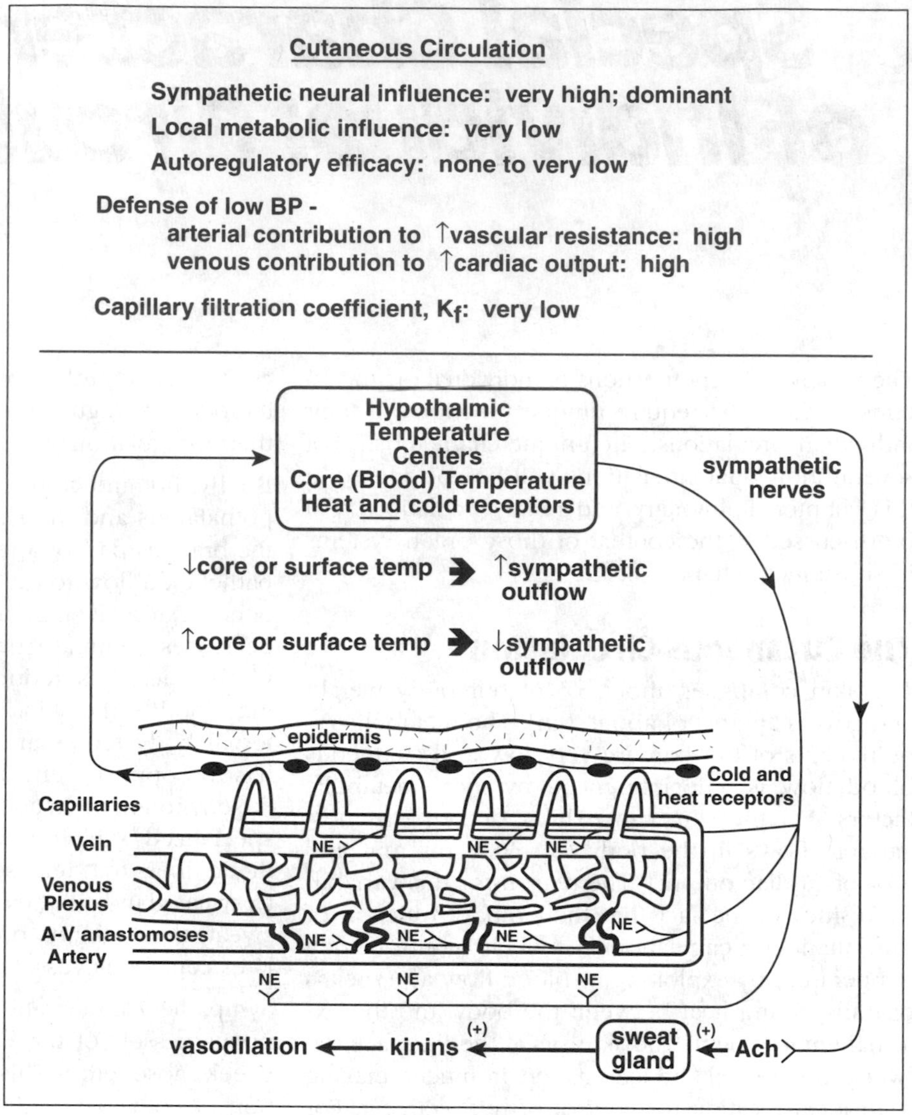

■ Fig. 15-1 ■
An overview of the special characteristics of the cutaneous circulation. Top: Quality of the characteristics of the circulation with respect to neural, metabolic, autoregulatory, and capillary dynamic factors. Bottom: The cutaneous circulation, showing sympathetic nerve connections and AV anastomoses between the artery and the venous plexus. Small upward arrow = increase, small downward arrow = decrease. Heavy arrows link effects resulting from change in the preceding variable. (See text for complete explanation.)

Circulation of Skeletal Muscle and the Small Intestine

Although the functions of skeletal muscle and the small intestine are markedly different, these two organ systems possess similar broad cardiovascular characteristics. **■ Fig. 15-2 ■** Both organs can exhibit highly variable flows based on differences in metabolic requirements at rest versus activity (exercise in muscle, digestion in the intestine). During high metabolic demands, local metabolic influences dominate control of blood flow. In both organs, autoregulatory efficiency is highly variable, being weak in some conditions and very strong in others. Finally, because both circulations are very large (each consuming ≈ 20% of resting cardiac output), they are recruited by neurogenic reflexes to support blood

pressure (with increased vascular resistance) and cardiac output (with increased venous tone) in response to circulatory collapse.

The arteries and veins of skeletal muscle and the intestine are innervated by the sympathetic nervous system and contain predominately α- over β-adrenergic receptors. Therefore, activation of sympathetic nerves to these organs increases vascular resistance and reduces venous capacitance. Sympathetic contractile tone is significant in both vascular beds; denervation results in significant vasodilation and hyperemia, although not as marked as that seen in the cutaneous circulation. In both organs, circulating chemical agents and myogenic responses also contribute significantly to resting contractile tone in their arteries.

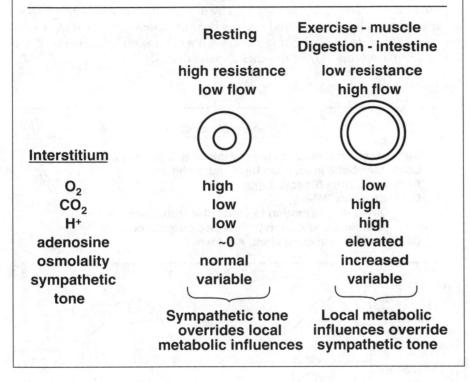

Skeletal Muscle and Intestinal Circulation

Sympathetic neural influence: moderate to very high to dominant
Local metabolic influence: low to very high to dominant
Autoregulatory efficacy: low to high (MVO_2-dependent)
Defense of low BP -
      arterial contribution to ↑vascular resistance: high
      venous contribution to ↑cardiac output: high
Capillary filtration coefficient, Kf: muscle = low
                                    intestine = high

	Resting	**Exercise - muscle** **Digestion - intestine**
	high resistance low flow	low resistance high flow
Interstitium		
O_2	high	low
CO_2	low	high
H^+	low	high
adenosine	~0	elevated
osmolality	normal	increased
sympathetic tone	variable	variable
	Sympathetic tone **overrides local** **metabolic influences**	**Local metabolic** **influences override** **sympathetic tone**

■ **Fig. 15-2** ■
Overview of special characteristics of the skeletal muscle and intestinal circulations. At top are quality descriptions of neural, local metabolic, autoregulatory, and capillary dynamic factors. Small upward arrow = increase. These vascular beds are characterized by the ability to either be dominated by sympathetic neural or local metabolic influences as the needs of the body require. (See text for complete details.)

In both organ systems, an increase in metabolism of the tissues results in a metabolic mediated vasodilation and active hyperemia that is strong enough to override basal sympathetic tone. ■ **Fig. 15-2** ■ Intestinal blood flow as much as doubles during digestion, whereas exercise can elicit a more than twentyfold increase in skeletal muscle blood flow despite marked sympathetic nerve activity to muscle arteries.

Autoregulatory control of blood flow in skeletal muscle and intestine is much stronger when their O_2 consumption or metabolism is high than when the organs are at rest; at rest, their arteries may actually respond passively to changes in intraarterial pressure.

When arterial pressure and hence organ blood flow and O_2 delivery are low in these organs, two vascular mechanisms are set into motion. In response to low flow, precapillary sphincters open prior to any significant dilation of the arterioles feeding the vascular bed. As a consequence, these organs take what blood is delivered to them and distribute it through more capillaries, with little alteration of vascular resistance. This allows each organ to extract more O_2 from the blood it gets. Thus, oxygen delivery to the tissues is returned toward normal in the face of reduced perfusion pressure without the need for arteriolar dilation and alteration of total blood flow.

However, once O_2 extraction is maximized (i.e., all capillaries are perfused) through the demands of increased tissue metabolism (such as exercise or digestion), arteriolar resistance must be altered to maintain oxygen delivery to the tissue if arterial perfusion pressure should happen to change (i.e., an autoregulatory response is needed).

The net result is that although blood flow autoregulation may be weak in some instances, the combination of an ability to alter perfused capillary density and total blood flow allows skeletal muscle and the intestine to autoregulate O_2 *delivery* over a wide range of physiological conditions.

Skeletal muscle and intestinal circulations contribute significantly to the increase in total peripheral vascular resistance and venous contraction (and thus stroke volume) associated with the barorecep-

tor reflex. In this situation, neurogenic influences dominate over the metabolic needs of the organs to the extent that muscles weaken, digestion becomes impaired, and intestinal ischemia ensues.

The intestinal circulation possesses a couple of anatomical liabilities in terms of overall cardiovascular control. First, intestinal capillaries have a very high capillary filtration coefficient. This aids in material transport during digestion but makes the intestinal circulation susceptible to significant fluid loss whenever intracapillary pressure rises. This can result from extreme arteriolar vasodilation caused by peritonitis and intestinal inflammation, or from elevated venous pressure due to obstruction of portal blood flow, such as that seen in cirrhosis of the liver or other hepatic diseases.

▪ Fig. 15-3 ▪

Special characteristics of the coronary circulation. The qualitative listing of sympathetic neural, local metabolic, autoregulatory, and capillary dynamic characteristics of this circulation are listed at the top of the figure. (a) Aortic pressure pulses and coronary flow in the left coronary artery perfusing the left ventricular and in the right coronary artery. (b) Representation of blood flow autoregulation in the epicardial and endocardial portions of the myocardium.

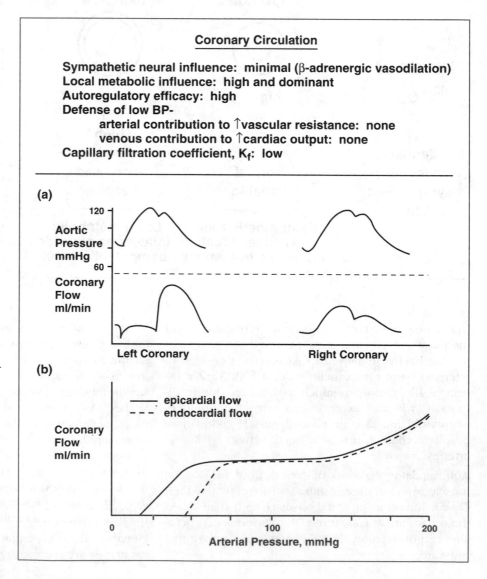

When venous pressure rises in the intestinal circulation, however, the upstream arterioles actively constrict. This phenomenon, called the *venous-arteriolar response,* helps maintain normal capillary pressure in the face of elevated venous pressure.

The mucosa of the intestine contains many villi, which serve to increase the surface area available for transport of digested food products from the intestine to the circulation. The arterioles and venules in the villi are arranged in close enough proximity to one another, however, to allow direct diffusion of O_2 from arteriole to the venules, thus bypassing the capillaries. Consequently, O_2 delivery to intestinal mucosal cells is poor, which results in high cell turnover and increased tissue susceptibility to ischemic damage whenever intestinal blood flow is restricted. This often occurs with the intense sympathetic vasoconstriction caused by shock.

Circulations of the Heart and Brain

The coronary and cerebral circulations are excluded from whole body reflex defense mechanisms employed to control arterial pressure. ■ **Figs. 15-3 and 15-4** ■ Indeed, arterial pressure is controlled so blood flow to these organs can be maintained. Compromising blood flow to either organ compromises the survival of the organism as a whole. Consequently, local regulatory factors dominate blood flow control in these organs. Both the heart and the brain are ex-

cellent autoregulators of blood flow and both show strong links between tissue metabolism and organ blood flow, i.e., active hyperemia.

Coronary Circulation

The heart is extremely active, even when the body as a whole is at rest. Its O_2 consumption per gram of organ weight is the highest of any organ in the body. In addition, all coronary capillaries are perfused at rest and thus the heart is unable to significantly increase O_2 extraction to meet an increased tissue O_2 demand.

Myocardial contraction interferes with myocardial blood perfusion; that is, the heart gets in the way of its own blood flow. ■ **Fig. 15-3a** ■ During systole, left ventricular muscle contraction compresses intramuscular arteries, effectively reducing or even stopping flow. Consequently, unlike other organs in the body, left ventricular blood flow is low in systole, when arterial pressure is high, and high during diastole, when arterial pressure is low. The thinner-walled, low-pressure right ventricle does not show this blood flow pattern. ■ **Fig. 15-3a** ■

Cardiac muscle compression is greatest in the endocardial layers of the heart and diminishes through the ventricular wall toward the epicardial surface. As a result, blood flow is more constrained during systole in the endocardium than in the epicardium and the endocardial arterioles must dilate more during diastole to compensate. For this reason, the low pressure limit for autoregulation in the endocardial

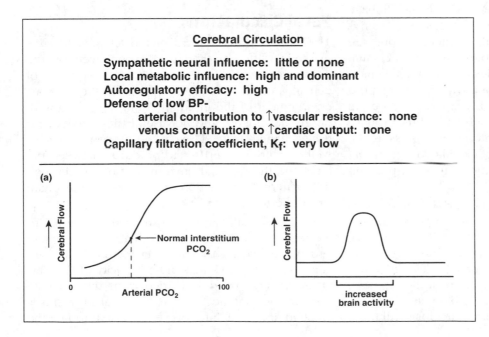

Cerebral Circulation

Sympathetic neural influence: little or none
Local metabolic influence: high and dominant
Autoregulatory efficacy: high
Defense of low BP-
    arterial contribution to ↑vascular resistance: none
    venous contribution to ↑cardiac output: none
Capillary filtration coefficient, K_f: very low

(a) Cerebral Flow — Normal interstitium PCO_2 — Arterial PCO_2 — 0 — 100

(b) Cerebral Flow — increased brain activity

■ **Fig. 15-4** ■
Special characteristics of the cerebral circulation. Qualitative influence of the sympathetic neural and local metabolic factors, as well as autoregulatory efficiency and capillary dynamics, are listed at the top of the figure. (a) Relationship between cerebral blood flow and carbon dioxide concentration surrounding the cerebral arteries. (b) An example of cerebral blood flow in response to local increased brain activity.

layer is greater than in the epicardial layer; endocardial arterial dilation reaches a maximum when arterial pressure drops to < 70 mmHg; maximum dilation in the epicardial arteries is not reached until pressure is < 40 mmHg. ■ **Fig. 15-3b** ■ For this reason, whenever blood flow to the heart is severely restricted, the endocardium is first to suffer damage and the resulting area of transmural myocardial infarction often is larger in the endocardium relative to the epicardium.

Activation of the sympathetic nervous system to the heart, such as during exercise or in response to a decrease in systemic arterial pressure, results in coronary vasodilation and a marked increase in coronary blood flow. This increase is primarily an active hyperemia in response to increased cardiac metabolism brought about by sympathetic nerve stimulation of heart rate and myocardial contractility. Coronary vessels, however, contain primarily β_2 rather than α adrenergic receptors and hence direct β-adrenergic–mediated coronary vasodilation also contributes to the sympathetic hyperemia. This obviously supports the metabolic demands of a heart trying either to maintain blood pressure in the face of hypotension or to increase cardiac output during exercise. The vasodilator metabolite, adenosine, appears to play a major role in metabolic hyperemia in the coronary circulation.

Cerebral Circulation

The blood vessels of the brain contain few or no adrenergic receptors nor sympathetic innervation and therefore are not influenced directly by the autonomic nerve system. The brain does exhibit a unique nerve reflex, however. Because the brain is encased in an inflexible skull, intracranial pressure will increase whenever the brain swells, in circumstances such as head injuries, intracranial hemorrhage, or a blockade of the outflow of cerebrospinal fluid (hydrencephalus). This increased pressure can collapse cerebral blood vessels and thus produce cerebral ischemia. When intercranial pressure increases, however, a neural reflex called the *Cushing response* increases arterial blood pressure, preventing vascular collapse.

Control of cerebral blood flow is dominated by local metabolic factors. CO_2 produced by tissue metabolism can combine with water to form carbonic acid, which produces an H+ assault on nerve function. Nerve function is very sensitive to alterations in the pH of its surroundings. In addition, brain function becomes deranged with even small degrees of hypoxia, hypercapnia, or acidosis. All these conditions dilate cerebral arteries and increase cerebral blood flow.

In particular, the cerebral circulation is the most sensitive in the body to changes in arterial P_{CO2}. ■ **Fig. 15-4a** ■ By linking increased cerebral flow to increased arterial P_{CO2}, the cerebral circulation protects the brain from damage due to acidosis. The brain also is a very strong local autoregulator of blood flow between arterial pressures of 60 to 160 mmHg and exhibits active hyperemia; increased activity in areas serving functions such as vision, hearing, thinking, etc., show increased flow when those systems are activated. ■ **Fig. 15-4b** ■

The cerebral capillary endothelial cells are joined by tight junctions in most areas of the brain. This markedly reduces diffusion of materials from the circulation into the brain, where they can cause aberrant cerebral function. These tight junctions form the anatomical component of what is called the *blood-brain barrier*. In addition, the capillaries in the brain have other barrier functions. There is minimal pinocytotic activity across cerebral capillaries and the endothelium contains enzymes that metabolize catecholamines, serotonin, and other compounds in the circulation that also happen to be CNS neurotransmitters. Exceptions to this arrangement occur in certain regions of the lower brain stem, where capillaries allow passage of angiotensin II and other hormones into the CNS, where they activate control functions over extracellular fluid volume and blood pressure.

Fetal Circulation

The external environment of the fetus *in utero* is markedly different than that experienced by the newborn. These differences impart a unique set of demands on the circulatory system. In the aqueous environment of the uterus the lungs are collapsed, poorly developed, and not useful (nor needed) for gas exchange. Instead, exchange of blood gases, as well as nutrients and waste products, between the fetus and the external environment occurs through the maternal circulation at a specialized organ called the *placenta*. ■ **Fig. 15-5** ■

Nevertheless, diffusion of O_2 from the maternal to the fetal circulation at the placenta is not complete and blood leaving the placenta for the fetus contains only 80% of its maximum capacity of O_2. This O_2-containing blood is carried from the placenta through the umbilical vein to the fetal liver and is emptied into the inferior vena cava through the

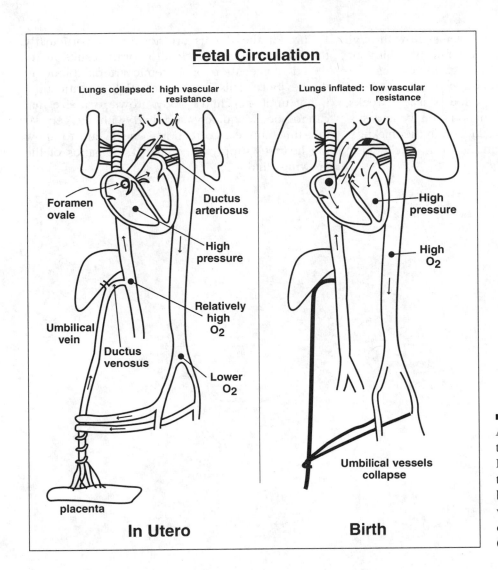

Fetal Circulation

Lungs collapsed: high vascular resistance

Lungs inflated: low vascular resistance

Foramen ovale

Ductus arteriosus

High pressure

Relatively high O_2

Umbilical vein

Ductus venosus

Lower O_2

placenta

In Utero

High pressure

High O_2

Umbilical vessels collapse

Birth

■ **Fig. 15-5** ■
Anatomical arrangement of the cardiovascular system. Left: In the fetal circulation. Right: In the newborn. Arrows within blood vessels and the heart indicate the direction of flow. (See text for explanation.)

ductus venosus. Blood is mixed there with O_2-depleted blood from the lower extremities of the fetus and eventually empties into the right atrium. The right atrium communicates with the left atrium through an opening called the *foramen ovale*.

Because the lungs are collapsed in the fetus, pulmonary resistance and pressure in the right heart are high. This forces blood to pass from the right atrium, through the foramen ovale, into the left atrium, rather than into the right ventricle and pulmonary circulation. What blood enters into the pulmonary artery is further shunted into the aorta through the ductus arteriosus. The net effect of these unique arrangements in the fetus is to deliver the most O_2-rich blood to the liver, the brain, and the upper extremities. (This pattern of O_2 delivery is

partly responsible for the larger head and upper torso of the newborn relative to their lower extremities.)

At birth, the transition from a water to an air environment elicits several changes in the fetal circulation. First, as the lungs fill with air, compression on the pulmonary vasculature is released, decreasing pulmonary vascular resistance and pressure. In addition, the umbilical vessels spasm in response to trauma, circulating catecholamines and O_2. This spasm collapses the ductus venosus and greatly increases systemic vascular resistance. This increase in resistance, coupled with decreased pulmonary vascular resistance, increases left atrial pressure above that in the right atria and closes a tissue flap over the foramen ovale.

This pressure difference also reverses flow through the ductus arteriosus. With the infant breathing air, high-O_2 blood now travels through the ductus arteriosus, causing constriction and eventual closure of that vessel. Finally, over a period of a few weeks, the different pressures of the pulmonary and systemic circulations cause a reduction in the thickness of the right ventricle and an increased thickness in the left ventricle.

Failure of the ductus arteriosus and particularly the foramen ovale to close at birth results in reduced oxygenation of systemic arterial blood in the newborn. This impairment might not affect the infant until the child's body grows to a size that cannot be adequately supplied with oxygen. At that time surgical correction is necessary to allow the heart to supply adequate O_2 demands of the growing child.

Circulatory Shock

Circulatory shock is a condition of generalized cardiovascular failure characterized by insufficient organ blood flow and often low blood pressure. This condition can result in deterioration of all tissues in the body and eventual death. The basic cause of shock is a loss of support of cardiac output. This may arise from direct cardiac dysfunction caused by myocardial ischemia, infarction, arrhythmias, etc., or from diminished venous filling pressure due to loss of blood, plasma volume, or venous tone.

Shock can be divided into three progressively serious subclassifications. ■ **Fig. 16-1** ■ The mildest form of shock is called *compensated* or *nonprogressive shock* because the body's own regulatory mechanisms will compensate for the initial decrease in cardiac output and/or arterial pressure. These mechanisms eventually will lead to recovery of the individual, and obviate the need for physician intervention.

The compensatory mechanisms in nonprogressive shock are much the same as those activated by a decrease in blood pressure and include activation of baroreceptor and other neurogenic pressor reflexes, stimulation of the renin-angiotensin system, and release of ADH. These reflexes and hormones tend to increase blood pressure and cardiac output by increasing heart rate, myocardial contractility, and vascular resistance (especially in skin, splanchnic organs, skeletal muscle, and kidney), while promoting renal Na^+ and H_2O retention to increase central venous pressure in support of stroke volume.

Low arterial pressure and increased arterial resistance in shock also reduces capillary hydrostatic pressure. This augments fluid reabsorption from the interstitial fluid, especially in the intestine and kidney. Collectively these compensatory mechanisms result in the initial clinical presentation of shock, which includes pale cold skin, rapid pulse, a sensation of thirst, hypotension, and reduced urine output.

If the initial causes of shock are severe, or the body is unable to compensate fully for the malfunctioning cardiovascular system, shock enters into a vicious positive feedback cycle known as *progressive shock.* This occurs when organs maintaining the cardiovascular system, notably the heart and brain, deteriorate due to poor blood supply. The body's own compensatory mechanisms cannot correct progressive shock and thus the physician must intervene with cardiovascular support (i.e., IV fluids, cardiac stimulants).

The most important factor involved in the progression of shock is deterioration of the heart. During progressive shock, myocardial contractility progressively decreases; the curve relating cardiac output to filling pressure becomes progressively shifted downward and to the right. Progressive shock is exacerbated by deterioration of vasomotor centers in the brain. Furthermore, both acidotic conditions in peripheral organs brought on by poor oxygen delivery, as well as release of toxins from deteriorating tissues, promote arterial blood clotting that further impairs tissue oxygen delivery. Acidosis and toxins also increase capillary permeability, which enhances fluid loss from the vascular compartment.

Without proper intervention, progressive shock will enter into an irreversible phase. In this phase, cardiac and cerebral function are so compromised that no intervention is able to restore normal cardiovascular function, and death is inevitable. In general, severe shock is characterized by decreased body temperature due to the effects of poor tissue oxygen delivery on tissue metabolism, depressed mental function or unconsciousness, renal failure, and generalized muscle weakness.

Several different conditions can lead to circulatory shock. In addition to blood volume loss due to hemorrhage, any loss of plasma volume, or *hypovolemia,* can reduce cardiac output and induce shock. This can occur from dehydration due to severe vomiting, sweating, diarrhea, decreased fluid and electrolyte intake, kidney damage, or adrenal cortical destruction that results in the loss of the hormone aldos-

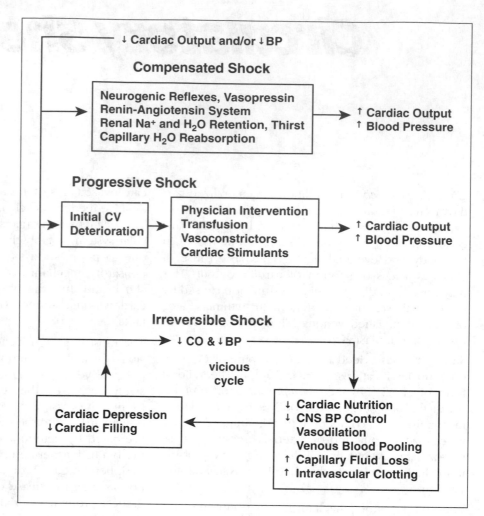

■ Fig. 16-1 ■

A flowchart representation of compensated, progressive, and irreversible shock. Depression of variables is indicated by small downward arrows, and stimulation by small upward arrows. Large arrowheads connect cause-and-effect relationships. CV = cardiovascular, BP = blood pressure, CNS = central nervous system. (See text for details.)

terone, which promotes Na^+ and H_2O reabsorption in the kidney.

Severe burns result in capillary destruction with loss of albumin from the vascular space. This causes transcapillary loss of plasma. A similar capillary fluid loss is associated with intestinal obstructions that greatly increase intestinal venous pressure. Capillary damage from severe physical injury or trauma also causes transcapillary loss of plasma. An important complication of shock due to plasma loss is an increase in blood viscosity, which further impairs the heart's ability to move blood through the peripheral circulation.

Neurogenic shock is a form of circulatory collapse brought about by loss of neurogenic tone to veins and arteries, secondary to inhibition or dysfunction of the central nervous system. This can result from general or spinal anesthesia (i.e., spinal blocks used in childbirth), traumatic brain injury, or depressed vasomotor center function due to fever, stress, in-

somnia, or even severe emotional distress (the latter resulting in emotional fainting).

Many people are severely allergic to certain antigens (bee venom, certain foods, etc.). In a serious antigen:antibody reaction, tremendous amounts of histamine and other toxins are released into the tissue spaces, resulting in anaphylactic shock. This results in destruction of surrounding tissue, which increases interstitial osmolality, thus promoting fluid efflux from the capillaries. Histamine also causes arteriolar dilation while increasing the permeability of capillaries and venules to water and proteins. These factors further exacerbate fluid loss from the vascular compartment and result in a decrease in circulating blood volume.

Septic shock, formerly called *blood poisoning,* is a form of shock caused by disseminated infection throughout the body. Next to cardiogenic shock, this is the leading cause of death from shock in the

United States. It is often brought on by peritonitis secondary to female reproductive organ infection, rupture of the gut during appendicitis, or the introduction of skin bacteria into the bloodstream. Unlike other forms of shock, septic shock is characterized by high body temperature, due to infection, and high cardiac output, due to intense vasodilation in the infected area.

This excess cardiac output, however, represents useless blood flow to infected regions at the expense of perfusion of other organ systems. Bacterial products and tissue destruction in this form of shock produce widespread microvascular blood clots, called *disseminated intervascular coagulation*. This condition greatly impairs O_2 delivery to tissues, thus exacerbating the primary shock condition.

CHAPTER 17

Overview of Respiratory Physiology

The primary function of the respiratory system is to exchange O_2 and CO_2 between the atmosphere and blood. Gas exchange between the circulation and the atmosphere occurs at the lungs. Atmospheric air enters the lungs through the respiratory passageways consisting of the nasal passages, trachea, and *bronchioles*. Bronchioles are lined with visceral smooth muscle that can contract and restrict air flow into the lungs. This is a common occurrence in asthma and in severe allergic reactions. Several substances produced by allergic reactions or inflammatory processes (e.g., histamine and SRS-A, or slow-reacting substance of anaphylaxis) can cause severe bronchiole constriction. Acetylcholine also is a bronchoconstrictor. Conversely, β-adrenergic agents dilate bronchioles, which is the basis for their use in the treatment of acute asthmatic attacks.

Bronchioles terminate in a set of thin, single-cell-layer sacs called *alveoli,* which are the primary exchange site between external gases and the pulmonary capillary circulation.

Respiratory function can be divided into the following processes:

1. Ventilation, or the physical process of moving air into and out of the lungs,
2. Diffusion of gas between the alveoli and pulmonary capillaries,
3. Transportation of gases in pulmonary blood (pulmonary blood flow),
4. Matching the level of ventilation and blood flow for efficient gas exchange,
5. Transportation of gases in the systemic blood,
6. Transfer of gases between peripheral capillaries and tissues, and

7. Tissue respiration (O_2 consumption and CO_2 production).

Feedback control mechanisms oversee these processes in order to adjust respiration to meet the needs of our bodies for O_2 and to remove CO_2 produced by oxidative metabolism.

The lungs also provide several ancillary functions. Because the lungs receive the entire cardiac output, they are an ideal location for biochemical transformation of substances carried in the blood. In addition to the conversion of angiotensin I to angiotensin II, the lung endothelium inactivates or removes compounds from blood such as bradykinin, serotonin, norepinephrine, and various prostaglandins.

Because the lungs communicate with the external environment, several respiratory functions are designed to limit undesirable intake of substances from the air. The respiratory passages produce mucous that traps particulate matter. Millions of cilia lining the bronchi and trachea move this mucus containing trapped particulates away from the deep lung tissues and to the pharynx, where it may be swallowed. Also, irritant receptors in the lungs and the nasal passageways are linked to cough and sneeze reflexes, which utilize deep inhalation in conjunction with rapid exhalation of air ($\approx$ 100 mph) to remove irritants from the pulmonary system.

The lungs also possess important immunological functions, the study of which is a growing subdiscipline within respiratory physiology. These aspects of pulmonary physiology are covered in other texts. Finally, the respiratory system is necessary for proper vocalization, as evidenced by the inability to speak during choking episodes.

CHAPTER 18

Ventilation

Basic Definitions

The amount of air inhaled or exhaled by the lungs with each breath is a small fraction of the maximum amount of air that can be moved into and out of those organs. In addition, not all inhaled air reaches the alveoli and it is not possible to exhale all the air in the lungs, even with the most forceful expiration. These and other factors have resulted in a categorization of four lung volumes and capacities that help describe pulmonary function in health and disease. ■ **Fig. 18-1a** ■

Inhalation of air into the lungs involves active muscle contraction. Exhalation normally is due to passive elastic recoil of the lungs and chest wall, although active muscle contraction can force expiration to greater than normal values. The volume of air inspired or expired with each normal breath is called the *tidal volume* and is about 500 mL in the adult male. An additional volume of about 3 L can be inhaled beyond a normal inspiration and is called the *inspiratory reserve volume*.

Similarly, the amount of air that can be forcefully expired beyond the end of normal expiration, about 1.1 L, is called the *expiratory reserve volume*. After such a maximum forceful expiration, however, a residual volume of air of about 1.2 L remains in the lungs. At the end of a normal expiration, about 2.5 L of air remains in the lungs. This volume is called the *functional residual capacity,* or *FRC*. The functional residual capacity and residual volume are important in that they provide aeration of the alveoli and allow gas exchange to occur even between breaths. Also, because only a portion of the FRC is exchanged with each breath, the FRC provides a buffer against rapid, large changes in the concentration of O_2 and CO_2 in the blood; several breaths are required to completely change alveolar gas composition. ■ **Fig. 18-1b** ■

Average total lung capacity in the adult male is slightly under 6 L. Of this, about 3.5 L can be inhaled maximally at the end of a normal expiration and represents the individual's inspiratory capacity. The total of inspiratory capacity and expiratory reserve volume equals the *vital capacity*. Vital capacity represents the maximum amount of air that a person can move into and out of the lungs with each breath and is an important clinical respiratory measurement because it is affected by disease. Vital capacity is decreased by paralysis of the respiratory muscles or by reduced lung compliance due to tuberculosis, asthma, lung cancer, bronchitis, pleurisy, or pulmonary edema. Vital capacity is less when an individual is lying down than when standing.

Minute Respiratory Volume and Alveolar Ventilation

The average individual inhales and exhales about 12 times per minute, with a tidal volume of about 500 ml. This corresponds to ventilation of the lungs with 6 L of air every minute and is called the *minute respiratory volume* or minute ventilation. About 30% of the tidal volume is contained in structures that are incapable of exchanging gases with the pulmonary circulation (e.g., bronchi, trachea, etc.). This nonexchangeable volume is called *anatomic dead space*. ■ **Fig. 18-1c** ■ Dead space can increase in pathological conditions whenever alveoli are ventilated but do not receive blood flow, as in the case of pulmonary emboli. In this case the useless ventilation is called *physiological dead space*.

Of the total minute ventilation, the air reaching the alveoli is of prime physiological importance. Normal resting alveolar ventilation V_A is 4–4.5 L/min and equals the ventilation rate times the difference in total and dead space ventilation. ■ **Fig. 18-1c** ■ As will be seen in subsequent chapters, alveolar ventilation is the key factor that determines the concentration of O_2 and CO_2 in the alveoli, and thus the diffusional exchange of these gases between the lungs and the pulmonary capillaries.

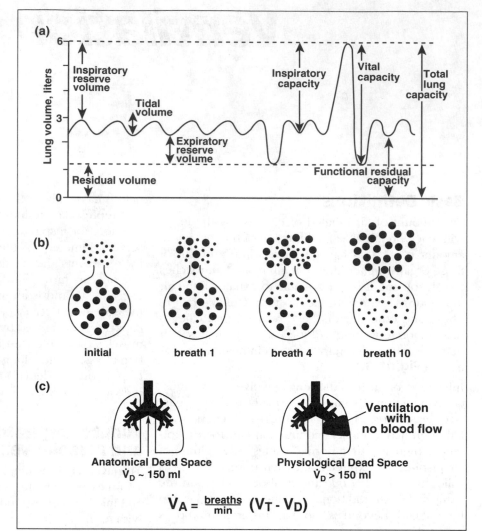

■ Fig. 18-1 ■

(a) Examples of important respiratory ventilation volumes and capacities in the human lung system. (b) A diagram showing the slow exchange of gases between the external environment at the alveoli due to residual air in the lungs at the end of exhalation. (c) Representation of anatomical and physiological dead space. Alveolar ventilation V_A is equal to the respiratory rate times the difference between total volume and dead space volume.

CHAPTER 19

Pulmonary Mechanics

General Characteristics of Inspiration and Expiration

The rhythmic inflation and deflation of the lungs maintains a flow of environmental gas through the alveoli. Inspiration requires that work must be done to overcome elastic recoil of the lungs and airway resistance. Consequently, inspiration is an active process, involving contraction of the diaphragm, sternocleidomastoid, anterior serrate, scaleni, and external intercostal muscles. Passive elastic recoil is responsible for normal expiration, although further, forceful expiration can be obtained by contraction of abdominal and internal intercostal muscles. Forceful expiration aids in rapid exhalation during exercise.

An understanding of breathing mechanics requires familiarity with the physical factors that alter lung volume. The pulmonary system is a "balloon within a balloon," that is, flexible lungs are contained within a flexible chest cavity. A change in volume in any flexible structure is dependent upon the transmural pressure across the wall of the structure and the wall compliance. In the pulmonary system we must consider three transmural pressures. ■ **Fig. 19-1a** ■

1. Transpulmonary pressure, which is alveolar pressure minus intrapleural pressure,
2. Transchest pressure, which is intrapleural pressure minus atmospheric pressure, and
3. Transtotal pressure, which is alveolar pressure minus atmospheric pressure.

In these cases atmospheric pressure is given the arbitrary value of 0. In respiratory physiology, pressure is often measured in cm H_2O instead of mmHg (1 cm $H_2O \approx 0.7$ mmHg) because of the often small pressures encountered in the pulmonary system.

Changes in volumes due to changes in transmural pressure across the chest, lungs, and the pulmonary system as a whole, are depicted in ■ **Fig. 19-1b** ■ .

The resting equilibrium volume of the chest, lungs, and the total system occurs when no transmural pressure exists across these structures. This volume occurs at the end of expiration in the total system, when alveolar pressure equals atmospheric pressure, and is equal to the *functional residual capacity* (FRC). The FRC is the capacity from which normal inspiration proceeds. The resting equilibrium volume for the lungs is much lower than the FRC and that of the chest is higher.

When no transmural pressure difference exists across the lungs, the lungs are collapsed with a volume ≈ 0. At a 0 transmural pressure difference, the chest wall is expanded beyond FRC to a value of ≈ 3.5 L. Therefore, at FRC the lungs are stretched beyond their equilibrium volume, creating a tendency for them to recoil inward, and the chest wall is held "crushed down" below its equilibrium volume, creating a tendency for it to recoil outward.

These opposite recoils create at the interface of these two adjacent structures a negative pressure, which equals about −5 cm H_2O. Thus at FRC the transmural pressure across the lungs is 0 − (−5), or +5 cm H_2O, which will expand the lungs beyond their resting equilibrium volume of 0 to a value of about 2.5 L (given a normal lung compliance of about 0.2 L/cm H_2O). The chest wall has a similar compliance; with a transmural pressure across this structure of −5 −0 or −5 cm H_2O, the chest is held down below its equilibrium volume, to 2.5 L. Combined, these two equal and opposite forces yield a transtotal pressure of 0, which is in equilibrium for the system as a whole.

Lung and chest wall compliances are fairly linear over a large range of transmural pressures. ■ **Fig. 19-1b** ■ The lungs resist further stretching at values near the total lung capacity, whereas the chest resists further compression below FRC. Both compliances can be altered by various physiological and pathological conditions. Chest wall compliance depends on the

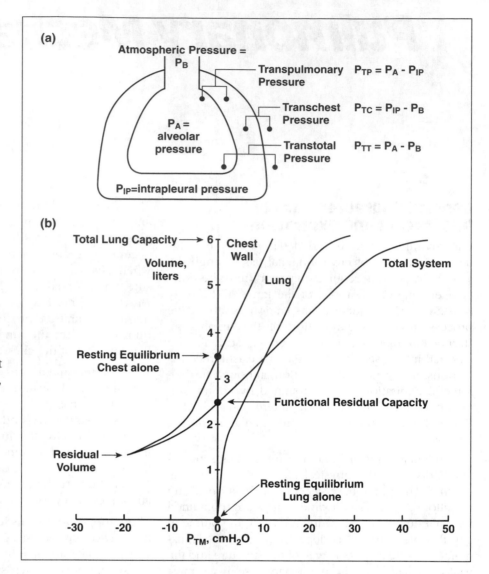

■ Fig. 19-1 ■
(a) Transmural pressures across the lungs, the chest wall, and the total pulmonary system. (b) Interrelationship between chest wall volume, lung volume, and volume in the total system as a function of transmural pressure. Equilibrium volume at the end of exhalation equals the functional residual capacity (FRC) and results from the combination of resting equilibrium volumes and compliances for the chest and the lung alone.

shape and rigidity of the thoracic cage, the diaphragm, and other abdominal structures. It is reduced significantly by scoliosis, polio, muscle paralysis, or even obesity. Decreased chest wall compliance makes it more difficult for the lungs to retract, or pull the chest down, toward normal FRC. Severe deformities such as scoliosis place anatomical constraints on FRC and thus reduce this volume.

Determinants of Lung Compliance

Only a small portion of the elastic recoil of the lungs is due to the elastic nature of lung tissue. Instead, elastic recoil is due primarily to the surface tension of water lining the alveolar surface and

other lung structures. **■ Fig. 19-2a ■** In explanation, water molecules have a greater attraction for one another than they do for surrounding air molecules; thus they tend to cling and pull together into the smallest possible volume. This is why water droplets coalesce into spheres or bead up on a surface, rather than spread into a thin layer. In the lungs, the attraction of water lining the alveoli for itself and for lung tissues tends to pull the lung structures inward. This is a very powerful force; an air:saline interface, which is analogous to the conditions in the lung, creates a surface tension of 72 dynes/cm of surface.

A structure like an alveolus requires greater transmural pressures to remain open at a given volume than would be required if it were filled with saline (a saline:saline interface) **■ Fig. 19-2b ■**. Applying

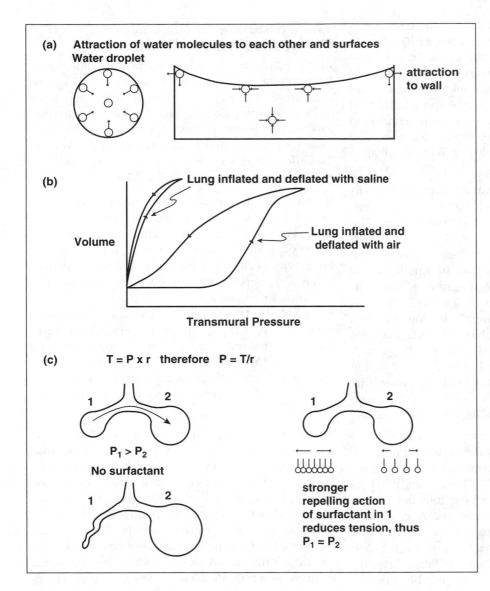

(a) **Attraction of water molecules to each other and surfaces**
Water droplet

attraction to wall

(b)

Volume

Lung inflated and deflated with saline

Lung inflated and deflated with air

Transmural Pressure

(c) **T = P x r   therefore   P = T/r**

1   2

$P_1 > P_2$

No surfactant

1   2

1   2

1   2

stronger repelling action of surfactant in 1 reduces tension, thus $P_1 = P_2$

■ **Fig. 19-2** ■
(a) An example of the effects of the attraction between water molecules; attraction for one another and for surfaces is greater than it is for air. (b) Graph showing that lung compliance is decreased when the lung is inflated or deflated with air. (c) A demonstration of the effect of pressure generated in alveoli of different sizes with and without the presence of surfactant. (See text for explanation.)

the *law of Laplace* to a typical alveolar radius, an individual would need to generate an intrapleural pressure of about −30 cm H_2O to create a transpulmonary pressure great enough to hold the lungs open at FRC against the recoil tension created by the air:saline interface. Actual intrapleural pressure in the thoracic cavity at FRC, however, is only −5 cm H_2O. Clearly some factor must be present at the alveolar-air interface that markedly reduces surface tension on lung surfaces, thereby making it easier for the lungs to remain open at FRC.

The type II granular pneumocytes in the alveoli produce a substance called *dipalmitoyl phosphatidylcholine* (DPPC) or *surfactant*. Surfactant is composed of two palmitate residues that are hydrophobic, connected to a hydrophilic tail. In water,

the hydrophilic portion of DPPC interacts with the water, projecting the palmitate residues out of the surface. ■ **Fig. 19-2c** ■ The palmitate residues repel each other and thus resist being crowded together. In a solution of DPPC and water exposed to air, as water molecules begin to pull together by virtue of their surface tension, they tend to crowd the DPPC molecules. The DPPC molecules then repel one another, providing a force that counteracts the surface tension caused by the water:air interface. In our lungs, DPPC greatly reduces lung surface tension and thus the tendency of the lungs to collapse. This enables us to use less force to inhale and yields a large FRC.

Surfactant possesses other valuable physiological properties. Our lungs contain alveoli of different sizes that are in communication with each other through the respiratory passageways. ■ **Fig. 19-2c** ■ Because pressure within a sphere = 2T/r, two alveoli with the same surface tension but different radii will experience different internal pressures; small alveoli will have larger internal pressures than larger alveoli. If two such alveoli were connected by an air passage, air would flow from the small alveolus into the larger alveolus until the small alveolus collapsed.

Collapse of alveoli would markedly reduce the surface area available for gas exchange in the lungs. Surfactant stabilizes alveoli of different sizes. The repelling force of DPPC and its ability to reduce surface tension is increased when these molecules are compressed closely together (as in small alveoli) and decreased when they are spread over large surfaces. Thus with DPPC, tension in small alveoli is reduced relative to large alveoli. This property tends to equalize pressure within alveoli of different sizes and thus prevents aveolar collapse. Finally, surfactant creates a type of oil seal over the alveoli that helps prevent influx of water from the interstitial spaces. This prevents the alveoli from filling with fluid, which would otherwise impair gas exchange.

DPPC is not produced until late in development of the fetus. Infants born prematurely often do not have enough DPPC to allow for normal respiratory function. Without sufficient DPPC, lung compliance is much lower than normal and these infants must expend large amounts of energy just to inhale. In addition, the lack of DPPC leads to alveolar collapse and formation of pulmonary edema, both of which impair O_2 delivery and CO_2 removal at the infant lung. Infants with this condition consequently become hypoxic, hypercapnic, acidotic, and exhausted. This condition is called *infant respiratory distress syndrome* (or *hyaline membrane disease* after the pulmonary inflammation present in this condition).

Less than three decades ago there was little a physician could do for an infant in this condition except administer O_2 and wait in the hope that the lungs would mature in time to produce enough DPPC before death occurred. Now, however, amniocentesis (sampling of the amniotic fluid) allows physicians to ascertain the extent of DPPC production in the infant prior to a potential premature birth. If this level is found to be insufficient, β-adrenergic drugs that relax uterine smooth muscle can be given to suppress labor and buy time for the fetus to mature. In addition glucocorticoids can be given to accelerate the production of DPPC.

The Influence of Airway Resistance on Ventilation

In the examples described previously, changes in lung volume did not take into account the fact that pressure is lost as air is brought across the resistance of airway passages. Like fluid flow in arteries, loss of pressure as air flows through respiratory passages is proportional to the resistance to airflow. The effect of airway resistance on respiratory function is diagrammed in ■ **Fig. 19-3a** ■ .

In this example, air is brought into the lungs at a rate of 1 L/s. This flow across the bronchiole resistance causes a loss in pressure from atmospheric levels of 0 cm H_2O to ≈ -2 cm H_2O. Expansion of lungs with normal compliance at this flow rate to a value 1 L beyond FRC requires generation of a transmural pressure of 10 cm H_2O across the lungs. See ■ **Fig. 19-1b** ■ In order to create this transmural pressure while taking in to account airway resistance, intrapleural pressure must decrease an extra 2 cm H_2O to -12 cm H_2O (i.e. an alveolar pressure of -2 cm H_2O minus an intrapleural pressure of -12 cm H_2O give a transpulmonary pressure of 10 cm H_2O).

This is a small requirement in terms of lung mechanics and one might expect that only a small amount of extra work is required to inflate our lungs in the presence of normal airway resistance. Indeed, the work of breathing uses only about 2% of the body's total O_2 consumption; even during exercise, when ventilation increases by a factor of 25, the work of breathing remains between 2% to 4% of the exercising total. As can be extrapolated from the example in ■ **Fig. 19-3a** ■, however, factors that increase airway resistance will require greater inspiratory work in order to obtain any given tidal volume. Large, pathological increases in airway resistance, such as those that occur in asthma and chronic emphysema, can greatly increase the work of breathing; such individuals can expend as much as 30% of their resting O_2 consumption simply to breathe.

Airway resistance is not constant during the respiratory cycle; see the left portion of ■ **Fig. 19-3b** ■ . During inhalation, intrapleural pressure becomes more negative and expands the bronchi, thus reducing airway resistance. During normal expiration this value decreases but nevertheless remains negative, keeping the airways open. During a normal expiration, the rate of expiratory flow depends on how much the lungs are first inflated during inspiration. Greater inflation stretches the lungs more, creating greater

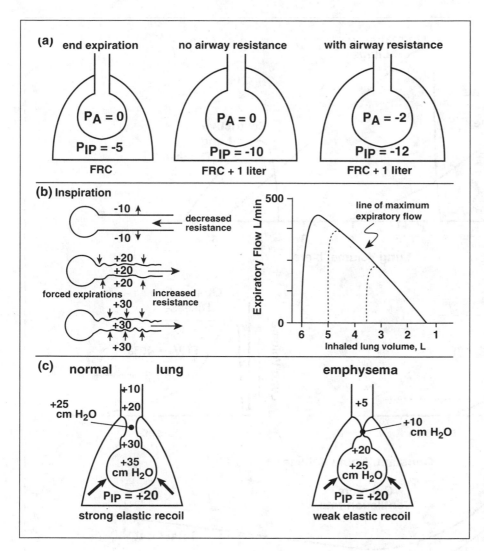

■ **Fig. 19-3** ■
(a) Effect of airway resistance on intrapleural pressure needed to inflate the lungs by one liter more than FRC. (b) Effect of inspiration and forced expirations on bronchial resistance. The maximum rate of expiratory flow during forced expiration is limited by the equal positive pressures created inside and outside the bronchioles, no matter how much the lung is inflated (right graph). (c) Pressure in the alveoli and bronchi during forced expiration in a normal lung with strong elastic recoil, and in a lung from a patient with emphysema (weak elastic recoil). The tendency to collapse the bronchioles is markedly increased in the patient with emphysema.

elastic recoil and hence greater airflow during expiration; see the right portion of ■ **Fig. 19-3b** ■

During forced expiration, however, exhalation is complicated because airway resistance increases as one forcefully exhales. During forceful expiration, contracting abdominal muscles create a positive pressure in the intrapleural space that adds to the pressure caused by the elastic recoil of the lungs. No matter to what volume we inflate our lungs, there is a certain limit beyond which expiration flow rate cannot be increased; again see the right part of ■ **Fig. 19-3b** ■ This occurs because any additional pressure created inside the alveoli by external compression of the thoracic cavity also increases pressure in the intrapleural space (outside the bronchi) by an equivalent amount. This "locks" bronchiole diameters and hence resistance at a certain set value.

Nevertheless, pathological conditions such as emphysema affect maximum expiratory flow, as shown in ■ **Fig. 19-3c** ■ At the beginning of a forced expiration, in the normal lungs the pressure inside the alveoli equals that due to the elastic recoil of the lungs plus any additional pressure caused by the forceful expiration. In our example, let this equal 35 cm of H_2O. This pressure is lost as air crosses the bronchial resistances on its way out of the lungs; in a normal lung this value remains above that in the intrapleural space and the bronchi remain open. In emphysema the lungs lose their elastic properties and thus have increased compliance. These "flabby" lungs produce very little elastic recoil, therefore adding little to alveolar pressure upon forced expiration.

In our example, perhaps only 25 cm H_2O pressure can be produced during a forced expiration. As

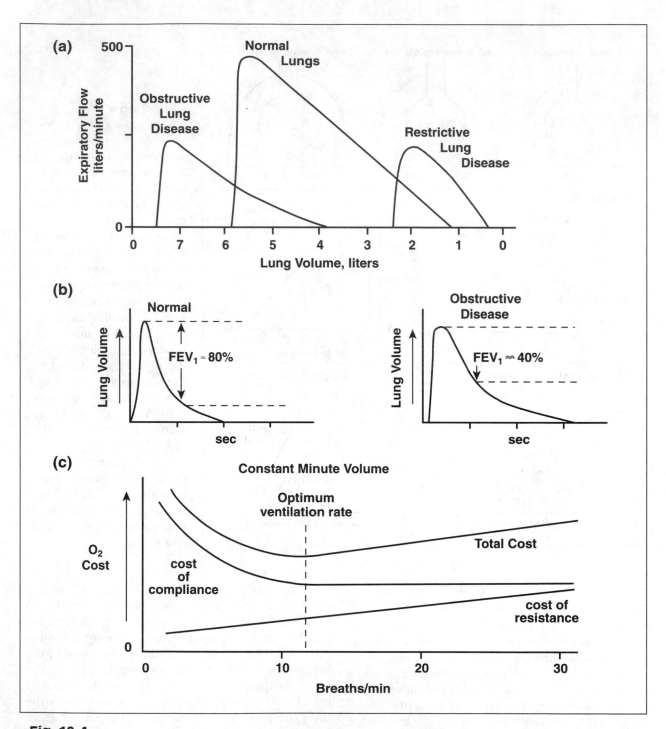

■ Fig. 19-4 ■

(a) Expiratory flow rates at given lung volumes in the normal lung, obstructive lung disease, and restrictive lung disease. (b) Forced expiratory volumes after one second (FEV_1) in a normal individual and in individuals with obstructive lung disease. (c) Oxygen consumption as a function of respiratory rate at a constant tidal volume. Energy is required to overcome lung elastic recoil and airway resistance. Differences in the effects of these variables on oxygen consumption result in a theoretical optimum ventilation rate for the individual.

pressure is lost from this value while air passes through the bronchi during expiration, airway pressure will drop below that in the intrapleural space *before* exiting the thoracic cavity. This will cause bronchiole collapse until enough pressure builds behind the bronchi, causing them to reopen, which again results in pressure loss and collapse, and so on. This rapid opening and closing of the bronchi creates the characteristic wheezing sound that is heard in these patients whenever they forcibly exhale. Patients with asthma have abnormal bronchial constriction and inflammation, which results in a greater tendency for bronchiole collapse during expiration as well as increased airway resistance during inhalation.

Patients with asthma and emphysema have trouble removing air from their lungs, even with forced expirations involved in coughing. Consequently, air stagnates in the lungs of these patients, making them prone to infections that further exacerbate lung destruction. Patients with emphysema have abnormally high FRC, total lung capacities, and residual volumes that result in the characteristic barrel-chested appearance of these individuals. Asthmatics and patients with emphysema are said to have obstructive pulmonary disease, because air movement out of the lungs is impaired; maximum expiratory air flow is markedly reduced in such patients. ■ **Fig. 19-4a** ■

Many respiratory diseases decrease lung compliance, making lung inflation difficult. These maladies are called *restrictive pulmonary diseases* and include pulmonary fibrosis, pneumonia, pulmonary edema, or other types of inflammatory lung diseases. Maximum expiratory air flow is decreased in restrictive pulmonary disease due to an inability to inflate the lungs to a high capacity where elastic recoil is large. Restrictive lung diseases are characterized by reduced vital and total lung capacity.

A low maximum expiratory flow rate can indicate the presence of pulmonary pathology in a patient, but alone can not distinguish between obstructive and restrictive pulmonary disease. To help distinguish between patients with obstructive or restrictive lung disease, the forced expiratory volume exhaled in 1 second is used, expressed as a percent of maximum inhaled volume. This is designated the FEV_1. ■ **Fig. 19-4b** ■ Patients with obstructive pulmonary diseases have reduced FEV_1 values; those with restrictive lung diseases do not. In obstructive diseases, increased airway resistance, or, in the case of emphysema, also weak elastic recoil of the lungs, markedly reduces the amount of air that can be forcefully exhaled in 1 second after a maximum inspiration; FEV_1 in restrictive lung diseases varies little from normal.

Work of Ventilation

Work of ventilation is normally just inspiratory work and is divided into two components: that required to overcome the elastic recoil of the lungs (compliant work), and that required to overcome airway resistance (resistive work). Compliant work is proportional to the magnitude of inspiration and therefore increases with an increased tidal volume. Resistive work occurs with each breath and therefore increases with an increased respiratory rate (breaths/min). A given constant minute volume of ventilation can be obtained in two ways; one can take frequent shallow breaths or infrequent deep breaths. Our respiratory rate and tidal volume are set at a value that tends to optimize the combined effects of resistance and compliance on ventilatory work. ■ **Fig. 19-4c** ■ It can be inferred from this figure that individuals with restrictive lung diseases benefit by taking frequent shallow breaths, whereas those with obstructive disease benefit from breathing deeply but less frequently.

CHAPTER 20

Principles of Gas Exchange

Getting air into and out of the alveoli by the process of ventilation is the first step in the transport of O_2 into and CO_2 out of the bloodstream. Exchange of O_2 and CO_2 between the alveoli and pulmonary capillary blood occurs by the process of simple diffusion and therefore is dependent upon the pressure gradient between these two locations.

In a mixture of gases, the diffusion of an individual gas is dependent only on the pressure difference for that gas alone. Inspired air is a mixture of several gases ■ **Fig. 20-1a** ■ In a mixture of gases, the pressure of any one gas is simply the percent of that gas in the mixture times the total mixture pressure. This value is called the *partial pressure* of the gas. Our atmosphere is approximately 21% O_2. At a standard atmospheric pressure of 760 mmHg, the partial pressure of O_2 (P_{O2}), is therefore 159 mmHg.

The P_{O2} in the alveoli is less than that in the atmosphere for several reasons. As air enters the lungs, it becomes completely saturated with water vapor. At body temperature (37°C), water vapor pressure is 47 mmHg and this gas dilutes the concentration of other gases in the lung (reducing P_{O2} to 149 mmHg). In addition, O_2 is continually being removed from the alveoli, while CO_2 is being added. The net effect of these transport phenomena is that the steady-state values of P_{O2} and P_{CO2} in the alveoli are 104 and 40 mmHg respectively. Typically, blood entering the pulmonary capillaries has a P_{O2} of 40 mmHg and P_{CO2} of 45 mmHg. Thus there is diffusion gradient for movement of O_2 from the alveoli into the capillaries, while CO_2 moves in the opposite direction.

Due to dead space ventilation, not all the air that enters the lung exchanges O_2 and CO_2 with the pulmonary circulation. Therefore, the concentrations of O_2 and CO_2 in expired air are between those in the alveoli and that in humidified atmospheric air. Consequently, expired air is a poor indicator of the gas tensions in the alveoli. However, because alveolar air is the last to exit the lungs, samples of air at the end of expiration closely approximate alveolar gas tensions.

Determinants of Alveolar O_2 and CO_2 Pressure

Alveolar P_{O2} and P_{CO2} are dependent on the rate at which fresh air can be brought into the alveoli (alveolar ventilation), as well as the metabolic rate of the individual (the rate of O_2 consumption and CO_2 production). *At a steady rate of oxygen consumption, alveolar gas tensions depend only on alveolar ventilation.* Increasing alveolar ventilation (hyperventilation) increases alveolar P_{O2}, (P_{AO2}) and reduces alveolar P_{ACO2}, as can be seen from ■ **Fig. 20-1b** ■. If alveolar ventilation could replace alveolar air as fast as O_2 was taken up and CO_2 deposited into the alveoli, the gas tensions in the alveoli would approach those of humidified room air. Conversely, if no fresh air were brought into the lungs, concentrations of O_2 eventually would approach 0 and those of CO_2 extremely large values.

Increasing O_2 consumption (MVO_2) decreases P_{AO2} and increases P_{ACO2} at any given alveolar ventilation. ■ **Fig. 20-1b** ■ This will reduce the driving force for these gases between the alveoli and the pulmonary capillaries. Therefore, when MVO_2 increases, alveolar ventilation must increase in order to maintain normal alveolar pressures for O_2 and CO_2 (i.e., P_{AO2} = 104 mmHg and P_{ACO2} = 40 mmHg).

The Respiratory Membrane

Gas exchange between the alveoli and the pulmonary capillaries must occur across a number of fluid and tissue barriers. These include the fluid:surfactant layer on the inner alveolar surface, the alveolar epithelium and its basement membranes, the interstitial space, and the capillary endothelium with its basement membrane. These various layers

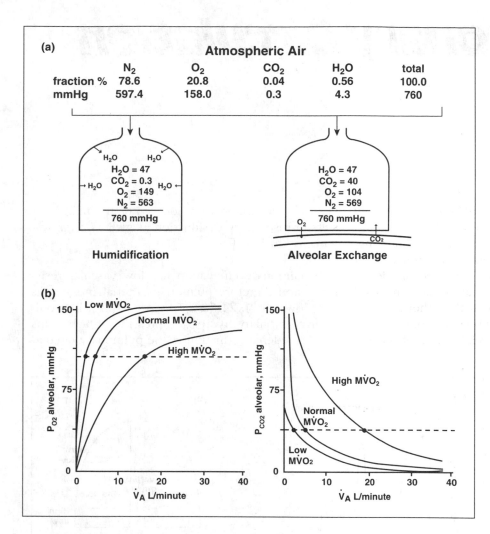

(a) Fra
partial
gen, c
ide, a
atmos
fied a
in the
alveo
alveo
(left)
bon
and
MVO
tion.

are referred to collectively as the *respiratory membrane,* which is approximately 0.2 to 0.6 μm thick and covers a surface area of 160 m².

Physical properties of the respiratory membrane and the blood gases themselves are additional determinants of the rate of diffusion between the alveoli and the pulmonary capillaries. Diffusion is impaired whenever the thickness of the respiratory membrane increases or its surface area decreases. Infections, fibrosis, and pulmonary edema all thicken the respiratory membrane. Lung edema reduces the effective alveolar surface area available for diffu-

sion. In emphysema, many s
mally would have a large col
alesce into a few large alv
smaller surface area, thus im
the lung. Finally, frank rem
surgery also reduces surface
sion and impairs gas exchar

CO_2 it is much more solubl
tory membrane. Therefore
times that for O_2. This mear
gas diffusion at the lung a
blood more severely than t

Circulation

entricle. For this reason, left ventricular failure re-
ults in respiratory dysfunction as well as poor sys-
mic perfusion.

e pulmonary circulation has low vascular resis-
ce and therefore pulmonary arterial pressure is
y low. ■ **Fig. 21-1a** ■ This results in a low pul-
nary capillary hydrostatic pressure, which helps
vent edema formation in the pulmonary circula-

20-1 ■
ctional content and
pressures of nitro-
xygen, carbon diox-
d water vapor in
pheric air, humidi-
ir in the lungs, and
alveoli. (b) Effect of
lar ventilation on
lar oxygen pressure
and on alveolar car-
dioxide (right) at high
ow metabolic rates.
$_2$ = oxygen consump-

mall alveoli, which nor-
lective surface area, co-
eoli with a collectively
pairing gas transport in
oval of the lung due to
area available for diffu-
ge.
e than O_2 in the respira-
it diffuses at a rate 20
s that factors that impair
ffect O_2 tensions in the
hey do CO_2 tensions.

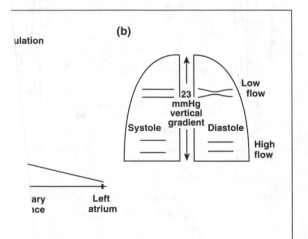

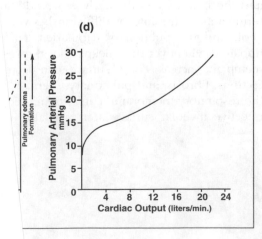

tion. Because the pulmonary circulation is required to receive the whole cardiac output, there is no reason for local autoregulation of blood flow in the lung and pulmonary arteries do not exhibit myogenic responses.

Pulmonary arterioles respond to alveolar O_2 and CO_2 in a manner opposite to that seen for systemic vessels. Pulmonary arteries dilate when exposed to high O_2 or decreased CO_2 and constrict when O_2 levels are low or CO_2 levels are high. This local response to gas tensions helps direct blood flow to well-ventilated alveoli and away from those that are poorly ventilated. Innervation of the pulmonary circulation is sparse and of uncertain function.

Pulmonary arteries are thin-walled vessels with little smooth muscle, or muscle tone. Consequently they respond passively to changes in arterial pressure. In a normal individual, approximately 10 cm of the lung is situated above the level of the heart, with the remainder below this level. When an individual stands, the effect of gravity subtracts up to 15 mmHg pressure from the pulmonary artery in the lung apex and adds about 8 mmHg to the pulmonary arterial pressure in the lung base. ■ **Fig. 21-1b** ■ As a result, blood vessels in the lung base are passively distended by the effect of gravity on blood in the lungs, whereas those in the apex tend to collapse during diastole when pulmonary arterial pressure is only about 8 mmHg. In the standing individual, blood flow to the lung base thus may be five times that in the apex. This condition makes vessels in the lung apex susceptible to collapse whenever pulmonary arterial pressure drops (e.g., during hemorrhage), or whenever alveolar or interstitial fluid pressure increases.

Like systemic capillaries, pulmonary capillary hydrostatic pressure is affected by pressure in the vasculature upstream and downstream to the capillaries. In the lungs, downstream pressure is related to pressure in the left atrium and hence is altered by changes in left ventricular function. Because of the passive nature of the pulmonary vessels, pulmonary arterial pressure changes very little over the normal range of left atrial pressures associated with normal ventricular function. ■ **Fig. 21-1c** ■ Furthermore, edema does not form in the lungs until left atrial pressure approaches 25 mmHg, which generally is seen only in left ventricular failure. The large safety margin against edema formation in the lungs is due to

1. The intrinsically low pulmonary capillary hydrostatic pressure,
2. The passive pulmonary vasculature distends with increased blood pressure, and
3. The fact that the lungs contain a very extensive and efficient lymphatic system.

Because cardiac output increases markedly during exercise, pulmonary blood flow also must increase significantly. This increased flow could cause a marked increase in pulmonary artery pressure and thus right ventricular afterload. However, an increase in cardiac output from 4 to 12 L/min results in only about a 15% increase in pulmonary arterial pressure. ■ **Fig. 21-1d** ■ This attenuated pressure rise in pulmonary circulation with high cardiac outputs again is a result of the passive nature of the pulmonary vasculature, which distends when exposed to volumes associated with high blood flow.

CHAPTER 22

Transport of O₂ and CO₂ in the Blood

Transport of O₂ in the Blood

Diffusion of O_2 into the pulmonary capillaries from the alveoli is a rapid process and capillary P_{O2} comes into equilibrium with alveolar P_{O2} long before blood reaches the venous end of the vessel. ■ **Fig. 22-1a** ■ This rapid equilibrium occurs even with high cardiac outputs associated with heavy exercise. Consequently, pulmonary blood flow is normally never a limiting factor in getting O_2 from the alveoli into the circulation of a normal individual.

Systemic arterial P_{O2} is slightly less than that in pulmonary capillaries. This arises from the fact that pulmonary capillary blood mixes with deoxygenated blood from the nutritional circulation of the lungs, and some blood perfuses pulmonary structures that do not exchanges gases with the pulmonary capillaries (i.e., trachea, bronchi). This is called a *right-to-left shunt*. Such shunts also can occur in any situation where deoxygenated blood, returning from the systemic veins, passes through the lungs and into the pulmonary vein without exchanging gases at the alveoli. This situation can occur when gas diffusion across the respiratory membrane is markedly impaired in large portions of the lung (e.g., pulmonary edema, infections, etc.). In this case, significant amounts of pulmonary blood flow will cross the lungs without becoming reoxygenated. This results in a significantly reduced arterial P_{O2} and reduced amount of oxygen reaching the systemic organs.

The P_{O2} of blood is a reflection of, but not equivalent to, the actual amount of O_2 in blood (known as O_2 content in mL O_2/100 mL blood). At a P_{O2} of 100 mmHg, only 0.3 mL of O_2 is contained in each 100 mL of blood as dissolved gas in plasma. Such O_2 carrying capacity is woefully inadequate to meet the metabolic needs of peripheral tissues, given the capacity of our heart to deliver blood to the systemic organs. Blood, however, contains red blood cells that, in turn, contain the molecule hemoglobin. Hemoglobin has the property of being able to bind large quantities of O_2. Hemoglobin is a complex molecule containing an Fe^{++} porphyrin ring system surrounded by globular proteins. Each gram of hemoglobin can bind reversibly with 1.34 mL of O_2. In normal individuals with a hematocrit of ≈ 45%, 100 mL of blood contains about 15 g hemoglobin and thus can hold about 20 mL of O_2.

The amount of O_2 contained in a given volume of blood obviously depends on the number of red blood cells present and their hemoglobin concentration. However, blood O_2 content also is dependent upon the relationship between P_{O2} and the resulting binding of O_2 to hemoglobin. This relationship is highly nonlinear. ■ **Fig. 22-1b** ■ As can be seen, the percent saturation of hemoglobin with O_2 is roughly proportional to P_{O2} between 0 and 70 mmHg and then relatively constant at $P_{O2} > 70$ mmHg; O_2 saturation of blood is about 97% at normal arterial P_{O2}. The flat portion of the oxyhemoglobin dissociation curve provides a large margin of safety for transport of O_2 in the blood. P_{O2} in the alveoli or the arterial system can drop approximately 30% without significantly affecting blood O_2 content. However, this same safety feature against low blood P_{O2} also means that little extra O_2 content can be added to blood by elevating P_{O2} above normal values.

The relationship between P_{O2} and saturation of hemoglobin also is influenced by physical and chemical factors. ■ **Fig. 22-1b** ■ High P_{CO2} or mild acidosis, such as that surrounding systemic tissues, decrease the affinity of hemoglobin for O_2. This favors unloading of O_2 from blood to tissues and increases delivery of oxygen to the tissues over that which would be obtained if arterial CO_2 tensions and pH were present. Lower CO_2 and slightly increased pH, which exists in the environment surrounding the alveoli, increases hemoglobin O_2 affinity and favors loading of O_2 from the alveoli into blood. Finally, increased temperature favors O_2 unloading from hemoglobin whereas decreased temperature has the opposite effect.

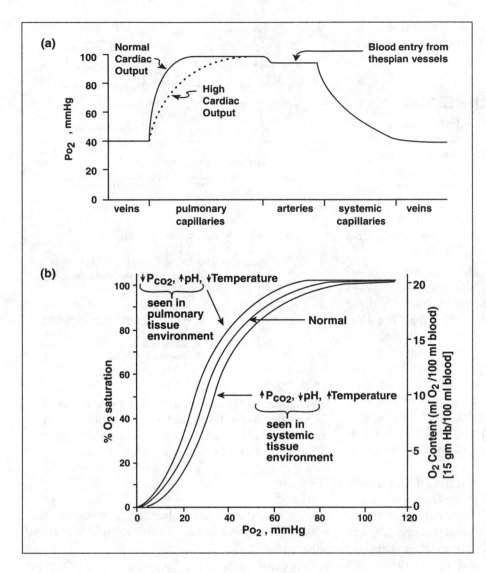

■ Fig. 22-1 ■
(a) A tracing of oxygen pressure in the pulmonary circulation during normal and high cardiac outputs. (b) The oxyhemoglobin dissociation curve, showing the relationship between either the percent saturation of hemoglobin or the oxygen content of blood, as a function of P_{O2}, in conjunction with conditions of low or high P_{CO2}, acidosis or alkalosis, and decreased or increased body temperature.

At the level of the systemic capillaries, the transfers of O_2 from hemoglobin back to plasma, through the capillary wall, into the interstitium, and then into cells, all occur by simple passive diffusion. O_2 transport is flow-, not diffusion-limited. Consequently increased organ blood flow favors O_2 delivery to tissues. Also, increased tissue O_2 consumption reduces interstitial P_{O2}. This increases the diffusional gradient for oxygen from blood to tissues and favors influx of oxygen from blood.

Hypoxia

Hypoxia is a general term used to describe conditions characterized by low oxygen tensions, or conditions in which O_2 delivery to systemic tissues is impaired. The term *hypoxic hypoxia* refers to conditions characterized by low P_{O2}. This can result from several respiratory diseases (e.g., emphysema, pneumonia, hypoventilation), or from breathing air at high altitude where atmospheric pressure, and hence P_{O2}, is low.

Circulatory hypoxia is a condition in which tissue O_2 delivery is reduced due to circulatory failure (shock, heart failure, etc.). *Histotoxic hypoxia* refers to the situation in which P_{O2} and O_2 delivery may be normal, but there is interference with the cells' ability to use O_2. This occurs with cyanide poisoning, which inhibits the mitochondrial respiratory chain. Finally, anemia, resulting from low hematocrit or low blood hemoglobin concentration, will result in hypoxic conditions even if blood flow and P_{O2} are normal because blood O_2 content will be reduced.

CO poisoning is a condition similar to anemia in that CO reduces O_2 content at any P_{O2}. CO has a much greater affinity for hemoglobin than does O_2, and hemoglobin will saturate with CO at only 0.4 mmHg CO pressure. CO levels of only 0.1% in environmental air produce lethal hypoxia.

Transport of CO_2 in the Blood

The uptake of CO_2 by blood from tissues and its transfer from pulmonary capillaries into the alveoli occur by simple passive diffusion. This is a very rapid process requiring only small pressure gradients because CO_2 is highly soluble in lipids and plasma. Total equilibration occurs between systemic tissues and capillaries as well as between pulmonary capillaries and the alveoli, before blood reaches the end of the capillary networks. ■ **Fig. 22-2a** ■

The CO_2 content of venous blood at a P_{CO2} of 46 mmHg is higher than that for O_2 in arterial blood (54 mL/100 mL vs. 20 mL/100 mL). There are three reasons for this situation. ■ **Fig. 22-2b** ■ First, CO_2 is more soluble in plasma than oxygen and thus about 3 mL of CO_2 is carried as dissolved gas in every 100 mL of blood, at a P_{CO2} of 46 mmHg. In addition, ≈ 4 mL CO_2/100 mL blood is transported as carbamino compounds in hemoglobin. There CO_2 combines with amino acid residues in the globin portion of the molecule. The majority of CO_2 transport in blood occurs as CO_2 complexed in bicarbonate, however.

CO_2 in plasma rapidly diffuses into red blood cells that contain large amounts of carbonic anhydrase. Carbonic anhydrase catalyzes the formation of H_2CO_3 from CO_2 and H_2O at a rate 1000 times greater than what would occur spontaneously in plasma. Inside the red blood cells, carbonic acid rapidly dissociates into HCO_3^- and H^+. The bicarbonate ions formed from H_2CO_3 dissociation are exchanged across the red blood cell membrane for Cl^- ions in a process called the *anion shift*.

The H^+ ions formed from this dissociation are rapidly buffered by amino acid residues on hemoglobin, thereby removing them from the intracellular environment. Removal of H^+ and HCO_3^- from the intracellular environment indirectly facilitates CO_2 transport in blood by "pulling" the reaction of CO_2 and water through the dissociation stage. This

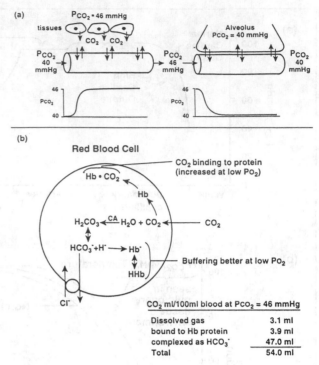

■ **Fig. 22-2** ■

(a) Diagrammatic representations of exchange of carbon dioxide at tissue (left) and pulmonary capillaries (right). (b) Carriage of carbon dioxide by red blood cells. Hb = hemoglobin. (See text for description.)

prevents buildup of intracellular P_{CO2} inside the cell, which would then impair diffusion of CO_2 into red blood cells.

The net effect of these processes is that 47 mL CO_2/100 mL of blood can be transported in the form of bicarbonate in the circulation. The binding of CO_2 and buffering of H^+ by hemoglobin is increased by low P_{O2}. Loading of CO_2 into blood thus is favored at the systemic tissues, whereas unloading of CO_2 from blood is favored at the alveoli. The CO_2 dissociation curve, or the relationship between blood CO_2 content and blood P_{CO2}, is essentially linear over a large range of P_{CO2}. In contrast to O_2 transport, changes in P_{CO2} have significant effects on blood CO_2 content and transport capacity.

CHAPTER 23

Matching Ventilation and Perfusion

The Ventilation Perfusion Ratio

The exchange of O_2 and CO_2 across the respiratory membrane would be most efficient if the volume of blood perfusing every alveoli at any given time were perfectly matched for the volume of air in the alveoli. That is, the ratio of alveolar ventilation to blood flow, or V_A/Q would equal 1. This situation never occurs, however, even in normal lungs.

Intrapleural pressure near the apex of the lungs is slightly more subatmospheric than that in the base. This tends to stretch the lung apex to a less compliant portion of its volume/pressure relationship, resulting in smaller changes in volume for a given change in transmural pressure. This reduces ventilation in the lung apex relative to that in the lung base. ■ **Fig. 23-1a** ■ This effect is not as dramatic as the effect of gravity on pulmonary blood flow. The net result is that the apex has a V_A/Q of about 3, and therefore is overventilated relative to its flow, whereas the V_A/Q of the base is about 0.6, signifying that it is underventilated relative to its flow. Overall, the average V_A/Q ratio in the lungs is approximately 0.8.

Alveolar and hence arterial blood gas tension are affected by the V_A/Q ratio. ■ **Fig. 23-1b** ■ As the V_A/Q approaches 0 (e.g., as alveolar ventilation approaches 0), the composition of alveolar gas and pulmonary capillary blood approaches that of venous blood. Furthermore the accompanying reduction of P_{O2} is much greater than the increase in P_{CO2}. As V_A/Q approaches infinity (e.g., due to low pulmonary blood flow), the composition of alveolar gas and any blood in contact with the alveoli approaches that of inspired, humidified air.

In the normal lung, low blood flow in the apex results in little O_2 transported in blood from that portion of the lung. The high V_A/Q ratio in that region allows for high amounts of CO_2 to be exhaled, however, and apical alveolar P_{CO2} is thus low. Conversely, the lung base, being relatively hypoventi-

lated, has low alveolar P_{O2} and high P_{CO2}. Nevertheless, the absolute quantity of blood flow in the base is so high that most of the oxygenated blood entering the systemic circulation comes from perfusion of the lower portions of the lungs.

Abnormal V_A/Q Ratio in Chronic Obstructive Lung Disease

Abnormal V_A/Q ratios in different parts of the lung result in inefficient gas exchange. This has the inevitable effect of reducing arterial P_{O2} and O_2 content. This situation can occur even though *total* lung blood flow and ventilation may be normal. This seemingly paradoxical situation is illustrated in ■ **Fig. 23-1c** ■ .

In this figure, two set of lungs units are represented; one unit is underventilated due to some form of respiratory disease, while the other is overventilated. Total lung ventilation is normal. Both these units have equal amounts of blood perfusing their alveoli. Consequently, one segment has a low V_A/Q and the other a high V_A/Q. Blood exiting the segment with low ventilation will contain a proportionally reduced P_{O2} and high P_{CO2}. Blood exiting the highly ventilated segment will have high P_{O2} and low P_{CO2}. Blood in the underventilated segment, with a P_{O2} of 65 mm Hg, will only be saturated with O_2 to 90% of its maximum value and thus have reduced oxygen-carrying capacity.

Unfortunately, increasing ventilation in the healthy alveoli gains next to nothing in terms of increased total blood oxygen content, because the oxyhemoglobin saturation curve is flat at $P_{O2} > 100$ mm Hg. When the two blood streams converge, blood saturated at 90% therefore is combined with blood saturated at 99% and yields blood with an average saturation of 94.5% in the pulmonary vein. At this saturation, the equilibrium plasma P_{O2} value only can be 78 mmHg. Because CO_2 contents in blood

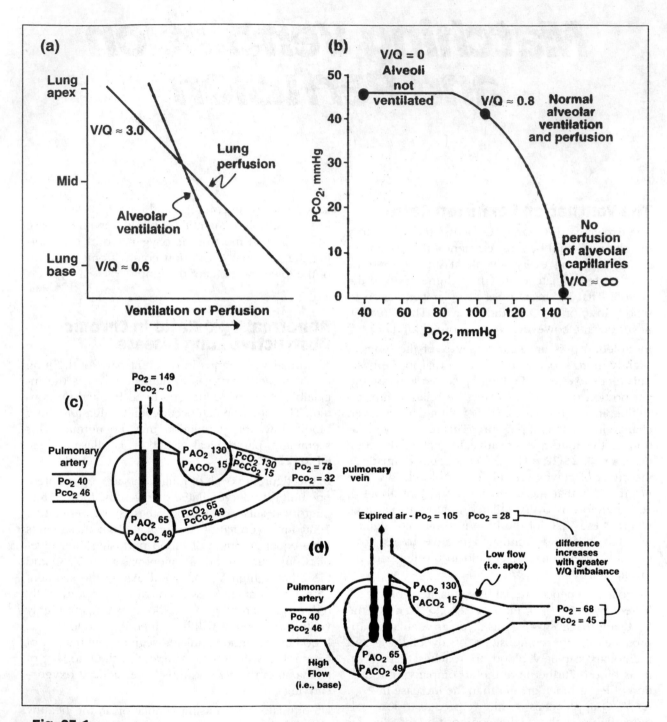

■ **Fig. 23-1** ■
(a) Ventilation, blood flow (lung perfusion), and V/Q ratios in the lung at the apex, midportion, and base of the lungs. (b) Carbon dioxide and oxygen tensions in the alveoli or pulmonary capillaries as a function of different V/Q ratios. (c) A ventilation perfusion abnormality. Some alveoli are hypoventilated relative to their blood flow. This results in a decrease in oxygen tension exiting in the pulmonary vein. This condition is exacerbated (d) if alveoli receiving little oxygen simultaneously receive high blood flow.

are essentially linearly related to P_{CO_2} values, the P_{CO_2} values in the two lung units in this example can be simply averaged to give P_{CO_2} in the pulmonary vein. Due to the high diffusibility of CO_2, the effect of V_A/Q mismatches on P_{CO_2} is not quite as dramatic as that seen for oxygen, although in our example arterial P_{CO_2} will be a little lower than normal.

V_A/Q imbalances can cause even more severe reductions in arterial O_2 tensions and even elevate CO_2 tensions if the underventilated alveoli happen to be perfused by a very large blood flow (e.g., at the base of the lung). ∎ **Fig. 23-1d** ∎ The severity of a V_A/Q imbalance generally is reflected as the difference between arterial and end-expired P_{O_2} and P_{CO_2}. End-expired P_{O_2} in a normal individual is approximately 5 mm Hg greater than arterial P_{O_2}, due in part to the normal, slightly underventilated state of the lungs. This difference widens as ventilation perfusion imbalances become more severe and is an indication of impaired pulmonary function.

CHAPTER 24

Control of Respiration

Neural Control

Alveolar ventilation is adjusted to meet almost exactly the changing and sometimes widely different metabolic demands of the body. Consequently, blood P_{O_2} and P_{CO_2} barely change, even during heavy exercise. Such adjustments to ventilation are due to reflex neural control systems. The central neural centers responsible for this control are not anatomically well-defined, nor are their functions completely understood. **■ Fig. 24-1 ■**

A dorsal inspiratory area has been located in the region of the nucleus tractus solitarius. Stimulation of this center leads to inspiration, although this center appears to fire spontaneous bursts of action potentials without any peripheral nerve inputs. An intrinsic rhythm exists in this center that starts with a latent period of a few seconds, followed by firing of

action potentials at progressively greater frequencies. Outputs from this center stimulate inspiratory muscle activity that is proportional to the frequency of action potential firing. This creates a "ramp" of increasingly stronger inspiratory muscle activity, resulting in a smooth inspiration, as opposed to a "gasping" inspiration. These inspiratory signals, however, inexplicably stop after a short period of time, allowing expiration to occur. The cycle of ramp action potentials then repeats.

Control of the stopping point in this cycle is not understood. It is reasonable to assume that changing the rate of increase of action potential firing, or limiting the time before the stopping point is reached, could change ventilatory rate (breaths/min). A pneumotaxic center has been identified in the upper pons of the brain in the area of the nucleus

■ Fig. 24-1 ■

Diagram of the medullary respiratory centers. These centers receive neural inputs from carotid and aortic bodies that are sensitive to changes in carbon dioxide, hydrogen ion, or oxygen tensions in the arterial blood. Inputs also are received from stretch and irritant receptors in the lung. Outflow from these centers proceeds to respiratory muscles to effect changes in ventilation. The respiratory center contains a chemosensitive area that is stimulated by increases in carbon dioxide or H^+.

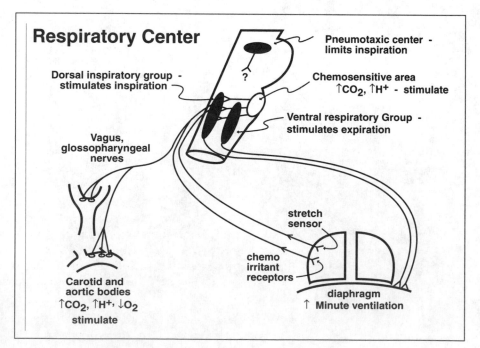

Respiratory Center

Dorsal inspiratory group - stimulates inspiration

Pneumotaxic center - limits inspiration

Chemosensitive area ↑CO_2, ↑H^+ - stimulate

Ventral respiratory Group - stimulates expiration

Vagus, glossopharyngeal nerves

stretch sensor

chemo irritant receptors

Carotid and aortic bodies ↑CO_2, ↑H^+, ↓O_2 stimulate

diaphragm ↑ Minute ventilation

parabrachialis. Strong signals from this center will reduce the duration of inspiration to < 0.5 second, whereas weak or no signals will prolong inspiration for more than 10 seconds. This center seems to control the cutoff point for the inspiratory ramp, thus limiting inspiration. It may secondarily be a means of affecting respiratory rate. This hypothesis has yet to be proven. Activity in the inspiratory center may be modified by signals from the vagus and glossopharyngeal nerves connected to chemoreceptors in the aortic arch and carotid arteries (see below).

A ventral respiratory group, located about 5 mm anterior and lateral to the dorsal inspiratory group, stimulates expiration. This may be important in helping exhalation during heavy breathing associated with exercise, but does not appear to affect normal expiration, which is a simple passive phenomenon.

Chemical Control

Minute ventilation is responsive to P_{O2}, P_{CO2} and H^+ concentrations in arterial blood and the fluids surrounding the brain stem. A chemosensitive area exists in the medulla of the brain. ■ **Fig. 24-1** ■ It is stimulated directly by increases in P_{CO2} or H^+ in the blood or cerebrospinal fluid perfusing this region. Oxygen, however, does not have a *direct* effect on the chemosensitive area. An increase in arterial P_{CO2} or H^+ also increases the rate and depth of lung ventilation through stimulation of this medullary chemosensitive area. ■ **Fig. 24-2a** ■

It is possible that H^+ ions are the only direct stimulus of this area; stimulation by CO_2 may occur secondarily to formation of carbonic acid through its reaction with water. Nevertheless, the chemosensitive area actually is more responsive to changes in *blood* P_{CO2} than *blood* H^+, because vascular and cerebral tissues are more permeable to CO_2 than to H^+. Consequently, blood P_{CO2} is a far more powerful regulator of alveolar ventilation than blood pH. ■ **Fig. 24-2a** ■

The chemosensitive area functions well as a regulator of alveolar ventilation in response to moment-to-moment changes in P_{CO2}. If P_{CO2} is elevated for more than a couple of days, however, this chemical respiratory control system loses its sensitivity. This may be due to increased bicarbonate production in the body, which elevates HCO_3^- in the blood and cerebrospinal fluid in response to systemic acidosis.

The carotid and aortic body chemoreceptors discussed in earlier chapters in the context of cardiovascular function are important regulators of alveolar ventilation. These sensors are stimulated by increases in arterial P_{CO2} and H^+, *and* by decreases in arterial P_{O2}, any or all of which results in stimulation of minute ventilation. When these three chemical signals are allowed to operate simultaneously, the effects of low P_{O2} to stimulate ventilation is feeble in comparison to that effected by high P_{CO2} or low pH. ■ **Figs. 24-2a and 24-2b** ■ The reason for this is as follows: Low P_{O2} is sensed by the arterial chemoreceptors, which begin to stimulate ventilation. This increase in ventilation tends to "blow off" CO_2 at the lungs, causing a fall in P_{CO2}. This then removes a potent stimulator of ventilation at both peripheral and medullary chemoreceptors, and the increase in ventilation caused by the hypoxia is attenuated.

The role of low P_{O2} in stimulating ventilation becomes more important in chronic respiratory diseases when the patient is hypoxic and CO_2 adaptation has already occurred. In such cases, low P_{O2} is the only factor left in the body that can stimulate ventilation in an effort to compensate for the hypoxia. Indeed, administering O_2 to patients in this condition can cause ventilation to cease and result in patient death. In the intact organism, changes in P_{O2}, P_{CO2}, and pH all synergize in their ability to stimulate ventilation. ■ **Figs. 24-2c and 24-2d** ■ For example, hypoxia is a more effective stimulus of ventilation if acidosis and/or hypercapnia are present.

As can be gathered from the preceding discussion, it appears that P_{CO2} rather than P_{O2} is the prime variable responsible for adjusting ventilation in the face of changes in blood gas tensions or pH. This appears logical when one recalls that P_{O2} can decrease by as much as 30% without radically affecting the O_2 content of the blood. It would therefore be of little benefit to stimulate ventilation to correct modest drops in P_{O2}, especially since such changes would alter P_{CO2} and pH.

Furthermore, because acidosis is detrimental to organ functions, linking ventilation to changes in P_{CO2} creates a means by which the body can exploit the respiratory system as a means of acid-base control (see subsequent chapters). Finally, a change in ventilation is an *effective* means of altering blood and tissue CO_2 levels; changing alveolar ventilation has a marked effect on arterial P_{CO2}, making it logical that ventilation is linked to P_{CO2}.

Several other factors can exert influence over respiratory function. Stimulation of the vasomotor center (which elevates cardiac output, vascular resistance,

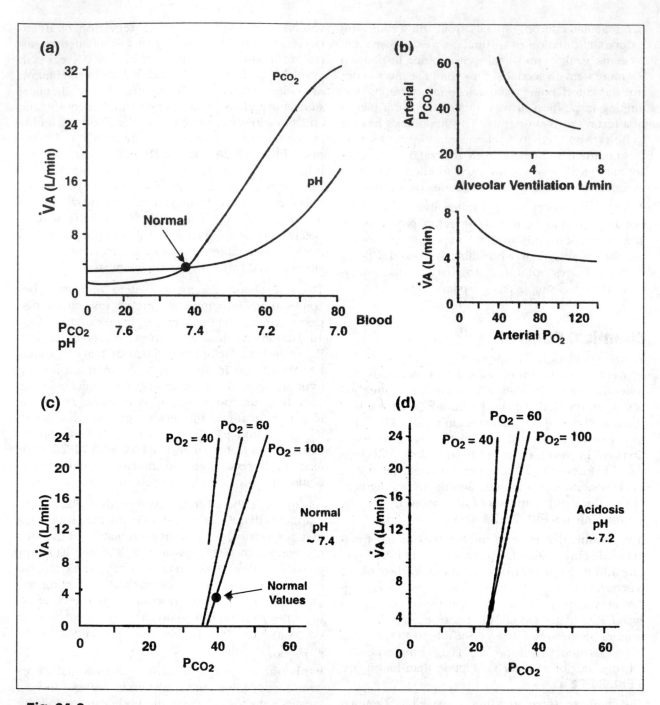

■ Fig. 24-2 ■

(a) The effect of changes in either arterial P_{CO_2} or pH on alveolar ventilation. (b) Top: The effect of alveolar ventilation on arterial P_{CO_2}. Bottom: This effect attenuates stimulation of ventilation caused by a decrease in arterial P_{O_2}. (c) Relationship between alveolar ventilation and arterial carbon dioxide tension at different arterial P_{O_2} with normal pH. (d) The relationship in acidotic conditions.

and blood pressure) also stimulates ventilation. Ventilation also can be altered voluntarily, at least for short periods of time (i.e., holding the breath, forced expiration, etc.).

In addition, several sensory receptors exist in the lung that are connected to reflexes that alter the normal respiratory cycle. For example, stretch receptors in airway smooth muscle, when activated, inhibit inspiration and promote expiration. This is called the *Hering-Breuer reflex* and prevents overinflation of the lungs. In addition, J (juxtacapillary) receptors are sensitive to irritants in the pulmonary structures. When stimulated by pollutants, toxins or particulates, they initiate laryngeal closure and cessation of breathing (apnea), which is quickly followed by rapid shallow breathing. This simultaneously prevents deep inhalation of toxic substances and promotes their removal from the lungs.

CHAPTER 25

Overview of Renal Function and Body Water Compartments

Basic Renal Function

Most people think of the kidney first as an excretory organ with the function of eliminating wastes. Certainly the function of the kidney to remove potentially injurious substances from the blood is important. Excretion of urea and uric acid, formed from catabolism of amino and nucleic acids respectively, as well as excretion of byproducts from the breakdown of blood cells and hemoglobin, form an important part of renal function. In addition, the kidney is an important route of excretion of hormones, drug metabolites, pesticides, and other chemicals.

In terms of the kidney's role in homeostasis and our overall survival, however, the kidney is more correctly viewed as the regulator of body fluid volume, electrolyte composition, and osmolality. In addition, the kidney plays a key role in acid-base regulation in our bodies. Without careful regulation of water, electrolyte and H^+ balance, the cells of all our organs would malfunction.

To perform important homeostatic tasks, the kidney must process plasma, adjusting the composition of this fluid in order to regulate circulating levels of several important physiological substances, as well as excrete substances that are not needed or potentially toxic. The functional unit of the kidney is called the *nephron,* which consists of two distinct parts: the *glomerulus,* which contains a capillary tuft through which plasma is filtered, and a *renal tubule,* which employs several different reabsorptive and secretion mechanisms to process the glomerular filtrate. ■ **Fig. 25-1a** ■

The amount of fluid passing out of the circulation through the renal glomeruli is enormous, equalling about 125 mL/min, or 180 L/day. Thus our entire plasma volume passes through our kidneys approximately 60 times in a 24-hour period. Just beyond the glomerulus, the filtrate is collected in a specialized end tube called *Bowman's capsule* and passed onto, in sequence, the *proximal convoluted tubule,* the *loop of Henle* (medullary or cortical loops), the *distal convoluted tubule,* and the collecting ducts. From this point, tubular fluid is passed out into the renal papilla and through the ureter to the urinary bladder, where it is stored until voided from the body (micturition).

The renal tubule is responsible for reclamation of important substances from the plasma filtrate/tubular fluid such as glucose, amino acids, Na^+, Cl^-, HCO_3^-, and H_2O. It also is the site of elimination of urea, uric acid, H^+, and other substances. It is the site of renal control of the plasma composition of Na^+, Cl^-, K^+ H^+, HCO_3^-, and osmolality. Specifics about functions of individual sections of the renal tubules will be discussed in subsequent chapters. Finally, the kidney is the site of the production of three important regulatory substances:

1. Renin, which, through its eventual stimulation of angiotensin II production, is involved in sodium, water, potassium and blood pressure maintenance,
2. Vitamin D, which is involved in calcium and phosphate metabolism, and
3. Erythropoietin, a hormone that stimulates red blood cell production in bone marrow in response to hypoxia.

Body Water Composition and Water Movement Among Body Water Compartments

Because the broad major function of the kidney is to maintain normal volume and composition in our body fluids, an understanding of the nature of these fluids and their interactions is important to the understanding of renal function. About 60% of lean body mass is made up of water. In a typical adult male this corresponds to a volume of $\approx$ 42 L. Total body water can be divided into intracellular fluid (ICF) and extracellular fluid (ECF) compartments, which

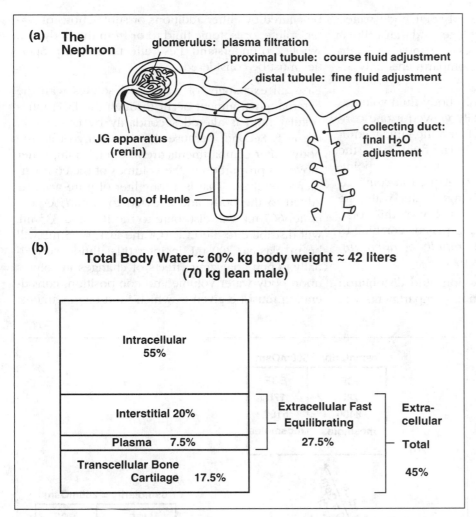

■ Fig. 25-1 ■
(a) Diagram of the nephron showing the filtering unit (glomerulus) and the processing unit for glomerular filtrate (the renal tubules). (b) Representation of body water compartments.

are separated by the cell membrane. **■ Fig. 25-1b ■** ECF includes interstitial fluid and plasma compartments that communicate with one another across the capillary endothelium. Technically ECF also includes transcellular fluid (fluid contained within organ structures such as synovial joints, bladders, etc.) and water complexed in cartilage and bone. **■ Fig. 25-1b ■**

The osmolalities of ICF, interstitial fluid, and plasma are essentially identical, although their chemical compositions differ. Na^+ and Cl^- are the major ions in plasma and interstitial fluid, with small but significant contributions from bicarbonate, glucose, and some proteins. Consequently Na^+ and its attendant anions are the major determinants of osmolality in the extracellular fluid. In fact, osmolality in this compartment can be estimated simply by doubling plasma Na^+ concentration. K^+ is the major cation in intracellular fluid, with proteins and organic phos-

phates contributing the major anionic components to intracellular osmolality.

The distribution of water among the various body water compartments can be represented in two ways. The volume in a given body water compartment can be expressed as a percentage of body weight; for example, plasma ≈ 4.5%, and ECF ≈ 16.5% of body weight. For the purpose of understanding transfer of water between body compartments, however, it often is more useful to express water compartments as a percentage of total body water. Thus ICF = 55% and ECF = 45% of total body water.

To understand movement of water between body water compartments it is important to realize that only the plasma and interstitial fluid compartments can rapidly equilibrate with ICF. Therefore only these compartments respond rapidly to changes in the composition and volume of total body water. Water contained in bone, cartilage, and transcellular compartments is largely inaccessible and comes into equilibrium with other fluid compartments only after long periods of time.

The rapid effects of changes in body fluid volumes or composition are more easily viewed if one considers only their effects on ICF and the rapidly equilibrating portion of extracellular fluid (i.e., the interstitial fluid and plasma). From this viewpoint, 82.5% of total body water is contained in compartments that can rapidly exchange water with one another. The ICF equals about 2/3 of this total, whereas the interstitial fluid and plasma combine to make up what is called the *rapidly equilibrating ECF,* which equals 1/3 of this total.

Body water volume, composition, and distribution among the rapidly equilibrating compartments will

be altered by either additions or subtractions of water, solute, or isotonic fluid to or from the body as a whole. To understand these effects, certain properties must be considered.

First, all exchanges of water and solutes with the external environment occur through the ECF; intracellular fluid is altered secondarily by changes in the ECF. Second, because the osmolality of all the body water compartments are in equilibrium, water moves in proportion to the volumes of the compartments involved. That is, if one liter of pure water is added to the body and allowed to *rapidly* equilibrate, 667 mL will distribute to the ICF and 333 mL will distribute to the ECF. (Of the ECF, ≈ 75 mL will be in plasma, 200 mL in interstitial fluid, etc.) Finally, when analyzing effects of changes in solutes upon body water volume and composition, consideration must be given to which fluid compartments

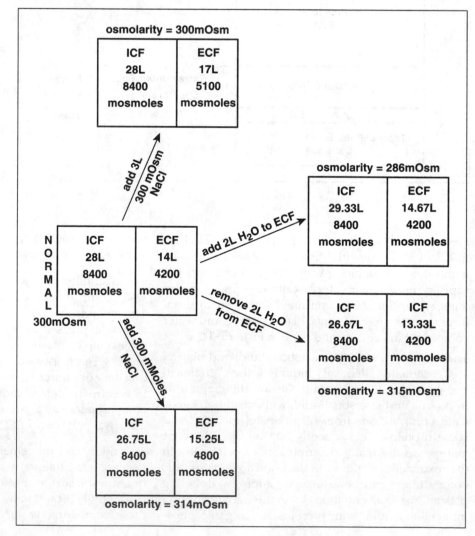

■ **Fig. 25-2** ■
Volumes and osmolar content of intracellular fluid (ICF) and rapidly equilibrating extracellular fluid (ECF) compartments in a normal individual. Effects of adding pure solute, isosmotic NaCl solution, and pure water, or removing pure water, on fluid osmolarity and ECF and ICF volumes.

exclude the solute in question. For example, Na+Cl− is confined to the extracellular fluid, large polymers will be largely restricted to the plasma, etc.

Examples of typical perturbations in body water distribution and osmolar composition are shown in ●**Fig. 25-2**●. This figure shows a total rapidly equilibrating body water of 42 L distributed as 28 L to the ICF and 14 L to the rapid ECF, with both having osmolarities of 300 mOsm. Thus, about 8400 mosmoles of solute exist in the ICF, with 4200 in the ECF. If 2 L of water is added to the body, this water would raise the total water volume to 44 L and be distributed 2/3 to the ICF and 1/3 to the rapid ECF. Since the total solute quantity is not changed, the effect of adding 2 L of pure water to the system will be to reduce the osmolarity in all compartments to about 286 mOsm. Opposite effects of the same proportion will occur with a 2 L water loss from the body.

If 2 L of isotonic NaCl is added to the body, all will be distributed to the ECF because NaCl is excluded from the cell interior. Total body water will again be 44 L, but ICF volume and osmolarity will not change. For a demonstration of what happens when 300 mmoles of NaCl (600 mosmoles) is added to the extracellular fluid as pure solute without the addition of water. See ●**Fig. 25-2**■ This addition of NaCl will be confined to the ECF, raising its osmolar effective solute total to 4800 mosmoles. Because total body water is not altered in this process, this extra ECF solute will osmotically draw water from the ICF. At equilibrium, the total osmolarity of all water compartments will be 315 mOsm (13,200 mosmoles in 42 L). The volume of ECF will increase to 15.25 L at the expense of 1.25 L from the ICF.

CHAPTER 26

Glomerular Filtration and Renal Blood Flow

Glomerular Filtration

An average adult male has a total renal blood flow of about 1.2 L/min, which represents ≈ 25% of total cardiac output, even though the kidneys comprise only 0.5% of total body weight. This high blood flow allows the kidneys to effectively regulate the quantity and composition of the body fluids through the processing of plasma. The rate of plasma flow through the kidney is about 650 ml/min. An average of 20% of renal plasma flow is filtered at the glomerulus and called the *glomerular filtration rate,* or *GFR.* The ratio of GFR to renal plasma flow is designated as the filtration fraction.

Renal plasma is filtered at the capillaries of the glomerulus, which present a selectively permeable barrier to plasma components. ■ **Fig. 26-1a** ■ Water, electrolytes, and small water-soluble molecules such as urea, glucose, and inulin are freely filtered at the glomerulus, whereas large proteins and cellular elements in the blood are not. Thus, fluid entering Bowman's capsule is essentially a protein-free plasma filtrate. The quantity of a freely filtered substance exiting the glomerulus per unit time is called the *filtered load* and equals the plasma concentration of the substance times GFR. ■ **Fig. 26-1a** ■

Many important plasma substances such as calcium, hormones, etc., are partially bound to plasma proteins in the circulation. The bound fraction of these substances cannot cross the glomerular capillaries; only the portion that is uncomplexed and free in plasma can be filtered at the glomerulus. The filtered load of such substances is equal to its total plasma concentration times its free fraction times GFR.

The physical forces that determine filtration at the glomerulus are analogous to the Starling forces for systemic capillaries, with some quantitative differences. ■ **Fig. 26-1b** ■ First, the glomerular capillary net is situated between an afferent and efferent arteriole. As such, glomerular capillary hydrostatic pres-

sure does not decrease significantly along the length of the capillary and provides a constant force favoring fluid efflux out of the glomerulus. A significant hydrostatic pressure of about 10 mmHg exists in Bowman's capsule. This pressure helps move glomerular filtrate through the renal tubules, but opposes glomerular filtration.

The oncotic pressure due to plasma proteins in the glomerular capillary is not constant along the length of the vessel. The filtration of plasma is so great at the glomerulus that plasma proteins become more concentrated as plasma travels from the afferent to the efferent end of the capillary net. Thus a progressively increasing osmotic force, retarding fluid efflux, is created along the length of the glomerular capillaries.

In a normal individual, there essentially are no proteins in the renal tubular fluid and oncotic pressure on the outside of the glomerular capillaries essentially is 0. Despite these quantitative differences in the Starling forces across the glomerular capillary, the net filtration force at the glomerulus is not much greater than that seen in systemic capillaries. The primary reason for a high GFR is that the glomerular K_f is very large relative to that in typical systemic capillaries.

Several factors can alter glomerular filtration rate. Degenerative diseases of the glomerulus increase the glomerular K_f, thereby greatly increasing water loss at the glomerulus; inflammation of the glomerular membranes decreases the filtration coefficient and results in water retention in the body. Ureter blockage, like that arising from kidney stones, can greatly increase tubular hydrostatic pressure and impair GFR. Loss of albumin in the blood results in a large efflux of plasma out of glomerular capillaries and can result in severe water loss in the body and shock.

Only two variables alter GFR under normal physiological circumstances; these are glomerular capillary

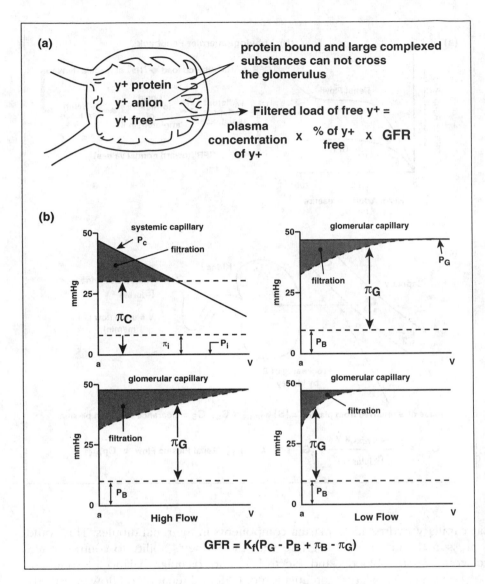

$$GFR = K_f(P_G - P_B + \pi_B - \pi_G)$$

(a) Only free substances can be filtered easily at the glomerulus. (b) Top left: Starling forces at a systemic capillary. Top right: Starling forces at a glomerular capillary during normal flow. Lower left: Starling forces of the glomerular capillary during high renal blood flow. Lower right: Starling forces at the glomerular capillary during low renal blood flow. P_C = capillary hydrostatic pressure, P_i = interstitial hydrostatic pressure, P_G = glomerular capillary hydrostatic pressure, P_B = hydrostatic pressure in Bowman's space, π_C = systemic capillary oncotic pressure, π_i = systemic interstitial fluid oncotic pressure, π_G = oncotic pressure in glomerular capillaries. The glomerular filtration rate (GFR) is a function of hydrostatic and oncotic pressure differences across the glomerulus and the conductance of the capillaries to water, as represented by K_f.

hydrostatic pressure and renal blood flow. Increases in capillary hydrostatic pressure increase GFR. Factors that increase capillary hydrostatic pressure include elevated arterial pressure, afferent arteriolar dilation, and/or efferent arteriolar vasoconstriction.

The effect of renal blood flow on GFR is shown in ■ **Fig. 26-1b** ■. The faster new plasma is brought into the glomerular capillaries, the less time there is for concentration of capillary plasma proteins due to glomerular filtration. Thus high blood flow facilitates GFR by reducing the average plasma oncotic pressure existing in the capillaries. Obviously, decreased blood flow has the opposite effect.

Renal Blood Flow and Control of GFR

Renal blood flow and GFR are tightly controlled under normal physiological conditions, varying less than 10% when arterial pressure varies between 80 to 180 mmHg. ■ **Fig. 26-2a** ■ The only way in which *both* renal blood flow and GFR can be controlled when arterial pressure changes is to have autoregulatory adjustments alter afferent arteriolar, but not efferent arteriolar, resistance. Indeed, the afferent arteriole shows strong myogenic vasoconstriction with an increase in arterial pressure. This has the dual effect of counteracting increases in both re-

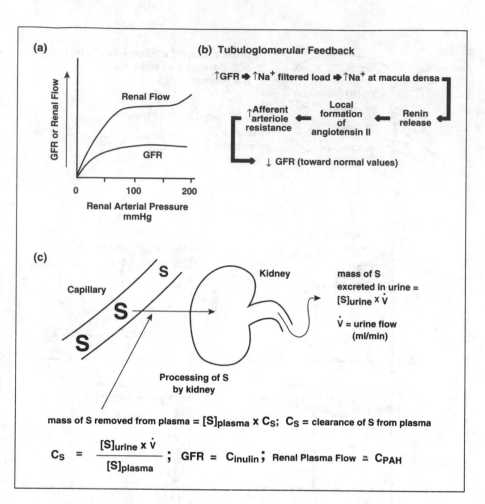

■ Fig. 26-2 ■
(a) Effect of changes in renal perfusion pressure on renal blood flow and GFR.
(b) Flowchart representation of tubuloglomerular feedback. Increases in variables are designated by a single upward arrow. Heavy arrows link variables by cause and effect. (See text for explanation.)
(c) Diagram showing the determination of rates of excretion of a given substance in the urine and its removal from the plasma. Clearance of any substance is given by the ratio of its urine to plasma concentration times the urine flow rate. Clearance of inulin is an estimate of GFR. Clearance of PAH is an estimate of renal plasma flow.

nal blood flow and glomerular capillary hydrostatic pressure when renal arterial pressure is increased. (Increasing efferent resistance would control blood flow but also would increase glomerular capillary pressure and GFR.)

The efficacy of local regulation of GFR is slightly better than that for renal blood flow. It has been shown that local formation of renin and release of angiotensin II may contribute to autoregulation of GFR by a process called *tubuloglomerular feedback*.
■ Fig. 26-2b ■ Basically, an initial increase in GFR increases in the filtered load of Na+ reaching the JG cells, where it is believed to stimulate the release of renin and formation of angiotensin II locally. The angiotensin II then constricts the afferent arteriole, returning GFR to normal.

The kidney works most efficiently if GFR and renal blood flow are not allowed to vary significantly, especially with changes in arterial pressure. Without regulation of GFR, such pressure changes could cause wildly varying filtered loads of important plasma components in the renal tubules. This could interfere with the kidney's ability to control water, and electrolyte and osmolar balance. Strong autoregulation of GFR and renal blood flow effectively uncouples renal function from potential vagaries in arterial pressure, thus helping maintain normal water and electrolyte balance in the event of cardiovascular malfunction.

Several other factors affect renal blood flow and GFR. Stimulation of renal sympathetic nerves constrict both the afferent and efferent arterioles, thereby decreasing renal blood flow and GFR, with the former being slightly more affected. Renal vasoconstriction, however, is part of the body's mechanism for controlling systemic arterial pressure rather than a mechanism for controlling renal blood flow and GFR. Circulating vasoconstrictors such as angiotensin II, vasopressin, and serotonin can restrict renal blood flow. Various prostaglandins, especially prostacyclin and PGE$_2$, are renal vasodilators. In chronic heart failure, these renal vasodilators help maintain enough renal blood flow to allow for reasonable renal function in spite of the tendency for renal flow to be restricted through sympathetic nerve activation in response to the failing heart.

The kidneys are unique in that changes in blood flow cause parallel changes in O_2 consumption, rather than the other way around, as seen in other systemic tissues. This is a consequence of the effect that increased blood flow increases GFR and thus the filtered load of substances entering the renal tubules. This in turn stimulates various energy-requiring transport mechanisms existing in the renal tubule and thus increases renal O_2 consumption.

Clearance

In the context of renal function, physiologists often are interested in what the kidney can eliminate from plasma. This function is called a *clearance*. To understand the concept of clearance, one must first examine excretion of a substance by the kidney.

■ **Fig. 26-2c** ■

The mass of a substance excreted by the kidney per unit of time equals the urine concentration of that substance times the urine flow rate. However, an important function of the kidney is to remove substances from plasma. The mass of a substance removed from plasma per unit of time is equal to the plasma concentration of that substance times the volume of plasma from which that substance is completely removed, or cleared.

It is important to understand that the volume of plasma *completely cleared* of a substance is a theoretical volume. No single milliliter of plasma has all of any substance removed from it by the kidney at any one time. Because of conservation of mass, however, the rate of removal of a substance, S, from the plasma traversing the kidney must equal its rate of excretion in the urine, or, $[S]_{plasma} \times$ Clearance S $= [S]_{urine} \times V$ (urine flow). This then rearranges to Clearance S $= [S]_{urine}/[S]_{plasma} \times V$. Clearance represents the volume of plasma entering the kidney per unit time from which all of S would have had to be removed, in order to create the urine excretion rate of S.

The clearance principle is a useful tool for measuring several renal functions and variables, including GFR and renal plasma flow. For example, the fructose polymer inulin is freely filtered at the glomerulus but neither reabsorbed or secreted by the renal tubules. The clearance of inulin must equal the GFR. That is, the GFR is the only route by which inulin could have been removed from plasma traversing the kidney.

By extension, clearance of a substance that is removed from renal arterial plasma at both the glomerulus and the renal tubular capillaries gives a measure of total renal plasma flow. Para-aminohippurate (PAH) is such a substance. Obviously, inulin clearance/PAH clearance can be used to measure the filtration fraction. This measure is useful in helping to determine whether GFR is altered by normal variations in renal blood flow or whether the alteration is due to renal malfunction. For example, low renal blood flow results in low GFR with low renal plasma flow and thus little alteration in filtration fraction.

Diseases involving the glomerulus alone (e.g., glomerular nephritis) can alter GFR without significant changes in renal plasma flow, and therefore result in an abnormal filtration fraction.

CHAPTER 27

Basic Principles of Reabsorption and Secretion by the Renal Tubules

The average glomerular filtration rate is 125 mL/min, which creates a tremendous filtered load of important plasma components such as glucose, amino acids, Na^+, Cl^-, HCO_3^-, K^+, and H_2O in the renal tubules. Therefore, reabsorption (and hence reclamation) of essential solutes and H_2O by the renal tubules is important for overall body homeostasis.

Also important is the kidney's secretion of urea, H^+, and several other waste products of metabolism into the tubules for eventual excretion. Reabsorption and secretion of substances by the renal tubules can occur by simple passive diffusion, facilitated diffusion, or active transport mechanisms. This chapter describes general principles of reabsorption and secretion by renal tubules.

Transport-Limited Reabsorption and Secretion

The reabsorption of a substance, X, by the kidney equals the amount of X filtered minus the amount excreted, or $T_x = P_x GFR - U_x V$, where P_x and U_x are the plasma and urine concentration of X respectively, V is urine flow rate, and T_x is the amount of X reabsorbed (usually in mg/min). Substances that are filtered and reabsorbed in the kidney have clearances less than the clearance of inulin.

Glucose and amino acids are reabsorbed across the renal tubule by transport maximum limited (T_m) secondary active transport. ■ **Fig. 27-1a** ■ Transport occurs via protein transporters on the apical membranes of tubular cells. The transporters have a limited number of binding sites and reabsorption rates that determine the limits of reabsorption. With this type of transport, the entire filtered load of glucose or amino acids will be reabsorbed providing that transporter sites are unsaturated.

Glucose will start to appear in the urine if its urine concentration exceeds the transport maximum. In our example, the theoretical glucose transport maximum occurs at concentrations of about 300 mg/100 mL. However, the effective glucose T_m is closer to 200 mg/100 mL, due to nephron heterogeneity as well as to the fact that free glucose in the tubule is in equilibrium with glucose bound to the transporter. Therefore, some free glucose always exists in the tubular fluid and starts to appear in the urine when the transporters approach their maximum capacity.

Similarly, certain substances in the peritubular capillaries, like PAH and other organic acids, can be transported across the capillary epithelium and secreted into the tubular fluid by transport-limited secretory processes. ■ **Fig. 27-1b** ■ For a substance, X, secreted by the renal tubules, $T_x = U_x V - P_x GFR$, and such substances have clearances that exceed that of inulin.

Not all important substances handled by the kidney use transporter systems. Urea is an example of a substance that can be passively reabsorbed from the tubules into the peritubular capillaries whenever its tubular fluid concentration exceeds that of plasma. Consequently, passive transport of urea is dependent upon the amount of water reabsorbed by the kidney. High water reabsorption concentrates urea in the renal tubule, allowing it to move down its concentration gradient into the peritubular capillaries.

Urine flow rate is an inverse reflection of water reabsorption by the kidney; low flow indicates high water reabsorption and results in high reabsorption and low clearance of urea; in contrast, high flow rates indicate low water reabsorption by the renal tubules which results in low urea concentration, impaired passive reabsorption, and thus increased excretion of urea in the urine. High urine flow rates

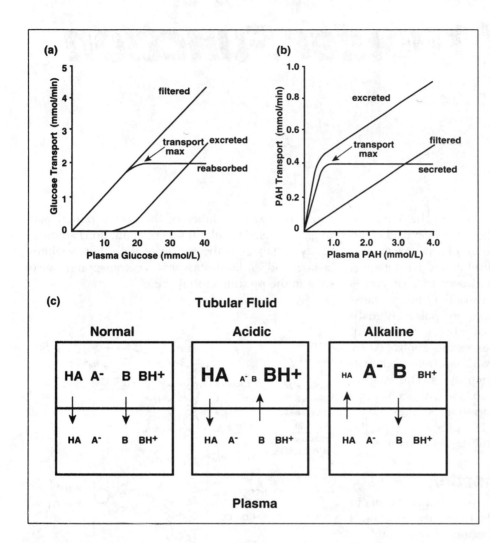

■ Fig. 27-1 ■
(a) Filtration, excretion, and reabsorption of glucose by the kidney as a function of plasma glucose concentration. (b) Excretion, filtration, and secretion of PAH by the kidney as a function of plasma PAH concentration. (c) Effect of tubular fluid acidification and alkalinization on the passive diffusion of weak organic acids (HA) and weak organic bases (B) between the tubular fluid and the plasma.

themselves augment excretion of the urea present in the tubules and clearance of urea increases when urine flow is high.

The acid-base status of tubular fluid influences the passive reabsorption or secretion of weak organic acids or bases by the renal tubules. **■ Fig. 27-1c ■** The nonionized form of organic acids or bases can diffuse easily across the tubular epithelium, whereas the ionized form cannot. Acidic urine favors the reabsorption of a weak organic acid (HA), whereas alkaline urine, by promoting dissociation of HA into H^+ and A^-, favors its secretion and eventual excretion. For a weak organic base, acidic urine will favor excretion and alkaline urine will favor reabsorption.

Clinically, the renal excretion of drugs or toxic substances can be altered by pharmacological agents that alter tubular fluid pH. This can be used either to increase the half-life of the substance in the circulation or accelerate its excretion. For example, removal of acidic aspirin or basic barbiturates may be desirable whenever these accidentally are ingested in excess. Conversely, the half-life of certain cancer chemotherapeutic agents or other beneficial drugs may be extended by manipulating tubular fluid acid-base conditions.

CHAPTER 28

Renal Tubular Function

Processing of glomerular filtrate by the renal tubules results from the interplay of specialized cellular transport systems, variable tubular permeabilities to solutes, and unusual peritubular environments. Many tubular reabsorptive and secretory processes involve carrier proteins and secondary active transport, whereas some substances are passively reabsorbed or secreted by the renal tubules. In addition, many tubular transport processes are controlled by hormonal mechanisms involved in whole-body balance of water and plasma electrolytes. This chapter will examine renal tubular reabsorption mechanisms for water and osmotically important solutes. Ca^{++}, Mg^{++}, phosphate, K^+, and H^+ processing by the kidney will be examined in subsequent chapters.

Proximal Tubular Function

The initial processing of glomerular filtrate occurs in the proximal convoluted tubule. Its primary function is basic reclamation of large amounts of water and essential solutes from glomerular filtrate. ■ **Fig. 28-1** ■ The proximal tubule reabsorbs about 2/3 of the filtered Na^+ and H_2O from the filtrate, significant amounts of Cl^-, HCO_3^-, Ca^{++}, Mg^{++}, and phosphate, and essentially all normal filtered loads of glucose and amino acids. The proximal tubule can reabsorb and secrete uric acid, urea, or K^+ and is a primary site for the secretion of many organic acids, bases, drugs, and toxins.

Sodium reabsorption in the proximal tubule occurs by several mechanisms which, nevertheless, are all ultimately linked to active transport of Na^+ out of the tubular cells by basolateral membrane Na^+/K^+ ATPases. ■ **Fig. 28-1** ■ These ATPases establish a low intracellular concentration of Na^+, which creates a gradient for passive reabsorption of Na^+ from the tubular fluid across the brush border of the apical membrane. Passive Na^+ entry is coupled to a protein cotransporter to the reabsorption of glucose and amino acids. Any factor that enhances reab-

sorption of one member of the cotransported pair (e.g., increased tubular fluid concentration) automatically enhances reabsorption of the other. Sodium-lactate and sodium-phosphate cotransporters also exist in the proximal tubule cells.

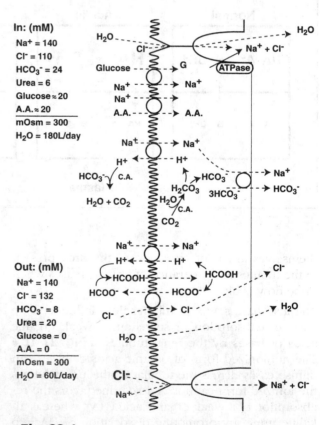

■ **Fig. 28-1** ■
Transport mechanisms in the proximal tubule. Fluid entering the proximal tubule is changed in composition as it traverses the tubule, although its osmotic concentration remains the same. Solid arrows indicate active transport and dashed arrows indicate passive transport. (See text for complete description.)

At the apical membrane, a countertransport protein reabsorbs Na^+ from tubular fluid in exchange for intracellular H^+. This H^+ arises from the dissociation of both carbonic and formic acid that is formed within the tubular cells. ■ **Fig. 28-1** ■ Thus intracellular acidosis promotes sodium reabsorption. Intracellular HCO_3^- from the dissociation of carbonic acid is cotransported with Na^+ across the basolateral membrane and into the peritubular fluid.

Formate ($HCOO^-$), arising from the dissociation of formic acid, crosses the apical membrane in exchange for tubular fluid Cl^-, which then diffuses across the basolateral membrane. In the tubular fluid, formate reassociates with H^+ to form formic acid ($HCOOH$), which easily back-diffuses into the cell. There it redissociates and runs the formate cycle again. Overall, formation of formic acid inside tubular cells results in the eventual reabsorption of $NaCl$ by the proximal tubule, whereas formation of carbonic acid results in reabsorption of $NaHCO_3$.

Tubular epithelial cells are joined by "tight" junctions that nevertheless are quite permeable to Cl^- and water. Consequently, Cl^- and H_2O follow Na^+ reabsorption in the proximal tubule, with the result that the osmolality of tubular fluid, peritubular fluid, and plasma are equalized at ≈ 300 mOsm. In addition, in the early proximal tubule, slightly more HCO_3^- accompanies Na^+ reabsorption than does Cl^-. This factor, coupled with water reabsorption by the proximal tubule, causes tubular fluid Cl^- concentration to increase as fluid moves down the proximal tubule. Near the end of the tubule, Cl^- passively diffuses through the tight junctions, down its concentration gradient, bringing Na^+ with it (paracellular reabsorption).

An important characteristic of sodium reabsorption in the proximal tube is its load dependence. The tubule reabsorbs the same *percent* of the filtered load of sodium, regardless of the size of the load. In other words, whether presented with large or small amounts of Na^+, the tubule still reabsorbs about 67% of the filtered Na^+ load. The net effect of proximal tubule processes is a 2/3 reduction in tubular fluid volume without a change in filtrate osmolality or Na^+ concentration. Cl^-, HCO_3^- and urea concentration are slightly modified by the end of the tubule, whereas that for glucose and amino acids are essentially 0. ■ **Fig. 28-1** ■

The Loop of Henle

The **loop of Henle** is a complex section of the renal tubule consisting of subsections with specialized permeability, active transport, and passive transport characteristics. In addition, the loop of Henle in juxtamedullary nephrons is slightly different than those in cortical nephrons (see below). ■ **Fig. 28-2** ■ The loops of Henle receive about 60 L of tubular fluid a day. Collectively the loops reabsorb about 25% of the Na^+ and 20% of the water filtered at the glomerulus while adding urea to the tubular fluid. The volume and osmolality of proximal tubular fluid is reduced in the loops; fluid exiting this section of the renal tubule is always hypotonic. The most important function of the loop of Henle is to create in the peritubular space specialized osmotic conditions that are essential for a kidney's ability to control water balance in the body.

An understanding of the function of the loop of Henle requires an understanding of the unique osmolar composition of the fluid surrounding that portion of the nephron. In this section, transport phenomena in the loop will be explained in the context of peritubular fluid composition as it is, before it is explained how that special composition is created and maintained. The peritubular fluid in the cortex of the kidney is isosmotic with plasma. However, a vertical osmotic gradient of 300 to 1200 mOsm exists in the renal medulla from the cortical-medullary boundary to the renal papilla. ■ **Fig. 28-2** ■ Na^+, Cl^-, and other nonurea solutes contribute 294 to 600 mOsm to this gradient, whereas urea contributes 6 to 600 mOsm.

The thin descending limb of the loop of Henle is highly permeable to water but impermeable to solutes. Consequently water is osmotically reabsorbed from the tubular fluid as fluid descends deeper into the medullary regions. Approximately 75% of the water entering medullary loops and 50% the water entering cortical loops is reabsorbed by the time fluid reaches the hairpin portion of the loop of Henle. ■ **Fig. 28-2** ■ At the hairpin, the osmolality of the tubular fluid in juxtamedullary nephrons equals the peritubular fluid osmolality of about 1200 mOsm. Tubule osmolality is due mostly to Na^+ and Cl^- with a small contribution from urea, in contrast to the peritubular fluid in which it is due to about 50% $NaCl$ and 50% urea.

The thin ascending limb of the loop of Henle is impermeable to H_2O but highly permeable to $NaCl$ and moderately permeable to urea. Thus, as tubular fluid travels up this limb, Na^+ and Cl^- passively diffuse out of the tubule and urea passively diffuses in, while water content remains unchanged. The quan-

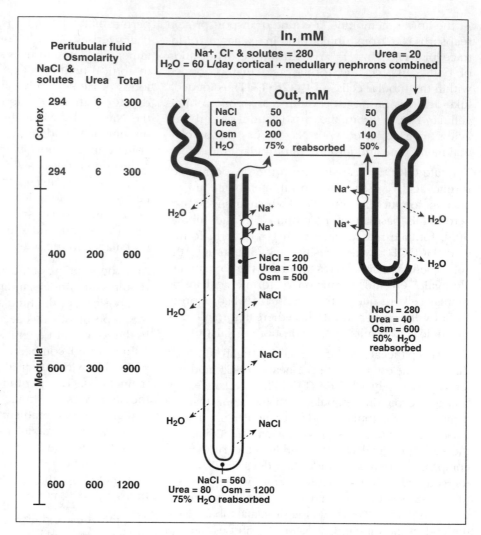

■ Fig. 28-2 ■
Water, sodium chloride, and urea movements in the loop of Henle in medullary and cortical nephrons. Solid arrows indicate active transport and dashed arrows indicate passive transport. Note the difference in composition of the peritubular fluid as one proceeds from the cortex to the medulla. Tubular fluid water content and solute composition is changed by an interplay of passive and active forces acting across the tubular epithelium. (See text for explanation.)

tity of Na^+ and Cl^- leaving the tubule is slightly greater than the amount of urea entering; therefore, osmolality of the fluid falls below that of the peritubular space.

The thick ascending limb of the loop is characterized by low water and urea permeability coupled with active reabsorption of NaCl from the tubular fluid. As a result, fluid exiting the thick ascending limb is hypotonic relative to plasma, although its urea concentration is unaltered and remains higher than that in the surrounding peritubular fluid. The overall effect of processes in the loop of Henle upon tubular fluid is a reduction of its NaCl concentration and osmolality, addition of urea, and further reabsorption of water.

The Distal Nephron: Distal Convoluted Tubule, Connecting Duct and Collecting Duct

The distal nephron is responsible for fine adjustments in the body's water, electrolyte, and acid-base balance. **■ Fig. 28-3 ■** The distal nephron reabsorbs 8% to 10% of the Na^+ and 10% to 15% of the H_2O filtered at the glomerulus. It secretes K^+ and H^+ into the renal tubule and is a major control site of water, Na^+, K^+, Ca^{++} and acid-base balance in the body. Many of these control processes involve the action of circulating hormones on distal nephron function. This section will focus on basic handling of NaCl, water, and urea by the distal nephron, including the role of antidiuretic hormone (ADH) in its transport

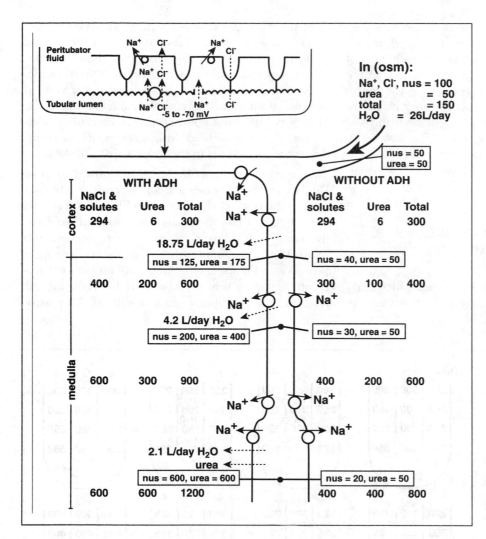

■ Fig. 28-3 ■
The top portion of the figure shows cellular handling of sodium and chloride in the distal convoluted tubule. Solid arrows indicate active transport and dashed arrows indicate passive transport. Reabsorption of sodium chloride creates a negative tubular electrical potential (-5 to -70 mV) that becomes more negative as sodium reabsorption increases. The final volume of fluid exiting the collecting duct and its osmolar and urea composition is dependent upon the actions of ADH on the collecting duct. (See text for complete explanation.)

properties. Details of other functions of the distal nephron will be explained in subsequent chapters.

The distal convoluted tubule has low water and urea permeability. Na^+ is actively transported at the basal surface of tubular cells by a load-dependent mechanism; see the top of **■ Fig. 28-3 ■**. This active transport is stimulated by the hormone aldosterone. Cl^- exits the distal tubule fluid via a $Na^+ Cl$ cotransporter at the apical membrane and by passive paracellular reabsorption mechanisms.

The tight junctions between distal convoluted tubule cells are not very permeable to anions, however. Therefore active transport of Na^+ out of the distal tubule creates a significant negative potential in the tubular lumen relative to the peritubular space. This value ranges from -5 mV, when Na^+ reabsorption is low, to -70 mV when Na^+ reabsorption is high. **■ Fig. 28-1a ■** This negative potential affects the re-

absorption and secretion of other ions such as K^+, H^+, and Ca^{++} in the distal tubule, as discussed in subsequent chapters. Active reabsorption of sodium along the distal tubule, without corresponding reabsorption of water, further reduces osmolality of tubular fluid. Na^+ and Cl^- concentrations become so low in the distal nephron that osmolal contributions of nonurea solutes become important in determining tubular fluid osmolality.

The connecting and collecting ducts also actively reabsorb Na^+ and Cl^-. The permeability of these structures to water is determined by the level of ADH in the circulation. With high levels of ADH, water permeability of all duct structures is high and the papillary region of the collecting duct becomes permeable to urea. With ADH, the collecting ducts reabsorb significant amounts of water, creating a urine with an osmolality and urea concentration identical to that of the hyperosmotic papillary peritubular fluid (i.e., a urine concentrating effect; see the bottom of ■ **Fig. 28-3** ■ . Under the influence of ADH, the kidney ultimately reabsorbs 99.5% of the water from the GFR, excreting < 1% in the urine. Without ADH, the collecting duct is impermeable to water. With continual reabsorption of Na+ and Cl– by the ducts, urine osmolality falls to as low as 70 mOsm (i.e., formation of dilute urine), and H_2O excretion by the kidney rises to about 15% of the filtered load.

Creation and Maintenance of the Medullary Osmolar Gradient

The vertical osmolar gradient in the renal medullary interstitium provides the driving force for water reabsorption by the collecting duct. This vertical osmotic gradient is created as the result of the unique anatomical arrangement, fluid flow, tissue permeability, and transport properties of the loop of Henle. The mechanism responsible for creating the vertical osmolar gradient in the medullary interstitium of the kidney is called the **countercurrent multiplier**, after the fact that tubular fluid flows in opposite, or countercurrent, directions in the loop. ■ **Fig. 28-4a** ■

The countercurrent multiplier in a cortical loop of Henle, which possesses a thick ascending limb but not a thin one, is depicted in ■ **Fig. 28-4a** ■ . To start, assume that tubular and peritubular fluid have the same osmolality as plasma (approximately 300 mOsm). Next, assume that active Na+ transport proceeds in the ascending limb until an osmotic gradient of 100 mOsm is established between tubular fluid and the peritubular space. ■ **Fig. 28-4a** ■, sub-

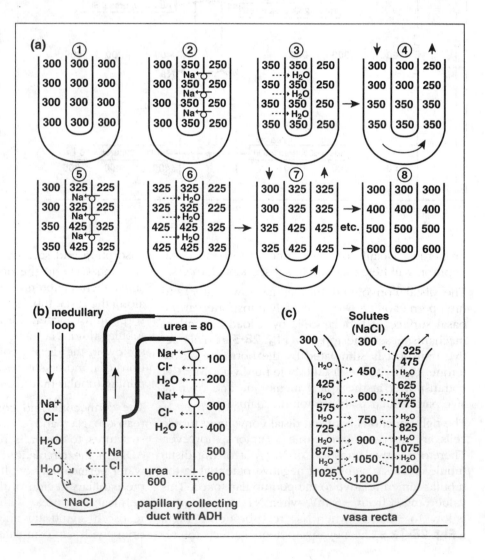

■ **Fig. 28-4** ■
(a) An example of countercurrent multiplying mechanism in the renal tubule; see text for explanation.
(b) Mechanism by which urea is added to the peritubular space of juxtamedullary nephrons. Solid arrows indicate active transport and dashed arrows in tubule wall indicate passive transport. The role of this mechanism in generating a countercurrent exchange in medullary loops is explained in the text. (c) Passive exchange of water and sodium chloride in the vasa recti. See text for the role of this process in maintaining hyperosmolarity of the peritubular fluid.

part 2. This hyperosmotic interstitium will draw water from the descending limb until osmolar concentrations of tubule and peritubular fluids are equal.

In the renal tubule, however, 300 mOsm fluid enters the descending limb continually from the proximal tubule. ■ **Fig. 28-4a** ■, subpart 4 As this process occurs, active Na⁺ transport reestablishes a 100 mOsm gradient, and osmotic equilibration of tubular and peritubular fluid further modifies peritubular osmolality. The result is that deep regions of the medullary interstitium become hyperosmotic relative to those near the top ■ **Fig. 28-4a** ■, subparts 5–7. As this process repeats itself, an ever-greater vertical osmotic gradient is created Fig. 4a, subpart 8.

A valuable consequence of this mechanism is that the only energy used to establish this significant vertical osmotic gradient is that used to establish the original 100 mOsm horizontal gradient between adjacent segments of the loop of Henle. The countercurrent mechanism is thus much more energy-efficient than that which would be required to establish 1200 mOsm in the deep medullary interstitium by direct active pumping of Na⁺ alone, without a countercurrent exchanger present.

The countercurrent mechanism also functions in medullary nephrons that have a thin as well as a thick ascending limb. Creating a vertical osmotic gradient around these nephrons would appear problematic, however, because Na⁺ and Cl⁻ are placed into the interstitium around the thin ascending limb by *passive* reabsorption only. Na⁺ and Cl⁻ must diffuse down a concentration gradient from high tubular concentration to lower peritubular levels in order to enter the peritubular fluid. This high concentration is created upstream by osmotic reabsorption of water from the descending limb and depends on the *prior* existence of a vertical medullary osmotic gradient.

The mechanism responsible for operation of a countercurrent multiplier in juxtamedullary nephrons is depicted in ■ **Fig. 28-4b** ■ . The distal nephron, up to the papillary collecting duct, is impermeable to urea and the concentration of urea entering the collecting duct is approximately 20 mM/L. If ADH is present, active Na⁺ and Cl⁻ reabsorption from the tubular fluid results in reabsorption of water from the collecting duct. This, in turn, progressively increases the concentration of urea in the duct fluid as this fluid flows down the duct.

With ADH present, the permeability of the papillary collecting duct to urea is high. Consequently, when duct fluid reaches this point, urea passively diffuses from the lumen into the papillary medullary interstitium. Accumulation of urea at this location increases peritubular fluid osmolality, which draws fluid from the descending limb of the loop of Henle and increases the concentration of NaCl contained therein. When this high concentration reaches the thin ascending limb, NaCl diffuses out of the tubule and into the peritubular space.

The Vasa Recta

The capillaries surrounding the renal tubules are highly permeable to solute and water. Blood flow through these vessels could easily wash out the vertical osmotic gradient created by the countercurrent multiplier. Special peritubular capillaries, called the *vasa recti*, prevent this from occurring because they are arranged in a unique parallel countercurrent orientation like that seen for the loop of Henle. ■ **Fig. 28-4c** ■ As these capillaries descend into the renal medulla, solute enters and H₂O exits until capillary osmolality equals that of the peritubular fluid. Solute would exit the medullary region at this point if the capillaries exited here. However, they traverse back through the same region from which they came, losing solute to the interstitium and gaining water as they go. ■ **Fig. 28-4c** ■

This process is just slow enough that total equilibration is not reached before the blood exits the vasa recti. In addition, plasma proteins in the vasa recti retard water efflux on the way down and favor influx on the way up through the capillaries. The net effect of both these phenomena is that blood exiting the medullary regions contains slightly more H₂O and solutes than blood that entered the recti. This represents the mechanism of Na⁺ and H₂O reabsorption in this portion of the kidney.

The medullary osmolar gradient is influenced by the rate of flow in both the collecting duct and the vasa recti; decreased flow favors the osmolar gradient, while increased flow dissipates the gradient. In addition, formation of the gradient depends on urea availability; decreased urea availability in protein-poor diets impairs the urine concentrating (i.e., water reabsorption) capacity of the kidney.

The terms *concentrating urine* and *formation of dilute urine* are often used to describe the handling of water by the kidney; these terms translate respectively to *reabsorption of water* and *excretion of water* by the kidney. A way of measuring renal urine concentrating and diluting ability is to calculate what is called *free water clearance*, or C_{H2O}. C_{H2O} is not a classic clearance; it is equal to urine flow rate minus the osmolar clearance, c_{osm}, which equals $u_{osm}/p_{osm} \times V$. When isotonic urine is excreted by the kidney, urine osmolality equals plasma osmolality and osmolar clearance is identical to the urine flow rate. When a dilute urine is being formed, the urine flow rate will be greater than that which would be needed to excrete the same amount of solutes in an isotonic urine. In this situation, C_{H2O} is positive and represents the volume of distilled, or "free," water that one would have to add to isotonic urine to make the actual urine.

Conversely, formation of concentrated urine results in urine flow that is less than what would occur if the same amount of solute were excreted in isotonic urine; C_{H2O} would be negative and represent the volume of free water that needs to be removed from isosmotic urine to make the existing hyperosmotic urine. In physical terms, the "free water" associated with positive C_{H2O} is formed by reabsorption of solute from water-impermeable regions of the nephron (i.e., thick ascending limb, distal tubule, and collecting duct with no ADH). A negative free water clearance arises by reabsorption of solute-free water through the actions of ADH on the collecting duct.

CHAPTER 29

Regulation of Water and Osmolality of Body Fluids

Because intracellular fluid is in osmotic equilibrium with extracellular fluid compartments, changes in the osmolality of the ECF can alter cell function by altering the water content and thus the chemical composition of intracellular fluid. In addition, the volume of plasma in the circulation is an important determinant of cardiac output and cardiovascular function. For these reasons, control of the volume and osmotic composition of body fluids is important in overall homeostasis.

The human body faces numerous and variable inputs of H_2O and Na^+ every day. Maintaining normal water volume and fluid osmolality requires that outputs of H_2O and Na^+ match their inputs. When H_2O volume or fluid osmolality deviate from the norm, our bodies must modify input and/or output processes involved with water and sodium balance in order to return fluid volume and osmolality to normal. This H_2O and Na^+ balance problem is illustrated in ■ **Fig. 29-1** ■ .

Water Inputs and Outputs

H_2O inputs to the body come in the form of water contained in food, that resulting from the metabolism of substrates, and that obtained by the consumption of liquids. Water consumed as liquid is the only regulated water input. H_2O consumption as a liquid can range from <1 to 20 L/day and results from physiological manipulation of the sensation of thirst. There are five sources of H_2O loss, or outputs, from our body: H_2O is lost in expired air, sweat and the feces, as well as by transpiration (evaporation through the skin) and through the production of urine. Urine output, the only regulated water output, is markedly affected by ADH and can range from 1 to 20 L/day.

Losses of water through expired air, the skin, sweat, and feces are called *obligatory water losses*, because these losses cannot be prevented from occurring. In addition, about 650 mOsmoles of electrolytes and other solutes must be excreted by the kidneys each day to maintain normal electrolyte balance and eliminate wastes. Because the maximum osmolarity of the medullary region of the kidney is 1200 mOsm, a minimum of 500 to 600 mL of H_2O must be excreted by the kidney to excrete the 650 mOsm of elec-

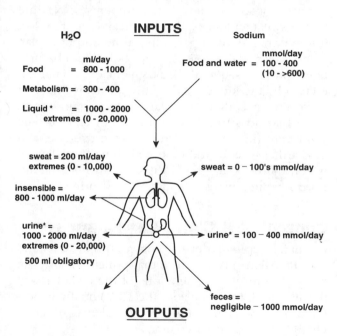

Primary change in H_2O balance changes fluid osmolality

Primary change in Na^+ balance changes fluid volume

■ **Fig. 29-1** ■

Schematic representation of water and sodium balance in the human body. Common inputs and outputs for water and sodium are listed. Values in parentheses show possible ranges for these variables in abnormal conditions. An asterisk (*) indicates physiologically controlled variables. Alterations in water balance affect fluid osmolarity, whereas alterations in sodium balance affect body fluid volumes.

trolytes and other solutes. This represents another obligatory H_2O loss in the body.

Even under normal physiological conditions, obligatory H_2O losses present a challenge to the H_2O balance problem. In pathological or abnormal conditions, some obligatory H_2O losses can become acutely life-threatening. For example, severe diarrhea (i.e., from cholera, gastroenteritis, etc.) can result in water loss of up to 5 L/day. Similar amounts can be lost in sweat during heavy exercise in hot climates. Diuretics or renal glomerular and tubular diseases also can result in abnormally large losses of water in the urine.

Sodium Inputs and Outputs

Na^+ contained in food and H_2O represent the major inputs of Na^+ to the body. Sodium inputs are not regulated in our bodies. Small amounts of Na^+ are lost in sweat and feces, but significantly more is lost in the urine. More importantly, urine output of Na^+ is the only variable regulated in the sodium balance equation. Consequently, adjustment of sodium excretion by the kidney is the only means we have of correcting a sodium imbalance. In certain conditions, Na^+ loss from sweat and feces can become significant (i.e., in sweat from severe exercise, and in diarrhea). As in the case with renal handling of water, diuretics and renal disease can result in abnormally high losses of sodium in the urine.

Control of H_2O and Na^+ Balance

An initial step in understanding control of water and sodium balance is to realize that primary changes in body H_2O results in alterations of the osmolality of the ECF and, by extension, the ICF. Equally important, primary deviations in Na^+ balance result in changes in body fluid volumes.

H_2O balance is controlled to a significant extent by thirst and plasma levels of ADH, which influence urine H_2O output. ■ **Fig. 29-2** ■ These factors are under the control of signals from the brain. Osmole receptors in the hypothalamic regions of the brain are stimulated by cell H_2O loss, which causes these cells to shrink. This can occur whenever H_2O is lost from the body as a whole or osmotically, whenever NaCl concentration increases in the extracellular fluid. Both factors result in increased osmolality of body fluids. When osmole receptors are activated, an increased sensation of thirst and an increase in plasma ADH levels ensue. These factors increase H_2O con-

sumption (water input) and increase H_2O reabsorption by the kidneys (i.e., decrease renal water output).

Additionally, water balance can be affected by baroreceptors in the atria, pulmonary vessels, carotid sinus, and aortic arch, which are sensitive to changes in plasma volume. These receptors are stimulated by stretch and send nerve impulses to the CNS to suppress ADH release. A decrease in plasma volume results in a decreased receptor firing, stimulation of ADH release, and increased H_2O reabsorption by the kidney. This stimulus also increases the sensation of thirst.

ADH release by hypothalamic osmole receptors is altered by as little as a 1% change in plasma osmolality. In contrast, plasma volume must change by more than 10% before circulating levels of ADH are altered significantly. Thus, the osmole receptors are more sensitive than volume receptors in the context of water balance. Changes in plasma volume primarily affect thirst and ADH in severe conditions such as hypovolemic shock. Although osmole receptors are more sensitive, however, the volume receptors can elicit a stronger overall response. This has given rise to the axiom that "volume overrides tonicity" in the control of water balance. ■ **Fig. 29-2a** ■ This statement means that a significant enough drop in plasma volume will stimulate thirst and ADH release, even if the plasma is hypotonic, whereas significantly high plasma volumes will suppress thirst in ADH release, even if plasma is hypertonic. These phenomena appear to set a priority on maintaining cardiovascular function over body osmolar composition in severe conditions such as shock.

Several other factors, not necessarily involved in day-to-day regulation of body H_2O volume, affect thirst, ADH release, and thus water balance. For example, angiotensin II, beta-adrenergic, and cholinergic agents, as well as barbiturates, stimulate thirst. ADH release is stimulated by pain, emotional stress, morphine, and nicotine. In contrast, ethanol suppresses ADH release, resulting in the well-known diuresis seen after episodes of consuming alcoholic beverages.

The body's response to acute dehydration is a good means of demonstrating the operation of H_2O balance mechanisms in the body. ■ **Fig. 29-2b** ■ Acute loss of H_2O from the body depresses plasma volume and increases plasma osmolality. These factors inhibit baroreceptors and stimulate osmole receptors, resulting in increased release of ADH and in-

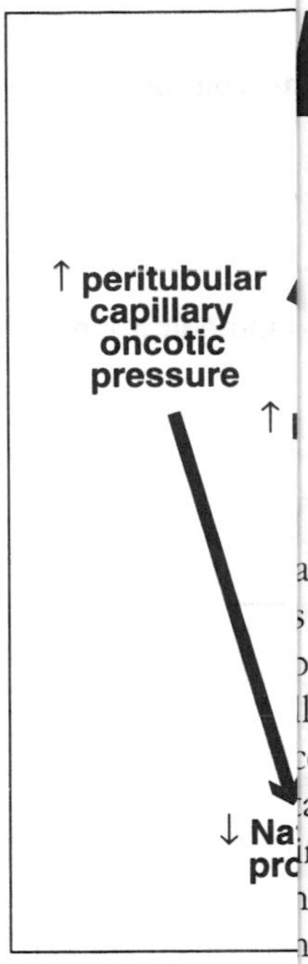

Balance

■ Fig. 29-3 ■
Response of the body to
an initial increase is
sodium intake. Small up-
ward arrows indicate in-
crease and downward
arrows indicate decrease.
Heavy arrows link effects
resulting from change in
the preceding variable.
GFR = glomerular filtration
rate, ANP = atrial natri-
uretic peptide. (See text
for complete explanation.)

↑ **peritubular
capillary
oncotic
pressure**

↓ **Na**
pr

ay with consumption of K+-rich fruits, or as
s 10 mM/day, due to malnutrition. However,
out does not appear to be regulated physio-
lly. K+ is lost from the body through sweat,
es, and urine. Sweat and fecal losses are not
ant except in severe conditions. K+ output in
ne is the only physiologically regulated vari-
the K+ balance equation, and hence is the
neans by which the body can ultimately con-
balance.

pressure baroreceptors, decreases plasma on**lling of K+ by the Nephron**
pressure, and stimulates the secretion of atrial
uretic peptide (ANP). Stimulation of barorece processed by all portions of the nephron, up
results in decreased sympathetic tone to the kic collecting ducts. It is reabsorbed in the first
which causes afferent arteriolar dilation and a rds of the proximal tubule, somewhat in pro-
crease in glomerular capillary hydrostatic pres to H_2O reabsorption, but substantially se-
ANP, released by atrial stretch from the incre in the latter portion of the proximal tubule
plasma volume, also dilates the afferent arterio e thin descending limb of the loop of Henle.
ching the hairpin loops actually may exceed
Coupled with the decrease of plasma oncotic filtered load. Secretion in this portion of the
sure caused by expansion of plasma water vol is proportional to K+ intake, but is not a fac-
this factor increases net filtration pressure at the he regulation of renal K+ output. This secre-
merulus and GFR. An increased GFR increase followed by substantial reabsorption of K+ in
tubular filtered load of sodium and is postulated n and thick ascending limbs of the loop of
sult in increased Na+ excretion, helping bring The net result of all these processes is that
into balance. In reality, however, changes in GFR of filtered K+ enters the distal nephron. K+
only a minor role in regulating Na+ excretion be e in the body is controlled by manipulation
autoregulation of GFR is strong and reabsorpti remaining 10% in the distal nephron.
Na+ by the kidney tubules is load-dependent; th
at increased loads the percent of Na+ reabsc eabsorption and secretion of K+ occur in the
(and hence that excreted) will remain the same. nephron, but reabsorption is relatively con-
Thus, physiological control of K+ secretion
Decreased sympathetic neural tone to the kic sible for controlling K+ excretion and, b
and dilation of afferent arterioles elevate rena , K+ balance in the body. Generally, K
fusion pressure, which then suppresses renin s ries directly in proportion to K+ i
tion and the formation of angiotensin II. AII mechanism by which K+ is se
potent stimulant of aldosterone secretion b nephron is diagrammed in ■ **Fi**
adrenal gland. Angiotensin II is the most imp ely pumped into the tub
action of Na+/K+ ATF
ort across the basola
negative electrical

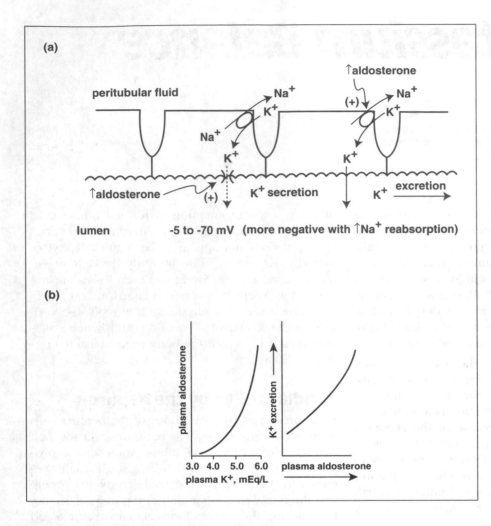

(a)

peritubular fluid

↑aldosterone

Na⁺

K⁺

Na⁺

(+)

Na⁺

K⁺

K⁺

↑aldosterone

(+)

K⁺ secretion

K⁺

K⁺ excretion

lumen   -5 to -70 mV (more negative with ↑Na⁺ reabsorption)

(b)

plasma aldosterone

K⁺ excretion

3.0 4.0 5.0 6.0
plasma K⁺, mEq/L

plasma aldosterone

■ **Fig. 30-1** ■

(a) Representation of the effects of aldosterone on potassium secretion in the distal convoluted tubule. Solid arrows indicate active transport and dashed arrows indicate passive transport. Aldosterone increases passive permeability of the apical membrane to potassium and enhances sodium reabsorption through effects on Na+/K+ ATPase pumps, which results in hypernegativity of the lumen fluid and increased secretion of potassium. Active potassium secretion at the apical membrane is speculative. (b) The effect of changes in plasma potassium concentration on plasma aldosterone levels (left), and the effect of changes in plasma aldosterone levels on potassium excretion (right).

lumen. Increased pump activity increases K+ secretion in two ways:

... potential ... t of K+

... to frank

... order or ... e K+ se-

... of aldos- ... etic ma- ... ce more ... ne. This ... a+ reab-

sorption and K+ secretion). In addition, aldosterone increases the permeability of the apical cell membrane to K+. Aldosterone plays a key role in the regulation of K+ secretion. Plasma K+ and aldosterone levels are interrelated. ■ **Fig. 30-1b** ■ Plasma aldosterone concentration is markedly enhanced by increased K+ concentration and K+ excretion is markedly enhanced by increased plasma aldosterone levels. This results in a negative feedback system that controls K+ balance. With aldosterone, a sevenfold range in dietary potassium intake results in <2% variation in plasma K+ concentration; without aldosterone, plasma levels over a similar range of intakes vary by as much as 30%.

The process of K+ balance in the body in response to an increase in K+ intake is depicted in ■ **Fig. 30-2** ■. An increased K+ intake elevates plasma K+ concen-

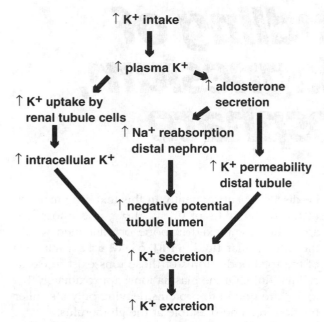

■ Fig. 30-2 ■

A summary of the body's adjustments to an increased potassium intake. Small upward arrows indicate increase and downward arrows indicate decrease. Heavy arrows link effects resulting from a change in the preceding variable. (See text for explanation.)

tration. This stimulates both aldosterone secretion and directly increases intracellular K+ in distal tubular cells. Aldosterone increases intracellular K+ by stimulating the Na+/K+ ATPase. This facilitates K+ secretion. Secretion is augmented by aldosterone's effect to increase the electronegativity of the tubular fluid (pump effect) and to increase the permeability of the luminal surface to K+. Increased K+ secretion in the distal nephron then serves to counteract the initial elevation of plasma K+ caused by increased K+ intake.

Other factors affect K+ secretion by the kidney. The presence of impermeant anions such as HCO_3^- and phosphate in the distal tubule attract positive K+ and hence enhance secretion. Also, secretion is favored by a high tubular flow rate that reduces tubular fluid K+ concentration, favoring efflux of K+ from the cell to the tubular lumen. Secretion, and hence excretion, is enhanced by alkalosis and impaired by acidosis; when excess plasma H+ diffuses into cells including those of the kidney, efflux of positively charged K+ ensues to maintain electric neutrality of the cell and cell K+ concentration falls.

Finally, several diuretic agents (agents that increase the excretion of Na+ and H_2O by the kidney) stimulate the secretion of K+ by the kidney. Loop diuretics such as furosemide impair Na+ reabsorption in the ascending limb of the loop of Henle, thereby increasing the Na+ load presented to the distal nephron. This enhances load-dependent Na+ reabsorption at the distal nephron, resulting in enhanced secretion of K+. "K+-sparing" diuretics do not affect K+ secretion. These agents decrease Na+ reabsorption directly in the distal nephron, decreasing the transepithelial negative potential difference and actually impairing K+ secretion. These diuretics are used whenever K+ loss due to diuretic action becomes a problem for the patient.

Renal Handling of Calcium, Magnesium, and Phosphate

CHAPTER *31*

Unlike Na^+ and K^+, the regulation of Ca^{++}, Mg^{++}, and phosphate balance are complicated by the fact that their inputs into the body do not arise only from dietary sources. Inputs and outputs of these multivalent ions are affected by hormonal and other factors that affect their absorption from the gastrointestinal tract, as well as their deposition in and reabsorption from bone; details of these processes will be discussed subsequently in this text. The majority of the body stores of Ca^{++}, Mg^{++}, and phosphate are either complexed in bone or contained within the intracellular fluid. ■ **Fig. 31-1a** ■ Less than 1% of the total body stores of these ions exist in extracellular fluid. Of the plasma ions, approximately 1/3 to 2/3 are bound to proteins, leaving only a smaller fraction free and filterable at the glomerulus.

■ **Fig. 31-1** ■
(a) An overview of body calcium, magnesium, and phosphate stores, their binding to plasma proteins, and the amounts of these ions that are free and filterable by the kidney.
(b) Response of the body to an initial decrease in plasma calcium or an increase in plasma phosphate concentration. PTH plays a central role in calcium reabsorption in the thick ascending limb and distal nephron, as well as in phosphate reabsorption in the proximal tubule. This latter effect alters eventual phosphate excretion.

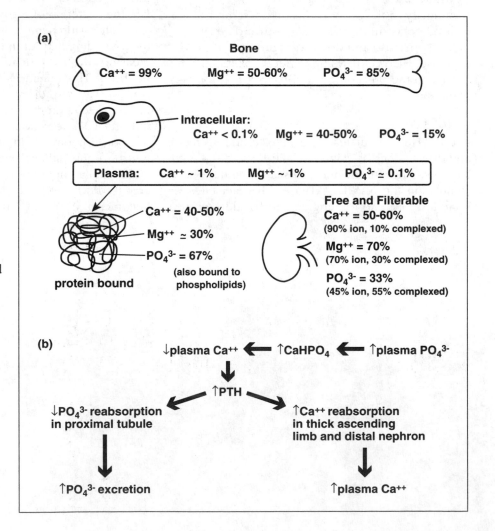

152

Of the Ca^{++} filtered at the glomerulus, 97% to 99% is reabsorbed by the kidney. Fractional reabsorption of Ca^{++} is similar to that of Na^+ prior to the distal nephron. Ca^{++} also is reabsorbed in the distal nephron—but by mechanisms that are poorly understood. Eventual excretion of Ca^{++} parallels the fractional excretion of Na^+; when plasma sodium is increased, the excretion of Na^+ to balance that ion increases Ca^{++} excretion as well, perhaps through the third factor effect. Loop diuretics, by creating a load-mediated increase in Na^+ reabsorption in the distal tubule and increased negativity of tubular fluid, impair Ca^{++} reabsorption and therefore cause Ca^{++} loss in the urine.

The primary physiological controller of Ca^{++} excretion by the kidney is parathyroid hormone, or PTH, which is produced by the parathyroid tissues whenever plasma Ca^{++} levels decrease. ■ **Fig. 31-1b** ■ In turn, PTH stimulates Ca^{++} reabsorption in the thick ascending limbs and distal nephron. The mechanism by which PTH does this is not understood. Because the distal transtubular potential is always negative,

however, the mechanism must involve some type of active Ca^{++} transport mechanism.

PTH also influences the renal handling of phosphate. When PTH levels are elevated, phosphate excretion increases to as much 40% of the filtered phosphate load. Without PTH, reabsorption of phosphate is stimulated, resulting in excretion of only 5% of the filtered phosphate load. In turn, plasma phosphate levels alter those of PTH, although this is an indirect effect. Whenever plasma phosphate levels are high, more Ca^{++} is complexed in the form of calcium phosphate, reducing the concentration of free ionized Ca^{++} in the plasma. This low Ca^{++} then stimulates PTH. PTH subsequently alters phosphate as well as Ca^{++} reabsorption in the kidney, restoring normal balance for both these divalent ions.

Little is understood about renal handling of Mg^{++}. Mg^{++} excretion is normally 1 to 10 mM/day but cannot be reduced to 0. Therefore, low Mg^{++} intake (i.e., a poor diet due to heavy alcoholism) results in Mg^{++} depletion. Generally, Mg^{++} excretion parallels that for Ca^{++} and is depressed by the actions of PTH.

CHAPTER 32

Acid-Base Balance

Changes in the H+ concentration of body fluids can have marked effects on protein conformation and function. It is hard to imagine any physiological process that would not be altered by changes in circulating H+ concentration. Normally, the pH of body fluids is maintained within an extremely narrow range of 7.38 to 7.42. This small range suggests both the importance of pH control to physiological functions and the efficacy of homeostatic mechanisms that maintain acid-base status within a narrow range.

Metabolic processes in the body produce acids that represent a threat to pH balance. CO_2 production alone, through its interaction of H_2O to form carbonic acid, can add $\approx$ 10,000 mM of H+ to body fluids, increasing H+ concentration more than 7 million times. In addition, sulfuric acid and phosphoric acid, formed from sulfur containing amino acids and phospholipids respectively, add another 50 to 100 mM of H+ to body fluids every day. Finally, organic acids such as lactic acid, acetoacetic acid, and β-OH-butyric acid, which are normally oxidized to CO_2 and H_2O, can accumulate in excess under abnormal conditions, such as diabetes mellitus, and present a further acid assault on the body.

Blood Acid-Base Buffers

The body's first line of defense against a daily acid assault is chemical buffering of the acid by a variety of blood buffer systems. Blood buffers are weak acids that exist in a mixture of protonated and unprotonated form, e.g., HA $\rightleftarrows$ H+ + A−. The dissociation constant of such a weak acid, K_a, equals [H+][A−]/[HA] (or the product of H+ and anion concentrations divided by the unprotonated acid concentration). By using this formula, rearranging, and substituting p for −log we arrive at the classical acid-base equation stating pH = pK_a +log [A-]/[HA]. Buffers work best when they are placed in a solution in which the pH is identical to the pK_a for the buffer. At this pH, the acid is 50% dissociated and has equivalent ability to buffer

added acid or added base. In addition, the ability to withstand changes in pH increases with greater quantities of buffer in solution.

Ideally, blood buffers should have a pK_a = 7.4 (normal body fluid pH) and exist in large quantities if they are to be most effective in countering alterations in the acid-base status of the body. No single blood buffer meets these criteria, however. Nevertheless, chemical buffering of acid and base is an important component of the body's ability to counteract changes in the pH of body fluids. Several buffers exist in plasma. For example, plasma proteins have considerable buffering capacity due to their C-terminal carboxyl and N-terminal amino groups. In addition, side chain carboxyls of glutamic and aspartic acid, amino groups of lysine, and the imidazole group of histidine all have buffering capacity; imidazole and terminal amino groups have useful pK_as close to 7.4.

The single most important plasma protein buffer is hemoglobin, which has 38 histidine residues. Its buffering capacity is about 6 times the buffering capacity of the other plasma proteins and twice that of albumin. Phosphate with a pK_a of 6.8 is another compound fairly well suited to serve as a blood buffer. Unfortunately, its quantity is low in the plasma. Phosphate is a more important pH buffer within cells and within the renal tubule.

Carbonic acid, H_2CO_3, is another source of plasma buffering capacity. The pK_a for the dissociation of carbonic acid into H+ and HCO_3^- is 3.7, so this would seem to preclude carbonic acid from being a useful buffer in our bodies. Carbonic acid is in equilibrium with CO_2 and H_2O, however. Therefore the pH balance equation may be rewritten in a form that takes into account CO_2. We can write

$$pH = pK_a + \log[HCO_3^-]/[CO_2]$$

where $0.03 P_{CO_2}$ may be substituted for $[CO_2]$ and the pK_a of this system is 6.1. This is still not an ideal blood buffer. Nevertheless, the bicarbonate/CO_2 system is the most important buffering system in the body because the concentrations of its components, HCO_3^- and CO_2, can be independently *regulated*, CO_2 by the lungs and HCO_3^- by the kidneys. No other blood buffer system has this property.

Respiratory Control of pH

CO_2 is a source of enormous additions of H^+ to the body fluids ever day. However, CO_2 can be removed by the lungs. At a fixed rate of CO_2 production, the arterial P_{CO_2} is determined by alveolar ventilation only; P_{CO_2} decreases when ventilation increases. Consequently, arterial pH is similarly related to V_A. ■ **Fig. 32-1a** ■ When coupled with the fact that alveolar ventilation is, in turn, altered by arterial pH, a negative feedback system for the control of pH, through respiratory control of arterial P_{CO_2}, is created. ■ **Fig. 32-1b** ■

The effectiveness of the respiratory system in controlling arterial pH is up to twice the buffering capacity of blood buffers. This system can compensate for a given disturbance in pH by 50% to 75% (i.e., a pH of 7.2 can be brought to 7.3 to 7.35 by the respiratory system alone). The reason the respiratory system cannot completely correct an acid-base disturbance in our body is that the CO_2 mechanism of ventilatory control is self-attenuating. As pH falls and stimulates ventilation, the increased ventilation blows off CO_2. The decreased arterial P_{CO_2} then impairs any further stimulation of ventilation by low pH. As can be seen, some other system is needed if correction of an acid-base disturbance is to proceed beyond that provided by the respiratory system alone. This function falls to the kidneys,

which control H^+ ion secretion and bicarbonate reabsorption.

Renal Control of pH

Addition of acid to body fluids in not the only way in which the pH of body fluids can fall (acidosis). For example, from the relationship pH = pK_a + log[HCO_3^-]/[CO_2], it can be seen that any bicarbonate lost in the body is equivalent to adding acid. The kidney plays a key role in acid-base balance in the body through its handling of plasma HCO_3^-. The kidney contends with two sources of HCO_3^- loss in the body. First, about 4000 mM of bicarbonate are filtered at the glomeruli each day. This bicarbonate must be recovered by the kidney, or pH of the body fluids will decrease. Secondly, the kidney must replace bicarbonate lost in buffering strong mineral and organic acids that arise as byproducts of metabolism.

As a means of reclaiming HCO_3^- lost from the plasma in the glomerular filtrate, the kidney links HCO_3^- reabsorption to H^+ secretion in proximal tubule cells, as well as in the intercalated cells of the collecting duct. ■ **Fig. 32-2** ■ The mechanisms used for this purpose are as follows.

In both renal sections, HCO_3^- and H^+ are formed within tubular cells from the dissociation of H_2CO_3, which is formed from CO_2 and H_2O in a reaction facilitated by carbonic anhydrase. In the proximal tubule, H^+ exits the apical membrane in exchange for Na^+. In the collecting duct, H^+ is actively secreted into the tubular lumen by a H^+ ATPase. In both sections, the dissociation of H_2CO_3 is facilitated if H^+ can be eliminated from the system. When tubular fluid H^+ is eliminated through reac-

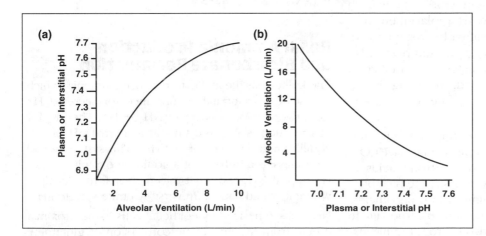

■ **Fig. 32-1** ■
(a) Effect of alveolar ventilation on plasma or interstitial fluid pH. (b) Effect of plasma or interstitial pH on alveolar ventilation.

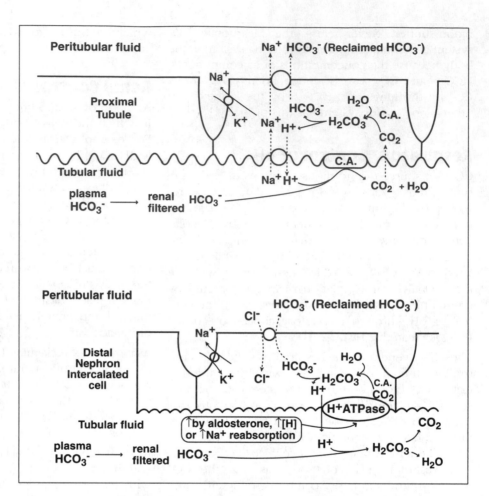

■ Fig. 32-2 ■
Cellular mechanisms involved with the reclamation of filtered bicarbonate by the proximal tubule (top) and the intercalated cells of the distal nephron (bottom). Solid arrows in cell membrane indicate active transport and dashed arrows indicate passive transport. Reclamation in the distal nephron can be enhanced by aldosterone, increased H+ inside the cells, or enhanced Na+ reabsorption in this portion of the renal tubule.

tion with a filtered HCO_3^-, a HCO_3^- molecule is left within the tubule cell. This ion is then reabsorbed across the basolateral membrane by co- or countertransport mechanisms.

The net effect of these processes is that every HCO_3^- filtered is replaced by reabsorption of another HCO_3^-. This is not the same molecule in each case, but is instead a simple 1:1 replacement process. This process can be modified by systemic acid-base conditions. For example, increased plasma H+ concentration (acidosis) stimulates the number of H+-ATPase molecules produced, resulting in increased H+ secretion and bicarbonate reabsorption, which helps correct the acidosis.

The mechanisms described in the renal tubules above are sufficient only to replace plasma HCO_3^- lost through glomerular filtration. Strong acids in the body (e.g., H_2SO_4, HCl) will dissociate bicarbonate from its Na+ salt, reforming H_2CO_3 and thence CO_2 and H_2O. The loss of plasma bicarbonate in this manner will result in acidosis. From the mecha-

nism of HCO_3^- reclamation described above, one can infer that bicarbonate lost in the titration of strong acids could also be "reclaimed" if some titratable substance were added into the renal tubule to eliminate H+. Such a system exists in the nephron and results from the kidney's ability to make ammonia (NH_3). **■ Fig. 32-3 ■**

Renal Ammonia Production and Bicarbonate Reclamation

The kidney has the ability to produce ammonia, which can serve as a titratable substance for secreted H+ ions; the reaction is $NH_4^+ \rightleftarrows NH_3 + H^+$. The pKa for this reaction is 9.3, and thus at a normal pH of 7.4, equilibrium is far in favor of NH_4^+. This system would be useless as a buffer, but it could be exploited as an H+ trap, if NH_3 could get into the renal tubular fluid where it would almost irreversibly titrate secreted H+.

NH_4^+ is synthesized by epithelial cells in the proximal tubule from the enzymatic conversion of glutamine

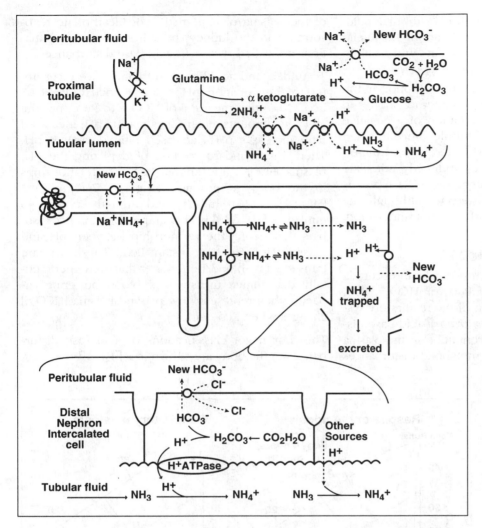

■ Fig. 32-3 ■
Mechanism used by the kidney to generate reabsorption of new bicarbonate to replace that lost in the titration of strong acids in the body. Solid arrows in cell membrane indicate active transport and dashed arrows indicate passive transport. (See text for description of the mechanisms involved.)

into 2 NH_4^+ (ammonium) and 2 HCO_3^-. **■ Fig. 32-3 ■** The HCO_3^- so formed is reabsorbed by the proximal tubule and represents some "new HCO_3^-" that can replace that lost in buffering strong acids. The more important new HCO_3^- generating mechanism involves a more complicated process, however.

First the ammonium ion formed in the proximal tubule is secreted into the tubular lumen in exchange for Na^+. It is then reabsorbed in Henle's loop and accumulates in the medullary interstitium, where it exists in equilibrium with NH_3. NH_3 diffuses into the collecting duct fluid, where it can rapidly titrate H^+ ions secreted by the distal nephron. This leaves a HCO_3^- in the intercalated cell which is reabsorbed, replacing that originally lost in strong acid titration. The NH_4^+ formed from this titration process is trapped in the collecting duct and is excreted. Secretion of H^+ ion by the collecting duct is essential for this excretion of ammonium.

Without H^+ ion secretion, ammonium eventually will be reabsorbed, where it will titrate intracellular bicarbonate and create an acidosis.

Factors Affecting HCO_3^- Reabsorption and H^+ Ion Secretion by the Kidney

The renal ammonium-ammonia system has the valuable property of being able to be regulated by several physiological factors. Production of the enzyme responsible for formation of NH_4^+ from glutamine is induced by acidosis, which then helps the kidney handle the increased acid load; this enzyme is reduced by alkalosis. Both adjustments require several days to reach full effect.

Theoretically, any anionic substance can titrate H^+ ions in the renal tubule. In the distal nephron, H_2O is reabsorbed in excess of phosphate, thereby in-

in tubular fluid. ... about 12–40 mM ...ate and result in ...a.

...sorption in the ...ertransporter in ... of a negative ... Since this Na+ ...ected by aldosterone and diuret-...s, aldosterone and diuretics indirectly stimulate H+ secretion. In addition, renal H+ ATPase also is stimulated directly by aldosterone, although the mechanism involved in this effect is not understood.

Acid-Base Disturbances

Deviations in arterial pH from normal can occur via changes in plasma levels of P_{CO_2} or HCO_3^-. P_{CO_2} can be altered by malfunction of the respiratory system. When this occurs, a *respiratory* acid-base disturbance results. HCO_3^- concentration in the plasma can change as the result of metabolic disturbances

of the plasma or malfunction of bicarbonate reabsorption in the kidney. In either case, such situations are called *metabolic* acid-base disturbances.

To understand acid-base disturbances we again refer to the equation pH = 6.1 + log[HCO_3^-]/0.03 P_{CO_2}. Note that the *ratio* of HCO_3^- to P_{CO_2}, not the absolute amounts, determines plasma pH; increased ratio increases pH, decreased ratio decreases pH. There is a standard method of depicting the pH, plasma HCO_3^-, and arterial P_{CO_2} interrelationships in the body, where normal pH is 7.40, plasma [HCO_3^-] is 24.0 mEq/L, and arterial P_{CO_2} is 40 mmHg. ■ **Fig. 32-4** ■ This graph contains P_{CO_2} isobars that depict the relationship between pH and plasma [HCO_3^-] at a constant P_{CO_2}. These bars are transected by blood/buffer lines that are experimentally determined measures of blood buffering capacity; they represent how pH and plasma [HCO_3^-] changes when P_{CO_2} varies.

The four major classifications of acid-base disturbances in the body are shown in ■ **Fig. 32-4** ■ . *Res-*

■ **Fig. 32-4** ■

Graphical representations of the interrelationships between plasma HCO_3^-, plasma P_{CO_2}, and plasma pH in the body. The point designated by "N" represents normal values for these three variables. Points at the ends of heavy arrows represent the equilibrium conditions for various acid-base disturbances. "A" represents the values during an acute disturbance; "C" the values after compensatory mechanisms are initiated in the body in response to a chronic disturbance. Metabolic acid-base disturbances rarely occur acutely, so these values are not listed on the figure. Explanation of acute disturbances and compensatory mechanisms are discussed in detail in the text.

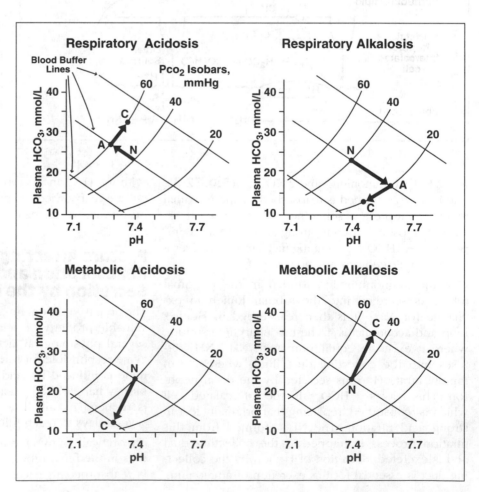

piratory acidosis is characterized by an increased P_{CO_2}. This commonly is caused by hypoventilation resulting from anesthesia, barbiturate overdose, brain trauma, or by severe lung diseases that impair gas exchange. In this condition, the system operates on a higher P_{CO_2} isobar. Note that $[HCO_3^-]$ increases slightly above normal because of the additional CO_2 in the system, but the ratio of $[HCO_3^-]$ to P_{CO_2} is below normal, and hence pH drops. If the P_{CO_2} remains elevated and the acidosis persists, renal compensation mechanisms that increase the amount of new HCO_3^- formed in the system are brought into play. With new HCO_3^- added to the system, the ratio of HCO_3^- and CO_2 approaches normal and pH returns closer to its original value.

In *respiratory alkalosis* (decreased P_{CO_2}), an opposite situation occurs to that described for acidosis. Common causes of respiratory alkalosis include hyperventilation secondary to hypoxia, CNS disorders, or simple anxiety. The renal compensatory mechanisms are analogous to that shown for respiratory acidosis, except they occur in the opposite direction.

Metabolic acidosis is caused by an effective loss of plasma $[HCO_3^-]$, either through frank loss of this anion or through titration with excess acids. This occurs in circulatory shock as a result of increased lactic acid production due to loss of oxidative metabolism; in diabetes mellitus, where production of acetoacetic and β-OH-butyric acids are increased; and in severe renal failure, where the H^+ ion secretory ability of the kidney needed to generate new bicarbonate is impaired. In addition, severe diarrhea often results in a loss of bicarbonate and thus metabolic acidosis.

In metabolic acidosis, the respiratory system is first to elicit compensatory mechanisms. Ventilation increases, blowing off excess CO_2, and returning pH nearly to normal. If the metabolic acidosis is not due to malfunction of the kidneys, the kidneys will help the body compensate for the acidosis by generating new bicarbonate. The opposite of this condition, metabolic alkalosis, can result from large loss of fluid containing acid, as seen with severe vomiting, or from the kidney under the influence of loop diuretics. Again, respiratory and renal compensations proceed analogous to that for metabolic acidosis, only in the opposite direction.

Metabolic alkalosis, however, is complicated if the alkalosis is accompanied by a plasma volume contraction (vomiting, diuresis). The decreased plasma volume will stimulate Na^+ reabsorption in the kidney, which will eventually stimulate renal H^+ secretion; $[HCO_3^-]$ in the plasma then may increase, perpetuating the alkalosis. When metabolic alkalosis is accompanied by plasma volume contraction, the kidneys therefore can correct the acid/base disturbance only *after* hypovolemia is corrected.

A graphical paradigm for the diagnosis of acid-base disturbances in the body is shown in ■ **Fig. 32-5** ■ , which also lists the quantitative magnitude of respiratory or renal corrections needed in the four major classes of acid-base disturbances. Whenever these compensatory mechanisms do not quantitatively equal what is indicated in the diagram, a mixed acid-base disturbance or an incomplete compensation is present.

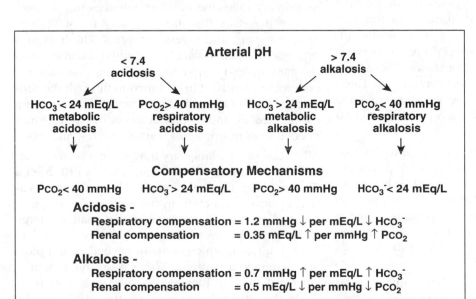

■ **Fig. 32-5** ■
A flowchart for the analysis of acid-base disturbances. Indicators of the primary cause of the disturbance and qualitative and quantitative changes in compensatory variables are listed.

CHAPTER 33

A Descriptive Overview of the Gastrointestinal System

The basic functions of the gastrointestinal system are to transform complex bulk foodstuffs into basic substrates and to absorb these substrates so that they may be used for metabolic processes needed to derive energy for all physiological functions in the body. The functions of the gastrointestinal system involve some of the most elaborate and elegant integrated control processes in the body. A high degree of integration of digestive, absorptive, and muscle activity at various locations in the GI tract, as well as coordination of accessory organ functions in the liver, pancreas, and salivary glands are involved in the digestive process. This process is all the more remarkable when one considers the complicated physical and chemical diversity of the substances ingested by an individual. The GI system must handle the breakdown, absorption, and coordinated processing of such diverse substances as carbohydrates, proteins, fats, electrolytes, H_2O, lipid- and water-soluble vitamins, bile acids, and poorly absorbed multivalent ions such as Fe^{++}, Ca^{++}, and Mg^{++}.

Secretory and absorptive processes in the GI tract are controlled by neural and humoral factors that are linked in complex interactions between the autonomic nervous system, a special enteric nervous system in the gut wall, and GI hormones. These three systems are involved in local and centrally mediated neural reflex control, endocrine control, paracrine control, and combinations of such controls over GI function.

Even the mouth, with its teeth, tongue and pharynx, are involved in the digestive process by physically breaking down food, mixing food with saliva to lubricate the food bolus and digest carbohydrate, and by initiating swallowing. The esophagus is not a passive tube but rather a transport conduit requiring coordinated neural reflexes to move food boluses from the pharynx to the stomach.

The stomach is responsible for both physical and chemical breakdown of food substances. It pro-

duces acid, a proteolytic enzyme pepsin, histamine, HCO_3^-, mucus, and the peptide hormone gastrin. It mixes foodstuffs with acid and pepsin and presents material to the duodenum in a controlled manner. Its function is modulated by several neural and humoral factors.

The small intestine, consisting of the duodenum, jejunum, and ileum is the primary digestive and absorptive organ for carbohydrates, proteins, fats, salts, and H_2O. It also controls and mediates gastric, biliary, and exocrine pancreatic function through the production of peptide hormones and plays an essential role in cholesterol reabsorption and the recycling of bile salts. The large intestine is a primary absorptive site of H_2O and salts. It also is involved in the elimination of waste in the body through the defecation reflex.

Salivary glands are an accessory digestive organ that secrete HCO_3^- containing fluid, mucus, and α-amylase, which initiates carbohydrate digestion in the oral cavity. The liver has many complex functions; its primary digestive function involves the production of bile salts that are necessary for solubilization, transport, and digestion of fats. The liver also processes fats, amino acids, and sugar absorbed from the intestine into various storage forms. The exocrine pancreas is involved in GI function through the production of HCO_3^- to buffer stomach acid entering the duodenum, and by production of myriad enzymes needed to digest proteins, carbohydrates, and fats.

All organs of the alimentary tract share a similar functional morphology in the gut wall. ■ **Fig. 33-1** ■ The inner, or mucosal, lining of the gut is the location of acid production in the stomach, and digestive and absorptive processes in the small and large intestine. Some secretory processes are located in the submucosa, which contains several neural plexi and submucosal ganglia. There is an inner circular layer and an outer longitudinal layer of smooth muscle in the gut wall that mediates the motility of the

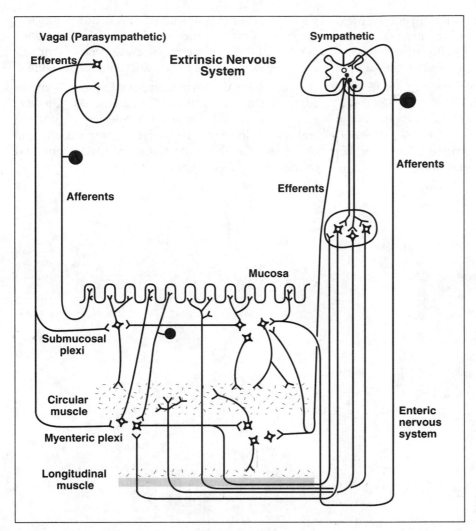

Fig. 33-1
A simplified schematic of the innervation of the gut wall by sympathetic and parasympathetic extrinsic nerves, and their interplay with neural networks associated with the enteric nervous system.

alimentary tract from the esophagus to the rectum. This layer also contains neural plexi called *myenteric ganglia*.

Neural factors that influence GI function are extremely complex and not understood fully. This text will focus on basic neural function in the gastrointestinal system. Neural influences on GI function are elicited through activity in two nervous systems. **Fig. 33-1** An *extrinsic nervous system* involves both branches of the autonomic nervous system and has afferent and efferent tracts in GI organs. As a very broad generalization, parasympathetic afferents stimulate motility and secretion in the alimentary tract, whereas sympathetic efferents have the opposite effect. Few fibers of either ANS branch innervate smooth muscle or secretory cells directly. Instead, the extrinsic nervous system serves to modulate GI function through actions upon the submucosal and myenteric plexi that form the *intrinsic* or *enteric nervous system*.

The enteric system contains over 100 million neurons in the wall of the alimentary tract, or about the same number of neurons that are contained in the spinal cord. Myenteric and submucosal plexi contain nerve cell bodies, axons, dendrites, and nerve endings. Their neuron processes innervate smooth muscle, secretory and absorptive cells, sensory receptors, and other neurons within and outside the plexi. Integration entirely within the enteric nervous system can take place independently; hence, the enteric nervous system has been called the "little brain" of the body.

The myenteric ganglia of the enteric nervous system contain primarily excitatory and inhibitory neurons to the muscle layers of the gut. Interneurons and sensory neurons also present in the myenteric plexi have receptive endings in any of the gut wall layers. Submucosal plexi primarily regulate secretory activities of the glandular, endocrine, and epithelial cells of the alimentary tract. Sensory neurons in the submucosal plexi elicit secretory motor reflexes.

The combined extrinsic and enteric nervous system contribute to the control of vascular tone, GI motility, secretomotor reflexes, hormone release and secretion, acid secretion, and mechano-, chemo- and nociceptive sensory functions. The neurotransmitters involved in these processes involve a tremendous number of different peptides, endorphins, nitric oxide, amines, and cholinergic and adrenergic agents.

The function of the gastrointestinal system is markedly affected by various hormones. All GI hormones are peptides and their role in GI function and interaction with neural GI control systems will be discussed in the context of individual systems and processes in subsequent chapters.

CHAPTER 34

Gastrointestinal Motility

The circular and longitudinal layers of smooth muscle contained within the alimentary tract are responsible for mixing of foodstuffs and the movement of their digestive products through the alimentary canal. Gastrointestinal motility is coordinated to optimize the digestion and absorption of food and to process meals in an appropriate, controlled, and timely manner in the various segments of the alimentary tract. This is accomplished through intrinsic and extrinsic neural reflexes interwoven with hormonal and paracrine control mechanisms.

Smooth muscle cells in the gastrointestinal system show a high degree of cell-to-cell electrical and mechanical coupling. The resting membrane potential in GI smooth muscle oscillates at a frequency ≈ 3/min in the stomach to as high as 12/min in the intestine. These oscillations are called *slow waves* and, except in the stomach, do not generate phasic muscle contraction unless they result in firing of action potentials. As a broad generalization, acetylcholine causes depolarization, increased action potential frequency, and increased smooth muscle motility, whereas norepinephrine has the opposite effect. It should be noted, however, that the enteric nervous system plays a significant role in the regulation of smooth muscle activity and motility in the GI tract and that other neurotransmitters also may modulate GI motility at specific locations (see below).

Motility of the Esophagus and the Process of Swallowing

The primary function of the esophagus is to transport materials from the pharynx to the stomach. This requires coordinated reflex interactions of the extrinsic and enteric nervous systems with the muscle layers of the esophagus. In addition, because the esophagus is located within the subatmospheric thoracic cavity, it must regulate muscle contraction at its pharyngeal and gastric ends in order to prevent entry of air and acidic gastric contents, respectively.

The esophagus is lined with longitudinal and circular layers of muscle that are innervated by branches of the vagus nerve. ■ **Fig. 34-1a** ■ The upper portion of the esophagus contains primarily striated muscle that transitions into entirely smooth muscle by its gastric terminus. The ends of the esophagus are constrained by heavy circular muscle layers that function as sphincters, called the *upper* and *lower esophageal sphincters* (UES and LES). When not involved in the process of swallowing, the LES and UES are closed and the esophagus is flaccid.

The esophagus is not a simple passive "tube" leading from the pharynx to the stomach. Instead, food substances are transported from the pharynx to the stomach by controlled, coordinated reflex activation of esophageal and other muscles that make up the *swallowing reflex*. Swallowing is initiated voluntarily; once food boluses contact tactile receptors in the pharynx, however, swallowing is under the reflex control of the swallowing center in the brain. This center sends signals through the nucleus ambiguous, which sends fibers to the pharynx and striated esophageal muscles, and the dorsal motor nucleus, which sends fibers to the esophageal smooth muscle.

Swallowing is divided into a pharyngeal phase and esophageal phase. The pharyngeal phase lasts <1 second and starts with presentation of a food bolus to the posterior pharynx. This initiates reflexes that pull the soft palate up to the posterior nares prevents exit of food particles through that cause medial approximat ryngeal folds to create ynx. This scree chewed food

The reflex also approximate an covering the glot entry of food par The pharyngeal ph contraction of the ph and relaxation of the upper esophageal sphincter, allowing the food bolus to enter the esophagus.

Upon entry of a food bolus to the esophagus, reflexes from the swallowing center send sequential signals to progressively more distal regions of the esophagus, resulting in a sequential, or peristaltic, wave of contraction. ■ **Fig. 34-1b** ■ The peristaltic wave is controlled primarily by efferent and afferent vagal fibers from the central nervous system, but the enteric nervous system also appears to be involved because bilateral vagotomy does not abolish esophageal peristalsis. Sensory afferents in the esophagus may modulate the strength of the peristaltic wave. If a food bolus does not exit the esophagus in one swallow, the trapped bolus is sensed by the esophagus, afferent signals are sent to the swallowing center, and second reflex peristaltic wave is initiated.

The lower esophageal sphincter has significant myogenic tone; this tone can be increased further by acetylcholine and gastrin or deceased by β-adrenergic stimuli and prostaglandin E2. When the food bolus reaches the lower esophageal sphincter, relaxation of the sphincter occurs via enteric nerve signals, possibly through release of *vasoactive intestinal peptide* (VIP) or nitric oxide. In conjunction with the relaxation of the LES, the orad portion, or *fundus,* of the stomach also relaxes, allowing "acceptance" of the bolus of food in the stomach. This receptive relaxation allows entry of large quantities of foodstuffs into the stomach without a great increase in gastric pressure.

Impairment of swallowing can have serious consequences, including severe pain, aspiration of food particles, and even malnutrition. Cerebral vascular accidents (CVA or strokes), can impair swallowing

■ **Fig. 34-1** ■
(a) A simple representation of the innervation of the pharynx and esophagus. Sensory neurons from the pharynx and esophagus send signals to a swallowing center in the reticular formation of the brain. Outputs pass through the nucleolus ambiguous (NA), the dorsal motor nucleolus (DMN), and nonvagal nuclei (NVN), and are sent to the myenteric plexi of the esophagus as well as the pharynx. UES = upper esophageal sphincter, LES lower esophageal sphincter. (b) An example peristaltic movement in esophagus initiated by swallowing reflex and relaxation of the fundus of the

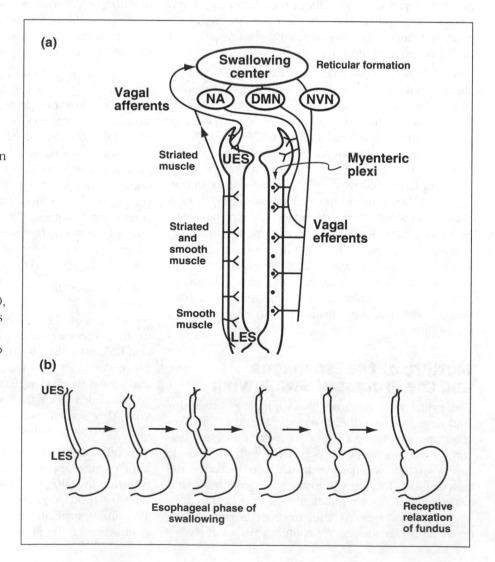

by inhibiting contraction of the pharynx and result in aspiration of food into the respiratory system. Incomplete closure of the LES allows reflux of gastric contents, causing painful spasms of the lower esophagus (heartburn) that mimic the pain of heart attack. Some individuals experience a condition called *achalasia,* in which the lower esophageal sphincter does not always open. These people have great difficulty swallowing, often aspirating food trapped in the esophagus, and can become malnourished.

Gastric Motility

In terms of the activity of its muscle layers, the stomach functions almost as two different organs. ■ **Fig. 34-2a** ■ The orad stomach is characterized by slow waves of low frequency and amplitude with very little contractile activity. The orad stomach is primarily a receptacle for food boluses delivered by the esophagus; food can stay essentially undisturbed in this region for more than an hour after a meal. Contractile activity increases in force and velocity from the mid-body to the pyloric sphincter of the stomach. In fact, this wave of contraction actually reaches the pyloric sphincter before the food bolus. This results in a retropulsion of the gastric contents back toward the mid-stomach region. A thorough mixing of the food bolus with acidic and enzymatic gastric contents results and creates a more efficient breakdown of large food boluses into smaller particles.

After a meal, the stomach may contain a liter of substances that empty into the duodenum over the next several hours. The process of gastric emptying is controlled to deliver substances into the duodenum in a manner that optimizes digestion and absorption

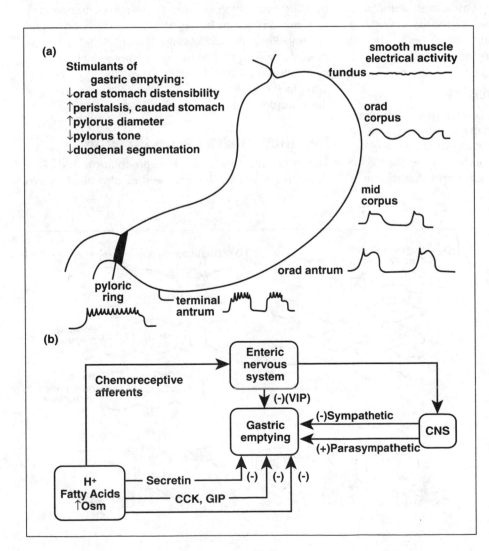

■ **Fig. 34-2** ■

(a) A list of stimulants of gastric emptying. Small upward arrows indicate increase and downward arrows indicate decrease. Smooth muscle electric activity is listed to the right of the stomach and increases from the level of the fundus to the terminal antrum and pyloric ring. (b) Representation of the control of gastric emptying, with (−) meaning inhibitory effect and (+) meaning stimulatory effect.

by the small intestine. ■ **Fig. 34-2b** ■ Distension of the orad portion of the stomach results in emptying of gastric contents into the duodenum, by stimulating peristaltic contractions in the caudal stomach while suppressing pyloric contraction and duodenal motility. Progression of digestion creates fatty acids, hypertonicity, and acid conditions in the duodenum, which then elicit neural and humoral reflexes that feed back and suppress further gastric emptying.

Although the mechanism of these reflexes is not understood completely, it is known that secretin as well as CCK and GIP are produced in the duodenum in response to acidification of duodenal contents and the presence of fatty acids, respectively. These suppress further gastric emptying. These hormonal effects synergize with chemoreceptive afferents in the intestinal wall, which sends signals to the intramural plexi of the enteric nervous system of the stomach. Vagal efferents stimulate the frequency and force of gastric contractions, whereas sympathetic stimulation has the opposite effect. These responses may stimulate and inhibit gastric emptying respectively, but their true physiological role is unknown.

Small Intestinal Motility

Contractions in the intestine occur more frequently (approximately 10–15/min) than those in the stomach. The predominant intestinal movement is *segmentation,* a "back-and-forth" contraction sequence resulting from sequential relaxation and contraction of small adjacent portions of the intestine. ■ **Fig. 34-3a** ■ This activity results in thorough mixing of intestinal contents. It insures good contact of intestinal chyme with digestive enzymes contained in the intestinal mucosa and passes digested products repeatedly over the high surface area of mucosal villi and microvilli, thereby enhancing product absorption.

Peristalsis occurs in the intestine and helps move digested contents down the alimentary tract. Peristaltic contractions consist of short-range (10–15 cm) contractions and are stimulated by mucosal irritation common in infectious diarrhea. Approximately every 75 to 90 minutes, a burst of electrical activity and wave of contraction proceeds from the stomach, through the small intestine, to the ileocecal junction. This activity, called the *migrating myoelectric complex* (MMC), is more vigorous during the interdigestive period and functions to sweep the small bowel clean of any remaining food particles left in the alimentary tract between meals. An intact enteric nerve system is known to be necessary for this coordinated activity. Recently, circulating levels of the hormone motilin, which is produced in the stomach, have been shown to correlate with the waves of contractions in the MMC, although the exact mechanism of this complex is not well understood.

Motility in the Large Intestine

The large intestine exhibits segmentation and peristaltic movements; the large intestine also displays two

■ **Fig. 34-3** ■
(a) Segmentation in the small and large intestine. (b) Haustration in the large intestine. (c) Mass movements in the large intestine resulting in sudden translocation of intestinal contents over large distances.

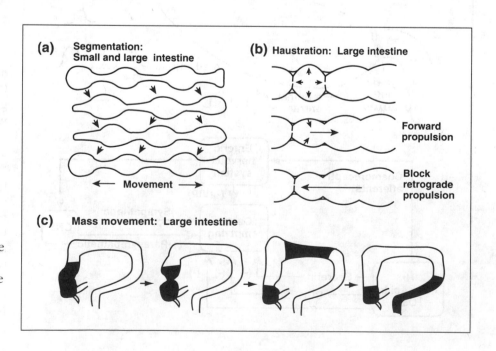

special types of contractile functions. ■ **Figs. 34-3b and 34-3c** ■ *Haustral movements,* unique forms of colonic motility, are characterized by a pinching of a segment of the colon at both an orad and caudad location that sections off one small portion of the bowel. As contraction continues, pressure increases in this portion and, when followed by reflex release of distal muscle tone, results in propulsion of the colonic contents in the caudad direction. Haustration also may be an important means of preventing retropulsion of colonic contents.

Most propulsion in the colon proceeds by a process called *mass movement.* ■ **Fig. 34-3c** ■ This is a reflex sequence starting with cessation of segmentation and haustration in a section of the colon followed by a large, sweeping, peristaltic-like contraction that moves large boluses of intestinal content toward the rectum.

Intestinal Reflexes

GI motility is strongly influenced by interactions and reflexes involving the extrinsic and enteric nervous systems, which contain an evergrowing number of different neurotransmitter and neurocrine substances. Details about the role of these neuro/endocrine substances in the elegant control of GI motility during digestion remain to be resolved. Certain important GI reflexes have been described, however.

There is an overall tendency for substances to be moved in the intestine from an orad to a caudad direction. A bolus presented to the intestine stimulates reflex orad contraction and caudad relaxation of the intestinal wall; this is called the *law of the intestine.* The small and large intestines display intestino-intestinal and colono-colonic reflexes in response to overdistension; when one area of the small or large intestine is overdistended, the rest of the intestine relaxes. These reflexes are known to require extrinsic nerves and may be partly mediated by branches of the sympathetic nervous system.

Gastroileac and gastrocolic reflexes are initiated by increased stretch in the stomach, such as that occurs with a meal, and result in reflex increases in motility in the terminal ileum and in the proximal and distal colon. They also increase mass movements. In addition, distension of the ileum suppresses gastric motility (the ileogastric reflex), which may prevent premature gastric emptying into an already full small intestine.

Finally, significant amounts of solid material remain in the terminal colon after all digestion, H_2O, and mineral reabsorption has taken place. The colonic contents at this point weigh about 100 to 200 g and are about 65% water with undigested particulate matter (i.e., cellulose fiber), mucus, intestinal secretions, epithelial cells, indoles, pigments, and bacterial products. These remaining products must be eliminated from the body as feces.

When colonic contents empty into the rectum, which otherwise is usually empty, they distend the rectal wall and elicit the *intrinsic reflex.* This reflex results in stimulation of efferent signals in the myenteric plexus of the rectum, initiating a peristaltic wave in the colon and rectum. This wave forces the remaining contents toward the anus, where they cause relaxation of the internal anal sphincter. This intrinsic reflex will result in defecation only in individuals who do not have control over the external anal sphincter, such as infants or individuals with spinal cord injuries. Defecation otherwise is under conscious control mediated by voluntary relaxation of the external anal sphincter.

CHAPTER 35

Salivary Secretion

Proper function of the salivary glands is not essential for survival even though salivary secretions facilitate the digestive process in several ways. These glands produce *mucins (glycoproteins)* that help lubricate food and facilitate swallowing. They also produce *ptyalin,* an α-amylase that cleaves the α1,4 glycosidic linkages in glycogen, and a *lingual-lipase,* which aids in lipid digestion in the mouth. Saliva contains lactoferrin, an antibacterial agent. Not surprisingly, an inability to produce saliva results in the acceleration of dental decay. A binding protein for the immunoglobin IGA, which helps transmission

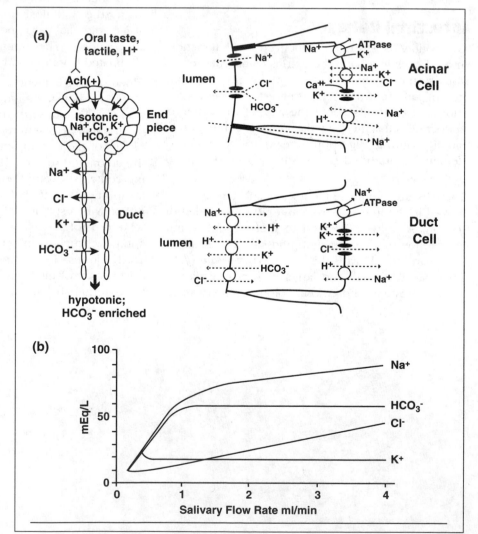

■ Fig. 35-1■

(a) Events involved in the production of saliva in the salivary ducts. Salivary secretion is stimulated by taste and tactile stimulation of the mouth through signals sent via the vagus nerve. The cellular mechanisms for these processes are listed at the top right. Passive transport is indicated by dashed arrows and active transport by solid arrows. (b) The effect of salivary flow rate on the composition of saliva.

of antibodies to nursing infants, also is present in saliva.

The salivary glands produce a fluid that is rich in K^+ and HCO_3^- in an aqueous volume of as much as 1000 mL/day. This is a high output for such a small organ. Metabolism and blood flow to salivary glands consequently is high relative to their weight. The production of large amounts of HCO_3^--rich fluid dilutes and cools ingested liquids and provides buffer for acidic substances in the mouth (hence the phenomenon of increased salivary secretion prior to vomiting).

Formation of saliva is a two-stage process. ■ **Fig. 35-1a** ■ A primary secretion is produced in the secretory endpiece of the salivary gland and contains amylase and an ionic composition similar to plasma. This is not a plasma filtrate, however, and may instead arise from active transport processes. Secondary active transport of Na^+, K^+ and Cl^- occurs into the cell from the serosal surface; this forms an electrochemical gradient for Cl^- to exit the cell into the acinar lumen. A Na^+/H^+ counter-transport at the serosal surface alkalinizes the cell and promotes HCO_3^- accumulation, which then exits with Cl^-, through specific channels in the apical membrane. These processes appear to be stimulated by increases in intracellular Ca^{++} and cyclic AMP.

The primary secretion is modified as it travels down the salivary duct, with a net removal of Na^+ and Cl^- and addition of K^+ and HCO_3^-. As shown in ■ **Fig. 35-1a** ■, a Na^+/H^+ countertransport at the serosal and luminal surfaces alkalizes the duct cell and promotes HCO_3^- accumulation, which then exits in exchange for Cl^- at the luminal surface. K^+ also exits the cell at this point in exchange for H^+ ions. This ion transport mechanism is enhanced by aldosterone. The removal of Na^+ from the system exceeds the addition of K^+; saliva is always hypotonic to plasma.

The composition of saliva is affected by secretory flow rate as shown in ■ **Fig. 35-1b** ■. Increased flow increases the alkalinity of the saliva to about 8.0, although its osmolality never exceeds more than 70% that of plasma. Salivary secretion is purely under neural reflex control, with the parasympathetic nervous system providing the principal stimulant signals. This system is activated by the sensation of taste, especially sour (i.e., H^+), and tactile stimuli in the tongue and mouth. Odors, nausea, or emotional considerations interacting with higher CNS centers also may stimulate or inhibit secretion. Sympathetic fibers to salivary glands primarily innervate blood vessels, although they appear to have a small, transient stimulant effect to produce a saliva rich in ptyalin, HCO_3^-, and K^+.

CHAPTER 36

Gastric Acid Secretion and Its Control

Cellular Mechanisms of Gastric Secretion

The gastric mucosa is responsible for secreting seven important substances, the most notable of which is acid from parietal cells in the gastric mucosa. ■ **Fig. 36-1a** ■ In addition, the gastric mucosa contains peptic cells that secrete pepsinogen, the precursor to the proteolytic enzyme pepsin, mucous cells that secrete mucus, and G cells that secrete the peptide hormone gastrin. The stomach also secretes H_2O and electrolytes, notably HCO_3^-, and intrinsic factor, which is a protein required for proper absorption of vitamin B_{12}, an essential factor for DNA replication in the development of red blood cells.

The cellular mechanism responsible for gastric acid secretion is depicted in ■ **Fig. 36-1b** ■ . First, carbonic anhydrase inside the cell catalyzes the conversion of carbonic acid to HCO_3^- and H^+. The parietal cells on their apical surface possess unique H^+/K^+ ATPase pumps that pump H^+ into the stomach lumen and K^+ into the cell against electrochemical gradients. This pumping of H^+ leaves in the cell an excess of HCO_3^-, which flows down its electrochemical gradient in exchange for Cl^-.

Cl^- concentrated in the cell is believed to exit into the stomach lumen by facilitated transport and creates an electronegative gradient in the lumen relative to the serosal surface of -60 to -80 mV. The energy for continual transport of Cl^- against this electrical gradient ultimately originates with the H^+/K^+ ATPase, which keeps intracellular HCO_3^- high, creating a driving force for the exit of Cl^- into the stomach lumen. The overall effect of these processes is to produce HCl in exchange for metabolic waste (CO_2) and reabsorption of $NaHCO_3$.

Mucins, along with quantities of NaCl, H_2O, K^+, and HCO_3^-, are secreted in the stomach by surface gastric epithelial cells, to form a mucous gel over the gastric mucosa. ■ **Fig. 36-1a** ■ The mucus layer traps secreted HCO_3^- and prevents it from mixing with the contents of the gastric lumen. The mucus/HCO_3^- combination forms a physical/chemical buffer barrier that protects the mucosa from HCl, without neutralizing H^+ in contact with food in the

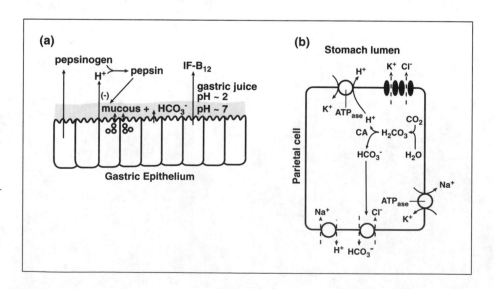

■ **Fig. 36-1** ■
(a) An overview of gastric secretion. (b) Cellular process of acid secretion by the gastric mucosal cells. Dashed line indicates passive processes, and CA = carbonic anhydrase.

gastric lumen. Further protection to stomach integrity is provided by the tight junctions between gastric epithelial cells that prevent back diffusion of H^+ into the serosal layers and circulation of the stomach. These tight junctions are destroyed by ethanol and such destruction is causative for gastric ulcers associated with chronic alcoholism.

Pepsinogen, the precursor of the proteolytic enzyme pepsin, is secreted into the stomach lumen, where it is cleaved by HCl. Low stomach pH favors the formation of pepsin. Pepsin itself is most active at a pH <3 and is responsible for digesting as much as 20% of protein in a typical meal. Importantly, pepsin degrades the stomach mucus barrier. Failure to continually produce mucins in the stomach thus results in gastric ulcer formation.

Stimulation of Gastric Acid Secretion

Acid secretion by the gastric mucosa is stimulated by three secretogogues: ■ **Fig. 36-2** ■

1. Acetylcholine released from cholinergic nerve terminals,
2. Gastrin released from G cells in the gastric mucosa, and
3. Histamine, released from enterochromaffin-like cells (ECL) in the stomach.

There is a significant synergism between these secretogogues. Histamine potentiates the actions of both gastrin and acetylcholine and causes the effect of gastrin and/or acetylcholine on H^+ to be much

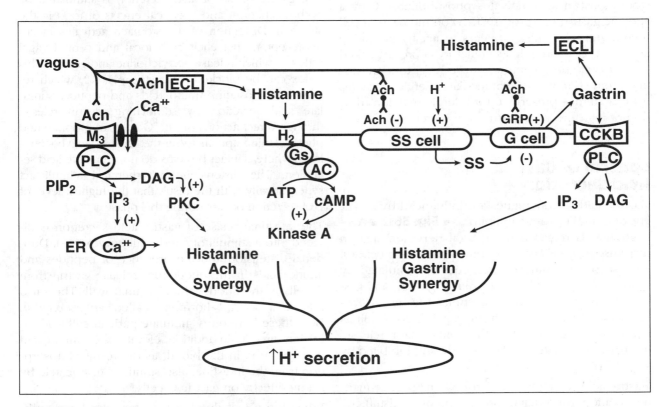

■ **Fig. 36-2** ■

Processes affecting gastric acid secretion at the cellular level. Small upward arrows indicate increase, (−) shows inhibition, and (+) shows stimulation. Abbreviations are as follows: Ach = acetylcholine, M_3 = acetylcholine muscarinic receptor, PLC = phospholipase C, DAG = diacylglycerol, PIP_2 = phosphotidylinositol-bis-phosphate, IP_3 = inositol triphosphate, PKC = protein kinase C, ECL = enterochromaffin-like cell, H_2 = histamine$_2$ receptor, G_S = stimulatory G-protein, AC = adenylate cyclase, SS = somatostatin, G = gastrin, CCKB = gastrin receptor, GRP = gastrin-releasing peptide. (See text for complete explanation.)

more than the sum of the individual effects. This synergism has two results:

1. Blocking one secretagogue will inhibit response to another, and
2. Specific blockers of either acetylcholine or histamine alone are unable to prevent HCl secretion.

Various intracellular mechanisms are believed to mediate the actions of the secretogogues on H^+ secretion. Acetylcholine activates Ca^{++} channels and phospholipase C, resulting in increased transmembrane influx of Ca^{++} and IP_3 stimulated release of Ca^{++} from the endoplasmic reticulum. Protein kinase-C and Ca^{++} from this process appear to activate proteins involved with the stimulation of acid secretion by mechanisms that are not well understood. Gastrin also activates phospholipase-C by a specific gastrin receptor (CCK-B) on the parietal cell membrane. Histamine appears to act by activating adenyl cyclase through a stimulatory G-protein linked to H_2 histamine receptors. These receptors are distinct from H_1 receptors that mediate allergic reactions. Antihistamines prescribed for allergic reactions thus do not interfere with gastric acid secretion.

Control of Gastric Acid Secretion

Gastric acid secretagogues are influenced by a variety of stimulants and inhibitors. ■ **Fig. 36-2** ■ Acetylcholine is released from vagal nerve endings in response to a variety of afferent signals (see below). Release of histamine by ECL cells is stimulated by acetylcholine from the vagus nerve, gastrin, and gastric injury. Gastrin release is stimulated by *gastrin-releasing peptide* (GRP) from vagal nerve endings and inhibited by somatostatin. Somatostatin release, in turn, is stimulated by H^+ directly and inhibited by acetylcholine.

Gastric acid secretion is controlled in a precise manner to allow for efficient processing of foodstuffs by the stomach. This control can be viewed best by examining gastric acid secretion in response to a typical meal. ■ **Fig. 36-3** ■

During a meal, gastric acid secretion is divided into cephalic, gastric, and intestinal phases. The cephalic phase of gastric acid secretion is initiated by the sight, smell, or taste of food. HCl secretory rate reaches 40% of maximum during this phase. The increase in gastric HCl secretion is mediated entirely by vagal reflexes, with both vagal-vagal and intermural neurons involved. HCl secretion is stimulated by the release of acetylcholine directly onto parietal cells, acetylcholine stimulated release of histamine, and by vagal-mediated release of gastrin via gastrin-releasing peptide.

GRP-mediated release of gastrin during the cephalic phase is responsible for the fact that atropine (a cholinergic muscarinic receptor blocker) will inhibit, but not block, the cephalic phase of gastric acid secretion, whereas total blockade occurs with bilateral vagotomy. This phase of gastric acid secretion is inhibited by low pH in the antrum, which suppresses HCl secretion directly and which stimulates somatostatin release. The latter inhibits gastrin release and uncouples its synergism with histamine.

The gastric phase of acid secretion is stimulated by both mechanical and chemical effects of food in the stomach. Distention of the stomach activates mechanoreceptors that elicit both local and central vagal reflexes, which release acetylcholine and gastrin. This reflex can be blocked by gastric pH <2, which releases somatostatin. Amino acids and peptides stimulate acid secretion by stimulating gastrin release through direct actions on the G cells; tryptophan and phenylalanine appear to be the most effective stimulates, whereas intact proteins do not stimulate acid secretion. The distension and chemical stimuli act synergistically with the result that the highest level of HCl secretion occurs during this phase.

The intestinal phase of gastric acid secretion is divided into a stimulatory and inhibitory period. Duodenal distension and the presence of peptides and amino acids in the duodenum release gastrin from G cells in the duodenal and jejunal wall. They also release a second hormone called *enterooxyntin*. Both these hormones stimulate parietal cell acid secretion directly. In addition, elevations in amino acid concentration in the blood, as the result of absorption from the intestine, also stimulate gastric acid by acting directly on gastric G cells.

When the pH of duodenal contents becomes sufficiently acidic (pH <3) and fat products and hyperosmolality also appear at this location, hormonal and neural reflexes are brought into play that inhibit gastric acid secretion. Duodenal H^+ releases secretin from the duodenal mucosa into the bloodstream. Secretin inhibits gastrin release and acid secretion directly. Duodenal acid inhibits HCl secretion via a local reflex as well as through the release of bulbogastrone, which inhibits the action of gastrin.

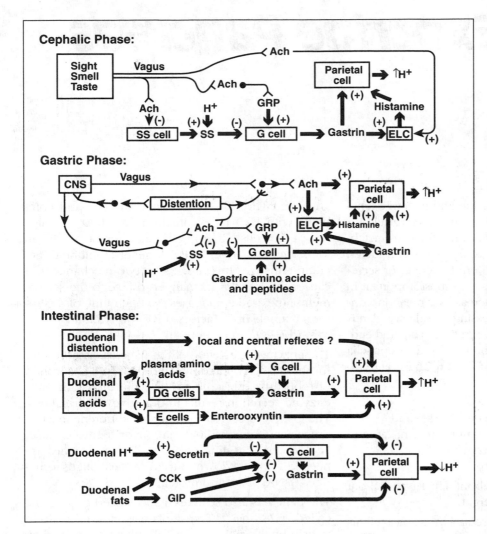

Cephalic Phase:

Gastric Phase:

Intestinal Phase:

■ Fig. 36-3 ■
Depiction of the events involved in stimulation of acid secretion during the cephalic, gastric, and intestinal phases of digestion. Forked lines represent nerve terminals, (+) represents stimulation, and (−) represents inhibition. Heavy arrows link effects resulting from change in the preceding variable. Ach = acetylcholine, GRP = gastrin-releasing peptide, G = gastrin, SS = somatostatin, ELC = histamine-secreting cell, DG = duodenal gastrin-secreting cells, GIP = gastrointestinal inhibitory peptide. (See text for complete description.)

Fatty acids release gastric inhibitory peptide (GIP) and CCK from the duodenum. GIP inhibits hydrochloric acid secretion directly and secondarily through the inhibition of gastrin release. CCK has similar amino acid homology with the functional site of gastrin and binds weakly to the gastrin receptor, thus competitively inhibiting gastrin stimulate HCl secretion.

Several nonphysiological factors are known to alter gastric acid secretion. For example, decreased glucose concentration in cerebral arterial blood stimulates acid secretion. Nicotine, through stimulation of the central nervous system, stimulates acid secretion. This may be the mechanism of higher incidences of ulcers in cigarette smokers. Caffeine stimulates acid release. This and other methylxanthines (i.e., theophylline in tea) release intercellular stores of calcium and inhibit cAMP phosphodiesterases. These increase intracellular Ca^{++} and cAMP levels, which may stimulate cellular HCl generation. Interestingly, decaffeinated coffee also stimulates acid secretion, as does ethanol. Conversely, opiates such as opium and morphine suppress HCl secretion.

Secretion of Pepsinogen

The control pepsinogen secretion is similar to that of HCl in the stomach except that secretin and CCK stimulate pepsinogen secretion. Also, β-adrenergic agonists, acetylcholine, and CCK are known secretogogues for pepsinogen, but the exact mechanism of control of pepsinogen secretion is not known.

CHAPTER 37

The Exocrine Pancreas

The pancreas has both endocrine and exocrine functions. Although its endocrine function related to production of insulin and glucagon influences metabolism of glucose and fatty acids, this is not considered a purely gastrointestinal function. Exocrine, or secretory, functions of the pancreas are most important in terms of digestion. The pancreas is similar in construction and secretory processing to salivary glands in that it produces a primary secretion in a gland endpiece (acinar cells) that is modified by duct epithelia before it is excreted. ■ **Fig. 37-1a** ■ There are two types of pancreatic secretions:

1. An aqueous, HCO_3^--enriched phase, and
2. An enzymatic phase containing protein, fat, and carbohydrate digesting enzymes.

Flow of pancreatic juice is about 1 L/day, or about 10 times the organ's own weight.

The aqueous portion of secretion by acinar cells is similar to that in salivary glands except that H_2O and HCO_3^- secretion is stimulated by secretin. In the duct, the pancreatic juice is enriched with HCO_3^-; enrichment is enhanced by high rate of juice production in exchange for Cl^- in the juice. Cl^- secretion is important in the duct. This is markedly impaired in cystic fibrosis and results in severe decrease in secretion of pancreatic juice from the duct. Without this secretion, pancreatic enzymes concentrate and eventually precipitate in the pancreatic ducts, blocking outflow and eventually destroying the pancreatic glands.

The mechanism of HCO_3^- enrichment in the duct is not well understood, but it appears that the HCO_3^- originates from the plasma rather than cell sources directly; see the right portion of ■ **Fig. 37-1a** ■. This process is called the *acidification of blood*. At the serosal membrane of duct cells, H^+ ions are secreted into the blood in exchange for Na^+. There they combine with circulating HCO_3^- to form CO_2

and H_2O. The CO_2 diffuses into the cell and combines with H_2O to eventually form HCO_3^-, which leaves the cells either in exchange for Cl^- or via an ion-specific channel at the luminal membrane. Secretin enhances this process by two mechanisms: it causes the Na^+/H^+ exchanger to fuse to the serosal membrane, and it increases the open time of the anion channel. Both factors drive the overall process toward HCO_3^- secretion.

The enzymatic secretion of the pancreas is necessary for the normal breakdown and therefore absorption of foodstuffs by the intestine. Failure of pancreatic enzyme secretion results in digestive abnormalities. The pancreas secretes numerous different inactive proenzyme forms of lipid, carbohydrate, nucleic acid, and protein-digesting enzymes. These enzymes are needed for breakdown of triglycerides, oligosaccharides, DNA, RNA, and proteins.

The pancreas also secretes a specialized proenzyme called *trypsinogen*. Trypsinogen is cleaved to form trypsin by the action of an enterokinase secreted by the duodenum. (This kinase is not a phosphate kinase but rather a proteolytic enzyme.) Trypsin's essential function is to convert the proenzyme forms of pancreatic digestive enzymes into active forms in the pancreatic juice. The pancreatic juice normally contains a trypsin inhibitor that prevents autodigestion of this organ.

Control of Pancreatic Exocrine Secretion

Both hormonal and neural influences modulate pancreatic secretion. ■ **Fig. 37-1b** ■ Secretin stimulates the aqueous form, whereas CCK stimulates the enzymatic form of pancreatic secretion. During digestion, pancreatic secretion can be divided into cephalic, gastric, and intestinal phases, but stimulation is weak in the cephalic and gastric phases. This results from release of gastrin, which has amino acid homology to

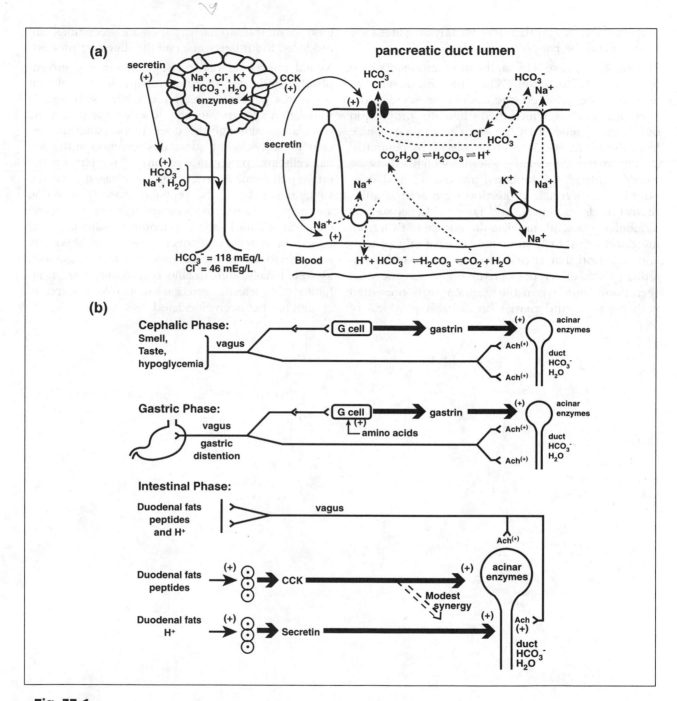

■ Fig. 37-1 ■

(a) Left: Representation of exocrine pancreas secretion by pancreatic acinar cells and ductal epithelium. The (+) indicates stimulation. Right: Effects of secretin on pancreatic duct cells. Bicarbonate secretion into the duct lumen results from the acidification of blood; see text for explanation. (b) A representation of factors affecting pancreatic secretion during the cephalic, gastric, and intestinal phases of digestion. Forked lines represent nerve endings, (+) means stimulation, and (−) means inhibition. Heavy arrows link effects resulting from change in the preceding variable. Ach = acetylcholine, G = gastrin.

portions of CCK and therefore weakly activates CCK receptors on the pancreatic glands.

The intestinal phase is by far the most important phase of pancreatic secretion. When the duodenal contents become acidified, the duodenum secretes the hormone secretin, which then stimulates production of a large volume of HCO_3^--enriched aqueous juice from the pancreas. This obviously helps neutralize acidity in the duodenal contents, which otherwise would damage the duodenal mucosa. (The duodenum has no intrinsic protection from acid assault.) Amino acids, peptides, and fatty acids, as well as monoglycerides, all stimulate the release of CCK from the duodenum. CCK stimulates release of a pancreatic secretion that is rich in enzymes and also potentiates the effect of secretin on pancreatic duct secretion. Thus, when the duodenum is presented with peptides and partial breakdown products of food from the stomach, pancreatic secretions are produced to further accelerate the digestive process.

Neural effects on pancreatic secretion are incompletely understood. Parasympathetic stimulation stimulates pancreatic secretion where sympathetic stimulation appears primarily to effect the pancreatic vasculature, although this does inhibit pancreatic secretion. Acetylcholine stimulates secretion in the acinar cells and potentiates actions of secretin on the duct epithelium. Acetylcholine is released from the vagus nerve during the cephalic phase of secretion and may play a role in vasovagal reflexes connecting chemical stimuli in the duodenum to stimulation of pancreatic enzyme and aqueous secretion. Vagotomy is known to decrease pancreatic secretion by as much as 50%. Finally, somatostatin is recognized as an inhibitor of pancreatic secretion but its role in secretory control has not been elucidated.

The liver has many important physiological functions. Most of these involve biochemical processes of synthesis, storage, detoxification, etc., that generally are covered in detail in courses of biochemistry. Details of all the chemical processes that occur in the liver will not be presented in this chapter.

A partial list of important hepatic functions is shown in ■ **Fig. 38-1a** ■ . The liver plays an important role in glucose regulation, as a site of glycogen synthesis and storage, glycogenolysis, and gluconeogenesis, all of which are under hormonal control. In addition, the liver takes up glycerol and fatty acids, synthesizes and secretes lipoprotein necessary for cholesterol transport, and provides a source of cholesterol for steroid synthesis. The liver forms ketones that can be used for energy sources in metabolism. In the liver, ammonia, a toxic substance formed from catabolism of amino acids, is converted to less toxic urea, which can be excreted by the kidney. Synthesis of all nonessential amino acids and all plasma proteins, except gamma globulins, occurs in the liver. The liver is an important storage site of vitamins A, D, and B_{12}.

The liver is a primary biochemical "factory" for th degradation and excretion of hormones, steroi catecholamines, and peptides, as well as for transformation and excretion of drugs and toy can inactivate, activate, detoxify, or intoxify ety of substances. Generally, transformatic upon drugs and chemicals by the liver ar to increase their H_2O solubility so that r excreted from the body more easily by

The primary digestive function of production, secretion, and reupta emulsifies lipids. This emulsificat requirement for proper diges forms that can be absorbed by more than half of the dry weight posed of bile acids that are synthesize lesterol. Bile is an amphoteric molecule, mea

has both a hydrophilic and h droxyl, carboxyl, and peptide are all on one surface of the hydrophilic portion. ■ **Fig**.

Bile acids are conjugated rine, which increases t' values of these amino that they are almost solutions, allowing Bile salts coalesc lipid sides facin the outside ac celle is com increase th celle. This ported i

Bile is body 2-n m

■ **Fig. 3**
(a) A sim important functions (b) Bile sal Pathic com form cylindr In aqueous s celles contain acids, phospho lesterol, and m erides. (See text details.)

into the canaliculi as of the bile duct resem patocytes secrete an iso ulated by CCK wher secretion with HCO_3^- w duodenum. Bile is not continually no bile is diverted into the gall to 20 mL of bile is stored one time. A sphincter calle prevents bile stored ing the duodenum. Na^+ trans membrane of gallbladder cells traction of H_2O from the blad

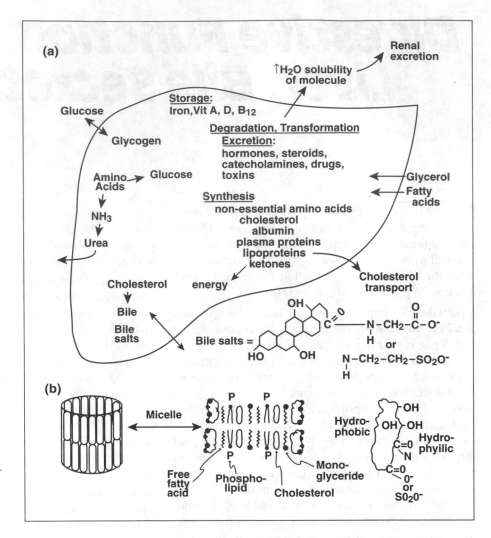

(a)

Renal
excretion

↑H_2O solubility
of molecule

Glucose

Storage:
Iron, Vit A, D, B_{12}

Glycogen

Degradation, Transformation
Excretion:
hormones, steroids,
catecholamines, drugs,
toxins

Glycerol
Fatty
acids

Amino → Glucose
Acids

NH_3

Synthesis
non-essential amino acids
cholesterol
albumin
plasma proteins
lipoproteins
ketones

Urea

Cholesterol   energy

Cholesterol
transport

Cholesterol

Bile

Bile
salts

Bile salts =

(b)

Micelle

Hydro-
phobic

Hydro-
phyilic

Free
fatty
acid

Phospho-
lipid

Cholesterol

Mono-
glyceride

3-1 ■

ple overview of
physiological
of the liver.
s are amphi-
ounds and
cal micelles.
lutions, mi-
free fatty
lipids, cho-
noglyc-
for

well. The secretory processes
le those of the pancreas; he-
tonic primary secretion stim-
as duct cells enrich the
en stimulated by secretin.

directly secreted into the
the interdigestive period,
ladder. Approximately 15
the gallbladder at any
the *sphincter of Oddi*
all bladder from enter-
port at the basolateral
results in osmotic ex-
er interior, resulting

in a five- to twentyfold effective increase in bile
concentration in the gallbladder. This concentrating
effect promotes micelle formation.

During the intestinal phase of digestion, fat products stimulate the release of CCK, which then stimulates gallbladder contraction, relaxation of the
sphincter of Oddi, and hence emptying of bile into
the duodenum. Thus, when fat breakdown products
are present in the duodenum, a hormonal reflex is
initiated that increases the solubility of these lipids
in the otherwise aqueous environment of the duodenum. Release of secretin, stimulated by presence
of acid in the duodenum, stimulates an aqueous
HCO_3^- secretion in the gallbladder ducts, which

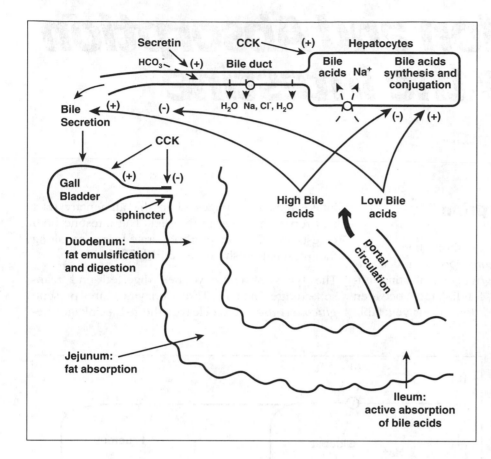

■ Fig. 38-2 ■
A representation of bile production and secretion by the liver, release of bile by the gall bladder into the duodenum, and reabsorption of bile acids into the portal circulation from the terminal ileum. The (+) symbol represents stimulation, (−) represents inhibition, and dashed lines represent passive movements of molecules.

adds to HCO_3^- from the pancreas, thus helping to neutralize duodenal H^+.

During digestion of a typical meal, bile acids are recycled in the gastrointestinal system by the *enterohepatic circulation*. **■ Fig. 38-2 ■** Dehydroxylation and deconjugation of bile acids by bacteria in the gut increase their lipid solubility and facilitate their reabsorption in the terminal ileum. Once reabsorbed, they enter the portal circulation. When the concentration of bile acids in the portal blood is high, secretion of bile acids in the liver is stimulated while, simultaneously, synthesis of new bile acids is inhibited.

Near the end of the digestive process, CCK levels fall, resulting in closure of the sphincter of Oddi and diversion of bile secretion into the gallbladder. Concentration of bile acids in the portal circulation, and thus those reaching the liver, begin to fall. This fall inhibits further secretion of bile acids while simultaneously stimulating their synthesis *de novo* in the liver. Overall, bile salts are recycled at least two times during a typical meal.

CHAPTER 39

Digestion and Absorption in the Intestine

Digestion and Absorption of Carbohydrates

The major sources of complex carbohydrates in the diet are the plant starches *amylopectin* and *cellulose,* and the animal starch *glycogen.* Intestinal enzymes cannot digest the β-1,4 linkages between glucoses in cellulose. This portion of our vegetable intake remains undigested in the alimentary tract and represents *fiber* in the diet. The intestine both digests and reabsorbs carbohydrate fragments along the intestinal brush border. ■ **Fig. 39-1a** ■

The types of carbohydrates digested and reabsorbed are limited. Three enzymes are present: *glucoamylase,* which cleaves the α-1,4 linkages be-

■ **Fig. 39-1** ■

(a) Handling of carbohydrates by the intestine. Enzymes on the intestinal brush border metabolize complex carbohydrates to release glucose (G), galactose (Ga), and fructose (F). These monosaccharides are reabsorbed by the brush border cells by passive cotransport or facilitated diffusion mechanisms. (b) Handling of proteins and peptides by the intestine. Proteins are broken down into peptides of greater than four amino acid residues by pancreatic proteases. Peptidases on the intestinal brush border further hydrolyze these peptides, which then can be transported into the intestinal cells for further reduction to single amino acids by intercellular intestinal enzymes. Single amino acids also can be transported across the cell membrane. Dashed lines signify passive reabsorptive processes.

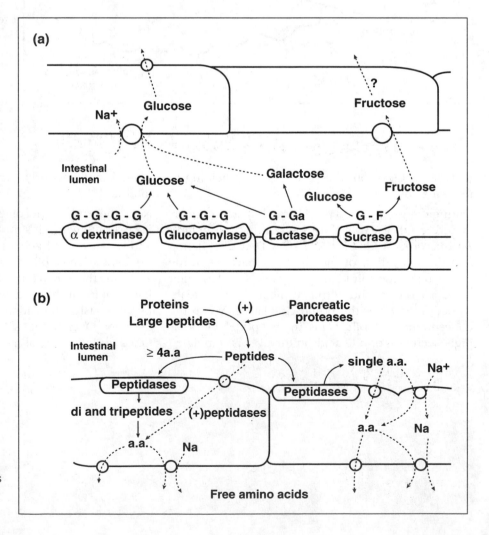

tween joined glucose molecules and is identical to pancreatic and salivary amylase; *α-dextrinase,* the only enzyme able to cleave the *α*-1,6 branch linkages in glycogen; and *sucrase,* which cleaves the glucose-fructose linkages in sucrose. Brush border transport proteins carry only the monosaccharides *glucose, galactose,* and *fructose.* Glucose and galactose are cotransported by these carriers with Na+, and the two sugars compete for the same carrier. Na+ stimulates absorption of glucose and galactose and the sugars reciprocally stimulate the absorption of Na+. Fructose transport does not involve a Na+ mechanism.

Monosaccharides leave the intestinal cells and enter the bloodstream by facilitated diffusion. Sugar absorption is higher in the duodenum and upper jejunum relative to that in more distal parts of the intestine. Malabsorption of carbohydrate invariably leads to osmotic retention of H_2O in the gut, excess bacterial production, and bacterial degradation products, resulting in bowel irritation, hypermotility, and diarrhea. Lactose malabsorption, hence *lactose intolerance,* results from lack of *lactase* (the enzyme responsible for digestion of milk sugar) and is common in about 50% of the adult population. Other, rarer forms of genetic defects in the glucose carrier also are associated with glucose malabsorption.

Digestion and Absorption of Proteins

Protein digestion results from the actions of proteases originating from the pancreas, the intestinal brush border, and the cytosol of intestinal mucosal cells. The enzymatic selectivity favors smaller peptides as one travels from the intestinal lumen to the brush border and into the cytosol. ■ **Fig. 39-1b** ■

Only small peptides and individual amino acids are transported into the cell. This occurs by numerous different brush border transport proteins. These proteins reabsorb amino acids and di- and tripeptides by secondary active transport with Na+, or by basic facilitated diffusion. Absorbed di- and tripeptides are cleaved to single amino acids by proteases in the cytosol. Large peptides and proteins are not absorbed by the intestines; some peptides diffuse enough into the circulation to elicit immunological reactions. Single amino acids within the cytosol cross the *basolateral membrane* into the circulation by a variety or sodium-dependent and -independent transport proteins.

Digestion and Absorption of Fats

All stages of fat processing during digestion are complicated by the poor H_2O solubility of lipids. Fats often form an oily upper layer in the stomach and are the last to exit the gastric chamber during digestion. Lipases in the intestine break down complex fats into free fatty acids and their lipid components (e.g., triglycerides into 2-monoglycerides, cholesterol esters into cholesterol, and phospholipids into lysolecithins). These breakdown products enter bile acid micelles. ■ **Fig. 39-2** ■ Micelles containing monoglycerides, cholesterol, and phospholipids are believed to diffuse among the microvilli of the intestinal brush border in an *unstirred layer,* bringing lipids close to the cell surface for easier diffusion across the lipid cell membrane. There are no known transport proteins for lipid; lipids are absorbed across the brush border through simple diffusion.

The eventual transport of lipid digestion products into the circulation is complicated. The digestion products are reformed within the intestinal cells into the same complex lipids from which they originated. This process occurs along the smooth endoplasmic reticulum of the intestinal mucosa cells. Triglycerides, cholesterol esters, phospholipids, and cholesterol, along with lipoproteins, are combined inside the cell to form chylomicrons which, in a manner analogous to bile salts, have a lipid core surrounded by a hydrophilic (in this case protein) exterior. The chylomicrons are transported out of the cell by exocytosis and taken up by lacteals inside the intestinal villi. These lacteals are blind-end lymph channels. Chylomicrons are transported in the lymph and then into the circulation via the thoracic duct.

Malabsorption of lipids occurs more frequently than malabsorption of amino acids or carbohydrates. Pancreatic lipase deficiency from pancreatic injury or disease is a common form of lipid malabsorption. Without this lipase, 2-monoglycerides and lysolecithins are not available for micelle formation and hence emulsification of lipids cannot occur. By extension, any factor that impairs emulsification, such as a decrease in conjugated bile salt availability, results in lipid malabsorption. This can be caused by a biliary fistula; obstruction of the gallbladder from gallstones; ileectomy that removes the primary intestinal reabsorption site for bile acids; and bacterial deconjugation. Lipid malabsorption also occurs whenever the surface area available for diffusion of lipids

■ Fig. 39-2 ■
Handling of fat by the intestine. Free fatty acids, monoglycerides, lysophospholipids, fatty acids, and cholesterol are in equilibrium with micelles at the brush border of the intestine. These compounds recombine with free fatty acids in the intestinal cells to form triglycerides, phospholipids, and cholesterol esters. These are combined with β-lipoprotein in the form of large chylomicrons, which are removed from the intestine by exocytosis into the interstitial fluid, to be reabsorbed by specialized lymph channels, called lacteals, in the intestinal villi.

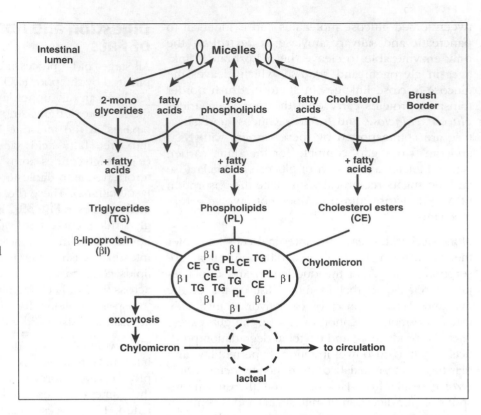

is reduced. This results from surgical bowel resection, or from diseases such as tropical sprue and gluten enteropathy that destroy the mucosal lining of the intestine.

Absorption of Salts, Water, Vitamins, and Minerals

Salts, H_2O, vitamins, and several other essential minerals that are important for our overall health and survival are components of food and are liberated during the digestive process. Ninety-nine percent of the H_2O in food, as well as that resulting from GI secretions, is reabsorbed in the alimentary tract at a rate of about 8 L/day. **■ Fig. 39-3 ■** Na^+, Cl^-, HCO_3^-, and K^+ are predominantly reabsorbed in the intestine, with some secretion of K^+ and HCO_3^- occurring in the ileum. The process for Na^+ occurs by active transport in the small and large intestine; Cl^- and HCO_3^- follow passively. K^+ is passively reabsorbed whenever its concentration in the gut exceeds that in the gut interstitium. This occurs secondarily to reabsorption of H_2O. K^+ reabsorption can convert to secretion in the colon whenever the colonic concentration of K^+ falls below 25 mM.

Transport of ions across the intestinal lumen depends ultimately on the activity of Na^+/K^+ ATPase

in the basolateral membrane. The specific electrolyte transport mechanism differs in the jejunum, ileum, and colon. **■ Fig. 39-3 ■** In the jejunum, Na^+ reabsorption is coupled to the reabsorption of glucose and amino acids, and each process facilitates the other. A Na^+/H^+ exchanger in the jejunum alkalinizes the cell, which helps increase intercellular bicarbonate concentration. Bicarbonate then exits into the basolateral space by facilitated diffusion.

Cl^- reabsorption occurs through tight junctions and follows Na^+. The reabsorption of Na^+ with its attendant anions causes the osmotic reabsorption of water from the intestinal lumen. With minor exceptions, the processes of salt and water reabsorption in the ileum and colon are similar to those in the jejunum. The colon does not have sugar or amino acid/ Na^+ cotransporters.

Na^+ reabsorption in the colon is facilitated by the presence of a specific Na^+ channel in the apical membrane that is sensitive to amiloride. This channel, as well as the activity of the Na^+/K^+ ATPase, is stimulated by aldosterone. The lumen of the colon is −30 mV relative to the basolateral surface; this factor attracts K^+, resulting in its secretion into the lumen of the colon. Consequently, severe forms of diarrhea can result in hypokalemic conditions.

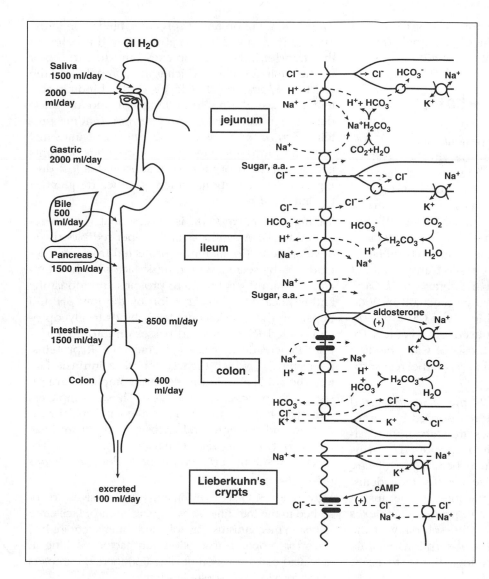

■ **Fig. 39-3** ■

An overview of handling of water by the gastrointestinal system (left), and cellular mechanism of reabsorption of water and electrolytes by intestinal cells (right). Mechanisms for reabsorbing water are linked to sodium chloride reabsorption throughout the intestinal system, although exact cellular mechanisms differ slightly between the jejunum, ileum, and colon. Dashed lines indicate passive transport. (See text for details.)

The autonomic nervous system alters reabsorption of Na+, Cl−, and H₂O by the intestine; sympathetic activation stimulates and parasympathetic stimulation inhibits reabsorption. These effects result, in part, secondarily from inhibition of motility with sympathetic stimulation and an increase in motility with parasympathetic stimulation. Decreased motility slows the transit time of intestinal contents through the alimentary tract, allowing more time for reabsorption. Opioids decrease motility and thereby increase NaCl and H₂O reabsorption in the intestine. This effect is responsible for the constipating effects of opioids and their former, now obsolete, use as treatments for diarrhea.

Abnormalities of salt and H₂O reabsorption in the intestine can result in disturbances of H₂O, electrolyte and acid-base balance in the body as a whole. Impaired Na+ and Cl− reabsorption can result secondarily to a primary malabsorption of carbohydrate with a combined result of creation of significant osmotic diarrhea. In some instances, Cl−/HCO₃− exchanger is missing or deficient in the intestine, resulting in impaired reabsorption of Cl− in the ileum; this results in diarrhea complicated by alkalosis.

Secretory diarrhea is the most important salt and H₂O malabsorption syndrome recognized. The most significant mechanism of secretion of salts and H₂O in the intestine occurs in the crypt cells of the small intestine. This secretion is driven by Cl− efflux at the brush border, through a channel the open time of which is stimulated by cAMP and Ca++. Cholera, which causes life-threatening diarrhea, produces a toxin that irreversibly activates adenylate cyclase, thereby producing excessive amounts of cAMP and excessive opening times of the Cl⁻ channel. This results in excessive Cl⁻ and water secretion.

Intestinal Handling of Ca⁺⁺, Fe⁺⁺, and Vitamins

Other important dietary components such as Ca^{++}, Fe^{++}, and vitamins are reabsorbed in the small intestine by mechanisms that are less well understood than those for monovalent ions and H_2O. Ca^{++} is actively reabsorbed in all areas in the intestine at rates much slower than that for Na^+, but 50 times greater than any other cation. A binding protein on the intestinal brush border and in the cytosol facilitate Ca^{++} entry into the cell. Ca^{++} is transported out of the cell at the basolateral membrane by a Ca^{++} ATPase and a Ca^+/Na^+ exchange mechanism. Vitamin D is essential for normal levels of Ca^{++} absorption by the intestine (see subsequent chapters for details). It increases the synthesis of Ca^{++} binding protein and stimulates all phases of the reabsorption process.

Less than 1 mg of the 15 to 20 mg of iron ingested daily in a normal diet can be reabsorbed by the intestine. Excess iron depresses iron absorption capacity; iron deficiency has the opposite effect. This calls into question the putative benefits of dietary iron supplements in otherwise healthy individuals. Iron absorption is limited in the intestine because it tends to form insoluble salts and protein complexes in the gut. Low pH enhances the solubility of the complexes and enhances iron absorption. Vitamin C, or other organic acids, reduce Fe^{+++} to Fe^{++}, which is more easily absorbed.

An iron-binding protein, *transferrin*, binds iron in the gut and is involved in iron absorption. It is believed that transferrin:Fe^{++} complexes bind to a receptor on the luminal surface, which is then brought into the cell by endocytosis. The levels of this binding protein increase during iron depletion and decrease during high iron intakes. Another iron binding protein, *ferritin*, exists within the cytosol of intestinal cells and forms a storage pool for iron; this prevents excess iron reabsorption. Iron so stored is lost during cell desquamation, which is rather frequent at the intestinal border.

Vitamin B_{12}, *cobalamin*, is an essential vitamin required for DNA synthesis and proper red blood cell development. Cobalamin is protected from acid degradation by secretion of intrinsic factor by the stomach. Vitamin B_{12} is bound to proteins and foodstuffs and is released upon digestion by the low pH and pepsin in the gastric contents. It binds to glycoproteins called *R proteins* and passes on into the intestine. Pancreatic proteases degrade the R proteins, releasing B_{12}, which then is bound to intrinsic factor. The cobalamin:intrinsic factor complexes are resistant to pancreatic proteases. These complexes dimerize, bind to receptors in the intestinal brush border, and undergo endocytosis. Without intrinsic factor, only 1% to 2% of ingested B_{12} will be absorbed, resulting in a condition called *pernicious anemia*.

Most other H_2O-soluble vitamins are passively reabsorbed in the intestine by Na^+ cotransport or facilitated diffusion mechanisms. Fat-soluble vitamins require bile acids for proper reabsorption; any factor resulting in fatty acid malabsorption or digestion therefore impairs the absorption of fat-soluble vitamins.

atures

Function

form ATP is lost as heat and another 35% to 40[...]
lost when ATP is used in body functions. Almo[...]
of these functions eventually dissipate the energ[...]
heat, with the exception of skeletal and ca[...]
muscle activity that can do external work.

Because heat is the eventual end product of al[...]
all energy released in the body, heat generatio[...]
the body is a measure of metabolism. This can b[...]
pressed in several units, the most common bein[...]
Calorie, which is equivalent to the standard ch[...]
cal term of 1 kcal. Other units include the *J*[...]
which is a unit of work (1 kcal = 4186 J). The [...] and *steroid hormones* are synthesized by
or the rate of heat production per unit time, e[...]tic reactions in specialized cells in the body.
1 joule per second. [...]is of peptide hormones, however, requires
[...]duction, transcription, translation, and inter-
[...]peptide processing associated with protein

Determinants of Metabolic Rate

At rest, metabolic rate varies roughly in prop[...]
to body surface area. It equals ≈ 45 W/m^2 or, [...]
typical adult body surface area of 1.8 m^2, abo[...]
W. This rate corresponds to a typical O_2 cons[...]
tion of 240 mL/min. A little over half of restin[...]
production is due to the visceral organs an[...]
trunk, with additional significant contributio[...]
humans from the brain. During exercise, up t[...]
of heat production is liberated from skeletal m[...]
and skin, which make up a little over one-half [...]
body mass.

Many factors alter metabolic rate. ■ **Fig. 40-1b**[...]
tosterone, catecholamines, growth hormone[...]
thyroid hormone all stimulate metabolism, pri[...]
through their effects on protein synthesis and [...]
of substrates in oxidative metabolism. Diges[...]
an energy-requiring process. Loss of digestic[...]
synthesis during malnutrition can reduce me[...]
rate by 20% to 30%. Metabolism increases i[...]
climates and decreases in warm tropical [...]
Overall, metabolism is slightly less in female[...]
in males and decreases as we age. ■ **Fig. 4**[...]
Muscle activity is a prime determinant of de[...]
from resting metabolism, as seen during e[...]
and shivering.

[...]is. *Amine* and *peptide hormones* are released
[...]eir parent cells through second-messenger–
[...]ed exocytosis (i.e., Ca^{++}, cAMP), whereas
[...] which are lipid-soluble, can diffuse easily
[...]cell membranes.

[...] feedback systems play a major role in the
[...]of hormone secretion and the physiological
[...]es that they influence. For example, a pri-
[...]crease in hormone secretion may stimulate a
[...]output of product from the target cell. This
[...]may then serve as a negative feedback sig-
[...]suppresses further hormone secretion in the
[...]e secreting cell.

[...]vely, a primary decrease in the output of
[...]from a target cell will feed back to stimulate
[...]ocrine gland to secrete hormone. The hor-
[...]en stimulates the target cell to increase its
[...]output. Hormone-to-hormone, substrate-to-
[...], and mineral-to-hormone negative feedback
[...]systems are involved in endocrine regula-
[...]e body.

[...]on, overlying neural control mechanisms in-
[...]drenergic, cholinergic, dopaminergic, sero-
[...]and endorphin and enkephalinergic nerves
[...]various endocrine functions. Discussion
[...]mechanisms is not within the scope of this
[...]re are higher CNS regulatory involvements
[...]ocrine functions, such as diurnal rhythms,
[...]ke cycles, menstrual rhythm, and the de-
[...]ntal rhythms involved in puberty.

[...]s initiate their effects on target cells through
[...]o mechanisms. Many hormones initiate re-
[...]n target cells by binding to cell membrane
[...]. Responses often are affected by the num-
[...]ceptors present in the cell membrane. (i.e.,

enhanced by increased number of receptors, or depressed by decreased number of receptors). Receptor number often is regulated by the hormone itself; receptor production is up-regulated when hormone levels are low or absent and down-regulated when levels are high.

Responses in many hormone target tissues are mediated by intracellular second messengers, the production of which is stimulated or inhibited once hormone binds to the appropriate receptor. An example of this second messenger mediation between extracellular hormone and the cellular response is shown in ■ **Fig. 41-1** ■ .

In this diagram the relationship of G-protein linkages between the hormone receptor and the effector systems is shown using the adenyl cyclase/cAMP system as the second messenger. G-proteins are trimers with α, β, and gamma subunits. Scores of different G-proteins in the cells of the body link receptor activation to effector responses. The α subunit is unique to each G-protein. This subunit binds the receptor to the effector, which can be an enzyme, ion channel, regulatory protein, etc. It also binds either GDP or GTP. A given α subunit may have a stimulatory or inhibitory effect on the effector mechanism.

In the illustration, a stimulatory G-protein is linked to adenyl cyclase. When hormone binds to the receptor, the α subunit of the G-protein binds to the receptor:hormone complex, releasing GDP while binding GTP. The binding of GTP dissociates the alpha subunit from the rest of the G-protein. The α subunit-GTP complex then activates the effector, in this case adenylate cyclase, which stimulates the production of cAMP. Cyclic AMP activates cAMP-dependent protein kinases, which then elicit the cell response. Hydrolysis of GTP provides the energy to recombine the alpha subunit with the remaining beta and gamma units and shuttle the trimer-GDP complex back to the membrane.

This repetitive cycling of the system results in a marked amplification of effector stimulation and hence of the effect of the initial hormone. As a result, little hormone is needed to activate the target tissue (indeed, effective plasma levels of many hormones are in the picomolar to nanomolar range). The particular response elicited by a hormone in a cell depends in part on what type of intracellular process is altered by activated kinases.

In addition to cyclic nucleotides (cAMP, cGMP), hormones also may initiate cellular response by modifying activity of membrane Ca^{++} channels.

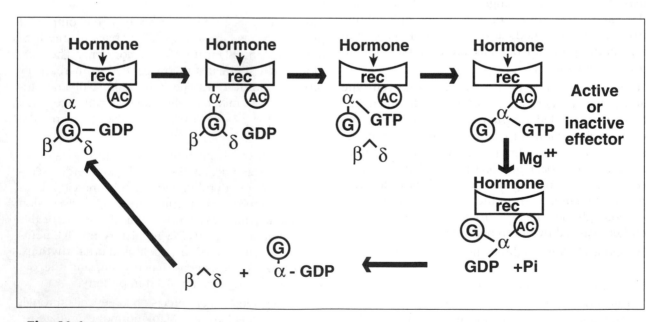

■ **Fig. 41-1** ■
A representation of the mechanism whereby G-proteins are linked to hormone action in cells. rec = hormone receptor. AC = adenyl cyclase. (See text for explanation of mechanism.)

Ca++ can form complexes with calmodulin within the cell, and these in turn serve to activate or inactivate several intracellular regulatory enzymes by activating Ca/calmodulin-dependent protein kinases. In some instances, binding of membrane receptor by a hormone will activate phospholipase C, with the formation of second messengers diacylglycerol (DAG) and IP_3. DAG results in subsequent activation of protein kinase C, whereas IP_3 releases Ca++; both may activate or inactivate cell processes.

Thyroid hormones and steroids are examples of hormones that do not act through membrane cell surface receptors to effect responses in target tissues. Instead, these hormones bind to receptors in the cell nucleus and alter cell function by controlling gene transcription. In target cells, steroids bind to steroid receptors in the cytosol. The receptor/hormone complex in turn binds a specific DNA domain called the *hormone response element*. In the presence of other transcription factors, activation of the response element initiates protein synthesis by starting transcription. Posttranscriptional and posttranslational modulation of protein synthesis often occurs, resulting in the final desired product. It is now known that some hormones cause gene induction through classical second messenger systems; cAMP and its dependent kinases are but one example.

CHAPTER 42

A Survey of Hypothalamic-Pituitary Function

The *pituitary gland* is a pea-sized organ at the base of the brain. It resides in the cella turcica, which is a superior depression in the sphenoid bone, and is divided into two sections. The posterior pituitary, or *neurohypophysis,* is a neurocrine organ that receives the neurohormones ADH and oxytocin from the hypothalamus through a specialized portal circulation. The anterior pituitary, or *adenohypophysis,* is an endocrine organ that produces six peptide hormones involved in the control of functions in several target tissues. ■ **Fig. 42-1** ■

The pituitary is the most complex of all endocrine organs. Its hormones are involved in the regulation of body fluid composition, growth, the body's response to stress and trauma, reproduction, and birth. Anterior pituitary function is regulated by internal and external signals that are processed by the brain. Not surprisingly, the hypothalamus influences the synthesis and release of pituitary hormones through the production of peptide-releasing factors.

The anterior pituitary produces six peptide hormones, two of which affect target tissues directly and four that affect the function of other endocrine glands. *Adrenocorticotrophic hormone,* or *ACTH,* has positive trophic influences on cortical cells in the adrenal glands and stimulates their synthesis and secretion of glucocorticoids (cortisol and corticosterone). Through its action on these glucocorticoids, ACTH participates in the body's defense against hypoglycemia.

ACTH is released from the pituitary in response to hypothalamic *corticotrophin-releasing hormone,* or *CRH,* which also stimulates the synthesis of ACTH. CRH affects ACTH synthesis and production by activating membrane receptors linked by G-proteins to cAMP production in the corticotrophin-producing cells. This triggers gene expression for *pro-opiomelanocortin,* or *POMC,* which is the precursor protein for ACTH.

Pituitary *thyroid-stimulating hormone,* or *TSH,* maintains thyroid cell size and integrity while stimulating the synthesis and secretion of the thyroid hormones, T_3 (triiodothyronine) and T_4 (thyroxin) in thyroid follicular cells. These hormones are essential for proper differentiation of the central nervous system early in development, overall body growth and development, energy production, and regulation of metabolism.

TSH is released from the pituitary by hypothalamic *thyrotropin-releasing hormone,* or *TRH.* TRH stimulates thyrotrophs through action on membrane receptors linked to phospholipase C. This results in production of IP_3 and DAG and subsequent release of intercellular Ca^{++} and activation of protein kinase C. These factors stimulate the synthesis and secretion of TSH. TRH also stimulates gene expression for the α and β subunits of TSH.

Follicle-stimulating hormone and *luteinizing hormone,* or *FSH* and *LH* respectively, participate in reproductive function and sexual development in both males and females. FSH is essential for production of sperm and ovum and is involved in the events of the menstrual cycle. LH stimulates the synthesis and secretion of testosterone, estrogen, and progesterone by testes and ovaries. It is responsible for causing ovulation and influences various aspects of the menstrual cycle.

FSH and LH are secreted in response to *gonadotrophin-releasing hormone,* or *GnRH.* Another pituitary reproductive hormone, *prolactin* or *PRL,* does not stimulate production of other endocrine-secreting cells, but rather stimulates milk production in lactating mammary glands. Synthesis of prolactin by lactotrophes in the pituitary is stimulated by TRH, whereas synthesis and release of prolactin is inhibited by dopamine released from neurons in the hypothalamus.

Finally, *growth hormone,* or *GH,* is produced by other pituitary somatotrophs. It is important in regulating body growth during childhood and exerts significant influence over carbohydrate and lipid

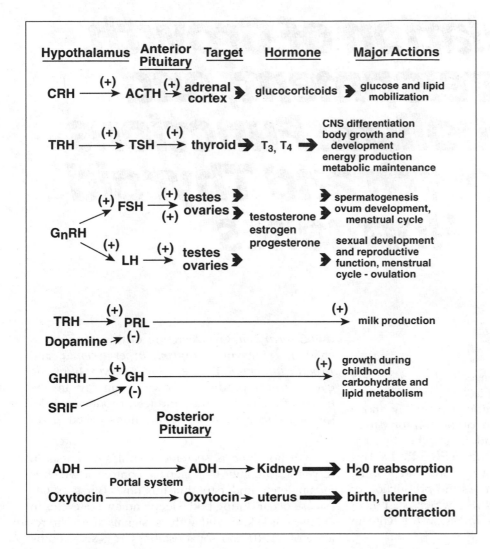

■ **Fig. 42-1** ■

A summary of pituitary hormones, hypothalamic releasing factors, primary target tissues for pituitary hormones, hormones produced by target tissues, and the major actions of hormones involved with several endocrine functions. Symbols (+) and (−) indicate stimulation and inhibition, respectively. (See text for description.)

metabolism. GH is released from the pituitary by *growth hormone–releasing hormone,* or *GHRH.* Somatotroph membrane receptors for GHRH are linked to stimulation of GH synthesis, secretion, and gene expression through increased cAMP production. TRH also stimulates growth hormone gene expression.

Somatostatin, also called *somatotropin release-inhibiting hormone* or *SRIF,* is a ubiquitous inhibitor of endocrine function. Its primary effect in the hypothalamic pituitary axis is to act through an inhibitory G-protein to suppress cAMP production in pituitary somatotrophs, thus inhibiting the action of GHRH and suppressing secretion of growth hormone.

Stimulation and inhibition of the synthesis and release of pituitary hormones and, in some cases their releasing factors, are subject to complicated multiple negative feedback loops involving products of target tissues, production of secondary hormones, and interrelationships between pituitary hormones and their releasing factors. These mechanism of control of endocrine function will be discussed in the context of individual hormones in subsequent chapters.

CHAPTER 43

Regulation of Growth, Development, and Metabolism: Functions of Growth and Thyroid Hormones

Growth Hormone

Growth hormone is essential for normal growth during childhood and adolescence. It does not affect fetal growth or development in the very early newborn. The primary, general action of growth hormone is to stimulate differentiation of *progenitor* (stem) cells into cells capable of undergoing the repeated cell division needed for growth. ■ **Fig. 43-1** ■ This effect is especially prominent in bone and muscle. Growth hormone also stimulates the production of *insulinlike growth factor,* or *IGF-I,* which is a potent mitogen, by inducing gene expression for IGF-I in the liver.

Growth hormone has metabolic effects that are consistent with increased energy needs for cell division and growth. This generally involves release and utilization of metabolic substrates while inhibiting their storage in the body. GH stimulates triglyceride mobilization and lipolysis, freeing up glycerol and fatty acids for entry into oxidative metabolism for the generation of ATP. It also counteracts the increased storage of excess glucose and fatty acids in muscle and fat cells caused by insulin and produces insulin resistance in these tissues. Growth hormone inhibits glucose use by muscle and fat while simultaneously stimulating glucose production in the liver. All these factors free more substrates in the body to be used for generation of energy for growth rather than for other cell activities.

A lack of growth hormone results in the inability of an individual to grow to a normal height, although normal body proportions are maintained, a condition called *dwarfism.* Oversecretion of this hormone in children results in *gigantism, hyperglycemia,* and *hyperinsulinemia.* In the adult, growth hormone oversecretion produces growth primarily in the bones of the face, hands, and feet, producing a deforming condition in these locations called *acromegaly.*

Growth hormone is secreted in pulsatile bursts in response to higher CNS signals, control of which is incompletely understood at this time. Bursts of GH release occur during both sleep and awake cycles in children. It is known that these signals affect the release of GHRH and somatostatin; GH is secreted by simultaneous stimulation of GHRH and inhibition of the release of somatostatin. In addition to GHRH, thyroid hormones are needed for GH production and thyroid deficiency leads to GH deficiency. Other ancillary factors are known to stimulate GH secretion. For example, GH levels are elevated by emotional or physical stress, vigorous exercise, hypoglycemia, or elevated levels of arginine and leucine in the blood.

Somatostatin is the primary inhibitor of GH secretion through its effect of inhibiting the ability of GHRH to stimulate pituitary somatotrophs. IGF-1 represents a feedback inhibition on GH secretion by inhibiting GHRH secretion, inhibiting the action of GHRH on GH production in the pituitary, and stimulating the secretion of somatostatin. Finally, growth hormone itself is involved in a negative feedback loop, suppressing secretion of GHRH and stimulating somatostatin secretion directly.

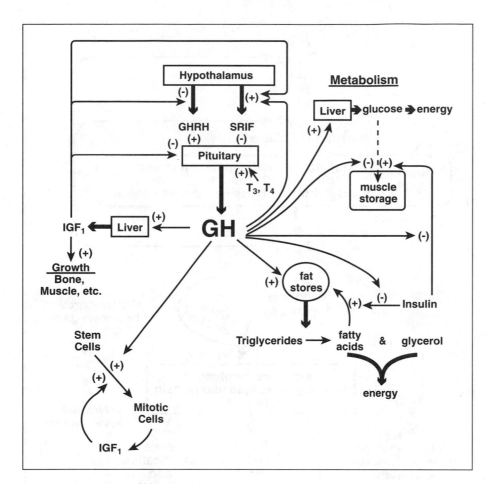

■ **Fig. 43-1** ■
A summary of the effects of growth hormone and its control in the body, where (+) indicates stimulation and (−) indicates inhibition. Heavy arrows point to substances released by designated tissues. GHRH = growth hormone–releasing hormone, SRIF = somatostatin or somatotropin release-inhibiting factor, T3 and T4 = thyroid hormones, IGF$_1$ = insulinlike growth factor. Growth hormone affects growth directly and affects processes in metabolism that support its growth-promoting function.

Thyroid Hormones and Regulation of Metabolism

Growth, development, body maintenance, and repair all require a system that can provide energy, synthesize new structures, and break down the old. The gastrointestinal system gets the basic building blocks required for these processes into the circulatory system, which then transports them to the cells of the body. Under the influence of growth hormone, glucose and fatty acids are freed up from storage forms and enter into the metabolic pathways so that cells can differentiate and grow. These processes will not function sufficiently if metabolic pathways are not maintained in a state that allows for normal cell development and function. In a broad sense, maintenance of metabolic pathways is the primary function of the thyroid hormones, *triiodothyronine* (T3) and *thyroxine* (T4).

Thyroid hormones are produced in the thyroid gland. They are not essential for life but are indispensable for normal growth, development, and maturation.

■ **Fig. 43-2** ■ They are crucial for normal development of the central nervous system in the fetus (second and third trimester) and the neonate (0–6 months), where they stimulate differentiation, dendrite formation, and myelination of nerves. Thyroid hormones stimulate production and maintenance of the enzymes responsible for the synthetic and degradative pathways of carbohydrate, lipid, and protein metabolism. Consequently, it is not surprising that thyroid hormone "sets" the basal rate of oxidative metabolism in cells and hence O_2 consumption and heat production in the body.

Synthesis of Thyroid Hormones

The synthesis of thyroid hormones is a complex process. Thyroid hormones are synthesized in spherical follicles within the thyroid gland. These follicles consist of a wall composed of a single layer of epithelial cells, which produce a thyroglobulin precursor protein. This precursor is packaged into vesicles and released into the lumen of the follicle via vesicular fusion. Follicular cells also take up io-

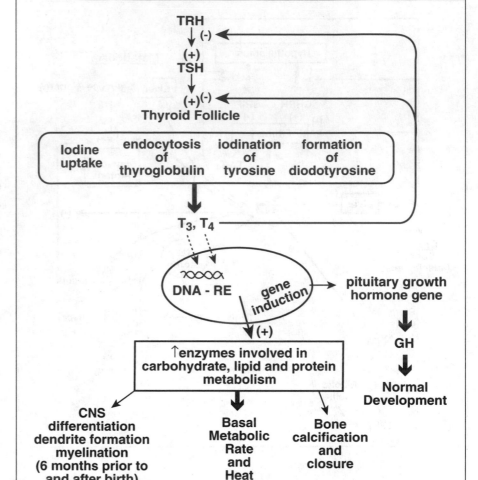

■ Fig. 43-2 ■

A summary of thyroid hormone production, cellular mode of action, and effects in the body. The (+) symbol indicates stimulation; (−) indicates inhibition. TRH = thyrotropin-releasing hormone, TSH = thyroid-stimulating hormone, T3 and T4 (thyroxin) = thyroid hormones, DNA-RE = DNA response element. Factors at the end of heavy arrows result from a change in the preceding variable. Thyroid hormones play a key role in early CNS development, bone development, and basal metabolic rate and heat production.

dine at the basal membrane through an active saturable transport mechanism. Iodine is added one or two at a time to tyrosine residues on thyroglobulin precursor molecules in the follicle lumen to form mono- and diototyrosines. A coupling reaction fuses iototyrosines to form either T3 or T4 (thyroxine), which is then taken up from the lumen, along with the thyroglobulin, back into the follicular cells. T_3 and T_4 are lysed from thyroglobulin within the cells and released into the circulation.

Of the circulating T_3 and T_4, 70% is bound to a special thyroxine-binding globulin and >29% is bound to albumin or a thyroxine-binding prealbumin. These forms are in equilibrium, with the 1% remaining free and in circulation, and serve as a buffer against loss of free hormone via the kidney. Many tissues convert T4 into T3, which is the primary active form

of thyroid hormone, and receptors in target cells primarily react with T3 rather than T4.

Biochemical Action of Thyroid Hormones

The basic mechanism by which thyroid hormones influence growth, development, metabolism, and heat production is through gene induction. **■ Fig. 43-2 ■** Steroid receptors in the cytosol of target cells bind thyroid hormone, which then binds to response elements on DNA, either initiating or inhibiting transcription of target genes.

Thyroid hormones stimulate the formation of the enzymes in the intermediate pathways of carbohydrates, fat, and protein metabolism, thus amplifying cell metabolic activity and heat production. They also stimulate production of mitochondrial proteins and possibly Na^+/K^+ ATPase molecules, thus increasing the calorigenic effect in most tissues. This effect is most prominent in skeletal muscle, liver, heart, kidney, and the developing brain and less so in skin, lymphoid organs, gonads, and the adult brain. Thyroid hormones stimulate anabolic protein pathways as well as lipolysis and lipogenesis and have positive chronotropic and inotropic effects on the heart.

Control of Thyroid Hormone Production

Production of thyroid hormones is increased by the action of TSH on thyrotrophs, where it increases iodine uptake by the follicles, stimulates iodination of tyrosine, and increases pinocytotic collection and hydrolysis of thyroglobulin molecules. TSH also maintains normal follicular cell size and stimulates thyroid growth and vascularity. Overproduction of TSH produces hypertrophy of the thyroid gland, called a *goiter.*

Secretion of TSH by the pituitary is stimulated continually by the tonic release of a tripeptide *thyrotropin releasing hormone,* or *TRH.* Eventual control of thyroid hormone levels results from an unusual negative feedback involving T_3 and T_4. High levels of thyroxine and T_3 decrease the sensitivity of the pituitary thyrotrophs to TRH by decreasing the number of TRH receptors present on the pituitary TSH cells. Down-regulation of the system with eventual decrease in thyroid hormone levels therefore occurs. Low levels of thyroid hormone have the opposite effect. Although circulating T_4 is more effective in producing feedback inhibition of hormone production, its effect is due to deiodonation in the pituitary to T_3, which works intrapituitarily to inhibit TRH receptor expression.

Hypothyroidism and Hyperthyroidism

Decreased production of thyroid hormone, or *hypothyroidism,* impairs growth and produces mental retardation in children. These effects are exacerbated in that thyroid hormones normally stimulate GH release as well. In the adult there is an overall decrease in metabolism, development of cold intolerance, cutaneous vasoconstriction due to decreased heat production, impaired mentation, depressed nerve conduction velocity, and a suppression of food intake.

Hypothyroidism can be caused by iodine deficiency, autoantibody destruction of the thyroid, hypothalamic or pituitary disease resulting in decreased TRH or TSH, surgical removal of the thyroid gland, or inheritable diseases that interfere with the biosynthesis of the thyroid hormone. If hypothyroidism is due to a primary problem in the thyroid gland, the low levels of circulating T_3 and T_4 stimulate TSH release, which stimulates thyroid growth, producing a goiter.

Hyperthyroidism produces a condition called *Graves' disease,* an autoimmune disease resulting in a "locked" activation of adenyl cyclase in follicular cells, which then stimulates excess thyroid hormone production. This condition is associated with a diffuse toxic goiter and results in nervousness, irritability, fatigue, heat intolerance, cutaneous vasodilation, profuse sweating, increased heart rate and cardiac output, increased degradative processes, and weight loss.

CHAPTER 44

Defense Against Starvation and Storage of Metabolic Substrates: The Functions of Adrenal Glucocorticoids and Insulin

Generation of ATP for use in cellular functions is necessary for survival. In our bodies, special metabolic pathways generate ATP primarily from the oxidation of glucose, fatty acids, and, in extreme conditions, even amino acids. However, these substrates must be obtained originally from complex food sources, the availability of which can be intermittent, unpredictable, or insufficient. Furthermore, the brain can utilize only glucose to generate ATP. In order to prevent life-threatening declines in circulating levels of essential substrates, the body must have some mechanism by which it can draw on substrate stores during starvation and build up these stores when food is readily available. Such functions have obvious survival value. The utilization and storage of substrates is under the control of two hormone systems: the adrenal glucocorticoids and insulin, the latter secreted by the pancreas. ■ **Fig. 44-1a** ■

Adrenal Cortical Function

The *adrenal cortex* produces two families of steroid hormones, both of which are essential for life. *Aldosterone* is necessary for proper regulation of salt and water balance as well as for volume regulation in support of the cardiovascular system. These functions have been discussed previously in this book. The adrenal cortex also produces two steroid *glucocorticoid hormones: corticosterone* and *cortisol*. ■ **Fig. 44-1b** ■

The best-understood function of the adrenal glucocorticoids is their role in reactions to fasting, or starvation. During starvation, glucocorticoids mobilize glucose stores, thus elevating blood glucose and preventing fast-induced hypoglycemia. They also permit lipolysis in fat cells, releasing high ATP-generating fatty acids into the circulation, and promote protein breakdown for gluconeogenesis (formation of glucose from amino acids). As a result, glucocorticoids greatly extend the tolerance of an individual to starvation. Without these hormones, an individual unable to obtain food sources would die from hypoglycemia within 24 hours.

The glucocorticoids have several other clinically important but poorly understood functions. Glucocorticoids have anti-inflammatory properties. This may involve their ability to inhibit prostaglandin synthesis through the production of macrocortin, an inhibitor of phospholipase A. The anti-inflammatory properties of glucocorticoids have led to the use of cortisone and related derivatives to treat rheumatoid arthritis and trauma-induced inflammation.

High levels of glucocorticoids are immunosuppressive; they prevent antibody production and interfere with cell-based immunity by killing immature T and B lymphocytes. This has led to their clinical use in the prevention of organ transplant rejection. Finally, the glucocorticoids are important in allowing the individual to cope with both emotional and physical stress. Without glucocorticoids, even minor daily stresses can be incapacitating. This effect of glucocorticoids is not understood.

Synthesis and Actions of Glucocorticoids

Glucocorticoids are derived from cholesterol, which is brought into adrenal cortical cells by low-density lipoproteins. ■ **Fig. 44-1b** ■ Steroid synthesis involves mitochondria and an initial rate-limiting step of conversion of cholesterol to pregnenolone by cytochrome P450scc. Pregnenolone can be converted to progesterone and then, through many enzymatic reactions, to corticosterone (an active glucocorticoid), aldosterone, or 17 α-OH-pregnenolone, and then to *cortisol,* the most active glucocorticoid. Inherited genetic defects in any of the enzyme systems involved in the biosynthesis of these steroids

can lead to life-threatening disease due to malfunction of glucocorticoid actions.

Most corticosteroids are bound to plasma-binding proteins and albumin, which protects them from renal elimination and increases their circulating half-life. Glucocorticoids, being steroids, produce their effects on target tissues through action on nuclear receptors, which bind to DNA response elements and then either initiate or inhibit gene transcription. The primary target tissues are the liver and kidney, where glucocorticoids stimulate gluconeogenesis during the first two days of starvation. To do so, glucocorticoids first inhibit protein synthesis from free amino acids. This effect synergizes with an added effect of starvation: suppression of the inhibitory effect of insulin on protein breakdown.

In this manner, glucocorticoids prevent amino acids released from protein breakdown from being rein-

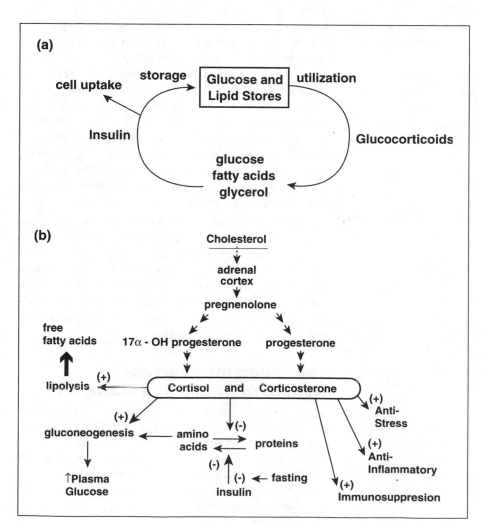

■ **Fig. 44-1** ■
(a) A simple overview of the interrelationship between insulin and glucocorticoids as they affect glucose and lipid stores. (b) Production of glucocorticoids and their actions in the body. The (+) indicates stimulation and the (−) indicates inhibition.

corporated into proteins. This creates a larger amino acid pool for gluconeogenesis. The glucocorticoids also play a permissive role in gluconeogenesis by maintaining the expression of genes that code for several enzymes involved in generation of glucose from amino acids. The net effect is that glucocorticoids buy time for brain survival by providing glucose substrate levels sufficient for brain metabolism until lipolysis can provide enough ketone bodies for that purpose.

Regulation of Secretion of Glucocorticoids

The primary stimulator of glucocorticoid secretion is ACTH. ■ Fig. 44-2 ■ In the adrenal cortex, ACTH stimulates adenyl cyclase via a membrane-associated stimulatory G-protein, which increases cAMP and activates cAMP-dependent protein kinases (kinase A). Kinase A phosphorylates several regulatory proteins, stimulates cholesterol uptake into the mitochondria, and maintains expression of enzymes necessary for steroidogenesis in the adrenal cortical cells.

Glucocorticoids inhibit their own production and secretion by inhibiting CRH and ACTH secretion, as well as inhibiting POMC gene expression, which codes for the precursor of ACTH. ACTH production is stimulated by stress and trauma, which in turn stimulate CRH.

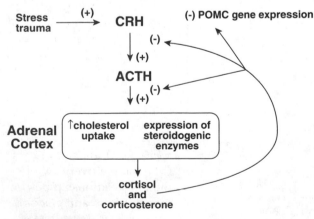

■ Fig. 44-2 ■
Feedback control mechanism for glucocorticoid secretion. The (+) indicates stimulation and the (−) indicates inhibition. CRH = corticotropin-releasing hormone, ACTH = adrenal corticotropin. (See text for details.)

Without glucocorticoids the body loses enzymes needed for gluconeogenesis. An individual then cannot accelerate this emergency source of glucose production when threatened with starvation, and death from hypoglycemia results. This effect also causes insulin hypersensitivity.

Cushing's disease is a condition associated with oversecretion of glucocorticoids, usually caused by corticotroph adenomas that secrete excess ACTH. Individuals with this condition have increased breakdown of peripheral tissue protein, hyperglycemia, hyperinsulinemia, and insulin resistance. There also are characteristic excess fat deposits in the face (creating a "moonface" appearance), as well as in the abdomen and between the shoulders.

Adrenal Medullary Function

The major hormones released from nerve endings in the adrenal medulla, epinephrine and norepinephrine, are important in the body's ability to cope with stress, trauma, exercise, and hypoglycemia. Cardiovascular and renal actions of these hormones have been discussed in preceding chapters. These hormones mobilize glucose needed to help the body cope with increased activity or stressful, traumatic conditions. They promote glycogenolysis by stimulating glycogen phosphorylase in liver, muscle, and adipose cells, thereby liberating glucose from its storage form. They also stimulate gluconeogenesis from lactate and amino acid. This is mediated by α_1 receptors in the liver and β-receptors in muscle and adipose tissue.

Epinephrine activates a hormone-sensitive lipase in adipose tissue, increasing lipolysis, thereby releasing free fatty acids and glycerol into the bloodstream. It inhibits insulin secretion (which promotes glucose and fatty acid incorporation into cells), thus allowing blood glucose and fatty acid levels to rise. The net effect is a mobilization of substrates that can be used for energy stores.

The Endocrine Pancreas: Actions of Insulin and Glucagon

The pancreas produces two hormones that regulate the storage and utilization of metabolic substrates. *Insulin* is a peptide hormone of nutrient abundance; it promotes storage of glucose and lipid in liver, muscle, and adipose tissues, and prevents protein breakdown when food intake is plentiful. *Glucagon* is similar in its action to the glucocorticoids; during starvation it stimulates glucose and lipid mobilization in the liver.

An overview of the mechanisms of action of insulin is illustrated in ■ **Fig. 44-3** ■. Insulin's actions are mediated through binding of cell surface membrane receptors. There are two binding sites on alpha chains of this receptor. When bound by insulin, these receptors undergo autophosphorylization of tyrosine residues on β-side chains, which then promotes the tyrosine kinase activity of the hormone:receptor complex. This results in phosphorylation of tyrosine on other cell proteins and initiates a cascade effect involving serine and threonine phosphorylation, which results in the ultimate actions of insulin on target cells.

The overall function of insulin is to promote glucose uptake and storage in target cells. It does so by promoting the insertion of the Glut 4 transporter into cell membranes and by increasing the number of these transporters in the cell membrane. Insulin promotes formation of glycogen from glucose by stimulating glycogen synthase while simultaneously inhibiting glycogen phosphorylase, which otherwise promotes glycogen breakdown.

Insulin stimulates several enzymes involved in glycolysis while inhibiting enzymes of the citric acid cycle. This would appear to be a counterproductive mechanism that accelerates glucose usage. The acceleration of glycolysis, however, provides precursors for the formation of triglycerides, which can be considered longterm storage forms of glucose and high-energy fatty acids. Acetyl CoA and α-glycerol formed from glycolysis is used to form fatty acids and the glycerin backbone of triglycerides, respec-

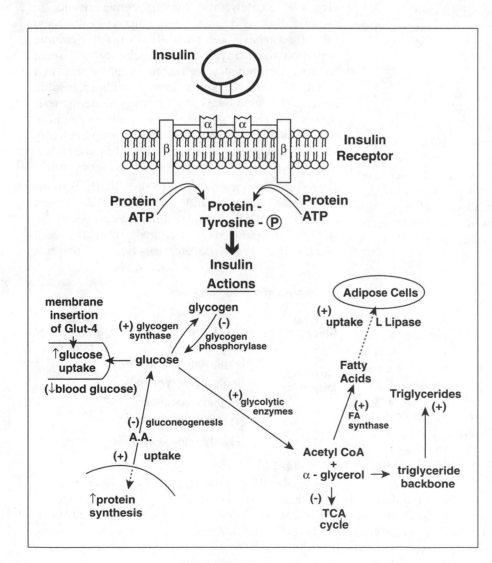

■ **Fig. 44-3** ■

A representation of the insulin receptor and the cellular action of insulin (top), and the complex actions of insulin on fat and glucose handling in the body (bottom). The (+) indicates stimulation and the (−) indicates inhibition. (See text for detailed explanation.)

tively. Insulin further facilitates this process by stimulating fatty acid synthase and lipoprotein lipase (which increases fatty acid uptake into adipose tissue) while inhibiting hormone-sensitive lipase. This latter effect prevents triglyceride breakdown. The final net effect on lipid handling in the body is a promotion of accumulation of triglycerides in target cells.

Insulin promotes ribosome synthesis, increases protein synthesis initiating factors, promotes the start of translation, and increases amino acid uptake in cells. Collectively these effects promote protein accumulation, primarily in liver, muscle, and adipose tissue. Insulin also helps maintain protein structure by inhibiting lysosome activity that causes protein breakdown.

The overall effect of insulin is to promote the incorporation of metabolic substrates into cells and then produce storage forms of those substrates so that they can be drawn upon when needed during fasting or starvation.

The primary stimulant of insulin secretion is hyperglycemia, which occurs when plasma levels exceed 100 mg/dl; insulin secretion is suppressed by hypoglycemia. In addition, amino acids (particularly arginine) and long-chain fatty acids stimulate secretion of insulin. Stimulated secretion of insulin is biphasic; an initial 10 to 15 min burst occurs due to release of packaged insulin, followed by a sustained release that results from increased synthesis of insulin. Somatostatin is an inhibitor of insulin secretion, although its role in insulin's many effects is unclear.

Glucagon and Promotion of Substrate Mobilization

Glucagon is a pancreatic hormone involved in promotion of fuel mobilization during times of fasting or starvation. ■ **Fig. 44-4** ■ The effects of glucagon are primarily exerted on the liver, where they are mediated by cAMP-dependent mechanisms. Glucagon increases blood glucose levels by promoting glycogen breakdown through stimulation of glycogen phosphorylase and inhibition of glycogen synthase. It also stimulates hepatic gluconeogenesis by increasing the transcription of the mRNA coding for phosphoenolpyruvate carboxykinase.

Glucagon also provides the substrates needed for gluconeogenesis by promoting amino acid transport into hepatocytes and by stimulating hepatic protein breakdown. One of the problems of catabolizing protein into glucose is the formation of ammonia,

which is toxic. Glucagon helps the liver dispose of excess ammonia by stimulating the activity of urea cyclase.

Glucagon lowers levels of melanyl CoA in the liver, which allows fatty acids to enter mitochondria so that they can be oxidized to ketones. Ketones are used as an energy source by the heart and muscle during times of starvation, thus freeing up glucose for tissues that can only use that substrate (i.e., the brain) in such extreme conditions. Glucagon secretion is stimulated by hypoglycemia and paradoxically by amino acids; it is inhibited by insulin, fatty acids, and somatostatin.

Diabetes Mellitus

Diabetes mellitus is a condition in which malfunction of the pancreatic insulin system causes hyperglycemia. Acutely, the hyperglycemia results in osmotic diuresis due to excess glucose in the renal tubules as well as ketonuria. This causes a volume depletion that can result in circulatory and renal collapse; accumulation of ketone bodies results in a metabolic acidosis (ketoacidosis). Without insulin, enhanced protein breakdown from gluconeogenesis occurs and results in toxic accumulation of ammonia in the blood. The combination of circulatory and renal failure, acidosis, and blood ammonia accumulation results in coma and subsequent death.

There are two forms of diabetes mellitus, *insulin-dependent* (IDDM) and *non-insulin–dependent* (NIDDM). IDDM is most commonly caused by inability of the pancreas to produce insulin. This condition causes *Type I diabetes*. It is believed that this

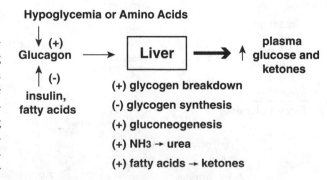

■ **Fig. 44-4** ■

Simple overview of the effects of glucagon on glucose handling by the liver. The (+) indicates stimulation, and the (−) indicates inhibition. Variables at the end of heavy arrows result from a change in the preceding variable. Glucagon increases plasma glucose and ketone concentrations.

type of diabetes results from autoimmune destruction of pancreatic β-cells that produce insulin. This form of diabetes can be treated successfully by replenishing insulin in the body with daily injections of the hormone. Management of the disease is facilitated by careful control of the diet and exercise, which increases glucose uptake into muscle cells.

The most common form of NIDDM results from an inability of the target cells to respond to circulating levels of insulin; this is called *Type II,* or sometimes *adult onset diabetes*. Insulin levels may be normal or high, but insulin secretion in response to glucose is blunted in this form of diabetes. Type II diabetes is thought to result from either malfunctioning insulin receptor or post-receptor processes.

Diabetes mellitus can result from excess glucocorticoid secretion (Cushing's syndrome) or the effects of circulating hormones during pregnancy. In spite of reasonable control of either Type I or Type II diabetes, the chronic outcome of the disease is poor.

Diabetes is known to damage the vascular endothelium with resultant acceleration of atherosclerosis; it is particularly devastating to the microcirculation, resulting in impaired transport of O_2 and nutrients to tissues. This is especially problematic in the extremities and often results in tissue death, necessitating amputation of fingers, toes, or even limbs. Poor circulation in the retina of the eye results in blindness associated with chronic diabetes. In addition, high glucose levels damage nerves, with resultant loss of sensation. This results in an inability to perceive pain and recognition of developing ulcerations of the skin.

Diabetes impairs endothelial nitric oxide production due to damaging effects on arterial endothelium. NO is released from the nonadrenergic/noncholinergic nerves that are necessary for penile erection; therefore, male impotence is a common consequence of diabetes. Deterioration of glomerular filtration caused by hyperglycemia can lead to renal failure.

CHAPTER 45

Endocrine Control of Calcium and Phosphate Balance

Input/Output Relationships for Calcium and Phosphate

Ca^{++} and phosphate play essential roles in physiological functions. Consequently, the plasma concentration of these ions is maintained within narrow limits. Balance of these substances is complicated by the fact that inputs into the plasma arise from a variety of sources other than that entering through the digestive tract. ■ Fig. 45-1 ■

On average, about 1000 mg of Ca^{++} is ingested in a daily diet. Of this, only about 350 mg is absorbed in the intestine (absorption is inversely proportional to dietary intake), whereas about 150 mg of Ca^{++} is secreted into the intestine. Total fecal loss of cal-

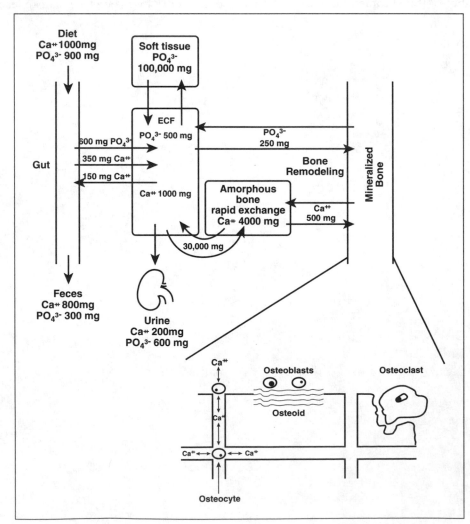

■ Fig. 45-1 ■
Diagrammatic representation of exchanges of calcium and phosphate among various body compartments. (See text for detailed mechanisms.) The lower right corner is a diagrammatic representation of calcium transfer from the interior of the bone to the extracellular fluid through osteocytes. Osteoblasts are involved with the laying down of new bone matrix, whereas osteoclasts destroy bone.

cium amounts to approximately 800 mg. Thus, on average, only 200 mg of Ca++ enters the extracellular fluid through the gut. This intake is balanced by a daily urine excretion of 200 mg, or 2% of the filtered calcium load. However, extracellular fluid Ca++ concentration is in equilibrium with an enormous Ca++ store of more than 1 million mg in mineralized bone.

Ca++ exchange between bone and plasma occurs through a rapidly exchanging Ca++ pool consisting of amorphous, or partial formed, bone at bone plate surfaces. ■ **Fig. 45-1** ■ In addition, about 500 mg of calcium is exchanged in remodeling of completely formed bone every day. Reabsorption of Ca++ from bone, its deposition to bone, urinary Ca++ excretion, and intestinal absorption of Ca++ are controlled by *parathyroid hormone* (PTH), produced by parathyroid glands on the inferior aspect of the thyroid, and vitamin D (see below).

Dietary intake of phosphate is approximately 900 mg/day. Two-thirds of this intake is absorbed in the gut regardless of the size of intake and therefore the gut is not a site of the control of phosphate balance; phosphate balance is controlled by altering urinary phosphate excretion. The kidney filters about 6000 mg phosphate/day and reabsorbs 70% to 100% of this load. Most phosphate resides within the soft tissues of the body. An extracellular pool of 500 mg exchanges with this soft tissue. About 250 mg enters and leaves bone in remodeling every day.

The role of bone in Ca++ and phosphate homeostasis is mediated through three different cell types; see the lower right of ■ **Fig. 45-1** ■ . Osteoblasts produce a collagen matrix for the deposition of Ca++, phosphate, hydroxide, and HCO_3^- to form *hydroxyapatite,* a marblelike crystalline structure. In support of bone structure, it also produces *osteonectin,* a protein that with collagen forms a complex that then binds hydroxyapatite crystals and osteocalcin, a high-affinity Ca++-binding protein.

Osteocytes in the fluid within the calculi function as transferors of Ca++ from the bone interior to the extracellular fluid by a process called *osteolytic osteolysis*. This transfer only involves recently formed crystals in amorphous bone and does not reduce already completely formed bone mass. Formed bone mass is reduced through enzymatic degradation of collagen and all other bone structures by osteoclasts. These cells literally "eat" the bone away, destroying the entire matrix and liberating its components, including Ca++ and phosphate.

Factors that stimulate bone formation include androgens, vitamin D, insulin, and growth hormone. Parathyroid hormone and cortisol inhibit bone formation. (This latter effect is responsible for bone fractures in patients given cortisol for arthritis.) Bone reabsorption is stimulated by vitamin D, parathyroid hormone, thyroid hormones, and cortisol. Reabsorption is inhibited by estrogen. This may relate estrogen loss at menopause to osteoporosis in postmenopausal women.

The Role of Parathyroid Hormone in Ca++ and Phosphate Balance

Plasma levels of Ca++ and phosphate are influenced in a negative feedback control system involving PTH. ■ **Figs. 45-2a and 45-2b** ■ *Hypocalcemia* stimulates the production of PTH, which then stimulates the elevation of plasma Ca++. Increased plasma phosphate concentrations, by combining with Ca++, reduce plasma calcium concentration and therefore also stimulate PTH secretion.

Parathyroid hormone increases plasma Ca++ levels through a variety of mechanisms. It stimulates osteoclasts to reabsorb completely mineralized bone, which then liberates Ca++ and phosphate. It also stimulates osteolysis by surface osteocytes, which transfers liberated Ca++ from the bone canaliculi to the extracellular fluid. Finally, PTH suppresses collagen synthesis in bone, thus depriving the bone of its underlying crystalline support matrix.

Liberation of calcium from bone by PTH increases the filtered load of calcium in the kidney. Nevertheless, plasma calcium rises because PTH increases the fractional reabsorption of Ca++ in the distal tubule and possibly the thick ascending limb of Henle's loop by a cAMP-dependent mechanism. This decreases fractional renal calcium excretion. In the kidney, PTH stimulates formation of the most potent form of vitamin D, which then stimulates reabsorption of Ca++ and phosphate by the intestine.

PTH suppresses reabsorption of phosphate by the proximal tubule of the kidney, thus increasing its excretion. This is a most important renal effect of PTH as it prevents Ca++ phosphate crystals from precipitating in the plasma after both calcium and phosphate are liberated from bone. PTH also inhibits renal reabsorption of HCO_3^-, which is liberated from reabsorbed bone, thus preventing alkalosis due to bone reabsorption.

■ **Fig. 45-2** ■

(a) Effects of PTH and vitamin D on calcium and phosphate movement between the gut, plasma and bone. The (+) indicates stimulation and the (−) indicates inhibition; see text for explanation. (b) Interrelationships between vitamin D parathyroid hormone, phosphate, and calcium. PTH elevates serum calcium levels, whereas high serum calcium levels suppress PTH levels. Calcium levels also are chemically reduced by complexing with phosphate. The interrelationship between PTH and calcium is modified by vitamin D, whose production by the kidney in turn is either stimulated or inhibited by a variety of variables. Small upward arrows indicate increase and downward arrows indicate decrease.

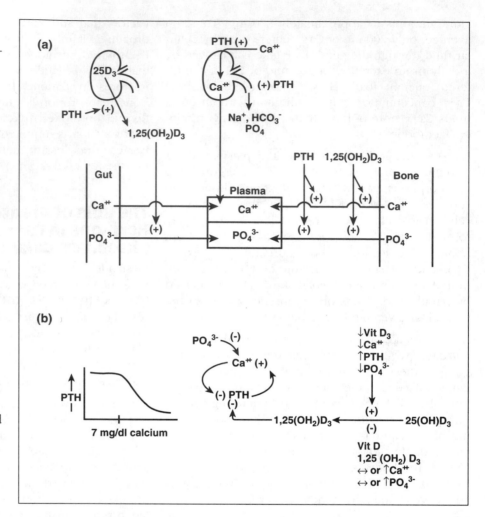

Vitamin D

Vitamin D works along with PTH to aid in Ca^{++} mobilization in response to decreased plasma Ca^{++}. Vitamin D, or *cholecalciferol,* is produced in the skin by the action of ultraviolet light. Cholecalciferol is converted to a more active metabolite in the liver and finally to 1,25 $(OH)_2$ D3, the most potent form of vitamin D, by the enzyme 1α-hydroxylase in the proximal tubule of the kidney. The kidney also can convert the liver metabolite to a 24,25 $(OH)_2$ D3, which is relatively inactive. Production of the active form of D3 by the kidney is stimulated by PTH or hypophosphatemia, both of which stimulate 1α-hydroxylase activity. Production of 24,25 D3 in the kidney is stimulated by sufficient amounts of 1,25 D3 and normal or hypercalcemia or phosphatemia.

Vitamin D is a highly lipid-soluble molecule and is transported in bile by the enterohepatic circulation. This recycling is needed to maintain normal vitamin D levels in the body; intestinal diseases or lipid malabsorptive syndromes can cause vitamin D deficiency. Vitamin D's primary effect in Ca^{++} homeostasis is to stimulate the absorption of Ca^{++} in the intestine. It does this by increasing intracellular levels of calcium-binding protein. It increases plasma calcium and phosphate levels by stimulating bone reabsorption, where it synergizes with PTH. Vitamin D stimulates cartilage development, which helps strengthen bone. Consequently vitamin D deficiency results in weak bones, or *rickets.*

During hypophosphatemia, increased levels of vitamin D3 stimulates the reabsorption of Ca^{++}, which suppresses PTH secretion and results in a decreased renal excretion of phosphate, allowing phosphate levels to come into balance.

Consequences of PTH and Vitamin D Dysfunction

Hyperparathyroidism (high PTH) results in hypercalcemia. Such high plasma Ca^{++} levels suppress membrane excitability in nerve and muscle. Therefore, hyperparathyroidism causes depressed neuromuscular excitability, lethargy, muscle weakness, dulled mentation, anorexia, and constipation. High plasma Ca^{++} predisposes the kidney to the development of renal stones and promotes gastric ulcer formation. Sustained high levels of PTH weakens bones, resulting in stress fractures and bone deformities.

Hypoparathyroidism can be caused by accidental surgical removal of the parathyroid glands during thyroidectomy or by autoimmune atrophy. The resulting hypocalcemia results in enhanced neuromuscular excitability and hyperreflexia, which can result in convulsions and muscle/laryngeal spasms sufficient to cause airway obstruction.

Excess vitamin D (usually from artificial vitamin overdose) results in excess bone reabsorption and enhanced gut absorption of Ca^{++}. This condition is similar to hyperparathyroidism except that plasma phosphate levels are increased because the resulting excess plasma Ca^{++} shuts off PTH secretion. Vitamin D deficiency can result from lack of sunlight, poor dietary intake, decreased absorption in the intestine, or defective hydroxylization in the liver. This results in depressed bone mineralization and weakened or deformed bone structure.

CHAPTER 46

Male Reproductive Physiology

The male contribution to production of viable progeny requires *spermatogenesis,* or the development of mature sperm. This requires the steroid hormone *testosterone* and FSH. ■ **Fig. 46-1** ■ Not only does testosterone promote spermatogenesis, but it is responsible for the development of "maleness," or secondary male sex characteristics. These include proper growth of external genitalia, enlargement of seminal vesicles, and stimulation of production of fructose as an energy source for sperm.

Ancillary effects of testosterone include enlargement of the larynx and vocal cords, resulting in a deep voice, as well as promotion of body hair growth while often inhibiting scalp hair growth. Testosterone promotes skeletal muscle development and adds to the effect of GH on bone growth during puberty and adolescence. Increased sebaceous gland secretion (which might promote acne) is yet another effect of testosterone. Finally, testosterone is known to result in aggressive, active attitudes, increased libido, and interest in the opposite sex.

Testosterone is synthesized from cholesterol in the *Leydig cells* of the testes from its initial precursor, pregnenolone. The enzymes for the conversion of pregnenolone to corticosteroids, such as seen in the adrenal gland, are absent in the testes. Instead, pre-existing enzymes favor the formation of 17 α-OH-pregnenolone (rather than progesterone), which then leads to testosterone formation. Once secreted into the circulation, testosterone is approximately 67% bound to gonadal steroid-binding globulin, and the rest to albumin.

Like all steroids, the general actions of male sex steroids are mediated via binding of nuclear steroid receptors with resulting gene induction. In target tissues, testosterone is converted to *dihydrotestosterone* (DHT), which is a better binder to DNA, resulting in amplification of testosterone effects. DHT can mediate several effects of testosterone and is essential for the development of external male genitalia.

The primary stimulant for testosterone production by Leydig cells of the testes is LH. This is accomplished through a cAMP/kinase A mechanism that stimulates the formation of cholesterol from cholesterol esters and promotes the conversion of the freed cholesterol into pregnenolone.

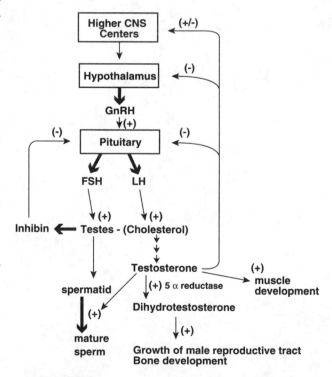

■ **Fig. 46-1** ■

A review of male sex steroid hormone regulation. The (+) indicates stimulation and the (−) indicates inhibition. GnRH = gonadotropin-releasing hormone, FSH = follicle-stimulating hormone, LH = luteinizing hormone. Items listed at the ends of heavy arrows are either factors released by the structure at the beginning of the arrow, or factors resulting from the item at the beginning of the arrow. (See text for details.)

Testosterone promotes the maturation of spermatids into sperm by stimulating protein synthesis and inhibiting protein breakdown. Proper spermatogenesis also requires FSH. This peptide hormone is trophic to sertoli cells and stimulates the production of an androgen-binding protein in these cells. This ensures that a pool of androgen in the cells is present to support spermatogenesis. FSH and LH must be released in a specific fashion in order for proper spermatogenesis to occur; this is accomplished by a unique pulsatile release of *gonadotropin-releasing hormone,* or *GnRH*. Release normally occurs at a rate of about 1 burst per hour; circulating levels of LH closely follow that of GnRH. FSH levels are not as well coordinated with the GnRH burst. Over- or understimulation of GnRH results in an underproduction of LH and FSH, with the result of suppressed testosterone production, reduced spermatogenesis, and possible infertility.

The secretion of testosterone is inhibited by testosterone itself. Testosterone exerts a feedback inhibition on LH release by decreasing the secretion of GnRH (decreasing pulse frequency). It also decreases the sensitivity of the pituitary to released GnRH. FSH secretion is not affected by testosterone, but is inhibited by the hormone *inhibin,* produced by the testes in response to FSH.

CHAPTER 47

Female Reproductive Physiology

The Menstrual Cycle

The female contribution to production of viable progeny requires a highly coordinated repeating cycle of events that is responsible for the production of a mature ovum about once every 4 weeks. This cycle has been termed the *ovarian cycle,* or *menstrual cycle,* after the characteristic periodic monthly shedding of uterine mucosa, or *menstruation.* ■ **Fig. 47-1** ■ This cycle involves changes in ovarian function and uterine growth in response to cyclic changes in gonadotropins and female sex steroids; it can be viewed as a preparation of the reproductive system for fertilization and pregnancy.

Menstruation is characteristic only of primates. The days of the cycle are numbered, with day 1 equaling the first day of menstruation. The menstrual cycle can be viewed as two cycles: an ovarian cycle that depicts the changes in the ovary and the developing ovum, and a *uterine cycle* that depicts the changes in the uterine wall. ■ **Fig. 47-1** ■

Day 1 of the menstrual cycle initiates follicular development in the ovary, and therefore initiates the follicular phase of the menstrual cycle. In this phase, the ovum is surrounded by a fluid-filled sac containing *estrogen* (primarily 17-β-estradiol) produced by the theca interna and granulosa cells in the follicle. Estradiol levels increase daily during the first 14 days of the ovarian cycle.

About the sixth day of the cycle, one follicle becomes dominant and by day 14 this follicle bursts, releasing an ovum; the process is called *ovulation.* This is correlated just prior to the ovulatory event with a surge in LH and FSH levels that result from a reinforcing positive feedback between estrogen production and hypothalamic and pituitary factors (see below).

The ruptured follicle fills with blood, and the bleeding into the abdomen may actually cause abdominal pain. Blood in the follicle is then replaced by lipid-rich cells, which create the *corpus luteum.* This initiates the luteal phase of the cycle. During this phase, the theca and granulosa cells proliferate and produce estrogen as well as large quantities of progesterone. If pregnancy occurs, the corpus luteum is maintained and the menstrual cycle stops; without pregnancy, the corpus luteum eventually atrophies and is replaced with scar tissue, *corpus albicans,* and the cycle eventually repeats.

Various changes occur in the uterine lining during the menstrual cycle in preparation for the possibility that a fertilized egg might need to implant and develop. By days 5 to 12, the uterine lining grows and the subepithelial glands lengthen, representing the proliferative phase of the ovarian cycle. This phase is stimulated by estrogen from the developing follicle.

After ovulation, the endometrium becomes more vascularized and edematous. Uterine glands become coiled and tortuous, which is characteristic of the luteal or secretory phase of the cycle. This phase is stimulated by the combined effects of estrogen and progesterone. As the corpus luteum regresses, the hormonal support for the endometrium declines. This causes a thinning of the endometrium, arterial spasm, spotty hemorrhage, and necrosis. A loss of most of the uterine lining results, and this then is shed in the process of menstruation.

Other effects occur during the uterine cycle. In response to estrogen prior to ovulation, the cervical mucus thins and becomes more alkaline, a condition that favors sperm transport. Under the influence of progesterone later in the cycle, cervical mucus thickens, inhibiting sperm transport and thus making it more difficult to become pregnant shortly after ovulation. Finally, progesterone also increases body temperature, which is why body temperature increases in women shortly after ovulation.

Ovarian Hormones

Estrogen is synthesized from cholesterol via androstenedione in the ovarian follicle, due to the

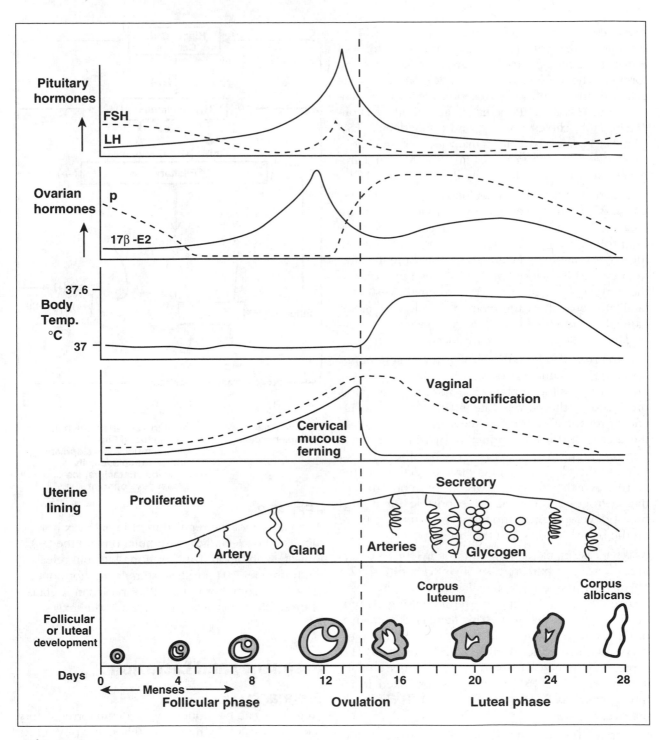

■ **Fig. 47-1** ■

An overview of changes in pituitary hormones, ovarian hormones, body temperature, cervical mucous composition, vaginal cornification, changes in the uterine lining, and follicular/luteal development during the menstrual cycle. P = progesterone. Details are provided in the text.

presence of an aromatase in the thecal cells. 17β-estradiol is the primary and most important form of estrogen, although estrone and estriol also are formed. The production of estrogen by the thecal cells is stimulated through receptor mechanisms activated by LH, via cAMP-mediated facilitation, and conversion of cholesterol to androstenedione. FSH stimulates granulosa cell aromatization of androgens to estrogen through increases in cyclic AMP and aromatase activity. Granulosa cells also respond to LH.

Estrogen stimulates the development of the uterus. ■ **Fig. 47-2** ■ It increases uterine blood flow and increases the amount of uterine muscle and contractile protein present. Estrogen also increases smooth muscle excitability, facilitates action potential frequency and formation, and sensitizes the uterus to the contractile effects of oxytocin. Finally, estrogen facilitates growth of the ovarian follicles, promotes vaginal development, and is responsible for secondary development of breast ducts.

Progesterone can be thought of as a *pro-gestational* hormone the function of which is to prepare the uterus for possible implantation and pregnancy. It is produced in the corpus luteum in response to LH and is responsible for the luteal phase changes in the uterus. It does this primarily by reducing estrogen receptors in the uterus. This has the effect of calming the electrical and contractile activity to the uterus, which otherwise would promote miscarriage. Progesterone is also responsible for normal breast development, although its primary effects are on the breast lobules and the areola.

As is the case in males, LH production in females occurs in response to a burst release of GnRH. ■ **Fig. 47-2** ■ This GnRH frequency in females, however, increases before ovulation, leading to ever increasing LH production, termed *LH surge*. This increased frequency of GnRH secretion increases sensitivity of the pituitary to GnRH, which further contributes to the LH surge. Generally, GnRH and LH secretion are inhibited by estrogen; FSH secretion is inhibited in inhibin, which, is in turn produced by FSH effects on the ovary.

During the follicular phase of the ovarian cycle, levels of inhibin are low and FSH levels are moderate, promoting follicular growth. LH is low due to the negative feedback of estrogen. As estrogen rises, a *positive* feedback is provided to the pituitary to alter GnRH sensitivity, producing the LH surge in ovulation. In the luteal phase, LH and FSH are low due to feedback effects of estrogen, progesterone, and inhibin. ■ **Fig. 47-2** ■

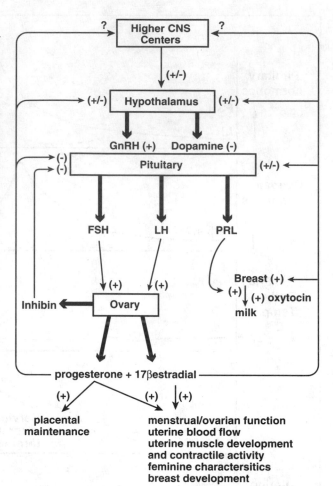

■ **Fig. 47-2** ■
An overview of the regulation of female sex hormones. The (+) indicates stimulation and the (−) indicates inhibition. GnRH = gonadotropin-releasing hormone, FSH = follicle-stimulating hormone, LH = luteinizing hormone, PRL = prolactin. Details of these mechanisms are provided in the text.

Pregnancy and Lactation

Pregnancy

Pregnancy can be thought of as a counterregulatory state in terms of the mother in that many physiological functions normally designed for maternal maintenance are transformed to support the development of the fetus.

Pregnancy ensues upon fertilization of the ovum and implantation of a properly developed zygote into a properly prepared uterine lining. Progesterone released from the corpus luteum calms the activity or motility of the uterus and aids in implantation. Progesterone and estrogens are necessary for the maintenance of pregnancy. Levels of these hormone do not cycle monthly, as in the nonpregnant female, but increase continually throughout the 40-week gestational period. Early in pregnancy, production of estrogen and progesterone by the corpus luteum is maintained by the action of *human chorionic gonadotropin,* or *hCG,* an LH-like hormone produced by the placenta. hCG levels can be detected in maternal serum as early as 1 week after conception and are used to confirm pregnancy by laboratory test.

After 8 weeks of gestation, steroidogenesis in the placenta itself is sufficient to maintain the pregnancy. The placenta can synthesize cholesterol from acetate but receives most of its cholesterol from the maternal circulation. The placenta can produce pregnenolone and progesterone but lacks the enzymes necessary to make dehydroepiandrosterone (DHEA) needed for production of androgens and estrogens. Conversion of pregnenolone to DHEA requires the fetal adrenal cortex, which also converts placental progesterone to androstenedione. These products are then converted to estradiol and estrone in the placenta. The fetal liver is necessary for the production of estriol, the most abundant estrogen in pregnancy.

The placenta also produces the hormone *human placental lactogen* (hPL), or *human chorionic somatomammotropin,* which has growth hormone- and prolactin-like functions. hPL mobilizes maternal nutrients for the benefit of the fetus, which uses glucose as its major energy source. hPL has antiinsulin actions that decrease maternal use of glucose and promote lipolysis and proteolysis. This antiinsulin activity is the basis for pregnancy-induced diabetes mellitus. Maternal prolactin (PRL) has similar effects during pregnancy. Both hPL an PRL act as fetal growth hormones and stimulate the production of fetal IGF-I.

Other hormones are altered during pregnancy. The placenta is a source of ACTH, TSH, and a parathyroid-like hormone that increases placental calcium transport. Production of thyroid hormones increases markedly during pregnancy. In addition, estrogen stimulates the production of transcortin, thus increasing circulating levels of cortisol.

Several physiological changes occur in the pregnant woman as a result of the developing fetus and the endocrine and cardiovascular changes associated with the pregnancy. Blood volume increases by 50% during pregnancy, with heart rate and stroke volume increases combining to elevate cardiac output by as much as 40%. The growing uterus can exert pressure on leg veins, creating edema in the lower limbs or venous damage.

Uterine growth also impinges on functional residual capacity and residual volume in the lungs. Because of the high metabolic rate of the growing fetus, maternal oxygen consumption increases, stimulating respiratory minute and tidal volume. Increased ventilation in pregnancy is aided by progesterone, which increases CNS sensitivity to CO_2.

The placental circulation represents an AV shunt to the mother, lowering maternal vascular resistance and blood pressure. This results in reflex production of renin, AII, aldosterone and ADH. Estrogen and progesterone also stimulate renin release. It is not surprising that salt and water retention is a normal consequence of pregnancy.

Lactation

Mammary growth and development is stimulated by hPL, PRL progesterone, and estrogen in pregnancy. Progesterone and estrogen, however, suppress milk synthesis during pregnancy. Synthesis occurs after birth when estrogen and progesterone levels decrease. This is thought to result from a burst of cortisol release at parturition. Reflexes from suckling produce milk expulsion from the breast through the action of oxytocin from the posterior pituitary.

CHAPTER 48

Thermoregulation: Regulation of Heat Balance in the Body

Chemical and physical processes in the body are influenced by temperature. An organism that can regulate its body temperature removes the potential for functional problems that otherwise would result from changes in external environmental temperature. Our internal, or core, body temperature rarely varies more that ±1°F even when we're exposed to external temperatures of 55° to 140°F. This suggests the existence of a powerful temperature control system. Normal body temperature is in the range 98.0° to 98.6°F (36.7° to 37°C). Body temperature is slightly higher in children and becomes slightly elevated by exercise or emotionally stressful conditions. It is slightly lower upon waking after restful sleep, or after prolonged exposure to cold weather.

The challenge to control of internal body temperature is to balance inputs and outputs of heat. ■ **Fig. 48-1** ■ The major interface between the body and the external environment is the surface of the skin, which plays a pivotal role in heat balance. Skin and fat provide thermal insulation for the body (fat conducts heat only one-third as well as other tissues), and every millimeter of fat increases tolerance to cold by 2° to 3°F. More important, heat is transferred to the environment/body interface through the *cutaneous circulation*. Cutaneous blood flow is the major determinant of heat conduction between the body and the external environment.

Heat Inputs

The primary heat input to the body results from metabolism of food. Fifty percent of food energy results in heat production, with protein processing stimulating metabolic rate more than that for carbohydrates or fat; this is called *the specific dynamic action of protein*. Basic metabolism is under the influence of thyroid hormone, which can increase metabolic rate and heat production 100%.

The sympathetic nervous system and circulating catecholamines also stimulate chemical thermogenesis by stimulating glycogenolysis and metabolism of brown fat. This latter effect contributes to heat production only in infants. Exercise, growth hormone, and testosterone also have at least temporary or modest stimulatory effects on heat production in the body. Radiation of heat from the environment, in the form of infrared energy to the body, occurs if the environmental temperature is greater than body temperature. Mechanisms that prevent the loss of heat from the body (i.e., cutaneous vasoconstriction) can be thought of as having the same effect as adding heat.

Shivering is an important means of increasing heat production in the body. Shivering is not an actual shaking of muscles but rather an oscillation of muscle tone mediated through spinal reflexes and stretch sensors in muscle spindle fibers. Shivering results in a high production of heat without frank gross movement of the body. Finally, *piloerection,* or "goose bumps," raises hair that traps air next to the skin, thus preventing removal of heat through air convection. This response is a noneffective vestige in humans and conserves heat only in other furry mammals.

Heat Loss

The primary source of heat loss in the body is through direct radiation of infrared energy to the environment ($\approx 60\%$). A small percent of heat is lost in direct conduction to any objects that are in contact with the body and also in conduction to air. Heat loss through conduction to air ceases, however, if the air is motionless across the skin and allowed to reach equilibrium with skin temperature. More heat can be lost if this air can be moved off the surface of the skin (as noted by the effect of fanning ourselves when we feel hot). This process is called *convection*.

Heat also is lost through the insensible evaporation of water from the respiratory tract and from uncontrolled transpiration through the skin. The high heat capacity of H_2O causes the body to lose more heat when it is exposed to water than when exposed to air. Wet clothing or immersion in large bodies of H_2O (i.e., swimming) results in great heat loss directly to water. This heat loss is exacerbated by removal of any air insulation zone on the body's surface. Wet conditions invariably cause detrimental loss of heat from the body that cannot be compensated by an individual's heat generating or conserving mechanisms.

Sweat and Heat Loss

Although exposure to water can be detrimental to heat balance, the high heat capacity of water is exploited as a cooling mechanism whenever body temperature rises. The skin contains specialized glands that produce an aqueous fluid, called *sweat,* that is secreted onto the surface of the skin. Evaporation of sweat is an effective mechanism of extracting heat from the body. More important, the production of sweat is the *only* cooling mechanism available to the body when environmental temperature is greater than skin temperature.

Like many glandular organs, sweat glands produce a primary, protein-free, plasmalike secretion that is modified by ductal epithelial cells. These cells basically remove NaCl from the primary secretion. Sweat production is stimulated by sympathetic *cholinergic* fibers. As sweat evaporates off the surface of the skin, it cools the skin and thus creates a temperature gradient between the body core and the skin's surface. This facilitates heat transfer to the environment.

Basal sweat production produces a secretion that contains high concentrations of urea, K^+, and lactate, but very low amounts of NaCl, due to reabsorption of Na^+, Cl^-, and H_2O from the duct. In an unacclimatized person (someone exposed acutely to a hot environment), sweat production is about 700 mL/hr and the Na^+ concentration of the sweat equals approximately 60 mEq/L. This would result in a daily Na^+ loss of 15 to 30 gm, which is considerably greater than normal intake.

If an individual is exposed to a hot climate for several days, sweat production increases to about 2 L/hr but with a daily loss of only 3 to 5 g of Na^+. This reduced sodium loss is due to stimulation by aldosterone of Na^+ reabsorptive mechanisms in the sweat gland. In addition to Na^+ conservation, increased sweat volume in the acclimatized individual creates an even greater temperature gradient between the skin and the body core, allowing for more rapid extraction of heat from the body.

Actual removal of heat from the body requires getting excess heat to the lower-temperature skin through transport in the blood. Heat can be removed from the skin according to the heat capacity for water; 1 kcal of heat per degree of gradient per liter of blood

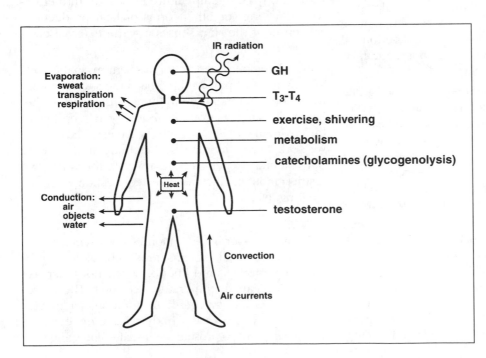

■ **Fig. 48-1** ■

Representation of heat exchange between the body and the external environment, and factors that affect heat generation and dissipation in the body.

in contact with the skin. Thus, greater sweat production and cutaneous blood flow results in greater heat removal. Total heat loss is a product of the core-to-skin temperature gradient and the cutaneous blood flow. For example, if sweat produced a 5°C gradient between the skin's surface and the body core, and blood flow in the cutaneous circulation were 2 L/min, approximately 600 kcal could be removed from the skin per hour. This is considerably greater than resting heat production of 60 kcal/hr or that of ≈ 360 kcal/hr in strenuous exercise; it would easily prevent any rise in temperature caused by this heat production.

In maximum exercise, marked muscle vasodilation has a tendency to lower blood pressure, resulting in reflex cutaneous vasoconstriction. In this condition, the ability of the body to remove heat, even within a 5°C gradient due to sweating, is reduced. Heat production then exceeds heat loss, and body temperature rises.

Temperature Regulation

Body temperature regulation is mediated through sensors in a heat-sensitive area in the preoptic region of the hypothalamus and through peripheral sensors, primarily in the skin. The rate of firing of the hypothalamic area increases whenever blood temperature increases even a fraction of a degree Celsius. The hypothalamus contains a cold temperature sensitive area in the septum and reticular substance that increases firing rate when temperature decreases. There are both hot and cold peripheral skin receptors. (The number of cold receptors is about 10 times that of hot receptors.)

The value of normal body temperature is set in the hypothalamus. Whenever body temperature deviates from this temperature "set point," appropriate heat producing or reducing mechanisms are brought into play. ■ **Figs. 48-2a and 48-2b** ■ The efficacy of the human temperature regulating systems is extremely strong; feedback control is 10 times greater than the highly sensitive baroreceptor control of blood pressure.

When an individual's temperature rises, several mechanisms combine to reduce temperature back to normal. First, inhibition of the sympathetic centers in the posterior area of the hypothalamus occurs, reducing cutaneous vascular resistance and increasing blood flow. Also, sweating is stimulated and shivering is inhibited. Whenever body temperature drops below the hypothalamic set point, cuta-

neous vasoconstriction is produced via stimulation of posterior hypothalamic sympathetic centers. Shivering is activated through actions of the primary motor center for shivering in the dorsomedial portion of the posterior hypothalamus. This shivering center is normally inhibited by heat centers in the preoptic area, but is stimulated by both peripheral and visceral cold receptors.

Increased muscle tension brought about by shivering can increase body heat production 400% to 500%. Release of circulating catecholamines also creates chemical thermogenesis through glycogenolysis. Additional metabolic heat-generating mechanisms such as adrenergic activation of brown fat and thyroxin output are primarily of more benefit to heat production in infants than in adults. Finally, piloerection occurs, but is only a symptom of cold exposure in humans.

Interaction Between Peripheral and Central Temperature Regulating Mechanisms

The hypothalamic temperature set point is changed by signals from peripheral receptors. ■ **Fig. 48-2b** ■ The set point for initiating sweating is lowered whenever skin temperature rises. In other words, sweating will ensue at a lower internal core temperature if the skin senses a warm external environment. In addition, whenever skin temperature rises, the set point for initiating shivering is lowered. That is, the body core temperature must drop further before shivering (or other forms of heat production) will ensue if the skin senses a warm external environment.

Although temperature control mechanisms in the body are elegant and powerful, perhaps the strongest control of body temperature in humans is conscious behavioral changes brought about by perception of the environment. For example, when exposed to cold, we seek warm environs, add clothing, and increase our voluntary activities. When we are too warm, we restrict motion, increase air convection, remove clothing, etc.

Fever

Fever is an abnormal elevation of body temperature. Infectious bacterial proteins, protein breakdown products, endotoxins, and lipopolysaccharides increase the hypothalamic temperature set point. These products are called *pyrogens*. In addition, leukocytes and macrophages in the body release endogenous pyrogens, perhaps prostaglandins, after ingesting bacterial products. Aspirin inhibits prostaglandin synthesis, perhaps explaining why aspirin reduces fever but does not alter body temperature in a normal individual.

By elevating the temperature set point in the hypothalamus, pyrogens "trick" the brain into thinking that the current body temperature is too cold. The body's response, understandably, is induction of shivering and cutaneous vasoconstriction, or what occurs normally when core temperature is perceived to be below normal. This results in the characteristic "shakes," pale skin, cold hands and feet, etc., associated with initial stages of infection.

When the new set point is reached (at a higher temperature), the symptoms of the body's exposure to cold disappear, and fever is present. Once the infection is controlled and pyrogens are removed from the body, the set point of the individual returns to normal. At this point then, the body correctly perceives that it is too warm and initiates factors to remove heat, including sweating and flushing of the skin. The point at which this happens is called the *crisis point* and was used long ago as an indication that the patient was going to overcome the infection.

Body temperature regulating mechanisms do not have infinite efficacy and in certain conditions the body temperature can exceed normal functional or even survivable ranges. When body temperature rises above 106°F, such as in individuals with AIDS or during heavy work in extremely hot environments, the

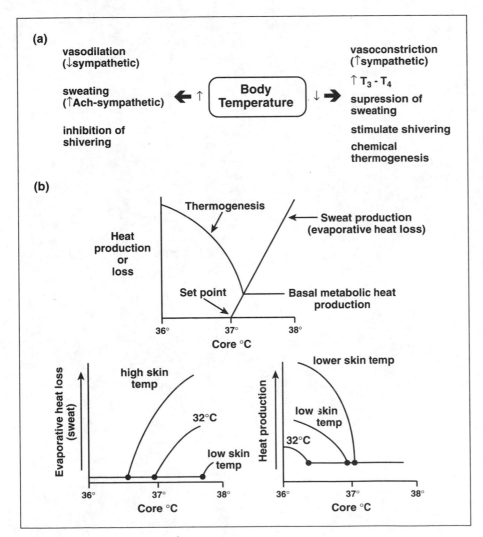

■ **Fig. 48-2** ■

(a) A list of the effects of changes in body temperature on variables involved with body temperature regulation. Small upward arrows show increase, and small downward arrows show decrease. (b) Relationship between heat production via thermogenesis or heat loss via sweat production in response to changes in body core temperature. Lower left: Relationship between body core temperature and sweat production as modified by different skin temperatures. Lower right: Body heat production as a function in changes in body core temperature as modified by different skin temperatures.

hypothalamus becomes inefficient as a thermal regulator and normal temperature control mechanisms fail to function properly. The symptoms of this hyperthermia include evidence of abnormal brain function such as dizziness, delirium, potential loss of consciousness, and abdominal pain.

A loss of consciousness also can occur from mild circulatory shock due to brain damage. Without immediate, appropriate intervention, *hyperthermia* will result in death. Treatment through exposure to extreme cold, such as an ice bath, is not advised, as this cold will be sensed by peripheral cold receptors that might induce shivering and exacerbate the hyperthermia. Generally, a rapidly evaporating substance such as alcohol is applied to skin to accelerate evaporative heat loss.

Hypothalamic temperature control is greatly impaired when body temperature drops below 94°F and is lost completely at a core body temperature below 85°F. In addition, the body's ability to produce heat through metabolism is depressed twofold for every 10° drop in temperature. Hypothermia by itself will not necessarily damage tissues; hence the often observed phenomena of individuals being able to recover after 30 minutes to 1 hour of unconsciousness in very cold water. Hypothermia eventually will result in collapse of the cardiovascular system and death if it is not corrected by external means.

CHAPTER 49

Exercise

Exercise is synonymous with physical activity. This is a condition that is so ubiquitous and varied in its form that perhaps true physiological "rest" is the exception rather than the rule in our daily lives. Although exercise is defined ultimately in terms of muscle contraction, exercise affects every organ in the body. Furthermore, different forms of exercise evoke quite different responses in various organ systems, as well as in the individual as a whole. These responses depend on whether exercise involves small or large muscle masses, is rhythmic or isometric, acute or chronic (training), intense or mild, or of long or short duration. Even sitting can

be considered exercise, as the calories used in this activity are about 50% more than those in the recumbent sleeping individual. With severe exercise, or even walking up a few flights of stairs, we consume 10 to 20 times more energy than we consume when at complete rest.

Exercise intensity is quantified in terms of O_2 consumption. ■ **Fig. 49-1a** ■ The energy needed for exercise comes from ATP. During strenuous bursts of activity, ATP already stored in cells and that replenished by creatinine phosphate stores provides only about a 15 second supply of ATP. Additional

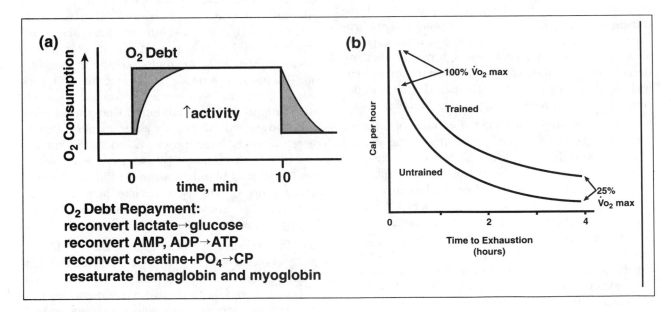

■ Fig. 49-1 ■
(a) Representation of increased oxygen consumption during an interval of increased physical activity. Oxygen debt and repayment are represented by the shaded areas. (b) The relationship between the onset of exhaustion in an exercising individual as a function of their maximum oxygen consumption. Trained individuals have higher maximum oxygen consumption capacity than untrained individuals. Intensity of exercise at the same percent of maximum in each individual produces the same time to exhaustion, however.

ATP then, must then come from metabolism. During heavy bursts of exercise, anaerobic metabolism can provide enough ATP for 1 to 2 minutes of strenuous activity. After that time, the slower ATP generating process of aerobic metabolism is used to generate energy for any further exercise.

After a bout of exercise, an individual continues to consume O_2 at a higher rate than at rest. This excess O_2 consumption is called the O_2 *debt* and is used to reconvert lactic acid into glucose, AMP and ADP to ATP, creatinine and phosphate to phosphocreatine. It also is used to reestablish normal hemoglobin and myoglobin saturation. O_2 debt is a poor indicator, however, of exercise intensity.

Evaluation of Exercise Intensity

Every individual has a maximum O_2 consumption, about 20 times BMR, that cannot be exceeded unless the individual goes through longterm training. This maximum value is called the V_{O2max}, or maximal O_2 uptake. V_{O2max} represents the physiological limit to O_2 transport and use in an individual, and therefore is a valuable predictor of exercise endurance. The V_{O2max} limit appears to arise from the fact that all factors involved in O_2 delivery and use during exercise, from cardiac output to O_2 utilization by the mitochondria, reach maximum capacity about the same time. This means, however, that any defect in the cardiovascular, pulmonary, or musculoskeletal systems, as well as in blood itself, can depress V_{O2max} and reduce exercise endurance.

Exhaustion ensues with long durations of exercise due to depletion of glycogen stores in the muscle and liver, and thus a lack of glucose as substrate for oxidative metabolism. The time it takes to reach this depletion depends on the intensity of exercise relative to an *individual's own* V_{O2max}. ■ **Fig. 49-1b** ■ Thus, a marathon runner and an untrained runner, when both are exercising at 50% of their V_{O2max}, will become exhausted in the same amount of time and for the same reasons, even though the absolute energy expenditure of the trained individual is much higher than that of the untrained.

Acute Cardiovascular Responses to Dynamic Exercise

Acute responses of the cardiovascular system to dynamic, or aerobic, exercise starts with activation of the motor cortex. Increased metabolism in exercising muscles causes local decreases in vascular resistance. ■ **Fig. 49-2a** ■ This decrease is proportional to the size of the muscle mass involved, as well as to the intensity of its activity. Neural reflexes also result in positive chronotropic and inotropic effects on the heart. In addition, increased muscle pumping further augments stroke volume, which increases in spite of decreased filling time due to high heart rates. The net effect is that cardiac output increases, almost in proportion to the decrease in resistance caused by the exercising muscle. Consequently, blood pressure changes little during exercise.

In very intense exercise, muscle vasodilation represents a threat to blood pressure maintenance and is countered by vasoconstriction in other organs, primarily the splanchnic region. During exercise, blood flow is not compromised to the brain because of the lack of arterial adrenergic receptors coupled with strong blood flow autoregulation capacity in that organ. Active hyperemia- and β-adrenergic-mediated blood flow increases occur in the coronary circulation. Increased flow also occurs in the cutaneous circulation due to increased heat production from exercising muscle.

The response of the cardiovascular system to isometric exercise, i.e., lifting weights, is different than that in aerobic exercise. Although cardiac output and muscle blood flow increase during isometric exercise, the extremely high intramuscular pressures generated by this form of activity compresses muscle arteries and thus limits metabolic vasodilation. This results in too little flow for too much O_2 consumption, which is why isometric exercise is quickly exhausting. In addition, although mean arterial pressure changes little during dynamic exercise due to correspondingly large muscle vasodilation, antagonism of this vasodilation by isometric exercise results in elevated blood pressure during that form of activity. This is why isometriclike activities (e.g., shoveling heavy snow) are more dangerous to individuals with various forms of heart disease.

The differences in responses of the cardiovascular system to isometric and aerobic exercise cause different adaptive changes during long periods of these forms of exercise (training). With chronic aerobic exercise, the heart chamber size increases with no change in wall thickness. There is increased vagal and decreased sympathetic drive at rest, resulting in a resting bradycardia. Stroke volume is augmented both at rest and during exercise, and resting blood pressure decreases in many individuals. There is an enhancement of muscle capillary density and coronary arteries are more responsive to vasodilators. Not surprisingly, exercise endurance is enhanced after training.

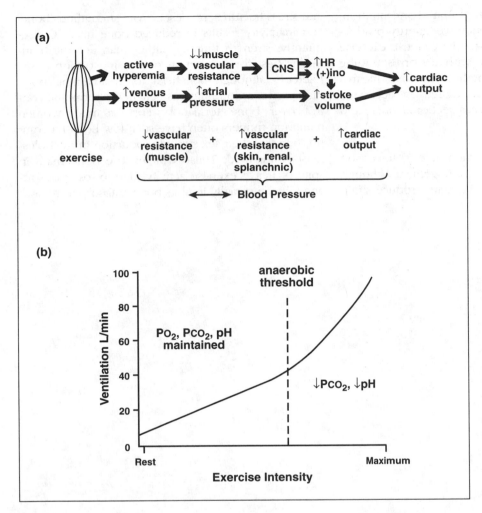

■ **Fig. 49-2** ■
(a) A representation of the response of the cardiovascular system to exercise. Small upward arrows show increases, and small downward arrows show decreases. Variables at the ends of heavy arrows result from a change in the preceding variable; see text for explanation. (b) The effect of exercise intensity on ventilation rate, showing the anaerobic threshold.

The primary cardiovascular adaptive effect of anaerobic, or isometric, exercise is *myocardial hypertrophy*. As this condition is characterized by an increase in cardiac muscle mass without a corresponding increase in capillary density, this situation is not particularly good for the individual.

Acute Respiratory Adjustments During Exercise

Increased ventilation is the most recognizable physiological response to exercise. ■ **Fig. 49-2b** ■ Increased ventilation during exercise is essential for both increasing O_2 uptake and removing excess CO_2 from the body. In light and moderate exercise, ventilation precisely maintains blood gas and pH homeostasis. With severe exercise, anaerobic lactate production further reduces pH, which in turn further stimulates ventilation and results in hypocapnia. Because CO_2 equilibrates in the cerebrospinal fluid easier than does H^+ ions, this low P_{CO_2} results in brain alkalinization.

It is unclear what sensory system is responsible for stimulating ventilation during exercise. Clearly, alterations in classic chemoreceptor control of ventilation cannot be responsible, because the receptors for this control exist on the arterial side of the circulation, whereas the primary change in blood gases with exercise is in the tissues or venous circulation.

Training has essentially no effect on the respiratory system, and therefore, enhanced V_{O2max} during training is not the result of increased efficiency of the respiratory system. However, lung diseases can markedly affect lung capacity and limit V_{O2max}.

Adjustments of Other Organs to Exercise

Muscle and bone respond positively to aerobic exercise. In muscle, training increases capillary and mitochondrial density, myoglobin concentration, enzymatic machinery for oxidative energy production, etc. In addition, high-load isometric exercise causes muscle hypertrophy with a corresponding increase in isometric strength. This also means, however, that low activity, for any reason, decreases capillary density, muscle cross-sectional area, and strength.

The force of muscle contraction exerts forces on bones, which stimulate bone remodeling. Although heavy repetitive physical activity can produce strain and stress fractures, modest activity strengthens bone, and inactivity results in reduced bone mass. Consequently, strength training, rather than aerobic training, is best for preventing or slowing osteoporosis. Exercise, although beneficial for maintaining bone mass, is not as important as genetic or hormonal control over bone formation. For example, women marathon runners often have such low body fat composition that their sex steroid production from cholesterol is impaired. These women lose bone mass in spite of heavy exercise activity, due to loss of estrogen which normally inhibits bone reabsorption.

CHAPTER 50

Hemostasis

Frank loss of blood from the cardiovascular system will result in shock and death. Although such a major cardiovascular disruption usually results from severe trauma, injury, or severing of blood vessels, the vascular system experiences many tiny tears and "leaks" every day. Given enough time, these too will result in shock if not stopped and repaired. Thus, a mechanism for stopping blood loss due to disruption of arteries and veins is required to maintain integrity of the cardiovascular system.

When blood is exposed to foreign substances, or when it is exposed to the vascular collagen matrix from tears in blood vessels, extremely complex sequences of biochemical events set into motion result ultimately in the construction of a fibrous patch that traps blood cells and forms a plug that prevents further blood movement or loss. ■ **Fig. 50-1** ■

There are two known biochemical pathways that result in eventual blood clot formation and hemostasis. One pathway, called the *intrinsic pathway,* is initiated when blood comes in contact with foreign substances or with collagen. This contact stimulates conversion of a factor in the blood coagulation cascade, *factor XII* or the *Hageman factor,* to its active form. The activated form of this factor activates a secondary factor, which activates another, and so on until the biochemical cascade converges on a *prothrombin activator component.* This activator converts prothrombin into thrombin in a process that requires Ca^{++}. Thrombin in turn converts the protein fibrinogen into a fiber monomer unit. With the addition of a fibrin stabilizing factor and Ca^{++}, these units form fibrin threads that help trap blood cells and, by themselves, seal over the broken areas of blood vessel.

A simpler extrinsic pathway is initiated for blood clot formation whenever tissue trauma occurs. When tissue is traumatized, several proteins and phospholipids are liberated, collectively called *tissue thromboplastins,* which converts *factor X,* or the *Stuart factor,* into its activated form, resulting in eventual fibrin thread formation by the same mechanism as that in the intrinsic pathway.

Blood platelets also play an important role in this process. During tissue traumatization, blood platelets, which contain many agents, undergo transformation in a burst of activity called the *release response.* Upon initiation of the release response, platelets become sticky, adhering to collagen matrix and each other, forming a type of *"papier-mâché"* over torn areas of the vasculature. In addition, platelets produce phospholipids, which help activate factor X, as well as thromboxane and ADP, which help promote further platelet aggregation.

Several of the clotting factors in the coagulation cascades require vitamin K, which is processed in the liver, for their formation. These include *factor IX,* also called the *Christmas factor; factor VII; factor X* or Stuart factor; and *prothrombin,* or *factor II.* Without vitamin K, clotting defects occur. Various genetic defects, resulting in faulty or missing factors from the clotting cascade, can result in absent or insufficient clotting, called *hemophilia.* Classic hemophilia (hemophilia A), is the most common hereditary defect of the intrinsic pathway. It results from suppressed ability to make *factor VIII:C,* or *antihemophilic factor.*

Clinical anticoagulants, such as heparin, interact with certain anticoagulation factors (Antithrombin III) to prevent activation of the coagulation cascade. In addition, because calcium plays an essential role in many of the steps in the coagulation cascade, Ca^{++} chelating agents such as sodium citrate block blood coagulation. This has led to their use as anticoagulants in blood sample containers.

The coagulation cascade normally is prevented from activation in the intact circulation by production of NO and prostacyclin from the vascular endothelium, and by the presence of heparin-rich proteoglycans on the endothelial surface. ■ **Fig. 50-1** ■ Once clots are formed, they eventually are dissolved by *plasmin,* a proteolytic enzyme that dissolves fibrin threads. Plasmin is formed from plasminogen by a tissue plasminogen activator, or tPA. This agent has been employed clinically to dissolve coronary thrombi responsible for sudden heart attack.

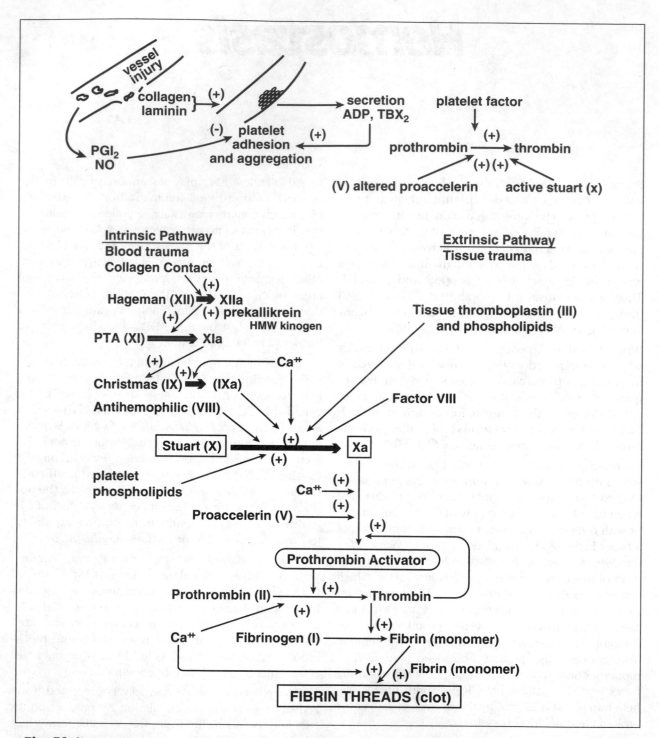

■ Fig. 50-1 ■

Top: Events in the formation of platelet plugs in response to vascular injury.
The (+) symbol indicates stimulation and the (−) symbol indicates inhibition.
TBX_2 = thromboxane, PGI_2 = prostacyclin. Details of this process are explained
in the text. (b) The intrinsic and extrinsic blood coagulation pathways. Both
cascades lead to the activation of Stuart factor, which results in the formation of
thrombin, then fibrin monomers and eventual fibrin threads that form the blood
clot. Details of these mechanisms are provided in the text.

Page numbers followed by *f* refer to figures.